Understanding SQL and Java Together

A Guide to SQLJ, JDBC, and Related Technologies

THE MORGAN KAUFMANN SERIES IN DATA MANAGEMENT SYSTEMS

Series Editor: Jim Gray, Microsoft Research

Understanding SQL and Java Together: A Guide to SQLJ, JDBC, and Related Technologies
Jim Melton and Andrew Eisenberg

Database: Principles, Programming, and Performance, Second Edition
Patrick and Elizabeth O'Neil

The Object Data Standard: ODMG 3.0
Edited by R. G. G. Cattell and Douglas K. Barry

Data on the Web: From Relations to Semistructured Data and XML
Serge Abiteboul, Peter Buneman, and Dan Suciu

Data Mining: Practical Machine Learning Tools and Techniques with Java Implementations
Ian H. Witten and Eibe Frank

Joe Celko's SQL for Smarties: Advanced SQL Programming, Second Edition
Joe Celko

Joe Celko's Data & Databases: Concepts in Practice
Joe Celko

Developing Time-Oriented Database Applications in SQL
Richard T. Snodgrass

Web Farming for the Data Warehouse
Richard D. Hackathorn

Database Modeling & Design, Third Edition
Toby J. Teorey

Management of Heterogeneous and Autonomous Database Systems
Edited by Ahmed Elmagarmid, Marek Rusinkiewicz, and Amit Sheth

Object-Relational DBMSs: Tracking the Next Great Wave, Second Edition
Michael Stonebraker and Paul Brown with Dorothy Moore

A Complete Guide to DB2 Universal Database
Don Chamberlin

Universal Database Management: A Guide to Object/Relational Technology
Cynthia Maro Saracco

Readings in Database Systems, Third Edition
Edited by Michael Stonebraker and Joseph M. Hellerstein

Understanding SQL's Stored Procedures: A Complete Guide to SQL/PSM
Jim Melton

Principles of Multimedia Database Systems
V. S. Subrahmanian

Principles of Database Query Processing for Advanced Applications
Clement T. Yu and Weiyi Meng

Advanced Database Systems
Carlo Zaniolo, Stefano Ceri, Christos Faloutsos, Richard T. Snodgrass, V. S. Subrahmanian, and Roberto Zicari

Principles of Transaction Processing
Philip A. Bernstein and Eric Newcomer

Using the New DB2: IBM's Object-Relational Database System
Don Chamberlin

Distributed Algorithms
Nancy A. Lynch

Active Database Systems: Triggers and Rules for Advanced Database Processing
Edited by Jennifer Widom and Stefano Ceri

Migrating Legacy Systems: Gateways, Interfaces, & the Incremental Approach
Michael L. Brodie and Michael Stonebraker

Atomic Transactions
Nancy Lynch, Michael Merritt, William Weihl, and Alan Fekete

Query Processing for Advanced Database Systems
Edited by Johann Christoph Freytag, David Maier, and Gottfried Vossen

Transaction Processing: Concepts and Techniques
Jim Gray and Andreas Reuter

Understanding the New SQL: A Complete Guide
Jim Melton and Alan R. Simon

Building an Object-Oriented Database System: The Story of O_2
Edited by François Bancilhon, Claude Delobel, and Paris Kanellakis

Database Transaction Models for Advanced Applications
Edited by Ahmed K. Elmagarmid

A Guide to Developing Client/Server SQL Applications
Setrag Khoshafian, Arvola Chan, Anna Wong, and Harry K. T. Wong

The Benchmark Handbook for Database and Transaction Processing Systems, Second Edition
Edited by Jim Gray

Camelot and Avalon: A Distributed Transaction Facility
Edited by Jeffrey L. Eppinger, Lily B. Mummert, and Alfred Z. Spector

Readings in Object-Oriented Database Systems
Edited by Stanley B. Zdonik and David Maier

Understanding SQL and Java Together

A Guide to SQLJ, JDBC, and Related Technologies

Jim Melton
Andrew Eisenberg

MORGAN KAUFMANN PUBLISHERS
AN IMPRINT OF ACADEMIC PRESS
A Harcourt Science and Technology Company
SAN FRANCISCO SAN DIEGO NEW YORK BOSTON
LONDON SYDNEY TOKYO

Senior Editor	Diane D. Cerra
Director of Production and Manufacturing	Yonie Overton
Senior Production Editor	Edward Wade
Editorial Coordinator	Belinda Breyer
Cover Design	Ross Carron Design
Text Design	Side-By-Side Studios/Mark Ong (based on a design by Rebecca Evans & Associates)
Composition and Technical Illustration	Proctor-Willenbacher
Copyeditor	Erin Milnes
Proofreader	Ken DellaPenta
Indexer	Steve Rath
Printer	Courier Corporation

ACADEMIC PRESS
A Harcourt Science and Technology Company
525 B Street, Suite 1900, San Diego, CA 92101-4495, USA
http://www.academicpress.com

Academic Press
Harcourt Place, 32 Jamestown Road, London, NW1 7BY, United Kingdom
http://www.hbuk.co.uk/ap/

Morgan Kaufmann Publishers
340 Pine Street, Sixth Floor, San Francisco, CA 94104-3205, USA
http://www.mkp.com

04 03 02 01 00 5 4 3 2 1

Library of Congress Cataloging-in-Publication Data is available for this book.
ISBN 1-55860-562-2

This book is printed on acid-free paper.

To Barbara, who is simply amazing!

Jim

To the memory of my father, who encouraged me to choose the profession that was right for me, and to my mother, for instilling in me both a love of learning and a strong work ethic

Andrew

A NOTE FROM THE SERIES EDITOR

Jim Gray, *Microsoft Research*

Database systems have been trying to add *objects* to their data stores for almost two decades. Each vendor has invented an object model and added it to its brand of SQL. The results have been mixed—the extensions add great power, but the object model is typically not very well thought out and differences between the DBMS and the host programming language object models have just increased the impedance mismatch between them.

SQLJ embraces the Java object model and integrates it with the SQL language. It allows programs to manipulate SQL tables using SQL embedded in Java, it allows a persistent form of Java, it allows stored procedures written in SQLJ, and it allows the SQL system to store Java objects as values within tables. The resulting language is quite elegant. The benefits go beyond just the object-oriented extensions. Iterators nicely model cursors and loops, SQL nulls are modeled with the Java undefined value, and error handling is performed by the Java structured exception handling mechanism.

The result is a huge improvement in simplicity and productivity. Simple programs are indeed simple. Much of the tedium of ODBC/JDBC programming is subsumed by the unification of SQLJ. Unfortunately, dynamic SQL still requires something like ODBC/JDBC or ADO. Still, for most database programming tasks, SQLJ will be a huge advance.

Most DBMS vendors have directly participated in the design of SQLJ. Their products are beginning to support the language, and the standards bodies are in the process of standardizing it. SQLJ may well become the COBOL of the next decade: the workhorse of data processing applications.

Jim Melton and Andrew Eisenberg are the ideal expositors of this new synthesis. They have been active participants in the design and implementation of SQL and now SQLJ. Jim Melton has edited the SQL Standard for more than a decade and participated actively in the SQLJ design. Andrew Eisenberg has been working on object-oriented SQL extensions for more than a decade as well. They are justifiably excited about SQLJ and communicate that enthusiasm in this book.

The book itself is an easy read. It first gives a crash course on Java and then on SQL in two chapters. It then develops the concepts of JDBC and SQLJ through a set of examples. All the examples and some programming tools are on the accompanying CD-ROM. It is a tribute to SQLJ that the examples are so compact and simple, but Melton and Eisenberg deserve a lot of credit for their clear exposition of the underlying concepts.

FOREWORD

Rick Cattell, *Sun Microsystems*

This book is about the collision of two important revolutions in the computer industry: SQL and Java. The book is important because relational databases have become the most popular way to store data and because Java is becoming the most popular way to write programs. At year-end 1999, there were 1.7 million Java developers, a number that has more than doubled annually since 1996. At least two-thirds of those developers were writing SQL database applications.

Neither Java nor SQL databases could stand on their own, however. Work on SQL3 strove to make SQL into an object-oriented programming language, and object databases strove to make Java into a database language. Nevertheless, most people still prefer to write their programs in Java and to store their data in SQL databases. Bridges between Java and SQL are therefore essential. This book is about those bridges.

JDBC provided the first bridge, by allowing SQL database calls to be made from Java. The three parts of SQLJ bridge Java to relational databases by allowing SQL to be used in Java programs, Java programs to be used in SQL databases, and Java data types to be used as SQL data types. Java Blend and similar products bridge Java to SQL databases by automatically mapping relational tables to Java classes. Java GUI builders bridge the technologies by generating Java programs by mapping relational tables to Java GUI elements. The authors devote a chapter to each of these bridges.

The book is well written for multiple audiences: those who are just learning Java, those who are just learning SQL, and those who already know something about both. The authors have been in the center of SQL and SQLJ development, and are well qualified to describe the use of these technologies with Java.

CONTENTS

PREFACE

SQL and Java—And Why They Matter

SQL remains the most accepted and implemented interface language for database systems. Many companies have implemented database management systems whose principal—or only—interface is the SQL language. Countless other companies have implemented tools of unimaginable variety that support the use of SQL for database management.

If you haven't heard about Java, then you're probably not an active developer of applications software—at least not software associated with the Internet or the World Wide Web! Since it exploded onto the scene just a few years ago, Java has become one of the more important programming languages in many developers' toolboxes. It is an object-oriented programming language designed with the express goal of allowing applications to be run on any platform without coding changes or recompilation. (Your mileage may vary, as they say.)

As the popularity of Java grew, it became obvious to some that there was immense value in being able to use Java and SQL together more easily than the initial interfaces allowed. Starting in 1997, a group of database and database tool vendors got together to develop a specification for embedding SQL statements in Java programs; this specification was initially called "SQLJ Part 0" and is referred to by that name in this book.

In 1998, that document was published as an American National Standard in the form of a new *part* to SQL-92.[1]

The SQLJ developers went on to create two additional specifications that enhance the use of the Java programming language along with SQL databases. One of those supports the use of Java methods—stored in SQL databases—from SQL code, while the other supports the definition and storage of data in SQL databases that are in fact instances of Java classes. These specifications were initially known as "SQLJ Part 1"

---

[1] ANSI X3.135.10:1998, *Information systems—Database language—SQL—Part 10: Object Language Bindings (SQL/OLB),* American National Standards Institute, New York City, 1998.

and "SQLJ Part 2," respectively. SQLJ Part 1 was adopted as a new NCITS (National Committee for Information Technology Standards) standard in October 1999.[2] SQLJ Part 2 is also being processed as a de jure standard.

Why We Wrote This Book

There are no books available today that deal with the subject of combining SQL and Java. While there are many books on the SQL language and countless more on Java, and even a few books on using SQL from Java programs through the use of the JDBC API, we are unaware of any that broadly address the combination of the two. We believe that this issue is extremely important and will be interesting to everybody who needs to write enterprise-class applications intended for today's distributed environment on the Internet.

Because we both were fortunate enough to have been around when the concepts presented in this book were initially conceived and were able to participate in the development of some of this technology, we believe that we are in a unique position to pass on useful and genuinely interesting information from which our peers in the information technology industry can benefit.

Who Should Read It

Because of the orientation and style chosen for the book, we believe that it will be useful to a broad range of readers. Application programmers who need to develop Java code that accesses SQL databases are the primary audience, but we also kept in mind the needs of database administrators and designers as well as system analysts.

We hope that this book will be a useful resource to programmers at every level. In addition, system designers and implementers can benefit from knowing the design rationale and choices represented in the standard. We have even included some fairly esoteric material from a new part of the SQL standard, called SQL/OLB (in fact, this specification of Object Language Bindings (OLB) was derived from SQLJ Part 0, mentioned earlier), and from other areas of Java database-related technology with the intent of clarifying some of the murkier concepts. This may be of help to engineers building the SQL DBMS systems that provide ways of combining the power of Java and of SQL.

---

[2] ANSI NCITS 311.1:1999, *SQLJ—Part 1: SQL Routines Using the Java™ Programming Language,* American National Standards Institute, New York City, 1999.

How This Book Is Organized

SQL is a large and complex language; Java is not nearly so large, but the object paradigm used by Java can be complex and confusing. No completely linear treatment of the combination of these two powerful and popular languages can satisfy every reader. Unfortunately, printed books are inherently linear. We have tried to organize the book so that you can read it cover-to-cover if you are so inclined. However, we know that most readers don't approach technical books in this manner. Instead, you might prefer to skip around and first read the chapters or sections of particular interest to you, or that contain information required for your current projects. Both the amount of material in each chapter and the structure of the discussions are intended to facilitate this kind of "real-world" use.

A possibly unfortunate result of this dual-use organization is that we occasionally repeat ourselves to ensure that important material is covered. We trust that you won't find this too repetitive, but it was the best way to serve readers who will use the book as a quick reference.

You'll probably be happier reading selected chapters instead of going through the book cover to cover. In Chapter 1, we suggest ways to determine which chapters will be the most interesting to you, based on your current interests and expertise.

We start off with basic concepts, move into foundation material, proceed through some rather complex areas related to all aspects of the language, and end up spending quite a lot of the book presenting different areas of using Java with SQL. In all cases, when a particularly important concept is used, we've tried to give you a cross-reference to the location where it is discussed in detail.

This book is meant to be used largely in lieu of the SQL/OLB standard and other documents related to the subjects of using SQL and Java together. It is not at all a rehash of the SQL/OLB standard—in fact, it discusses aspects of SQL used with Java that are quite outside the scope of SQL/OLB. Whereas the standard is designed to tell vendors how to implement SQL/OLB in the context of an SQL DBMS, this book is intended to tell application writers how to *use* those features. If you are interested in the details of the language specification, Appendix A tells you how to buy a copy of the standard and of other relevant specifications for your own use.

However, this book is *not* a substitute for product documentation. It discusses several ways to combine the power of Java with the capabilities of SQL, doing so in the context of various de facto and de jure standards, as well as current implementations, but we do not limit our discussion to only those parts implemented by a specific vendor or at any specific point in time. You will frequently need documentation for your specific products to write your applications, but this book may give you some idea of what your system will be capable of in future versions.

Examples

One thing that should distinguish this book from most others is the nature of the example application. Almost all database books choose one of two example applications to illustrate language features: a payroll application and a parts database. We have long since tired of these applications and have tried to find something that could be more fun. We are both big cinema fans, so we decided to build a database of movie information and write our sample code to extract information from and manipulate data in that database. Appendix B presents the database definition (schema) and the data that we used for this application.

Wherever possible, we have actually run our example code and recorded the output produced by the products we used. Unfortunately, not all of our examples can actually be run—a small number of them use features of the SQL language or of JDBC that have not yet been implemented (though implementations may be available by the time you read this book). To highlight those examples where we had to "invent" the output, instead of actually running them and recording the output, we precede their titles with an ↷.

We've used Sybase's Adaptive Server Anywhere 6.0 (ASA 6.0) to run most of our examples, either through its interactive interface or through its jConnect JDBC driver. We've tried to use standard SQL syntax wherever possible, but occasionally the use of some ASA 6.0 extension to the standard was necessary (or crept in without our realizing it).

Anybody who has ever read a programming language manual or text knows that the authors always have to present the syntax of the language elements (the statements, for example) in *some* form. One of the most common techniques for this is the use of Backus-Naur form (BNF), which is used extensively in this book.

Moving Targets

As we finish writing this book, we are basing our understanding of these topics on a number of specifications. This technology is moving quickly, and parts of it will almost certainly change by the time you read this, or reread this (if you found it valuable the first time)—indeed, even while we wrote the book, the technology kept evolving and required us to revise chapters we thought we had finished. SQLJ Part 0 (SQL/OLB) was approved as a formal American National Standard in late 1998 and is currently being updated to align with JDBC 2.0 in preparation for publication as an International Standard. SQLJ Part 1 was formally approved as an American National Standard in mid-1999. SQLJ Part 2 will be going through its review and final approval cycle in 2000. The specification for JDBC 1.20 is widely used, and the final Java Developer's Kit that supports that version is JDK 1.1.8. The JDBC 2.0 Core API specification is available, the API is part of the Java 2 platform, Standard Edition, and products supporting it are beginning to appear.

Additional Resources

When you bought this book, you got a CD-ROM disk along with it. That CD-ROM holds interesting and useful material, including evaluation kits of Sybase's SQL Anywhere Studio, Oracle's SQLJ Reference Implementation Translator, Informix's Cloudscape, and Oracle's JDeveloper; the complete database schema, including sample data; and the complete text of all "interesting" examples.

Unfortunately, we were not able to include the latest release of the Java Developer's Kit, due to licensing restrictions, but you can get it yourself from the Java Web pages identified a little later in this Preface.

In addition to the CD-ROM, Morgan Kaufmann maintains a Web site on which some of the resources associated with this book can be found, including the database schema, sample data, and example text. Possibly even more important, though, is that we will post on the Web site any corrections to errata discovered in this book. You can find Morgan Kaufmann on the Web at *www.mkp.com*. The Web page associated with this book is *www.mkp.com/books_catalog/catalog.asp?ISBN-1-55860-562-2*.

See the About the CD-ROM section at the end of this book for important information on the CD-ROM.

Relevant Products

Another moving target is the range of products that implement various interfaces and specifications discussed in this book. Although we know that readers of a book about using Java and SQL together are naturally interested in knowing whether their favorite product (e.g., database system, application development tool, etc.) provides the facilities we describe, we can only cite those products that are available at the time we write the book—knowing that the list is likely to grow longer every month.

We are willing to say this much now: The following companies are each known to be implementing or to have implemented one or more products that build on the facilities described in this book:

- Cloudscape, Inc. *(www.cloudscape.com)*
- IBM Corporation *(www.ibm.com)*
- Informix Software, Inc. *(www.informix.com)*
- Oracle Corporation *(www.oracle.com)*
- Sun Microsystems *(java.sun.com)*
- Sybase, Inc. *(www.sybase.com)*

There may well be other companies that should appear in this list; if so, we apologize for excluding them and will endeavor to correct the omission whenever possible.

Naturally, different versions of products may enhance the facilities already implemented. Keep in touch with your vendors for the latest information about products that implement these specifications.

Conventions

A quick note on the typographical conventions used in the book:

- Type in this font (Stone Serif) is used for all ordinary text.
- *Type in this font (Stone Serif Italic) is used for terms that we define, for emphasis, and for Web addresses.*
- `Type in this font (Courier) is used for all the examples, syntax presentation, SQL keywords and identifiers, and Java identifiers that appear in ordinary text.`
- **`Type in this font (Courier Bold) is used to highlight especially interesting parts of some examples.`**
- *`Type in this font (Courier Italic) is used occasionally to represent strings of text in BNF or example text to be replaced with user-provided text in actual code.`*

Acknowledgments

Writing any book is a labor of love, with the emphasis all too often on "labor." It's hard, but rewarding. It's rare to do it alone—the assistance of others is invaluable: for reviews, for bouncing ideas off, and often just for encouragement. We cannot fail to acknowledge and thank the wonderful and talented people who reviewed this book and offered help throughout the process. We especially want to thank Ames Carlson, Chris Farrar, and Rick Cattell for their extensive reviews—the depth and breadth of several chapters were inspired by their comments and suggestions—as well as Nelson Mattos for his review of the SQL:1999 user-defined type material. Chuck Campbell also deserves our thanks for reviewing the CD-ROM and suggesting ways to improve its useability.

Both of us want to acknowledge the support we have gotten from Don Deutch, longtime chair of NCITS H2 (the ANSI technical committee on databases) and our manager when we worked at Sybase. Jim also wishes to express his appreciation to Vishu Krishnamurthy and Andy Mendelsohn, his management at Oracle, for their support and encouragement. Andrew thanks Clark French, his manager at Progress, for supporting this book.

We'd also like to thank Diane Cerra, Belinda Breyer, Edward Wade, and others at Morgan Kaufmann Publishers for their outstanding support during the conception, writing, and production of this book. Diane provided us with tremendously helpful feedback and suggestions about the content and style of the book, Belinda kept the lines of communication open and ensured that our chapters were quickly reviewed, and Edward made the production process almost painless; to them and others, we are most grateful.

And, of course, while writing a book, lots of other things in life go neglected. We are immensely grateful to our Significant Others—Barbara Edelberg and Nancy Eisenberg—for picking up the load and keeping our lives on track while the book was in progress. We can't say whether or not it's true that we couldn't have done it without their help, but we're quite positive that it would have been more difficult and not nearly as much fun. Thanks!

CHAPTER 1

Introduction

1.1 Overview of the Book

Lest there be any confusion on this point, we want to be quite clear: This book is about using Java and SQL together. It is not a book about SQL per se—that is, you shouldn't expect to learn all about SQL (neither the SQL standard nor any specific product's implementation) in this book. There exist any number of books covering SQL thoroughly, and we encourage you to take advantage of them if your knowledge of SQL is limited. Neither is this a book about Java; there are considerable resources available for your use in learning that language, and what you get out of this book will benefit considerably if you have a working knowledge of Java. Instead, we will show you, sometimes in great detail and other times in a sketchier form, a number of ways in which you can use the power of SQL and the power of Java together to build your applications.

In this book, we're going to cover a great variety of material, for the very pertinent reason that there are several effective ways of combining Java and SQL in applications. Some of these methods have been available since shortly after Java exploded onto the scene in the mid-1990s; others were developed over a period of two or three years after that. No doubt, other ideas are still gestating as this book is being written; we can't cover those today, but perhaps a future edition will close the gap.

In Section 1.2, we'll give you a bit of a road map to suggest how you might consider using the book; in preparation for that, we will sketch out the material we cover in this book:

1. Brief introductions to Java and to SQL. We know that few professionals today are fluent in both the database language SQL and the object programming language Java. Although we have no intention of attempting to teach you either of those languages, we consider it important to provide those of you who are fluent in SQL enough information about Java to whet your appetite and to make this book useful to you, but we encourage you to turn to other resources to learn Java more completely.

   Similarly, we believe that those of you reading this book who are Java programmers, but aren't familiar with SQL, will be able to get a "feel" for SQL in this book, but we urge you to use the many other available SQL resources to become truly conversant with the language. See Chapters 2 and 3 for this material.
2. JDBC 1.0. Shortly after Java itself was made available, JavaSoft also published the specifications for a database interface (an application programming interface [API]), composed of a package of Java class and interface definitions, that allows convenient access to relational database management systems—SQL systems in particular. Although JDBC has both a name and a look-and-feel that resembles Microsoft Corporation's popular Open Database Connectivity (ODBC) API, it is not merely a clone of that interface. Instead, JDBC (which JavaSoft has stated is not an acronym and doesn't stand for anything like Java Database Connectivity) is better viewed as an object-oriented analog of interfaces like ODBC.

   We do not plan to teach you the JDBC API here. Several excellent books and other source material are already available covering that subject thoroughly. However, because it is both an important component of some of the other interfaces that we will cover in detail in this book and an interface of significance in its own right, we will introduce you to the API and give you enough information to follow the ways in which it is used in other areas covered by this book. As with SQL and Java, we encourage you to locate other resources to learn JDBC in detail. Chapter 4 addresses this subject. The JDBC 2.0 API builds on the JDBC 1.0 API. It contains several new features and support for SQL:1999 data types. The JDBC 2.0 API is addressed in Chapter 9.

3. Writing Java programs that use SQL. Undoubtedly, the first urge most Java programmers will have when they become aware of SQL and the advantages it gives applications—particularly enterprise-class applications—is to write a Java program that accesses an SQL database. One approach to writing such a program is to use JDBC, but we have found (as have many other people in this industry) that JDBC is not exactly user-friendly. Its style is clearly aligned with the style of using any Java-oriented interface, which makes it reasonably familiar to Java programmers. JDBC may be the right approach for applications that need to issue dynamic SQL statements, but for applications in which static SQL is sufficient, JDBC makes application writers remain unnecessarily aware of gritty details. . . clouding their ability to focus on the application itself.

   Another approach, called "SQLJ" by some, has emerged to allow application developers to embed SQL statements directly in their Java code, in much the same way that the SQL standard has long allowed coders to embed SQL statements in their C, COBOL, and PL/I programs. This "embedded Java" capability, in addition to catching on quickly with database vendors, is now part of the SQL standard; however, the precise mechanisms of embedding SQL into Java programs differs sufficiently from the mechanisms used for embedding it into other languages that a separate part of the SQL standard was developed. It is this embedding capability that forms the first really substantive section of this book. You'll find information about this in Chapter 5.

4. Writing SQL programs that use Java. Similarly, as soon as an SQL programmer becomes aware of Java—its power and popularity, and the advantages it can offer because of its object orientation and its ability to reuse code in the form of classes—his first question is likely to be "How can I invoke Java routines directly from my SQL code?" We believe that the most important use of Java routines in SQL code will be the ability for SQL routines that are stored in the database to invoke Java routines that are also stored in the database.

   Another aspect of "SQLJ" provides exactly this ability: to write portions of your application in Java and then invoke those Java routines from your SQL code. This offers tremendous advantages, particularly when the semantics of your applications demand that you perform certain operations both in code unrelated to database access and in the database-oriented segments of your programs: by using the exact same routines, written in Java, you can ensure that the exact same semantics are provided in both places. The specification for invoking Java routines from SQL has been standardized, but not as part of the SQL standard; instead, it constitutes the first part of a new two-part standard and is called "SQLJ Part 1: SQL Routines Using the Java™ Programming Language." Chapter 6 focuses on this technology.

5. Building databases that store Java objects. One of the principal shortcomings of using object-oriented programming languages (OOPL) in enterprise-class applications has been the inability of those languages to cause the objects they manipulate to persist for longer than the program runs. Obviously, there are many, many categories of application in which objects might be created one day and then used on many days following—perhaps for years afterward. A minor industry has arisen to address the issue of providing "persistent C++" or "persistent Smalltalk" or "persistent *X*" (insert your favorite OOPL here), but most of the solutions offered have been only the ability to "cache" programming language objects onto disk storage so they can be reacquired at a later time.

   There are considerable advantages to be had if applications can not only store their objects (values, or states, as well as the routines that manipulate them) in some persistent store, but manipulate them within that store as well—just as easily and using the same facilities as manipulating them in the programming language environment. SQLJ takes this additional step of permitting you to define SQL tables having columns whose data types are Java classes! This ability allows you not only to store your Java objects in columns of SQL tables, but also to operate on those objects *in the database,* without having to retrieve them to your application code, manipulate them there, and return them to the database. You can make significant performance gains in this way, of course, but you also benefit from reduced loss of semantic integrity through the elimination of several sources of impedance mismatch between SQL and Java.

   A second part of that new two-part standard, to be called "SQLJ Part 2: SQL Types Using the Java™ Programming Language," will support this capability, which is covered in Chapter 8.

   In Chapter 7, we introduce you to SQL:1999's user-defined types to show an alternative approach that your applications can choose—to build your "objects" using pure SQL. This alternative may be desirable if, for example, your application can be built to run entirely (or largely) within the database and to eschew most client-side operations. One reason this is interesting is that SQLJ Part 2 maps Java types and SQL's user-defined types to one another. As with other aspects of SQL, it is not our intent here to teach you all about SQL's user-defined types; instead, we suggest that you avail yourself of other resources that cover that subject thoroughly. Nonetheless, we have observed that JDBC has been extended with specifications to allow you to map your Java classes closely to SQL's user-defined types and—more importantly—to help you access your SQL user-defined type values through your Java code. In addition to Chapter 7, you'll find Chapter 9 helpful here.

6. Applying object-oriented capabilities to "legacy data" through Java. No matter how popular Java is now—or how popular it may yet become—the truth is that there are enormous quantities of data, extremely valuable data, in existence today that cannot be inexpensively accessed through Java, even using the facilities we've mentioned above.

   JavaSoft has responded to this situation with a product called Java Blend, which allows users to "map" Java classes onto existing SQL databases. Java Blend is an implementation of the ODMG 2.0 specification using the newly defined Java bindings. Java Blend requires no changes to your databases—it isn't necessary to create tables with columns whose types are Java classes or to create Java stored routines—but it does support accessing your SQL data through an interface that has an object-oriented look and feel about it. Happily, it allows you to avoid most of the pain associated with the use of JDBC, as well. This technology is still emerging, and it hasn't been proved in the furnaces of enterprise application development. Nonetheless, it offers some advantages (as well as disadvantages) and we give you a modest overview of the facility.

   Other vendors have products with similar goals, such as SoftwareTree's JDX, WebLogic's dbKona, and so forth. We have chosen to deal with Java Blend in our treatment of this technology for two reasons: First, we are limited in the space we can allocate to a single aspect of Java and SQL together; and, second, we believe that more readers will be familiar with Java Blend (if only by name). We have no intention of implying that the other products are less worthy of your attention; we simply didn't want the book to be overwhelmed with this particular area of technology. Chapter 10 is the place you can read more about Java Blend.

7. Building applications. Writing Java code isn't, necessarily, difficult, but it can be exceedingly tedious. Java, frankly, isn't a fourth-generation language (4GL) but is a powerful 3GL language roughly based on another powerful 3GL language, C++. A number of powerful application development environments have sprung up to help you build your applications more easily. These GUI tools are usually object-oriented themselves and offer tremendous efficiency advantages when building small client applications, larger Web applications, and complex enterprise applications. We survey several tools on the market and analyze their support for leveraging Java and SQL together. Chapter 11 covers this topic.
8. Seeing into the future. We give you our opinions—educated, but opinions nonetheless—about what we think will happen to the Java-SQL synergy in the future, discussing not only technology advances that are likely to come about, but how standards in this area will affect (and be affected by) those advances in the technology. Take a look at Chapter 12 for our view of the future of Java and SQL together.

We're sure that's not everything that could be usefully said about the subject of using SQL and Java together, but we believe it's the most important bits. It's a highly dynamic industry that we're examining in this book and things change very quickly. No book can be completely up to date, but we've covered the products and standards in use at the time we wrote this one, and we'll continue to monitor developments to see whether a revision of the book will help you.

We will provide updates to certain information contained in this book, as well as corrections of errors discovered after printing, on our publisher's Web site at *www.mkp.com.*

1.2 Road Map

In the Preface to this book, we acknowledged that a subject as complex as using SQL and Java together simply can't be satisfactorily presented in any linear arrangement. We recognize that some readers will have the motivation and time to read this book cover to cover—and we admire people with that level of dedication! But we also recognize that many readers will want to go directly to the meaty bits, based on their particular needs.

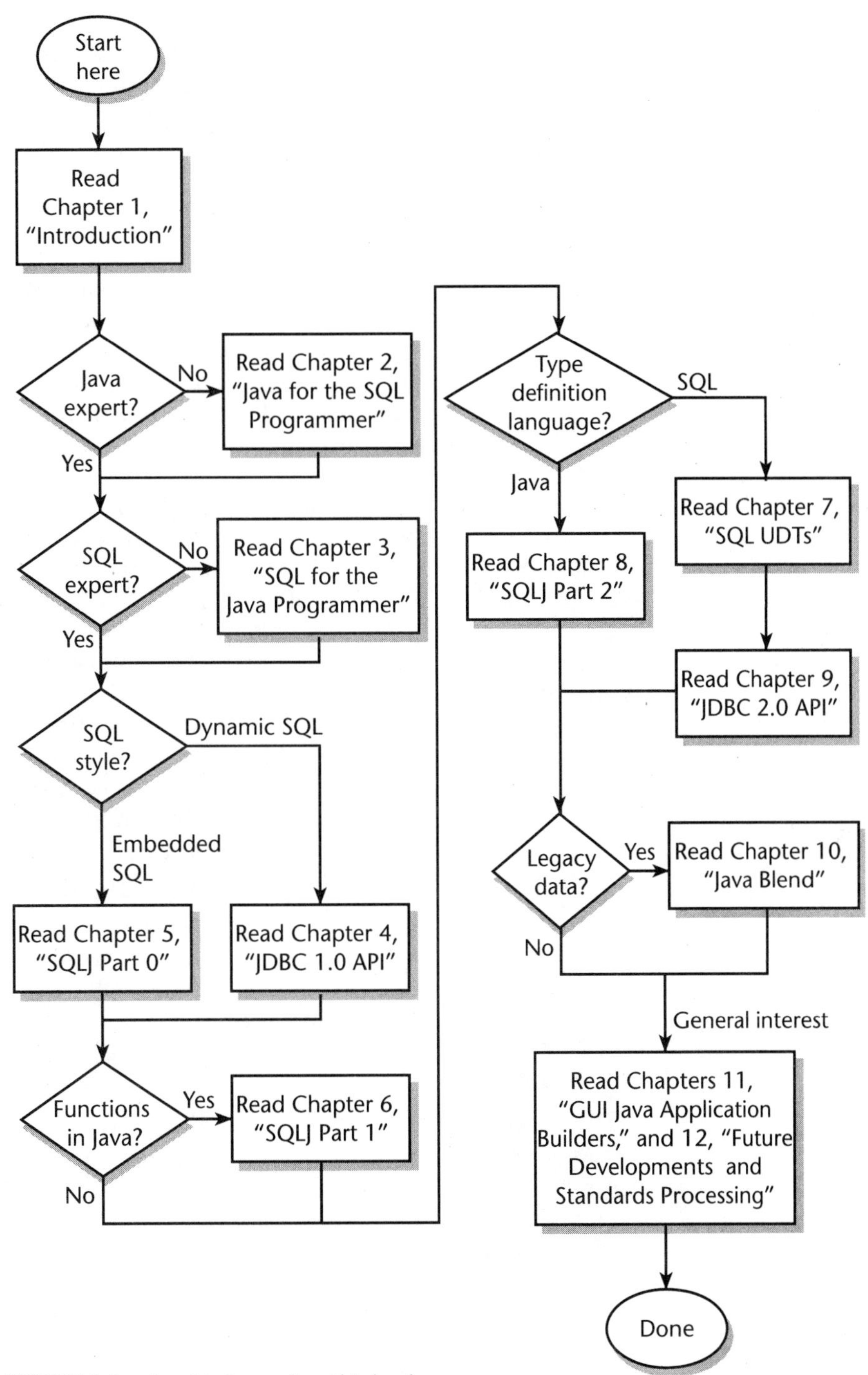

FIGURE 1.1 *A guide to reading this book.*

To that end, we've put together a sort of road map that we hope will guide you to the parts of the book that will benefit you most, given your interests, background, and current requirements. Figure 1.1 graphically illustrates the organization of the book and shows decision points where you might make choices.

1.3 What Problem Needs Solving?

We're going to talk an awful lot about how Java and SQL can be used together. Let's take a moment to consider the applications that might use these technologies to their best advantage.

Application architectures have changed considerably over time. Long, long ago, applications resided on mainframes, and terminals provided I/O and possibly simple validation. Figure 1.2 illustrates this architecture.

The emergence of client machines allowed small, self-contained databases, or parts of a larger centralized database, to be moved to the client machine. The emergence of local area networks (LANs) made feasible replication of all or parts of a database, as illustrated in Figure 1.3.

The emergence of LANs also allowed parts of an application to be moved to the client, with the data still residing on a server, as we illustrate in Figure 1.4. Finally, the emergence of higher speed modems made feasible the replication and synchronization of database fragments by occasionally connected users.

Most recently, we have seen the emergence of intranet and Internet applications. An intranet application, illustrated in Figure 1.5, may be installed by individuals or by an IT department. Within a company or organization, the choice of client hardware and operating system may be limited.

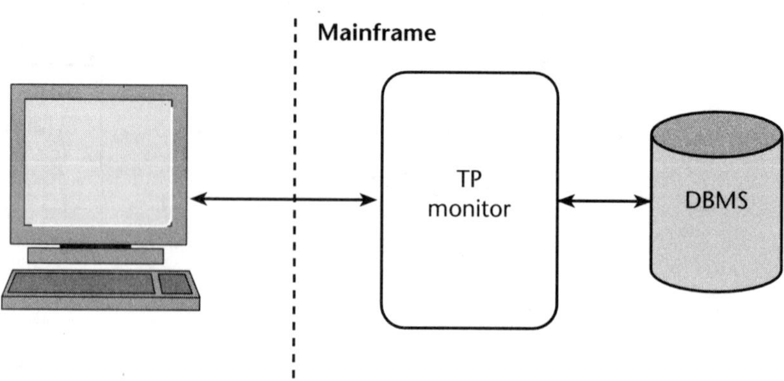

FIGURE 1.2 *Mainframe application architecture.*

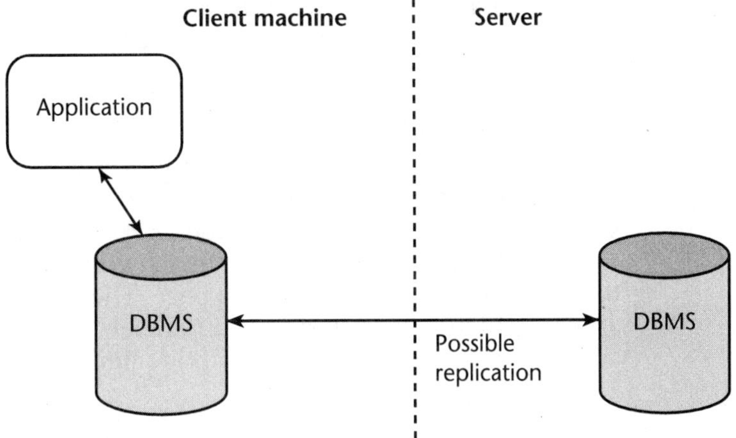

FIGURE 1.3 *Local application architecture.*

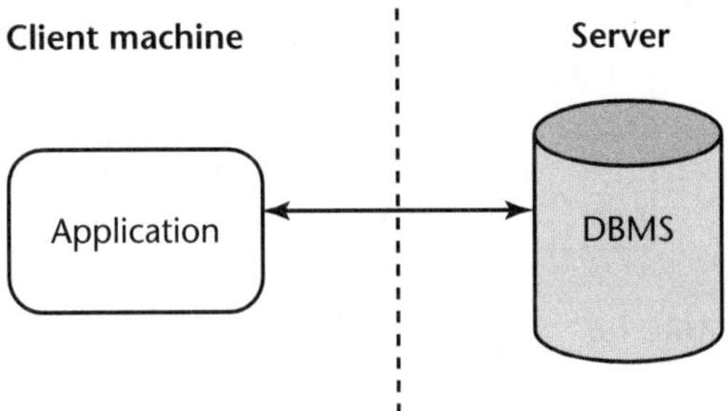

FIGURE 1.4 *Client/server application architecture.*

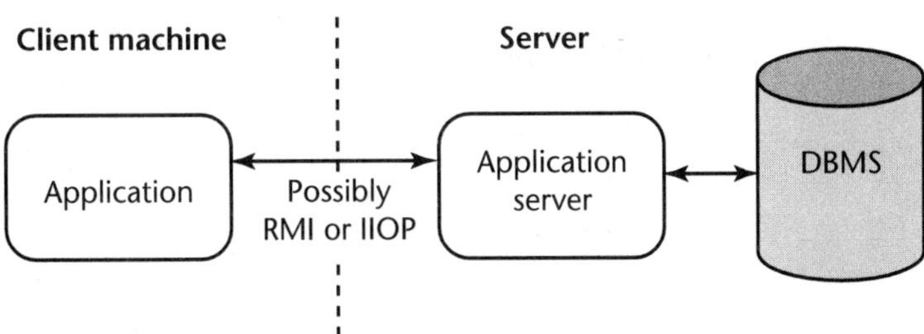

FIGURE 1.5 *Intranet application architecture.*

Internet applications are typically accessed by a browser, which may itself run on many different types of client machines. With this architecture, it is impractical to require that any type of application installation or configuration be done on the client machine. The end user generally does not want to be bothered with this chore, and the use of a number of possible client hardware platforms makes this prohibitive. Internet applications can take one of several forms. A Web server may serve up static HTML pages, as well as HTML pages that have been generated dynamically. Another approach is to bring the application over to the client along with the Web page. The Web server can serve up the applet, which can then access a database directly, or it can access an application server. These variations are illustrated in turn by Figures 1.6, 1.7, and 1.8.

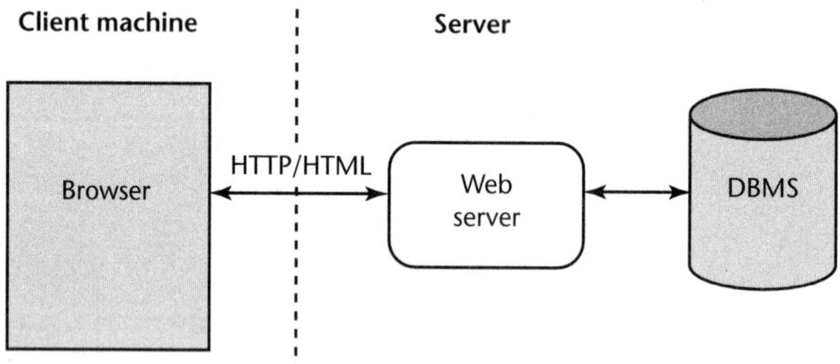

FIGURE 1.6 *Simple internet application architecture.*

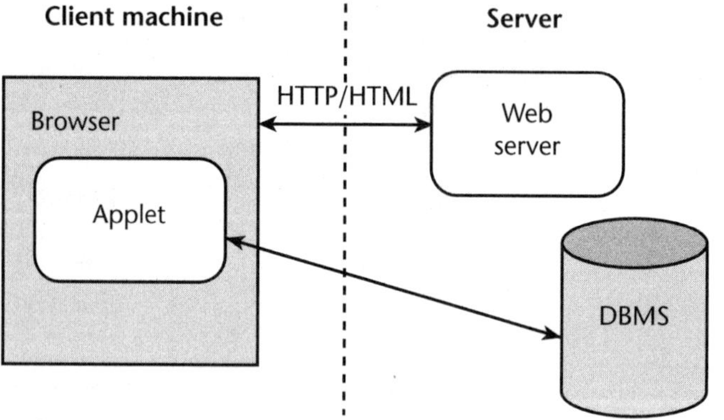

FIGURE 1.7 *Simple internet applet application architecture.*

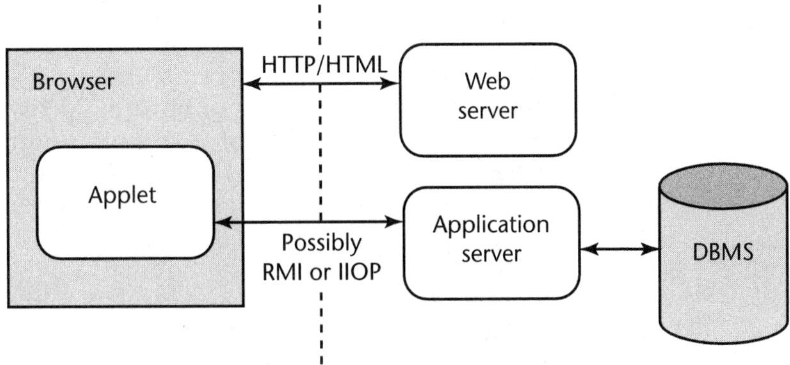

FIGURE 1.8 *Internet application server architecture.*

In all of these diagrams, we see access to a database. It is possible for a Java program to perform this function in almost all of these architectures (the exception is the mainframe application architecture). A Web or application server can be written in Java in whole or in part.

1.3.1 Putting Java and Persistent Data Together

Java is a relatively new programming language, but it is arguably growing—and maturing—faster and being adopted by more organizations more rapidly than any previous programming language. Although much of this rapid acceptance is driven by several possibly debatable perceptions (e.g., that Java is platform-independent and completely portable, that Java is finely tuned for the Internet and the World Wide Web, that Java offers independence from proprietary vendor interests), it is also true that Java offers attractive advantages as merely another programming language.

Because Java is clearly object-oriented and has been found to be powerful enough for use in developing enterprise-class applications, it quickly gained attention as a primary language for building new application systems. Simultaneously, because it was derived from one of the most popular non–object-oriented programming languages—C, via C++—the learning curve for a great many software professionals has proven easier to overcome than for other object-oriented languages, such as Smalltalk or CLOS.

SQL, of course, is not at all new, the first standard for the language appearing in 1986, not too long after the first products in the early 1980s. The SQL standard, however, is not static—new versions have been published in 1989, 1992, and 1999, and both observers and participants anticipate that future versions will be published at intervals of three to five years. There are a great many software professionals trained on SQL database systems, and we are confident that a significant fraction of those have been or are learning to program in Java as well. Combining the capabilities of both languages offers developers a lot of power for developing complex and robust applications.

Of course, SQL is not the only mechanism for accessing data—the world has a lot of important data stored in "flat file" systems, in hierarchical (e.g., IMS) and network (e.g., CODASYL) databases, and even on magnetic tapes. Java programmers will have to be able to access that data as well as SQL data. Nevertheless, this book will focus on accessing data stored in SQL databases simply because we believe that the great majority of new applications written in Java will focus on SQL technology more than those older alternatives. There are, of course, numerous gateway products on the market that provide SQL access to these legacy data sources, bringing us back into the area where we feel most comfortable.

1.3.2 Java and "Native" Interfaces

Java, as you may know, depends heavily on class definitions for most of its capabilities. The Java language itself is pretty small but is extensible through the ability to define new classes that perform whatever functions an application requires.

There are several ways to access an SQL database system from a Java program (which, of course, is the whole point of this book). If Java is augmented by JDBC—that is, if the JDBC-provided package of class definitions and interfaces, called `java.sql`, is available—then you can access SQL through JDBC.

But what if you need to access data stored in some non-SQL environment? JDBC doesn't offer any solution for that, and neither do the other approaches discussed in this book. Instead, you'll probably have to take advantage of what JavaSoft (recently renamed the Java Software division of Sun Microsystems) calls the "native interface" for that data store. This process entails writing the Java specification of the interfaces presented by that data store, using the Java keyword `native` to signal the Java environment that this code invokes non-Java code . . . which is no small task. Although the Java language and runtime environment have been designed very carefully to minimize the dangers associated with code from unknown sources, leaving the Java "sandbox" (that is, the carefully controlled runtime environment in which Java applications normally execute) and entering the realm of non-Java code eliminates most of those safeguards.

Another approach is to use the network messaging capabilities provided in the `java.net` package to communicate with a foreign data source or server.

It is quite beyond the scope of this book to cover writing and using either native methods or Java network communication, but we did feel that it was important to mention these capabilities at least briefly. If you find that you need to access non-SQL data stores, then you should take advantage of other resources, such as one of the many JDBC-oriented books or a book addressing Java Native Interface (JNI), that cover the subject in detail.

Of course, it is possible to access data stored in SQL databases by using a native interface, too; however, because the Java environment offers several all-Java (and several mostly-Java) alternatives for getting to SQL database systems, we believe that it will be rare for you to have the need to use a native interface for this purpose. The only reason that occurs to us is if your SQL store doesn't provide an ODBC (yes, we said "ODBC") interface at all, which is pretty uncommon these days. ODBC is the minimum necessary to support use of JDBC because, as we elaborate in Chapter 4, JDBC implementations can be based on a JDBC-to-ODBC bridge.

1.3.3 Java Serialization

During the course of this book, we'll talk about the need to store Java objects—that is, instances of Java classes—in some persistent way. Normally, this notion means "in a database" or "in a file" (but there might be other interpretations about which we aren't concerned at present).

If all you need to do in your application is preserve the state of one or more Java objects in a way that permits your computing environment to be "significantly disturbed" (for example, to protect against crashes and reboots), then you might be satisfied with just converting those objects into some format that permits them to be written to a disk or tape, keeping for yourself the responsibility of managing that storage medium. Java classes can be declared to implement an interface called `java.io.Serializable`, meaning that the class implementation provides methods to convert a class instance to a string of bits (perhaps a string of characters) and to convert one of those strings back into a class instance.

You can think of serializing a Java object as converting it to an external (but unusable!) format for temporary storage and deserializing as converting that external format back into a real object. Serialized objects aren't really objects at all any more, and you cannot invoke their methods without deserializing them first. But it's one way of making the state of an object persist across some span of time when the Java environment isn't active. It's even possible to use serialization as one way of passing an object from one Java environment to another; in fact, this is exactly what Java Remote Method Invocation (RMI) does. When using this method, however, the unique identity of the object isn't maintained—that is, the two environments probably won't know that they've merely got copies of the same object.

We'll talk more about object serialization in Chapter 2.

1.3.4 Static SQL, Dynamic SQL, and ODBC (SQL/CLI)

Several ways to access SQL databases are provided by the SQL standard and by various SQL implementations. Each method has positive and negative aspects. We'll discuss all three in more detail, especially the two that are most relevant to Java, later in the book. However, it's worth a couple of minutes to summarize them here (especially if you're not already familiar with building SQL applications).

For most of the time that SQL has been in existence, the most popular mechanism for using it has been to *embed* "static" SQL statements into otherwise-ordinary programs written in some more conventional programming language. This approach has the advantage of being quite efficient, since the embedded SQL programs can be compiled in such a way that the database access is pre-optimized and ready to go whenever the applications are run. This approach works very well for stable applications where the queries and operations against the database are well defined and known in advance.

However, that approach doesn't work as well when the database operations can't be confidently determined while the application is being written—for example, in an environment where a great many ad hoc queries are expected, when successive refinement of queries is required to acquire desired information, or when the user is performing on-line analysis of data. For such purposes, a more dynamic approach is required.

The first attempts to provide this more dynamic approach did so by defining SQL statements that accepted character strings representing other SQL statements and then preparing them (think "interactive compilation and optimization") for (possibly later and/or repeated) execution or else executing them one time immediately. This facility, called "dynamic SQL," worked quite well for certain classes of dynamic applications but was most successful when contained in a single-system setup such as that found in many mainframe computing environments.

As distributed computing capabilities, such as client-server, became more important to the user community, ordinary dynamic SQL began showing its limitations and a still more dynamic approach was required. The response from the database community was to provide call-level interfaces—functional interfaces—to SQL database management systems. This approach has been standardized under the name SQL/CLI, and the most popular implementation is Microsoft's ODBC.

CLI (or, if you prefer, ODBC) has truly captured the hearts and minds of database application programmers in any environment where highly dynamic capabilities are required.

You can learn a bit more about this in Chapter 3, although we suggest you take advantage of the numerous SQL resources available for detailed information on the subject.

1.3.5 JDBC, with and without ODBC

But where does that leave Java programmers—especially those who don't want to deal with native interfaces and the potential problems they involve?

Happily, Java can be accompanied by JDBC. JDBC is a Java interface to SQL database management systems and can operate in pure-Java mode if desired. However, in order to give Java programmers access to the maximum number of SQL database systems, JDBC can also interface with ODBC through something called the JDBC-ODBC bridge. It's also possible to interface Java to the database system's native drivers through a "partly Java driver" without too much violation of your desire for pure Java. Finally, JDBC allows the use of database drivers that translate the JDBC method invocations directly into network protocols used by the database systems, either the proprietary protocols specified by individual vendors or a DBMS-independent protocol.

These alternatives put different demands on your system management facilities, though. Some require installing additional software onto your client platforms, while others require additional software on the server platforms. Your choice of which to use will be governed by many considerations, including the number of client machines that need to access your databases, the number of database servers that your clients will access, whether all of the client and server machines are under your control or not, and so forth.

We don't cover this subject (system management and implementation-specific details of installing software) further in this book, but you can turn to JDBC resources for additional guidance. JDBC 1.0, however, is addressed in Chapter 4.

1.3.6 SQLJ Specifications and Standards

One of the most important developments related to database access from Java programs is known as "SQLJ" (which stands for "SQL-Java" but avoids trademark problems associated with the name "Java"). SQLJ is a multipart specification developed by a group of database experts from a spectrum of companies in the data management industry, including SQL database system vendors as well as database tools vendors.

The first part of SQLJ that was developed came to be known as "Part 0" and dealt with embedding SQL statements in Java programs. Although SQLJ Part 0 specifies a facility that is analogous to the SQL standard way of embedding SQL statements in programs written in a more conventional programming language, it contains significant differences arising from Java's object-oriented nature.

Because of those differences, the SQL-embedded-in-Java facility was not merged into the part of SQL:1999 dealing with host language bindings (SQL/Bindings), but was instead processed as a separate part of the SQL standard—called SQL/OLB (for Object Language Bindings). Furthermore, the style of the language used in the document for this new part 10 of the SQL standard (SQL/OLB) is noticeably different from the style of the other parts of SQL, owing largely to its heritage as a pseudo-consortium specification. Whether the SQL standard as a whole benefits or suffers from this style of specification remains to be seen, but one advantage is immediately clear: the SQL standards community was able to publish SQL/OLB much sooner than if it had been required to be rewritten in the more formal "standardese" used by other parts of the SQL standard. Chapter 5 will deal with this topic at length.

Another part of SQLJ, Part 1, deals with the ability to invoke methods written in Java from SQL code—that is, directly in SQL statements. The Java methods provide the implementation of SQL routines (procedures and functions). This offers a number of advantages for your applications. Perhaps the most important advantage is that you can write a routine (say, one that computes pro-rated interest on corporate debt) and use that routine in your client-side applications *and* in your database applications—and be assured that the identical results will be produced in both places. This assurance can be quite comforting when compared with the more typical environment in which routines used outside the database system are often written in one language and those inside the database are written in another; under that situation, it's difficult, at best, to be sure that the two routines produce exactly the same results in all cases. We'll address this in full detail in Chapter 6.

A third part of SQLJ, called Part 2 (isn't zero-based numbering *fun*?), provides the capability of storing and using Java objects directly in your databases! Although SQL:1999 does, as we'll see in Chapters 3 and 7, have a user-defined type capability that offers significant support for object orientation, you may benefit significantly from being able to use the same object definitions in the rest of your applications that you use within your database. Further, SQL:1999's user-defined types are available only in the SQL environment (although we admit that it's theoretically possible for someone to extend relevant parts of the SQL environment into the client side, we find it unlikely that this process will become a marketplace reality). SQLJ Part 2 allows you to "import" a Java package right into your SQL database and set up the metadata appropriately so that you can begin defining tables containing columns whose data types are specified to be a Java class. Once you have done that, you can store Java objects in those columns in rows of the table and manipulate those objects using ordinary Java method invocations. We'll cover this in great detail in Chapter 8.

1.3.7 Java Blend

In 1998, JavaSoft released a new tool to be used for developing database-oriented applications purely in Java. Developed in conjunction with the Baan Company, Java Blend provides automatic facilities that map SQL tables onto Java classes and map the columns of those tables onto fields of the classes.

Java Blend offers the promise of allowing you to write Java applications whose data are automatically transferred between Java objects and your SQL database. This capability might or might not affect your business, but we believe that there are certain situations where the automatic translation between the Java and SQL model of data is valuable. Java Blend uses JDBC to actually access the database to which a mapping is desired and accesses the metadata of the database through JDBC methods to "discover" the structures of the database—the tables, views, columns, and so forth. When you write your applications using Java Blend, you don't write SQL queries on the underlying database; you write OQL queries on your Java classes, which Java Blend then translates into SQL database queries. OQL is a query language derived from SQL by the Object Data Management Group (ODMG . . . not to be confused with the OMG, or Object Management Group).

We'll discuss Java Blend in some detail in Chapter 10.

1.3.8 Interfaces to (ODMG-Compliant) OODBMSs

An alternative to using SQL and Java together that we hear suggested every now and then is this: Why not just use an object-oriented database with an object-oriented programming language? In fact, the Object Data Management Group (ODMG) makes just that recommendation, having published a specification for an object model and a query language (OQL) with a Java binding. We don't agree with that recommendation, as you'll infer from the fact that this book doesn't pursue the OODBMS alternative, but you're right to ask us, "Why not?"

The "why not" boils down to the following points:

- There are a great many more installations of SQL database management systems—and a great deal more data stored under their control—than of OODBMSs. This means that, except for brand-new applications without any legacy data to consider, SQL is far more likely to be required than any other database language.

- The number of software professionals trained to write and maintain SQL code is significantly higher, probably by two or more orders of magnitude, than those trained in OODBMSs. This suggests that staffing an implementation project is likely to be both easier and less costly if you use SQL.
- The data model defined by SQL and used by SQL DBMS implementations is well defined and fairly constant across those implementations (although there are a regrettably large number of language differences among them), whereas the range of data model (and language) differences across OODBMS implementations is significantly larger. This suggests that you will have greater flexibility in changing vendors if required by economics or politics if you choose SQL.
- More people and more companies are working to integrate SQL with Java and to supply tools to enhance the synergy between the two languages; by contrast, the number of people and companies working to integrate Java with OODBMSs is small and not growing particularly fast. Although this may be a matter of perception and can certainly change overnight (unlike our earlier points), it supports our belief that SQL is far more mainstream.

If you have special interest in OODBMS technology and its use with Java, several resources are available on the subject, and we encourage you to look to them for help. We will mention this subject once again in Chapter 3, where we will identify the best resources we know on the issue.

1.4 Chapter Summary

In this introductory chapter, we gave you a broad overview of the book and the subjects that we cover in it. In addition, we suggested ways in which you might approach the book, based on your background and expected ways of using Java and SQL together. Finally, we discussed a number of topics concerning the use of SQL with Java (or is that "Java with SQL"?), as well as several issues related to accessing other sorts of data with Java.

With this introduction under your belt you're ready to dig into the more technical material we've got in store. So get out your shovels and pickaxes and let's move on!

CHAPTER

2

Java for the SQL Programmer

2.1 Introduction

As an SQL programmer, you are certainly familiar with one or more programming languages, possibly COBOL, C, or C++. You might have embedded SQL statements in one of these languages, or perhaps you have developed an application using the ODBC programming API, with the ODBC calls coming from one of these languages. This chapter is intended for those of you who have not yet encountered the Java programming language.

In any of these programming languages, or in any of the variants of SQL's stored procedure language, you have become familiar with constructs such as data types, functions, procedures, control flow, and exception handling. The Java programming language has its own particular flavor of all of these, as we shall soon see.

Many books are available to teach you the Java programming language in all of its glory. The best known of these is probably *The Java Programming Language,*[1] co-authored by James Gosling, the creator of the Java programming language. You may also want to look at the Sun Web site, *java.sun.com*. It contains a great deal of information on all aspects of Java.

---

1 *The Java Programming Language, 2nd edition,* Ken Arnold and James Gosling, Addison-Wesley, 1997.

Our goal in this chapter is to make you familiar with Java's most important elements, especially those that will be relevant to SQLJ. We will discuss JDBC, Java's method of making requests of an SQL database, separately. The JDBC 1.0 API will be discussed in Chapter 4, and the JDBC 2.0 API will be discussed in Chapter 9.

2.2 The Java Environment

A Java compiler accepts a Java source program and produces Java *bytecode* files. Unlike the output from a traditional language compiler, these bytecode files are independent of the machine and operating system that were used during compilation.

Bytecode files are interpreted by a Java Virtual Machine (JVM). JVMs are available on a wide variety of hardware platforms and operating systems. Although we won't discuss Java applets very much, it is worth mentioning that the Web browsers, such as Netscape Navigator and Microsoft Internet Explorer, that have been produced in the last several years include their own JVMs to support applets.

You may wish to experiment with Java by getting one of the Java Developer's Kits (JDKs) that are available without charge from the Sun Web site. A JDK contains a Java compiler, a variety of tools, and a Java runtime environment (JRE). The JRE contains a JVM, Java platform core classes, and some supporting files. The JRE will allow you to execute the Java applications that you create. Sun provides JDKs for the Windows 95/98/NT and Solaris operating systems.

In Example 2.1, we see a very simple Java program that prints the prime numbers between 1000 and 1050. This code might be placed in a file called `Primes.java`.

The compilation and execution of this program can be seen in the terminal session shown in Example 2.2.

We realize that some parts of the example above will be foreign to you. Don't worry—we'll explain all of them in just a little while. As you can probably guess, the `System.out.println` method prints a complete line to the system output device.

The Java compiler is invoked by the command `javac`. It processed a file named `Primes.java` and produced a file named `Primes.class`, which contains the bytecodes we mentioned. The `java` command invokes the JVM for the Windows 95 environment that we are using. We started the JVM and told it to begin executing the `Primes` class (actually the `main` method of the `Primes` class).

Java allows classes to be loaded dynamically. By this we mean that a class may contain references to other classes that are not themselves already loaded. When an application is running and one of these classes is needed, the JVM loads it and then continues execution of the application. Exactly how Java determines where to find the classes

EXAMPLE 2.1 JAVA CLASS THAT WILL DISPLAY A RANGE OF PRIME NUMBERS.

```
public class Primes {

   public static void main (String[] argv) {

      for (int i = 1001; i < 1050; i++) {

         // Test each value to see if it is prime

         boolean itsPrime = true;
         for (int j = 2; j <= i/2; j++) {

            // if j evenly divides i, then i is not prime

            if (i%j == 0) {
               itsPrime = false;
               break;
            }
         }

         // Display the ones that are prime

         if (itsPrime) {
            System.out.println (i);
         }
      }

   }

}
```

that it needs to load varies between implementations. In the Windows environment, the JVM looks at the `CLASSPATH` environment variable. This environment variable, if it is used, is expected to contain a semi-colon-separated list of file and directory names. Very often you will want to put a line in your `autoexec.bat` file to set the `CLASSPATH` variable. This will look something like the following:

```
SET CLASSPATH=.;C:\Progra~1\jdk1.1.8\lib\classes.zip
```

When a JVM needs to load a class file, it uses the names that it finds in the class path in the order that they are specified. Directories will be searched for the desired class file. When a name identifies a JAR or a ZIP file, then the contents of the file will be searched for the desired class file. Several of the Java tools, such as the `java` and `javac`

EXAMPLE 2.2 COMPILATION AND EXECUTION OF THE PRIMES CLASS.

```
Command>javac Primes.java

Command>java Primes
1009
1013
1019
1021
1031
1033
1039
1049
```

commands that we used, allow a `-classpath` option to override the class path in the environment variable.

Some parts of Example 2.1 will be familiar to C and C++ programmers because those languages strongly influenced the design of Java. In fact, the flow of control statements in Java are so similar to those of C and C++ that programmers of these languages may wish to skip the next section altogether.

2.3 Control Flow in Java

In this section we briefly describe Java's flow of control statements.

A *block* contains zero or more statements, enclosed in braces (`{` and `}`). A block is itself a statement and so can be used anywhere that a statement is allowed. The statements in a block are executed one after another.

```
{ }
```

or

```
{ statement ... }
```

An `if` statement provides conditional execution of statements.

```
if (boolean-expression)
   statement
else
   statement
```

The execution of the `if` statement first evaluates the boolean expression. If the result is true, then the first statement, the then statement, is executed. Otherwise, the second statement, the else statement, is executed. The `else` part of the `if` statement is optional. Multiple `if` statements will often be strung together in the following way:

```
if (boolean-expression-1)
   statement-1
else if (boolean-expression-2)
   statement-2
else if ...
   ...
else
   statement-n
```

The `switch` statement provides another type of conditional statement execution.

```
switch (expression) {
   case constant-1:
      statement ...

   case constant-2:
      statement ...

   ...

   default:
      statement ...
}
```

The execution of the `switch` statement first causes the `expression` to be evaluated. The cases are then tested one by one, until a match is found between the result of the expression evaluation and the constant value that the case provides. Once this match is found, the statements that follow the case are executed. If none of the constants contained in the `case` clauses match the result of the `expression`, then the statements in the `default` clause are executed. The `switch` statement can contain any number of `case` clauses; the `default` clause is optional; and each `case` clause can contain zero or more statements. The constant can either be a literal value or a static final variable.

A word of caution is in order here. Once the execution of a case's statements begins, it will continue through the end of the `switch` statement, and not just until the next `case` clause as you might expect. The `break` statement, which we'll discuss shortly, can be used to stop the execution of the `switch` statement wherever you desire. In most cases, the statements of each case are ended with a `break` statement.

Java contains several types of *loop statement* that provide repetitive execution of statements. The loop statements are the `while` statement, the `do-while` statement, and the `for` statement.

Let's look first at the `while` and `do-while` statements.

```
while (boolean-expression)
   statement
```

```
do
   statement
while (boolean-expression)
```

The execution of the `while` statement, shown first, evaluates its expression and then executes its statement if the result of the expression is true. This continues until the result of the expression evaluation is false. The evaluation of the `do-while` statement executes the statement that it contains, and then evaluates the expression. This process is repeated for as long as the expression evaluates to true.

The `for` statement is a bit more complicated than the two forms of the `while` statement.

```
for ( initial-expression ; boolean-expression ;
      increment-expression )
   statement
```

The execution of the `for` statement begins with the execution of the `initial-expression`. This expression usually provides an initial value for a variable or for several variables (an expression can include assignment operators and it can also be a comma-separated list of expressions). The `initial-expression` can also be a variable declaration that includes the variable's initialization. The `boolean-expression` is evaluated, and if the result is true, then the statement is executed. If the result is false, then the execution of the `for` statement is finished. After the statement is executed, the `increment-expression` is executed. This expression often increments an integer variable. After the `increment-expression` is executed, the loop continues with the evaluation of the `boolean-expression`. This statement is complicated enough that we provide a simple example of it.

In this example we've created a method that takes an integer argument called `limit` and returns the result of adding the numbers from 1 to `limit`. The `for` statement begins with the declaration of the variable `i`, with an initial value of 1. The "+=" operator in the `for` statement adds `i` to the value already in `result`. The "++" operator in the `increment-expression` increments the value in `i` by 1. Because we have chosen to declare `i` in the `for` statement, the scope of `i` consists

EXAMPLE 2.3 A SIMPLE `for` STATEMENT.

```
// Sum the numbers from 1 to limit

public static int sumTo (int limit) {
   int result = 0;

   for (int i = 1; i <= limit; i++)
      result += i;

   return result;
}
```

only of the `for` statement. An attempt to use `i` once the `for` statement has completed would result in a compilation error.

Although we haven't shown it yet, statements can be labeled, using the following syntax:

```
label: statement
```

Labeling a statement is useful in conjunction with the `continue` and the `break` statements.

The `break` statement ends the execution of any labeled statement. If it is used without a label, then it ends the innermost `switch` statement or loop statement that contains it.

```
break
```

or

```
break label
```

We mentioned earlier that the `break` statement is very useful in terminating the statements of a case within a `switch` statement. The following pattern is often used:

```
switch (...) {
   case VALUE1:
      statement ...
      break;

   case VALUE2:
      statement ...
      break;

   ...
}
```

The `continue` statement ends the execution of the statement in a loop statement without ending the loop statement itself. The loop statement continues as if the end of the statement it contains had been reached. If the `continue` statement is used without a label, then it applies to the innermost loop statement that contains it.

The final flow of control statement is the `return` statement. The `return` statement ends the execution of a method. If the method has a return type, then the `return` statement must provide a value of that type to be returned.

```
return
```

or

```
return expression
```

2.4 Java Data Types

Java provides a small number of primitive data types. It also has classes, which are the mechanism by which new data types are defined. The Java core classes, provided with the JDK, contain a lot of code that will prove useful when you develop your own applications.

In this section, we first introduce Java's primitive data types. We then discuss the Java core classes that are most relevant to the larger discussion of how Java and SQL can be used together.

2.4.1 Primitive Data Types

Java provides the primitive data types shown in Table 2.1.

For the SQL INTEGER and SMALLINT data types, the precision of these types is chosen by each product, whereas in Java the integer data types each have a fixed precision.

2.4.2 Object Wrappers for the Primitive Data Types

The primitive data types we have just mentioned are simple scalar values, just as they are when provided by COBOL, C, and so on. Very often, they are exactly what you need as you develop your application. Sometimes, however, you would like these data types to behave the way that all of the other objects in Java behave. There is no way to share a reference to a value of one of the primitive data types. Unlike C and C++, Java does not have pointers.

Java provides a series of object wrapper classes for the primitive data types. These classes are defined in the `java.lang` package. They are listed in Table 2.2.

Type	Description	Literals
`boolean`	Boolean	`true`, `false`
`char`	single 16-bit Unicode 1.1.5 character	`'A'`, `'\n'`, `'\154'`, `'\u0027'`
`byte`	8-bit signed 2's complement integer	`int` literal can be used for assignment
`short`	16-bit signed 2's complement integer	`int` literal can be used for assignment
`int`	32-bit signed 2's complement integer	`13`, `-7`, `054`, `0X1f`
`long`	64-bit signed 2's complement integer	`29l` (that's a lowercase *L*), `123456789L`
`float`	32-bit IEEE 754-1985 floating point number	`9.8e2f`
`double`	64-bit IEEE 754-1985 floating point number	`4.5e3`, `3.2e0d`

TABLE 2.1 *Java primitive types.*

Primitive data type	Wrapper class
`boolean`	`Boolean`
`char`	`Character`
`byte`	`Byte`
`short`	`Short`
`int`	`Integer`
`long`	`Long`
`float`	`Float`
`double`	`Double`

TABLE 2.2 *Java wrapper classes.*

Notice that the names of the wrapper class often differ from the name of the corresponding primitive data types in the case (upper or lower) of the first letter; since Java, like C and C++, uses case-sensitive identifiers, this difference is sufficient. SQL programmers may find this a bit subtle at first, since SQL's identifiers are not case sensitive.

2.4.3 Strings

You probably noticed that character strings were missing from the list of Java's primitive data types. Strings are, in fact, objects provided by the `String` class in the `java.lang` package. Strings also have an extra bit of support in the Java language. In Example 2.4, we define the `makePigLatin` method, which takes a string argument and returns the "pig Latin" string value for it.

EXAMPLE 2.4 A METHOD TO TRANSLATE A WORD INTO "PIG LATIN."

```
static final String vowels = "aeiouAEIOU";

static String makePigLatin (String s) {

   // If the word begins with a vowel, just add "way",
   // otherwise move the leading consonants to the back
   // and add "ay"

   if (vowels.indexOf(s.charAt(0)) == -1) {
      for (int j = 0;
            j < s.length() && vowels.indexOf(s.charAt(0)) == -1;
            j++) {

         char firstChar = s.charAt(0);
         String allButFirst = s.substring(1, s.length());
         s = allButFirst + firstChar;
      }
      return s + "ay";
   }
   else {
      return s + "way";
   }
}
```

This method is used as follows:

```
makePigLatin("Java")
```

returns

```
"avaJay"
```

We are, perhaps, getting ahead of ourselves a bit. This example shows methods being invoked on `String` objects (we'll cover this in Section 2.5.2), and possibly unfamiliar methods at that. Nevertheless, this method shows us several important things about strings. A string literal is written within double quotes. The "+" operator provides string concatenation. When string concatenation is taking place, non-string operands are automatically converted to strings. In the method above, strings and characters were being concatenated when consonants were being moved to the rear of the string. When the non-string operand is an object, then its `toString` method is implicitly invoked. Finally, we see that some useful methods are available for the String class: length, substring, and indexOf, just to name a few of them.

The String class provides us with immutable objects, meaning that operations on String objects may provide new String objects, but they do not change the value of their operands. Java also provides the StringBuffer class, which offers us mutable strings. In certain situations, it can be much more efficient to use StringBuffer than String.StringBuffer objects can easily be built from String objects, and vice versa.

2.4.4 The BigDecimal Class

The BigDecimal class, which is contained in the java.math package, can be used to create and manipulate decimal values. In Example 2.5, we use the BigDecimal class to calculate the value of 3/7.

EXAMPLE 2.5 WORKING WITH BigDecimal VALUES.

```
import java.math.*;

// Calculate the value of 3/7 to 6 decimal places

BigDecimal bd = new BigDecimal(3.0);
bd = bd.setScale(6);
bd = bd.divide(new BigDecimal("7"), BigDecimal.ROUND_HALF_UP);

System.out.println ("3/7 = " + bd + " with scale of " +
    bd.scale());
```

This fragment of code produces the following result:

```
3/7 = 0.428571 with scale of 6
```

This example is, perhaps, a bit confusing. While the SQL NUMERIC and DECIMAL data types have a fixed, user-specified decimal precision, the Java BigDecimal class provides an amount of precision that varies as needed. Only the scale (the number of digits to the right of the decimal point) can be set by the user of the class.

You might have noticed that we constructed our BigDecimal objects in two different ways, first with the float value of 3.0 and then with the string "7". There's even a constructor that creates one BigDecimal object from another BigDecimal object.

2.4.5 Arrays

Java arrays provide an ordered collection of elements. A Java array whose length is some value n has n elements. Those elements are identified by an integer index that runs from 0 to $n - 1$. The elements of an array can be values of any primitive data type, as well as objects from some class. Let's consider the situation in Example 2.6.

EXAMPLE 2.6 INITIALIZING AND OPERATING ON AN ARRAY OF `int` VALUES.

```
int[] a1 = {1, 2, 3};
int[] a2 = null;

a2 = new int[3];
a2[0] = a1[2];
a2[1] = a1[1];
a2[2] = a2[0];

int alen = a2.length;
```

The first array variable, `a1`, contains a reference to an array of three `int` elements. The second array variable, `a2`, will contain references to arrays of `int`. It has been created with a value of `null`, meaning a reference to no object. Immediately after its creation, `a2` is assigned a reference to a newly created array of three `int` elements, which are then given values.

A Java array is itself an object, with a length field that reflects the number of elements it contains. In the example above, the value of `alen` would be 3.

2.5 Java Classes

Classes are the single most important construct in the Java language—it's not an overstatement to say that classes are the entire point of Java. When an *object* is created, it is an instance of some class. *Classes* are analogous to data types, except that (in Java) they specify characteristics of objects, called *instances* of the class. Each instance of a class has a unique *identity* (it is that unique identity that references to the objects use) and a *state* that contains the values of the object's fields.

2.5.1 Fields, Methods, and Constructors

Classes consist of fields, methods, and constructors. The *fields* provide a place to store the state of an object, the *methods* provide the object's behavior, and the *constructors* provide the ability to create instances of the class. All of these constructs are shown in Example 2.7.

EXAMPLE 2.7 A CLASS TO REPRESENT A PLAYING CARD.

```
public class PlayingCard {

   private int rank;
   private int suit;

   public PlayingCard (int rank, int suit) {
      this.suit = suit;
      this.rank = rank;
   }

   public int getRank () {
      return rank;
   }

   public int getSuit () {
      return suit;
   }

   public boolean equals (PlayingCard comparand) {
      return (this.suit == comparand.suit &&
              this.rank == comparand.rank);
   }

   public boolean greaterThan (PlayingCard comparand) {
      return (this.rank > comparand.rank);
   }

   public boolean ties (PlayingCard comparand) {
      return (this.rank == comparand.rank);
   }

}
```

In this example, the fields of rank and suit are defined at the very beginning of the class. They are defined as being private, which means that only methods within this class can access these fields. Instead of private, the keyword public could have been used to indicate that methods in any class could access these fields. This ability—to decide how widely visible a field or a method is—is known as *encapsulation*.

In this example, we have made rank and suit private, so that they cannot be directly accessed—or, more importantly, modified—by a user of the class. We provided the getRank and getSuit methods to allow the user to "see" the values of these fields.

A method defines an operation on an object. A method is defined with a fixed number of parameters (possibly zero). A method may return a value, or it may be specified as returning void, meaning that no value is to be returned. The method name, along with the types of each of its parameters, is known as the *method signature*.

Some of the methods above use the keyword this to reference the object that a method is operating on. It was used above to distinguish references to the object's fields from those of its parameters.

The PlayingCard class contains one constructor. Constructors look very much like methods; however, they always include the name of the class that contains them and they do not specify any return type, nor do they specify void. The constructor, as its name implies, allows a user to create instances of the class.

Let us for a moment use the values 0 to 13 for the rank of a card (Two through King, Ace, and then Joker), and 0 to 3 for the suit (Hearts, Diamonds, Spades, and Clubs, respectively) of a card. This class can be used in the following way:

```
PlayingCard card1 = new PlayingCard (1, 1);      // 3 of diamonds
PlayingCard card2 = new PlayingCard (8, 3);      // 10 of clubs

System.out.println (card1.getRank() + " " + card1.getSuit());
System.out.println (card1.greaterThan (card2));
```

The new operator refers to a class constructor and, when it executes, it creates an instance of the class. The new operator allocates as much memory from the heap as is needed. Although it seems like the card1 variable contains the object, in reality the new operator provides a *reference* to the newly created object. This reference may be copied into several variables, and it can be used to invoke methods on the object. This reference serves to uniquely identify the object.

Some of you are probably familiar with C or C++ and the pointers that they provide. Java references are much simpler and less error prone than these pointers. Java does not provide an equivalent capability to that of pointer arithmetic, pointers to variables, or pointers to pointers. A very common error found in C/C++ programs involves the creation of a pointer to an automatic variable (sometimes called a stack variable) that contains an object. If this pointer is used after the block that contains the variable has completed, then the behavior of the program becomes very unpredictable. The designers of Java made an explicit decision to prevent this type of error by creating all objects on a heap and providing references to them.

More than one method can exist with the same name and more than one constructor may exist for a class, provided that their signatures differ. The signatures may differ in the number of parameters they have, or, if they have the same number of parameters, in the types of the parameters. This is known as *overloading*. If we wanted to, we could add the following constructor and method to the `PlayingCard` class.

```
public PlayingCard (int rank) {
        this.rank = rank;
        this.suit = 0;
    }

public boolean equals (int rank, int suit) {
        return (this.rank == rank && this.suit == suit);
    }
```

2.5.2 Method Invocation

Having already seen method invocation in several examples, you've probably already realized that the invocation of the method is written in the following way:

```
object.method ( argument, argument, ... )
```

The object specified in the invocation is sometimes known as the *receiving object*. The arguments to the method are all passed by value. Java does not have the ability to pass arguments by reference, nor does it have output parameters.

When an object is passed as an argument to a method, its reference is passed by value. This means that any change to the state of that object will be seen by the caller when the method completes.

Let us consider for a moment what can be done if it is necessary to have a method return several values or objects. It is, after all, fairly common for an SQL procedure to have several OUT or INOUT parameters. One way to solve this problem is to create a new class that has fields for each of the values and objects to be returned; the method can be defined with this class as its return type.

Another way to solve this problem is to have the method define parameters that are arrays of the types needed. The invoker creates arrays of one element for each value and object and passes them to the method. The method assigns the values and objects to the first elements of the arrays, and then returns to the invoker. Because Java arrays are themselves objects, using them as arguments to a method means that their references are passed by value and the changes made to the arrays are inherently visible to the method's invoker. This technique can be seen in the following method:

```
public void getSuitAndName (int[] suitOut, String[] suitNameOut) {
   suitOut[0] = suit;
   suitNameOut[0] = suitNames[suit];
   return;
}
```

The method could be invoked as follows:

```
int[] suit = new int[1];
String[] suitName = new String [1];

threeSpades.getSuitAndName (suit, suitName);

System.out.println (suit[0] + " represents " + suitName[0]);
```

2.5.3 Static Fields, Static Methods, and Static Initializers

The fields that we've described so far are created in each object of a given class. Java also allows the definition of *static fields* in a class, which are created once for the class itself. These are sometimes referred to as *class variables*. These fields can hold values or objects that are used by all instances of the class, in contrast to instance fields, which you must define and store in every instance of the class. Example 2.8 shows the addition of some useful static fields to our `PlayingCard` class.

Within the `PlayingCard` class, a suit can be referenced simply as `HEART`. Outside of the class, the suit can be referenced as `PlayingCard.HEART`. In a similar fashion we'll add static fields to represent the ranks of `TWO`, `THREE`, . . . , `ACE`, and finally `JOKER`.

Many of the fields in Example 2.8 are defined to be `final`. This means that their values cannot be changed by any other statements. The combination of `final` and `static` is a great way to define named constant values (analogous to C's manifest constants).

Java also allows the definition of *static methods* in a class. These methods are part of the class itself and may refer only to static fields. A static method is identified with `static`, but otherwise it looks very much like a nonstatic method. This invocation of a static method is written in the following way:

```
class.method ( argument, argument,...)
```

The definition and use of static methods can be seen in Example 2.9 and Example 2.10.

EXAMPLE 2.8 USING STATIC FIELDS TO REPRESENT SUIT VALUES FOR PLAYING CARDS.

```
final static int HEART    =  0;
final static int DIAMOND  =  1;
final static int SPADE    =  2;
final static int CLUB     =  3;
final static int NOSUIT   =  4;
final static int MAXSUIT  =  4;

final static String[] suitNames = { "Hearts",
                                    "Diamonds",
                                    "Spades",
                                    "Clubs",
                                    ""
                                  };

static PlayingCard[] CARDS = null;
```

EXAMPLE 2.9 DEFINITION OF A STATIC METHOD.

```
public static boolean red (int suit) {
   return (suit == HEART || suit == DIAMOND);
}
```

EXAMPLE 2.10 INVOCATION OF A STATIC METHOD.

```
PlayingCard card1
   = new PlayingCard (PlayingCard.THREE, PlayingCard.CLUB);

if (PlayingCard.red(card1.getSuit())) {
   ...
}
```

The closest thing that Java has to an SQL function is a static method that does not use any static variables. Similarly, the closest thing to an SQL procedure is a static void method.

Finally we come to *static initializers*. A class can be loaded explicitly, but class loading most often happens automatically. If a class contains static initializers, then these are executed at the time the class is loaded. Example 2.11 shows how a static initializer changes the value of the `CARDS` field to that of a newly constructed array that contains a complete deck of cards.

EXAMPLE 2.11 A STATIC INITIALIZER TO ADD TO THE `PlayingCard` CLASS.

```
static {
   CARDS = new PlayingCard[DECKSIZE];

   int i = 0;
   for (int r = 0; r <= MAXRANK; r++) {
      for (int s = 0; s <= MAXSUIT; s++) {
         if (r != JOKER && s != NOSUIT) {
            CARDS[i++] = new PlayingCard (r, s);
         }
      }
   }
   CARDS[i++] = new PlayingCard (JOKER, NOSUIT);
   CARDS[i++] = new PlayingCard (JOKER, NOSUIT);

}
```

With this static initializer, the user of the `PlayingCard` class can now use `PlayingCard.CARDS` to specify a complete deck of cards. The class will be loaded and the initializer will run without any additional action on the part of the user.

2.5.4 The `main` Method

The author of a class may choose to define a special method named `main`. Exactly how a Java application is invoked varies from system to system, but in all cases a class name must be provided by the invoker. The Java runtime environment invokes the `main` method of the class that has been specified.

This `main` method must have the following signature:

```
public static void main ( String[] argv )
```

If arguments were provided as part of the invocation of the application, then these will be used to create an array of strings (one array element per argument) that is passed to the main method. Of course, an application can also invoke the main method just as it would any other static method.

In Example 2.12, we see a class that provides a main method as well as the makePigLatin method that we looked at in Section 2.4.3 when we discussed strings.

EXAMPLE 2.12 main METHOD TO DISPLAY THE COMMAND LINE ARGUMENTS IN "PIG LATIN."

```
public class PigLatin {

   public static void main (String[] argv) {

      // Display the "pig latin" form of each
      // command line argument

      for (int i = 0; i < argv.length; i++) {
         String s = makePigLatin(argv[i]);
         System.out.print (s + " ");
      }
   }

   static String makePigLatin (String s) {
      ...
   }
}
```

This program generates the following results:

```
Command>java PigLatin This is a test
isThay isway away esttay
```

2.5.5 Garbage Collection

Java differs from the other languages that we've mentioned by providing *garbage collection.* An application does not have to keep track of how long an object is needed and then destroy it—Java takes care of that for you. When no further references to an object exist, the object becomes a candidate for garbage collection. The garbage collector runs periodically and reclaims the memory of such unused objects, destroying them as it goes.

2.6 Object-Oriented Aspects of Java

There are some capabilities that we expect all object-oriented languages to possess. We have already discussed how Java provides both encapsulation and object identity. In this section we will discuss how Java provides inheritance and polymorphism.

One of the advantages provided by an object-oriented language—some might claim it's one of the primary advantages—is the reuse of code. This reuse is achieved by allowing the creation of a class that has different, or more specialized, behavior than a class that has already been written and tested.

2.6.1 Inheritance

Java provides a mechanism to create a more specialized version of an existing class. This new class will have all the same methods as its parent and may have additional methods as well. It will also have all the fields of its parent and may have additional fields as well.

Consider the `PlayingCard` class. In some games, the Ace is considered to be lower than all other cards, rather than higher. Example 2.13 shows how a new class can be created with this behavior.

The class `PlayingCardAceLow` has extended the class `PlayingCard`. It contains all of the fields and methods of `PlayingCard`; however, the `greaterThan` method will now treat the Ace as low, rather than high. The implementation checks to see whether either card is an Ace, and, if it is, returns the appropriate result. Otherwise, it returns the value produced by the `greaterThan` method of its parent type.

Let us consider Example 2.14. We might want to extend our class to support the display of playing cards in a windowed GUI (graphical user interface) environment.

In this case we've provided the new `backgroundGIF` field to store a URL for a gif file. This file will contain an image that can be used when the display of the back of a playing card is required. The constructor for this class takes an additional argument for this URL. The constructor initializes the `rank` and `suit` fields by using the constructor of the superclass, using the keyword `super`, and then creates a `URL` object and assigns it to the field we have added.

The ability to extend a class is sometimes known as *single inheritance of implementation.* A subclass has a single parent and inherits both the signature and implementation of the parent's methods.

If a class is created without specifying that it is extending a class, then it implicitly extends the `Object` class. One, perhaps obvious, implication of this fact is that every Java class is a subclass of the `Object` class.

A class may be specified as `final`. This means that it cannot be extended any further. This guarantees to the author that no one will

EXAMPLE 2.13 EXTENDING THE `PlayingCard` CLASS TO TREAT THE ACE AS LOW CARD.

```
public class PlayingCardAceLow extends PlayingCard {

   public PlayingCardAceLow (int rank, int suit) {
      super (rank, suit);
   }

   public boolean greaterThan (PlayingCard comparand) {
      if (this.getRank() == ACE) {
         return false;
      }
      else if (comparand.getRank() == ACE) {
         return true;
      }
      else return super.greaterThan(comparand);
   }

}
```

EXAMPLE 2.14 EXTENDING THE `PlayingCard` CLASS FOR A GUI ENVIRONMENT.

```
public class PlayingCardGUI extends PlayingCard {

   public java.net.URL backgroundGIF = null;

   public PlayingCardGUI (int rank, int suit, String url) {
      super (rank, suit);
      try {
         backgroundGIF = new java.net.URL(url);
      }
      catch (java.net.MalformedURLException mue) {
      }
   }

}
```

extend the class in order to redefine some of its methods. With this additional knowledge, a Java compiler can also better optimize some operations on the class.

A little while ago we discussed an author's choice of `public` or `private` for the encapsulation level of a class, method, or constructor.

Another choice that can be made for the encapsulation of these elements is `protected`, which means that the element can be "seen" only by the containing class and its subclasses. A `private` element in a class is not visible to any subclass of the containing class.

2.6.2 The `Object` Class

The `Object` class is defined to have several "utility" methods. Some of these methods are shown below.

java.lang.Object Class

```
public boolean equals (Object obj)
```

Compares the values of the two objects (== and != compare the object references; a common error committed by Java neophytes is to use these two operators when the intent is to compare object values).

```
public int hashCode ()
```

Returns a hash code for the object. The hash codes for different objects are usually (but not necessarily always) different.

```
protected Object clone (Object obj)
    throws CloneNotSupportedException
```

Returns a clone of the object. The clone is a new object that is a copy of the original. The state of the clone will be the same as the state of the original, but they will have different references.

```
public String toString ()
```

Returns a string representation of the object. The `toString` method for `Object` returns a string that contains the class name and hash code for the object.

Specializations of the `Object` class may redefine these methods. In our `PlayingCard` class in Example 2.7, the `equals` method was redefined.

2.6.3 Polymorphism

An object is created with the `new` operator and the specification of a constructor. This new object is an instance of the class associated with the constructor. It may be used wherever an instance of any of its supertypes can be used. This is known as *substitutability.* An instance of `Integer` may be assigned to a `Number` variable, or even to an `Object` variable.

In Example 2.15, the variable `pc` holds the values of both `PlayingCard` and `PlayingCardAceLow` at different times. Twice in this example, we see the invocation of the `greaterThan` method. At compile time, the compiler checks to see that the declared type of `pc`, `PlayingCard`, actually has a `greaterThan` method. At runtime, it is the type of the object that is being referenced that is used to determine which `greaterThan` method to use. This process is known as *polymorphism,* or *late binding,* or *runtime binding.* The first invocation of `greaterThan` provides the Ace high version of the method and produces `false`. The second invocation uses the Ace low version of the method and produces `true`.

EXAMPLE 2.15 POLYMORPHISM.

```
PlayingCard ace =
   new PlayingCard (PlayingCard.ACE, PlayingCard.HEART);
PlayingCard c1 =
   new PlayingCard (PlayingCard.FIVE, PlayingCard.CLUB);
PlayingCardAceLow c2 =
   new PlayingCardAceLow (PlayingCard.FIVE, PlayingCard.CLUB);
PlayingCard pc = null;

pc = c1;
System.out.println (pc.greaterThan(ace));
pc = c2;
System.out.println (pc.greaterThan(ace));
```

Sometimes you will have a variable or field that is declared to be of one class, but you know that it contains an object of a specific subclass. In order to invoke a method that exists only for the subclass you must first *narrow* the type of the reference. This process can be seen in the following method:

```
public static void printInt (Object o) {
   int i = ((Number) o).intValue();
   System.out.println (i);
}
```

Before the `intValue` method can be applied to `o`, it must be narrowed to be a `Number`. If `printInt` is passed a `Float`, then it will execute correctly. If it is passed an object of a nonnumeric class, say `String`, then `ClassCastException` would be thrown.

2.6.4 Abstract Classes and Methods

In our examples, we have encountered several methods. Although we have not shown it, a method can be declared to be an *abstract method* (using the keyword `abstract`), meaning that it has a signature but no body. A class can also be declared to be an *abstract class,* meaning that no instances of the class can be created. A class with an abstract method must be declared to be an abstract class.

An abstract class can be extended, and in the subclass the abstract methods can be given implementations (with the same signatures as their abstract parents, of course). We could, for example, have written our `PlayingCard` class as an abstract class with `greaterThan` as an abstract method (all of the other methods could have implementations). We might then have created a subclass for Ace high and a subclass for Ace low, each with a different implementation of `greaterThan`.

The use of this feature can also be seen in the `java.lang` package. `Number` is an abstract class. It has several nonabstract subclasses; among these are `Byte`, `Double`, `Float`, `Integer`, `Long`, `Short`, and `java.math.BigDecimal`. The methods of `Number`, such as `intValue`, are implemented in each of these subclasses.

2.6.5 Interfaces

An *interface* is in some ways similar to an abstract class. The methods of an interface cannot have implementations, so they are implicitly all abstract. In order to create instances of the class, the author must provide an implementation for each of the interfaces' methods. An interface can contain fields, but these fields are implicitly both `static` and `final`.

The `java.util` package contains the `Enumeration` interface. Its definition is something like the following:

```
public interface Enumeration {
   public boolean hasMoreElements();
   public Object nextElement throws NoSuchElementException();
}
```

Example 2.16 shows the definition of a new class that implements the `Enumeration` interface.

A class can specify that it is implementing one or more interfaces. This class is implicitly extending the `Object` class and implements the methods of `Enumeration`. The class uses a private integer field to store the position of the enumeration in the deck of cards.

We have seen primitive data types and class names used to define variables, fields, and parameters. Interface names can also be used in these

EXAMPLE 2.16 CLASS THAT IMPLEMENTS THE Enumeration INTERFACE.

```
import java.util.*;

public class PlayingCardEnum implements Enumeration {
   private int currentCard = 0;

   public PlayingCardEnum () {
   }

   public boolean hasMoreElements () {
      return (currentCard < PlayingCard.DECKSIZE);
   }

   public Object nextElement () throws NoSuchElementException {
      if (currentCard == PlayingCard.DECKSIZE) {
         throw new NoSuchElementException();
      }

      return PlayingCard.CARDS[currentCard++];
   }
}
```

definitions. A method that expects an argument of type `Enumeration` can be passed an object of type `PlayingCardEnum`. This can be seen in the `Deck` class, shown in Example 2.17, which might also provide methods such as `shuffle` and `dealCard`.

A deck of cards can be created with the following statement:

```
Deck thisDeck = new Deck (new PlayingCardEnum());
```

Interfaces give classes *multiple inheritance of interface,* meaning that the class can inherit the method signatures from one or more interfaces.

2.7 Exceptions

When one is writing code in any language, one must always consider what kind of error conditions may occur and what actions to take when they do occur. In the C language, many functions were coded to return an integer value that indicated the success of the function. Every time such a function was called, the user checked the return value and then decided what to do if it indicated success or failure (or possibly different types of failure). The resulting code was often lengthy and difficult to read.

EXAMPLE 2.17 CLASS TO REPRESENT A DECK OF PLAYING CARDS.

```
import java.util.*;

public class Deck {

   private PlayingCard[] deckOfCards
      = new PlayingCard[PlayingCard.DECKSIZE];

   public Deck (Enumeration e) {
      int i = 0;

      while (e.hasMoreElements()) {
         deckOfCards[i++] = (PlayingCard) (e.nextElement());
      }
   }
}
```

In Java, an author can "throw" a special type of object, called an `Exception` object, when an error condition occurs. Usually an author will create a subclass of `Exception` for each specific error condition that needs to be thrown. By "throw an `Exception` object," we mean that the `throw` statement is executed, telling Java that an error condition has occurred and providing the `Exception` object.

The exceptions that may be thrown by a method must be declared in the method's signature—that is, signatures include not only the method name and the number and type of each parameter, but also the exceptions that can be thrown by the method. If a method can throw a particular exception and no code is prepared to handle it, then the author is presumed to have made a mistake, and the compiler will report an error. To see how an exception is thrown, we have rewritten the constructor for `PlayingCard` in Example 2.18.

In this example, we have defined the `InvalidCard` class. The class can be extremely minimal, as we have shown here, or it can have fields and methods to convey information about the exceptional condition that occurred. The `PlayingCard` constructor tests the values that it has been given, and if they are found wanting, it creates an instance of the `InvalidCard` class and throws it. You can also see that the constructor now declares that this type of exception may be thrown.

Having discussed how exceptions are thrown, we next need to discuss how they are "caught." Java provides the *try-catch-finally* block for this purpose. Example 2.19 shows how a user of our class would catch the `InvalidCard` exception.

EXAMPLE 2.18 A PlayingCard CONSTRUCTOR THAT THROWS AN EXCEPTION.

```
public class InvalidCard extends Exception {
}


public PlayingCard (int rank, int suit)
      throws InvalidCard {

   if (rank < 0 || suit < 0
       || rank > MAXRANK || suit > MAXSUIT
       || (rank == JOKER && suit != NOSUIT)
       || (rank != JOKER && suit == NOSUIT)
      )
      throw new InvalidCard();

   this.suit = suit;
   this.rank = rank;
}
```

EXAMPLE 2.19 USE OF THE TRY-CATCH-FINALLY BLOCK.

```
PlayingCard pc;
int x = PlayingCard.QUEEN;
int y = PlayingCard.NOSUIT;

try {
   pc = new PlayingCard (x, y);
}
catch (InvalidCard ic) {
   System.out.println ("Oops");
}
catch (SomeOtherException soe) {
   ...
}
finally {
   ...
}
```

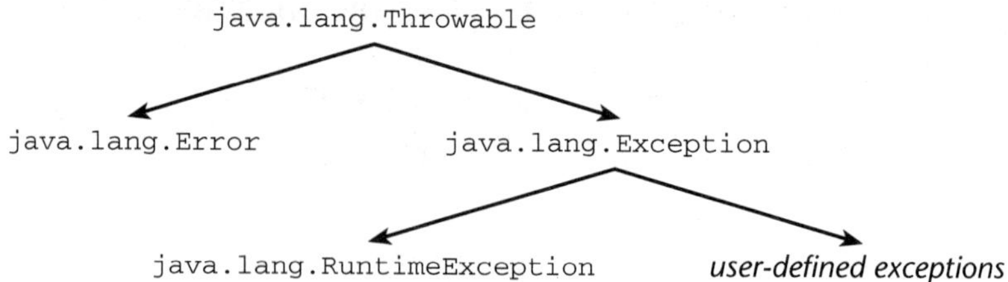

FIGURE 2.1 *Java exceptions class hierarchy.*

If an exception is thrown by a statement inside the `try` section, then each of the `catch` sections are checked in turn to see whether one of them is able to accept the exception object. This check is accomplished by determining whether the exception object is a legal argument for the parameter in the `catch` section. If it is, then the code in that `catch` section is executed. If this `try-catch-finally` block does not catch it, then any `try-catch-finally` blocks that contain this block are checked. If the exception has *still* not been caught, then the method that contains this code throws the exception to its invoker.

As you can see, once an exception is thrown, it travels outward through `try-catch-finally` blocks and through the call stack until it is caught. If by some chance an exception is not handled by the application, then it will be handled by the *default exception handler.* Usually, this handler will display the name of the exception and some information about the call stack.

The `finally` section of the `try-catch-finally` block, if it exists, will execute no matter why the block is being left. If the code in the `finally` section provides its own reason for leaving the block, such as a `return` statement or the throwing of an exception, then this reason will take precedence over the original reason for leaving the block. The `finally` clause is an excellent way to clean up and return resources that were acquired in the `try` clause.

Let us consider for a moment the part of the class hierarchy that is defined in the `java.lang` package and is shown in Figure 2.1.

The exceptions that we have been discussing, subclasses of the `Exception` class, are known as *checked exceptions*; these are exceptions that the compiler is aware of and provides checking for. Other exceptions, `Error` and `RuntimeException`, are known as *unchecked exceptions.* Any statement could throw one of these unchecked exceptions, so they are not included in the method signature. `NullPointerException` and `ArrayIndexOutOfBoundsException` are two examples of unchecked exceptions.

2.8 Packages

A *package* is a named group of classes and *subpackages*. This type of grouping allows for independent development of code and prevents the clashing of names. Package names are hierarchical in nature, with periods separating the parts of the name.

Sun supplies several useful packages with the JDK, all beginning with the "`java.`" prefix. The `java.util` package, for example, contains the `Hashtable` class. This class can be referred to as `java.util.Hashtable`. The `import` statement allows the classes in a package to be referred to by just their class name and would appear as

```
import java.util.*;

public class ... {

   Hashtable myHash = null;

}
```

The `java.lang` package is a special package that contains classes such as `Integer` and `String`. This package does not need to be imported, and its classes can be referred to without qualifying them with the package name.

Example 2.20 shows how the `PlayingCard` class can be created in the `games.util` package.

EXAMPLE 2.20 CREATING A CLASS WITHIN A PACKAGE.

```
package games.util;

public class PlayingCard {
   ...
}
```

In some environments, the name of the directory that contains a class file is determined by the name of its containing package. The hierarchical package name must be matched by a hierarchical directory structure with the same names. Our `PlayingCard` class might be stored in a file with the name

```
D:\MyJava\games\util\PlayingCard.class
```

For it to be found and loaded during the execution of an application, the JVM class path must include the `D:\MyJava` directory.

2.9 Serialization and Externalization

The objects that are created in a JVM do not have any form of persistence. When the application terminates, all of its objects are destroyed. *Serialization* is the process of generating a representation of a Java object that can be saved in a persistent location such as a file. This representation can later be *deserialized* to recreate the object. The deserialization of an object creates a copy of the original object. Serialization and deserialization take into account all of the fields of an object that are themselves objects and makes them part of the representation that is generated. The process of *externalization* provides the same capability as serialization, but gives the author a great deal of control over the bytes that are generated.

2.9.1 Serialization

The serialized representation of an object is independent of the operating system and hardware platform used. The sequence of bytes that makes up the representation of an object is defined in the Java Object Serialization Specification. An object can be serialized on one JVM, and then deserialized on another JVM once the serialized representation has been sent to it.

The process of serializing an object is somewhat complicated. The class name of the object has to be included in the serialized representation, as well as the value of each of the object's fields. Some of the object's fields are themselves objects, so all of this information must be included in the serialized representation as well. If several fields contain the same object reference, then it would be inefficient to include multiple copies of the same object in the serialized representation of the object. Instead, the process of serialization must recognize that this is the case and include only a single copy of the object in the serialized representation.

When we said that an object's fields are included in the serialized representation, we did not mean to include static fields. These fields belong to the class as a whole, not to the specific object being serialized. Static fields will have to take care of themselves when objects are deserialized in a new Java environment.

Although this process sounds cumbersome and error-prone, it has actually been made quite easy. The classes that you wish to serialize must implement the `java.io.Serializable` interface. Most of the time, when you implement an interface, you will be writing the body of one or more methods. In this case, because `java.io.Serializable` has no methods, simply adding `java.io.Serializable` to the list of interfaces in the method signature is sufficient. Implementing this interface simply identifies the class as one that can be serialized. You can mark any fields that you do not wish to be included in the serialized representation with the `transient` keyword.

Once this is done, the `writeObject` method of `ObjectOutputStream` can serialize an object, and the `readObject` method of `ObjectInputStream` can deserialize an object.

In Example 2.21, we have created a new class that extends `PlayingCard` and is serializable, adding some fields, one of which is marked `transient`.

EXAMPLE 2.21 IMPLEMENTATION OF THE `Serializable` INTERFACE.

```
import PlayingCard;
import java.io.*;

public class SerializableCard extends PlayingCard
   implements Serializable {

   String test1 = "One";
   transient String test2 = "Two";
   String test3 = "Three";

   ...
}
```

Example 2.22 shows how we serialize an instance of this class. After creating an instance of the `SerializableCard` class, we create a place (baos) to put the serialized representation, create an `ObjectOutputStream` object that knows where that destination is, and then write the object.

EXAMPLE 2.22 SERIALIZING THE ACE OF HEARTS.

```
SerializableCard sc =
   new SerializableCard (PlayingCard.ACE, PlayingCard.HEART);

ByteArrayOutputStream baos = new ByteArrayOutputStream();
ObjectOutputStream oos = new ObjectOutputStream (baos);

oos.writeObject(sc);
```

To deserialize the object, we create an `ObjectInputStream` object that knows where the serialized representation is, and then read from it to create the object. The serialized representation of our object has been placed in the byte array `serialized`. Note in Example 2.23 that the `readObject` method returns an `Object`, so we must narrow it to the correct subclass before we can assign it to the variable.

EXAMPLE 2.23 CREATING A PLAYING CARD FROM ITS SERIALIZED REPRESENTATION.

```
SerializableCard sc2 = null;

ByteArrayInputStream bais
   = new ByteArrayInputStream (serialized);
ObjectInputStream ois = new ObjectInputStream (bais);

sc2 = (SerializableCard) ois.readObject();
```

It is worth mentioning that the `SerializableCard` class requires that the `PlayingCard` class also be serializable. For a class to be serializable all of its superclasses must be serializable.

Customizing Serialization

If, for some reason, the default serialization is not sufficient, then the author of a class can choose to implement the following methods:

```
private void writeObject(java.io.ObjectOutputStream out)
   throws IOException

private void readObject(java.io.ObjectInputStream in)
   throws IOException, ClassNotFoundException
```

The methods of `ObjectOutputStream` and `ObjectInputStream` are written to look for methods with these signatures and will use them if they exist. In this way, the author determines exactly what fields are included in the serialized representation of the class. The fields could even be transformed (possibly encrypted or compressed) before they are placed in this representation. Of course, it is the author's responsibility to make sure that whatever is placed in the serialized representation can be interpreted later to recreate the object.

The implementation of `writeObject` for a class is only responsible for writing its own fields. The fields of its supertype and any of its subtypes will be written automatically.

An author may wish only to store some additional information that would not be included in the default serialization process. This can be easily accomplished by having the implementation of `writeObject` first invoke the class's `defaultWriteObject` method and then write the additional information that is desired.

2.9.2 Externalization

As we have seen, object serialization generates a byte stream that can be used to reconstitute an object at a later time. The byte stream is generated in a specific format defined in the Java Object Serialization Specification, and very little work is required on the part of the author of a class. The process of externalization provides the same capability as serialization, but the author is responsible for producing code to write, and later read, the byte stream. This gives the author a great deal of control over the bytes that are generated.

To use externalization, the author of a class implements the `Externalizable` interface, which has the following methods:

java.io.Externalizable Interface

```
public void writeExternal(ObjectOutput out)
   throws IOException

public void readExternal(ObjectInput in)
   throws IOException, ClassNotFoundException
```

In implementing the `writeExternal` method, the author will decide which fields to use and what bytes to send to the output stream. The author will implement the `readExternal` method to interpret these bytes and build the new object. The `writeObject` method of the `ObjectOutputStream` class will detect that the `Externalizable` interface has been implemented and will use the `writeExternal` method to send bytes to the stream. We're sure that by now you can see how the process is reversed for `readObject`.

The author must make certain that any necessary supertype information is included in the serialized representation of the class. The supertype fields will not automatically be included in the output stream.

2.10 JAR Files

A Java archive (JAR) file is a file that itself contains multiple files (the name must have been inspired by UNIX TAR, or tape archive, files). The JAR file was introduced in JDK 1.1 as a method of bundling all of the class files, image files, audio files, and any other files required by an applet into a single file to improve the applet's performance. This performance improvement is achieved by reducing the multiple network requests otherwise required to transfer the files from a Web site to a browser into a single request. The performance is improved still further by the JAR file's support of compression.

Although support of applets was the primary motivation for JAR files, their utility is much broader. We will see later that they are used in SQLJ Parts 1 and 2.

The JAR file format is based on the ZIP file format, which should be familiar to PC users. A JAR file contains the individual files of interest, and it may contain a *manifest file*. The manifest file lists some or all of the files in the JAR file (but not itself). The manifest contains different types of descriptive information for each of these files.

JAR files may be created with the `jar` utility, provided with Sun's JDKs. This utility allows for the construction of JAR files and the listing and extraction of their contents. This process is shown in Example 2.24.

EXAMPLE 2.24 CREATING A JAR FILE AND LISTING ITS CONTENTS.

```
Command>jar cf0 Test.jar *.class

Command>jar tf Test.jar
META-INF/MANIFEST.MF
Test.class
```

The first of these statements creates a JAR file with all of the class files in the current directory. The second statement lists the contents of the JAR file. The manifest file, shown below, has been created automatically.

```
Manifest-Version: 1.0

Name: Test.class
Digest-Algorithms: SHA MD5
SHA-Digest: DSV8una66X27MIg7uL7elhYRYY0=
MD5-Digest: riX7wQEccLlhRCmngrT7mg==
```

2.11 Other Features of the Java Programming Language

Java provides additional features, some of which we will mention briefly here. Java provides multithreading. Independent threads of control can be created and managed completely within the Java environment. A thread might, for example, be created to execute a synchronous call to some distributed service. That thread could wait for the response from the service, while other threads go about their business. Threads allow multiple concurrent operations to proceed simultaneously in a single application, offering sometimes substantial performance benefits.

We've briefly mentioned that authors do not have to track the usage of their objects or make explicit calls to destroy them when they are no longer needed. Java does, however, provide mechanisms to allow an application some control over the garbage collection process.

Several of the core packages that can be extremely useful to an application writer are the following:

`java.io`	Provides common I/O operations.
`java.util`	Provides classes for date and time, random numbers, and several type of collections.
`java.net`	Provides common network operations.

2.12 Chapter Summary

Via prose and examples, we've tried to give you a good start toward your understanding of the Java language. We've reviewed the primitive data types that Java provides, the object wrapper classes for these primitive types, and the very useful `String` class and `BigDecimal` class that are provided in the `java.lang` package and the `java.math` package, respectively. We've discussed how to define classes, the methods that they contain, and the exceptions that may be thrown by some of these methods. We've seen how to create a class by extending an existing class and how to use interfaces in the creation of a class to provide a form of multiple inheritance.

If this is your first experience with Java, then you may want to come back to this chapter from time to time to refresh yourself on particular topics. There is certainly a lot to absorb.

We've already suggested once that you install one of the JDKs provided on the Sun Web site (for the Windows and Solaris platforms). We've included the `PlayingCard` class and several related classes in Appendix I and on the CD-ROM that accompanies the book, as well as on the Morgan Kaufmann Web site.

With this foundation, we're ready to see how Java and SQL can be used together.

CHAPTER 3

SQL for the Java Programmer

3.1 Introduction

In this chapter, we're going to review the database language SQL for the benefit of readers who are Java programmers but don't have extensive (or, perhaps, any) experience with SQL or with database systems. We'll start off with an overview of SQL, including its purpose and use and its place in information technology life, and then we'll give you a number of examples of SQL statements with a brief analysis of some of them.

We'll also present various reasons why a Java programmer needs to know something about SQL, including a few paragraphs that compare and contrast SQL with object-oriented database systems. One important component of using SQL and Java together involves understanding the mappings between SQL's data types and Java's types and classes. Because of the fundamental importance of this subject, we'll include a significant amount of information on it.

As you may know already, SQL is rarely used alone to write applications (although the more modern facilities in the SQL standard permit application designers to build more and more of their systems purely in SQL when appropriate). Instead, it is almost always combined with code in one or more other programming languages, with facilities in each language used to satisfy requirements for which they are best suited. There are several ways in which traditional programming languages and SQL are used together:

- Embedded SQL, in which SQL statements are embedded in an otherwise ordinary programming language; these statements are executed by invoking database functionality whenever they are encountered during the normal flow of the program.
- Module language, which allows SQL statements to be gathered together into "pure SQL" modules containing procedures comprising the SQL statements; these procedures are invoked by the use of the host programming language's "call statements."
- Dynamic SQL, although invoked through normal embedded or module language statements, allows SQL statements to be executed even when they are not known at the time that the application is written—the statements can be created "on the fly," either in part or wholly.
- Call-level interfaces permit SQL functionality to be invoked from applications by invoking functions or procedures, some of which process SQL statements and some of which encapsulate frequently required actions into simple invocations of the interface.

We'll survey each of these mechanisms in this chapter without going into tremendous detail—other SQL resources, mentioned in this chapter, are available if you want to know more about this subject. Since the focus of this book is the use of SQL and Java together, we're going to concentrate on the variations of those techniques that support Java's use of SQL.

Many SQL implementations—as well as SQL:1999—provide a powerful, but poorly understood, facility for returning multiple rows of SQL data to application programs. This capability, called *result sets,* allows a database procedure written in (or with) SQL to return a set of rows to its caller, which then processes those rows one at a time. The most popular techniques for using SQL with Java depend heavily on the use of result sets, so we'll introduce the concept in this chapter (but discuss it in detail later in the book).

Finally, we have found that most programmers who don't spend much time using SQL or other database systems are not adequately familiar with the concept of *metadata.* Metadata is data that describes other data: for example, in SQL, there is metadata that describes each of the tables in a database. In this book, we're not going to burden you with all of the detail about SQL metadata as prescribed in the SQL standard or implemented in any specific product, but we'll introduce the subject, illustrate its importance, and show some of the relationships and differences between SQL metadata and the data that it describes.

3.2 SQL—What Is It and What's It Good For?

The short version is easy: SQL is a *data sublanguage* that is used for accessing relational databases. The longer answer will take a bit more effort, in part because we'll provide a few examples to illustrate the words.

As the name suggests, a data sublanguage is one that is used in association with another language for the specialized purpose of accessing data. SQL (correctly pronounced "ess cue ell," instead of the somewhat common "sequel") is a data sublanguage for access to relational databases that are managed by relational database management systems (RDBMS). Many books and articles "define" SQL by parenthetically claiming that the letters stand for Structured Query Language. Although this was true for the original prototypes, it is not true of the standard. When the letters appear in product names, they have often been assigned this meaning by the product vendors, but we believe that users are ill-served by assertions that the word "structured" accurately describes the language. The letters, by the way, don't stand for anything at all. They are not an abbreviation or an acronym, merely the result of the evolution of research projects.

3.2.1 Application Languages versus Data Sublanguages

Application languages are the sort of programming languages with which most people are familiar; they include COBOL, Fortran, C, and—more recently—Java. These languages were designed to allow application programmers to express their computational requirements efficiently. Fortran was designed primarily to support application programmers interested in building numeric or engineering applications, whereas COBOL is generally felt to be more suitable for writing business-oriented applications, and C is often cited as being well designed for systems programming applications. Java, of course, is the *wunderkind* of the World Wide Web—but you're obviously already aware of that or you wouldn't be reading this book.

Languages such as LISP and Prolog that may be less well known were designed for other classes of applications—primarily for building certain classes of artificial intelligence systems.

None of these languages was designed specifically for manipulating data stored under the control of database management systems. It has been found that specialized languages for this purpose are very useful because they permit application writers to accurately (and often concisely) express the data management requirements of the application and get the desired results.

However, a data language by itself is usually insufficient for writing real applications. In almost all cases, an application has a mixture of requirements: perform some calculations, manipulate some information, and manage some data. In this common sort of application, it is helpful if the application writer can build the calculation or manipulate portions of the application by using a language well suited for the purpose, reverting to a specialized data language only for those parts of the application that require it. In this way, the data language is often viewed as (and called) a data sublanguage with respect to the *primary programming language*, or *host language*.

There are several relational data sublanguages to choose from (e.g., QUEL from Relational Technology, Inc. [now CA/Ingres], and RDML from what used to be Digital Equipment Corporation's Rdb/VMS and is now OracleRDB), but only one has been formally standardized for access to relational databases: SQL. It is undoubtedly true that other relational languages have similar expressive power and that at least some are more faithful to the relational model, but SQL has the distinct advantage of being widely implemented and used. This, more than anything else, is the reason SQL has been selected for standardization.

3.2.2 Procedural versus Nonprocedural Languages

Another useful classification for computer programming languages is the degree of procedural support provided within the language's programming constructs, that is, within the basic building blocks inherent in most application programming languages. Constructs such as IF-THEN-ELSE, DO WHILE, DO UNTIL, CASE, and even the much maligned GO TO all deal primarily with *how* application functions should be performed. The order in which operations are to be performed is rigidly specified and created by the programmer.

Nonprocedural languages, on the other hand, are oriented more toward the results of certain operations, leaving the *how* aspects to the "black box"—the underlying software environment. The approach of nonprocedural languages tends to be that of a hands-off, goals-oriented boss, as contrasted with the style of the model above, which could be compared to that of the ultimate micromanager. Basically, the nonprocedural language says, "Look through this stuff, and get me results based on certain criteria; do it the best way you can, and don't bother me with the details."

SQL is heavily oriented toward a nonprocedural model, whereas C, COBOL, Ada, and most languages with which you are familiar tend to be procedural in nature. (Java, like C++ and Smalltalk, falls somewhere in between: there's a lot of procedural code involved in programs written in all three of those languages, but their philosophies encourage you to break down the functions you want performed into small chunks of behavior performed on a variety of *objects.*) In fact, most of the basic programming constructs don't even exist in SQL (although SQL/PSM and proprietary analogs—such as Oracle's PL/SQL or Sybase's Transact-SQL—do provide such constructs), which means your applications usually require a combination of SQL and some host language to perform your required functions.

This is not to say that SQL has no procedural aspects or features at all, however. Although it's true that most SQL statements are essentially nonprocedural in the sense that they specify often complex operations without saying how those results are to be obtained, it's also true that programs that contain two SQL statements that must execute sequentially have a procedural component to them: SQL's rules require that the results of the first statement are obtained before the second statement is executed.

3.2.3 SQL's Background and Focus

Like any other tool, SQL is particularly good for solving some problems and not very good at solving others. However, for good or ill, SQL is *the* primary database language available today; in fact, as the well-known database industry figure Michael Stonebreaker said, SQL has become "intergalactic dataspeak"—meaning, we presume, that it's the only database language that vendors need implement to sell to most of the marketplace.

SQL turns out to be extremely good for building applications that use "traditional data," but not quite as good at dealing with "complex data." Before we analyze that statement further, let's briefly describe the context in which SQL came about.

The Origins of SQL

SQL is based on the relational model of data originally described by Dr. E. F. Codd in a 1970 paper entitled "A Relational Model of Data for Large Shared Data Banks."[1] The relational model describes data that most of us envision as taking a two-dimensional tabular form; SQL, in fact, uses the word "table" to describe a collection of data (organized into "rows" and "columns"), whereas the relational model uses the word "relation" to describe a collection of data (organized into "tuples" and "attributes"). Even though SQL does not strictly implement the

---

[1] "A Relational Model of Data for Large Shared Data Banks," *Communications of the ACM,* Vol. 13, No. 6, June 1970, pp. 377–387.

relational model of data (that is, SQL has a number of extensions that go beyond the relational model—some actually violating basic principles of the model, such as SQL's permissiveness regarding duplicate rows and others irrelevant to the relational model but required by specific product needs), it is definitely *founded* on that model. As a result, most people will consider SQL to be a relational database language. While some might argue with that characterization, we recognize the intent of the phrase and are comfortable with it.

After Dr. Codd published his seminal paper on the relational model, IBM's San Jose Research Laboratory began research on a language to implement that model; the language, designed largely by Don Chamberlin and Raymond Boyce, was called SEQUEL (for Structured English Query Language). Part of this effort involved creation of a research database system called "System R," for which SEQUEL was the principle API (application programming interface). This language was first implemented in a prototype between 1974 and 1975. In the next couple of years, a revised version called SEQUEL/2 was defined; the name of this version was later changed to SQL because of trademark concerns. (No doubt, this is the source of the popular belief that SQL stands for Structured Query Language and is pronounced "sequel.") Further development of SEQUEL/2 eventually led to an IBM specification for the language that, with a few modifications, was proposed as a formal standard, published in 1986.

Dialects of SQL

SQL has been adopted as a standard in the United States by NCITS (formerly ANSI X3) and internationally by ISO. SQL-86 and SQL-89 were superceded by SQL-92,[2] and SQL-92 itself has been superceded by SQL:1999.[3]

SQL-92 introduced a number of identifiable new features that were divided into three levels of conformance: Entry SQL-92, Intermediate SQL-92, and Full SQL-92. In fact, FIPS 127-2,[4] a U.S. Federal Government document published by NIST (the National Institute of Standards

---

[2] ANSI X3.135-1992, *Information Systems—Database Language—SQL,* American National Standards Institute, 1992, and ISO/IEC 9075:1992, *Information technology—Database languages—SQL,* International Organization for Standardization, 1992.

[3] ISO/IEC 9075-1:1999, *Information technology—Database languages—SQL—Part 1: Framework,* ISO/IEC 9075-2:1999, *Information technology—Database languages—SQL—Part 2: Foundation,* ISO/IEC 9075-4:1999, *Information technology—Database languages—SQL—Part 4: Persistent Stored Modules,* and ISO/IEC 9075-5:1999, *Information technology—Database languages—SQL—Part 5: Host language bindings,* International Organization for Standardization, 1999.

[4] FIPS 127-2, *Federal Information Processing Standards Publication 127-2,* National Institute of Standards and Technology, 2 June 1993.

and Technology), enumerated the new features and came up with 83 of them. FIPS 127-2 also defined another conformance level approximately halfway between Entry SQL-92 and Intermediate SQL-92, called Transitional SQL-92.

SQL:1999 introduced quite a bit of new functionality beyond SQL-92, but it eliminated the *levels* used to claim conformance to that edition of the standard; instead, it introduced the notion of Core SQL, the minimum possible set of features that allows a product to claim conformance to the SQL:1999 standard.

The vendors of RDBMSs almost universally conform to Entry SQL-92. They also all provide many additional features, some of them from the higher levels of conformance or from SQL:1999, some of them similar to these features, but with differing syntax or semantics, and some of them completely proprietary. At the time that we wrote this book, no vendor had reached conformance to Core SQL:1999, but several vendors had indicated plans to do so in relatively short order—in our opinion, that means "in the next one or two releases." It is, perhaps, a less than optimal state of affairs for the industry to be in. The writer of a particular application needs to be aware of exactly which RDBMSs must be supported. This is somewhat the opposite of Java's "write once, run anywhere" philosophy.

Traditional Data

In the beginning of Section 3.2.3, we noted that SQL is well suited for dealing with traditional data. Let's look more closely at that. The relational model of data carefully defines the semantics of operations on "relations" of "tuples" of "attributes," but it doesn't state what the data type of that data must be. Most people seem convinced that the relational model requires that the data types fall into a few categories such as "integers," "floating point," and "character strings." That perception is an artifact of two things: the fact that most papers written about the relational model used such data types for illustrative purposes (probably because the discussions were simplified by not having to explain the semantics of other data types); and the fact that SQL traditionally supported only such data types.

In fact, most SQL products have, from the beginning, provided support only for such data types. The 1992 version of the SQL standard (SQL-92) provides only these data types: SMALLINT, INTEGER, DECIMAL, NUMERIC, FLOAT, REAL, DOUBLE PRECISION, CHARACTER, CHARACTER VARYING, BIT, BIT VARYING, DATE, TIME, and TIMESTAMP. (In fact, the last six of those were only added in 1992; previous versions of the SQL standard had only the first eight data types.)

Those data types are used to represent what we call "traditional" data—numbers, text, bit strings, and datetimes. Databases containing data represented exclusively by such data types have for many years held the vast majority of business data handled worldwide, and the DBMS products managing that data have been remarkably successful, supporting a $10 billion industry.

Complex Data

The world is a lot more complicated than numbers, text, bits, and datetimes. In fact, the fastest-growing types of data being generated by businesses and governments don't fall into those neat categories.

Instead, owners of computer systems are insisting on capturing, managing, and interrogating massive collections of unstructured text documents, photographs, drawings, radar images, seismic data, and so forth. And the truth is that SQL hasn't traditionally been very good for such requirements.

Sure, many SQL vendors have enhanced their products to add a data type often called "BLOB" (binary large object), intended to allow users to store and retrieve nontraditional data. But BLOB support has usually been limited strictly to storage and retrieval, without any other semantics applied to them (such as comparisons or using them in criteria for retrieving other data).

Beginning in 1991, even before SQL-92 was published, the standards community started work on the next major generation of the SQL standard, now called "SQL:1999" (and widely known as "SQL3" during its development cycle). The principle "theme" of the SQL:1999 development effort was support of complex data through a mechanism that gradually became known as "user-defined types," in which the ability to define new data types and their operations directly in SQL was provided—thus allowing language support of the sort of complex data increasingly required by industry.

Still, even with user-defined type capabilities, it is clear that SQL doesn't respond to every user's problems. One of several problems is that application developers were (and are) not thrilled with the idea that they might have to define data types and operations in SQL for use within the database system and in another language for use elsewhere. As we'll see in this book, vendors have responded to this problem by supporting Java in the database as well as outside it.

3.3 SQL Language Resources

The purpose of this book is to teach you how to use Java and SQL together, particularly through the use of SQLJ (otherwise known as SQL/OLB and the two parts of the new SQLJ standard), not to teach you how to write SQL programs per se. After all, there are many resources from which you can draw to learn the SQL language, ranging from database product documentation to specific books on the subject.

(One such book from Morgan Kaufmann is *Understanding the New SQL: A Complete Guide.*[5])

We must warn you that we'll use quite a bit of the SQL language in the examples of this book. More important, though, is that understanding many of the concepts in this book requires an understanding of the underlying SQL concepts. We will, whenever it seems appropriate to do so, provide at least a quick review of those SQL concepts, but we will assume that you are familiar with the more fundamental concepts.

In the spirit of getting you oriented (after all, we know you're not going to run right out and buy an SQL book right now!), however, we think it's worth spending a few pages outlining the principal features of the SQL language. Not at all incidentally, we're going to take this opportunity to introduce the example application that we've chosen for presenting the concepts discussed in the rest of the book.

3.4 SQL Examples

In order to illustrate some of the principal features of SQL, we'll start off by creating a table, shown in Example 3.1, that we'll then manipulate in this section. An SQL table is created, logically enough, with the CREATE TABLE statement.

As a convention, we tend to write SQL keywords in all uppercase letters ("`CREATE`" and "`CHARACTER`") and identifiers in all lowercase letters ("`title`" and "`director`"). In a very few cases, we write identifiers in mixed-case to illustrate the possibility of doing so ("`ReleaseDate`" could have been used instead of "`release_date`"), but you should remember that SQL's keywords and identifiers are not case sensitive.[6] By contrast, the case of character string literals is significant, as we'll see.

---

[5] *Understanding the New SQL: A Complete Guide,* Jim Melton and Alan R. Simon, Morgan Kaufmann, 1993.

[6] SQL does, however, have a special type of identifier in which case is important. This type of identifier is called a "delimited identifier" or "quoted identifier." It allows you to write identifiers that are spelled the same as a keyword, which is otherwise forbidden in SQL; it also allows you to write identifiers that use special characters. For example, although

```
TABLE
```

is a keyword in SQL and not permitted for use as the name (identifier) of any object, the identifier

```
"TABLE"
```

is a valid identifier! Similarly, the identifier

```
"This is a not-very-normal identifier!"
```

is also a valid identifier, even though it has normally prohibited characters—such as spaces and punctuation marks—in it.

EXAMPLE 3.1 CREATING AN SQL TABLE.

```
CREATE TABLE movies (
   title               CHARACTER VARYING (100),
   director            CHARACTER VARYING (50),
   year_introduced     CHARACTER(4),
   release_date        DATE,7
   runs                INTEGER
     CONSTRAINT runs_range
       CHECK (runs BETWEEN 0 AND 480),

   CONSTRAINT movies_pk
     PRIMARY KEY (title)
   );
```

The table created by the statement in Example 3.1 is usually visualized in a form something like that shown in Result 3.1. For convenience in illustrating some of the subsequent SQL statements, we've taken the liberty of populating the table with data, but don't assume that the CREATE TABLE statement had that effect! (By the way, the order in which SQL returns rows from a query is undefined—perhaps determined by implementation considerations—unless specified by the application's code.)

Although Result 3.1 is a great way to *visualize* a table, all those lines around the cells of the table are rather intrusive in the context of a book like this; to minimize that effect, we're going to present our results in a friendlier form, which you can see in Result 3.2.

[7] We use the DATE data type in the first few examples in this chapter for pedagogic purposes; however, this data type has not been widely implemented in its standard-conforming manner, so later examples—and our sample schema in Appendix B—omit this column entirely. Instead of repeating the CREATE TABLE statement and the visualizations of the resulting table, which are identical to this example except for the omission of the column, we will simply write examples and illustrate results without the DATE column. In fact, because of the conventions we use for writing SQL, the queries that omit use of the DATE column will function properly in any case, because they do not depend on, nor can they detect the presence or absence of, the DATE column.

Result 3.1 **Visualizing an SQL table.**

title	director	year_introduced	release_date	runs
Independence Day (ID4)	Roland Emerich	1996	1996-07-03	153
Deep Impact	Mimi Leder	1998	1998-05-08	120
Mars Attacks!	Tim Burton	1996	1996-12-13	106
The Terminator	James Cameron	1984	1985-10-26	107
Blazing Stewardesses	Al Adamson	1974	1974-06-30	80
Terminator 2: Judgment Day	James Cameron	1991	1991-07-03	152
Plan 9 from Outer Space	Edward D. Wood, Jr.	1958	1958-06-30	79
.	.		.	.
.	.		.	.
.	.		.	.
Lost in Space	Stephen Hopkins	1998	1998-04-03	130

Result 3.2 **Another way of visualizing an SQL table.**

title	director	year_introduced	release_date	runs
Independence Day (ID4)	Roland Emerich	1996	1996-07-03	153
Deep Impact	Mimi Leder	1998	1998-05-08	120
Mars Attacks!	Tim Burton	1996	1996-12-13	106
The Terminator	James Cameron	1984	1985-10-26	107
Blazing Stewardesses	Al Adamson	1974	1974-06-30	80
Terminator 2: Judgment Day	James Cameron	1991	1991-07-03	152
Plan 9 from Outer Space	Edward D. Wood, Jr.	1958	1958-06-30	79
.	.		.	.
.	.		.	.
.	.		.	.
Lost in Space	Stephen Hopkins	1998	1998-04-03	130

3.4.1 Data Retrieval

Arguably, the most basic operation in SQL is retrieval of data from an SQL table. In order to retrieve the names of movies and their directors for all films released in 1998, a statement like the one in Example 3.2 would be used.

EXAMPLE 3.2 A SELECT STATEMENT.

```
SELECT   title, director
FROM     movies
WHERE    release_date BETWEEN
            DATE '1998-01-01' AND DATE '1998-12-31'
```

Result 3.3 illustrates the result of that statement. Note particularly that the result of an SQL SELECT statement is another table! Furthermore, this table has only two columns, even though the source table has five—that's because our sample SQL statement has two columns in its *select list*. Of course, this table is not a *persistent table* (one that is stored somewhere in the database); instead, it's a *virtual table* (one whose value is computed upon demand). This example illustrates one important aspect of the SQL language: most SQL operations on tables produce other tables as their result. (There are a few exceptions to this rule because SQL needs some operations that extract data from tables in scalar or other nontabular form.)

Result 3.3 SELECT result.

title	director
Lost in Space	Stephen Hopkins
Deep Impact	Mimi Leder

The liberal use of multiple lines and spaces in SQL statements is also insignificant. In general, you can go to a new line anywhere and insert spaces (for readability, perhaps) within an SQL statement, except, of course, in the middle of a keyword, identifier, or literal. (You'll notice that our SQL code generally follows the advice we're giving you, but the patterns might vary among examples; if nothing else, you can deduce from this practice that you're going to have to develop your own SQL coding style.) The major exception to this rule is that one form of SQL comments always start with two or more hyphens and is terminated by the end of the line:

```
-- This is an SQL comment
-- This is a second SQL comment
This is not part of the second SQL comment and is an error
```

Let's take the SELECT statement of Example 3.2 apart a little bit, since it may not be obvious why it was written as it was. The keyword `SELECT` is followed by a *select list,* which is a comma-separated list of values to be retrieved; those values can be retrieved directly from columns in the table identified in the FROM clause, or they can be computed from those values stored in columns in the table and from literals.[8] The FROM clause specifies the table (or tables; one of the special talents of SQL is the ability to combine data from multiple tables in a single operation) from which data is to be retrieved. The WHERE clause specifies filter criteria to be applied to the data coming from the table specified in the FROM clause; in this example, we've instructed SQL to retrieve only those rows for which the `release_date` column has a value that falls between 1 January 1998 and 31 December 1998.

Our example earlier could have been written in many different ways with the same result. For example, instead of using the BETWEEN predicate to restrict the rows retrieved to those in which the `release_date` column values fall into a specified range of dates, we could have extracted the year component of the `release_date` column values and required that they be equal to the integer value 1998, as shown in Example 3.3.

EXAMPLE 3.3 ANOTHER SELECT STATEMENT.

```
SELECT   title, director
FROM     movies
WHERE    EXTRACT (YEAR FROM release_date) = 1998
```

---

[8] A *literal* is a sequence of characters in source code that represents a value of a particular data type. Thus, a literal representation for the number ten is `10` and a literal representation for the names of the two languages discussed by this book is `'SQL and Java'`. Datetime literals follow conventions of an international standard (ISO 8601) and are structured like this:

`yyyy-MM-dd:hh:mm:ss.ff...`

In this format, `yyyy` represents four digits of the year (no Y2K problem here!), `MM` represents the month, `dd` represents the date of the month, `hh` represents the hour (in 24-hour format), `mm` represents the minute, `ss` represents the seconds, and `ff...` represents fractions of a second (to an implementation-defined precision).

Now, there's a minor problem with that statement, at least if you're planning to use it in an application program. If you were to invoke the statement directly from some sort of interactive query tool, the result would probably be a lengthy list of data (made up of movie titles and director names, probably on a single line) scrolling up your screen. However, if the statement is invoked from, say, a COBOL program (or a Java program) that "lengthy list of data" becomes awkward to handle. Most application programming languages are unable to accept sets of data or lists of data returned from subprograms. After all, there's no place to store such a list of unknown—and effectively unlimited—length, so most programming languages require that you handle such data one piece at a time (in this case, one row at a time). We call this difference in SQL's set-at-a-time capabilities and conventional programming languages' datum-at-a-time orientation "an impedance mismatch"; there are other examples of SQL's impedance mismatch with other programming languages, such as the precise semantics of data types.

To help you deal with this set-at-a-time impedance mismatch, the SQL language provides something called a *cursor* (a more generalized term is *iterator,* because a cursor allows a program to iterate across the set of rows returned from a retrieval expression like that shown in Example 3.2 and in Example 3.3). Application programs declare a cursor and associate it with a retrieval expression, then they open the cursor, retrieve (fetch) rows from it, and eventually close it; they are normally allowed to update the rows they've retrieved and even delete them while the cursor is positioned on the row.

Another way to deal with this impedance mismatch is provided in many SQL implementations. This other approach is called a *result set* and allows applications to pretend that they can actually retrieve a set of rows from the database at once. In other words, the cursor is sort of hidden under the covers. We'll see a great deal more discussion of result sets and iterators as we look at SQL/OLB[9] later in this book.

3.4.2 Data Creation

Of course, data in an SQL table has to be put there somehow, normally through the use of an SQL statement. The INSERT statement is used for that purpose, as shown in Example 3.4.

[9] The standard for embedding SQL statements into Java code is sometimes called "SQLJ Part 0," but its acceptance as an American National Standard (X3.135.10: 1998) means that it is also properly known by its name there: SQL/OLB (Object Language Bindings).

EXAMPLE 3.4 AN INSERT STATEMENT.

```
INSERT INTO movies
VALUES ( 'Titanic', 'James Cameron', '1997', 194 )
```

That statement, of course, adds to our table a row of data describing the movie *Titanic*. (We've chosen, somewhat arbitrarily, to use movie data based on the USA release of the movies; naturally, data for releases in other countries may vary.) The results are illustrated in Result 3.4.

Result 3.4 Inserting into an SQL table, alternative 1.

title	director	year_introduced	runs
Independence Day (ID4)	Roland Emerich	1996	153
Deep Impact	Mimi Leder	1998	120
Mars Attacks!	Tim Burton	1996	106
Titanic	James Cameron	1997	194
The Terminator	James Cameron	1985	107
Blazing Stewardesses	Al Adamson	1974	80
Terminator 2: Judgment Day	James Cameron	1991	152
Plan 9 from Outer Space	Edward D. Wood, Jr.	1958	79
.	.		.
.	.		.
.	.		.
Lost in Space	Stephen Hopkins	1998	130

Note that the row we inserted (describing the movie *Titanic*) wasn't put at the end of the table—SQL, like the relational model, stores data in a completely unordered form (by which we mean that the location of any specific row is determined strictly by the implementation based on its own needs); if you want to retrieve data in some specific order, there are ways to do that, but that's beyond the scope of this book.

If, for some reason, you didn't want to provide values for all columns, or you wanted to provide those values in a different sequence, you can code the statement as shown in Example 3.5.

EXAMPLE 3.5 ANOTHER INSERT STATEMENT.

```
INSERT INTO movies (title, year_introduced, director)
VALUES ( 'Titanic', '1997', 'James Cameron' )
```

The results of Example 3.5 are shown in Result 3.5.

Result 3.5 Inserting into an SQL table, alternative 2.

title	director	year_introduced	runs
Independence Day (ID4)	Roland Emerich	1996	153
Deep Impact	Mimi Leder	1998	120
Mars Attacks!	Tim Burton	1996	106
The Terminator	James Cameron	1985	107
Blazing Stewardesses	Al Adamson	1974	80
Terminator 2: Judgment Day	James Cameron	1991	152
Titanic	James Cameron	1997	*(null)*
Plan 9 from Outer Space	Edward D. Wood, Jr.	1958	79
.	.		.
.	.		.
.	.		.
Lost in Space	Stephen Hopkins	1998	130

The (*null*) notation indicates that the row was stored with the default value in that column. According to our table definition earlier in this chapter, there are no explicit default values for the `year_introduced` and `runs` columns; SQL's default default is the null value. (We haven't covered this concept yet, but we will discuss it later in this chapter when we talk about SQL's data types and their relationships to Java types and classes.)

Of course, it would be tedious to manually code and execute the thousands of INSERT statements required to populate a serious movie database, but you might manually execute a few such statements to update your database in an emergency. Normally, you'd write a program to read the data from another source (such as a file supplied by a film distributor or studio) and invoke the SQL statements using parameters that provide the data, as you can see in Example 3.6.

EXAMPLE 3.6 INSERT STATEMENT WITH INPUT DATA.

```
INSERT INTO movies ( title, director, year_introduced, runs )
VALUES (:hv1, :hv2, :hv3, :hv4)
```

The *:identifier* (:hv1, for example) notation specifies the name of a host language variable[10] that the application program uses to pass data to the SQL statement or that will be used to return data from the SQL statement to the application program. The use of the colon (:) signals the SQL compiler that the identifier isn't the name of a column, for example, but is the name of a host language variable (in most implementations, there is an SQL preprocessor that performs this function).

Of course, the use of such an SQL statement is significantly complicated by the fact that no conventional programming language has data types that correspond directly to SQL's DATE type—another example of the impedance mismatch we mentioned earlier. To deal with this problem, most application programs will convert (or ask SQL to convert) between host program character strings and SQL types.

In the context of a C program, this statement might be used as shown in Example 3.7. (You may ask why we've chosen to use C for some examples instead of Java—it's simply because we haven't introduced the conventions for using Java to embed SQL yet, though we will do so in Chapter 5. In the meantime, C is among the most popular languages that has a "conventional" SQL embedding capability.)

The keywords EXEC SQL are used to signal to an SQL preprocessor that the remainder of the statement is SQL instead of the application programming language. The CAST function is how SQL does data conversion, in this case from C's character strings to an SQL DATE type, which is especially important when interfacing with languages that don't support a particular SQL data type.

3.4.3 Updating Data

Rarely is the data you put into your databases perfect and unchanging. Instead, it is sometimes corrected and very often updated as business conditions evolve. Some data is inherently meant to be updated—such as a database column intended to hold year-to-date sales. Perhaps our movie table should have looked like the one shown in Example 3.8.

---

10 As we'll see in Chapter 5, SQL/OLB allows host value expressions in addition to host language variable names. In addition, as we'll see in Chapter 4, dynamic parameter markers (represented by question marks [?]) are also allowed.

EXAMPLE 3.7 C PROGRAM WITH INSERT STATEMENT.

```
/* Declare host variables; allow for null terminator */

EXEC SQL BEGIN DECLARE SECTION;
char movie_title[101];
char director[51];
char released[11];
char year[5];
short runtime;
EXEC SQL END DECLARE SECTION;

/* Get values for all 5 variables and populate them */

...

/* Now, invoke the SQL INSERT statement */

EXEC SQL
  INSERT INTO movies ( title, director, year_introduced,
                       release_date, runs )
  VALUES ( :movie_title, :director, :year,
           CAST(:released AS DATE), :runtime );
```

EXAMPLE 3.8 ADDITIONAL TABLE CREATION.

```
CREATE TABLE movies_in_stock (
    title           CHARACTER VARYING (100) REFERENCES MOVIES,
    quantity        INTEGER,
    sale_price      DECIMAL(4,2),
    YearToDateSales DECIMAL(6,2),

    CONSTRAINT stock_pk
      PRIMARY KEY (title)
)
```

Result 3.6 shows how we visualize this table (and, again, we've taken the liberty of populating the table with sample data).

With the `yeartodatesales` column (yes, that's harder to read, but it means exactly the same to SQL as `YearToDateSales`, since case is unimportant!), we'd expect the application to update the column in a row every time we sold a copy of a movie. The statement to accomplish this might look like the one in Example 3.9.

Result 3.6 Visualizing the new table.

title	quantity	sale_price	YearToDateSales
Blazing Stewardesses	131	21.95	8942.85
Deep Impact	21	24.95	1247.50
Independence Day (ID4)	12	19.95	1995.00
Lost in Space	34	4.95	103.95
Mars Attacks!	17	17.95	2566.85
Plan 9 from Outer Space	9	10.00	680.00
Terminator 2: Judgment Day	42	12.95	3082.10
The Terminator	28	17.95	1310.35

EXAMPLE 3.9 EXAMPLE UPDATE STATEMENT.

```
UPDATE   movies_in_stock
SET      YearToDateSales = YearToDateSales + sale_price
WHERE    title = :hv1
```

Of course, if you're a fan of the genre, you'll know that we got both the `year_introduced` and `runs` values wrong for Arnie's *oeuvre, The Terminator*; Example 3.10 shows how we can fix this problem.

The effect of this statement looks something like that shown in Result 3.7.

EXAMPLE 3.10 ANOTHER UPDATE STATEMENT.

```
UPDATE   movies
SET      year_introduced = '1984',
         runs = 108
WHERE    title = 'The Terminator'
```

Result 3.7 An updated SQL table.

title	director	year_introduced	runs
Independence Day (ID4)	Roland Emerich	1996	153
Deep Impact	Mimi Leder	1998	120
Mars Attacks!	Tim Burton	1996	106
The Terminator	James Cameron	1984	108
Blazing Stewardesses	Al Adamson	1974	80
Terminator 2: Judgment Day	James Cameron	1991	152
Plan 9 from Outer Space	Edward D. Wood, Jr.	1958	79
.	.		.
.	.		.
.	.		.
Lost in Space	Stephen Hopkins	1998	130

3.4.4 Removal of Data

To bring your database up to date, you may have to delete data from it as well. SQL provides the DELETE statement for this purpose. Since we're running a family operation here, we might clean things up by executing a statement like the one shown in Example 3.11.

EXAMPLE 3.11 EXAMPLE DELETE STATEMENT.

```
DELETE   FROM movies
WHERE    title LIKE '%Stewardess%'
```

The LIKE predicate matches character strings through the use of wildcards such as the "%", which means "zero or more characters"; the other wildcard is "_", which means "exactly one character." In our example, any movie whose title contains the character sequence "Stewardess" (in exactly that case convention) will be deleted. Consequently, we'll lose *Blazing Stewardesses, Bedroom Stewardesses, Naughty Stewardesses,* and anything else with those ten characters in the title. Result 3.8 shows the result using our sample data.

Result 3.8 The SQL table, after delete operation.

title	director	year_introduced	runs
Independence Day (ID4)	Roland Emerich	1996	153
Deep Impact	Mimi Leder	1998	120
Mars Attacks!	Tim Burton	1996	106
The Terminator	James Cameron	1984	108
Terminator 2: Judgment Day	James Cameron	1991	152
Plan 9 from Outer Space	Edward D. Wood, Jr.	1958	79
.	.		.
.	.		.
.	.		.
Lost in Space	Stephen Hopkins	1998	130

3.4.5 More Complex Operations

While discussing data retrieval above, we mentioned that SQL's strengths include the ability to combine data from multiple tables. There are several SQL operations that combine data in different ways, and we'll define another table, as shown in Example 3.12, to help us demonstrate these.

EXAMPLE 3.12 DEFINING YET ANOTHER TABLE.

```
CREATE TABLE movie_stars (
    title             CHARACTER VARYING (100),
    star_first_name   CHARACTER VARYING (25),
    star_last_name    CHARACTER VARYING (25),

    CONSTRAINT movie_stars_pk
      PRIMARY KEY (title, star_first_name, star_last_name),

    CONSTRAINT movie_star_movies_fk
      FOREIGN KEY (title)
        REFERENCES movies
)
```

We've already seen the visualization and sample data for the `movies` table, so we won't repeat it here. However, the `movie_stars` table is new, so Result 3.9 shows you how we visualize it. (For convenience we collected all the rows dealing with each movie together; of course, this isn't necessarily how SQL stores the data, but it's easier on human readers.)

You've probably noticed the `CONSTRAINT` and `PRIMARY KEY` lines in the earlier CREATE TABLE statements, and noted that we've ignored them so far. A *constraint* is an SQL facility that allows you to specify rules (sometimes called *business rules,* because they are often used to state restrictions and requirements of the business or enterprise supported by the database) directly in your database, ensuring that the rule is enforced at all times without the necessity of your application code constantly having to enforce it (and perhaps getting it wrong some of the time, or enforcing it differently at different times). Constraints are enforced by the database management system, frequently at the end of the execution of every SQL statement. The statement fails if it has changed the database in such a way that the constraint is violated. SQL implementations often provide, as does the SQL standard, "deferrable" constraints, which are not enforced until activated; this activation takes place no later than the end of the transaction. Examples of business rules that you might specify as constraints are the following:

- All employee salaries must be greater than zero, but no employee salary shall be greater than the budget of the department for which the employee works.
- No temperature shall be less than –273 (°C, of course).
- Every department must be managed by an employee whose job title code is 46 or greater.

SQL allows you to define constraints on individual columns of a table ("column-level" constraints), on combinations of columns in a table ("table-level" constraints), and on multiple tables ("assertions").

The `CONSTRAINT` *`identifier`* syntax gives a name to a constraint; it's entirely optional, but we like to specify it in our code since the database system may use it for reporting errors involving violations of the constraint that it names. The `PRIMARY KEY` syntax specifies the names of the column or columns whose values uniquely identify each row in a table; without a PRIMARY KEY, SQL permits duplicate rows in tables, but we decided that we don't really need two different rows for *Plan Nine from Outer Space* (or any other movie). In a real-life situation, we'd probably define our primary key to specify both the `title` and the `release_date` columns so our database could contain rows for, say, two different movies with the same name (such movies, in our experience, aren't released in the same year, much less on the same date).

Result 3.9 **The `movie_stars` table.**

title	star_first_name	star_last_name
Deep Impact	Robert	Duvall
Deep Impact	Téa	Leoni
Deep Impact	Elijah	Wood
Deep Impact	Vanessa	Redgrave
Deep Impact	Morgan	Freeman
Independence Day (ID4)	Will	Smith
Independence Day (ID4)	Bill	Pullman
Independence Day (ID4)	Jeff	Goldblum
Independence Day (ID4)	Judd	Hirsch
Mars Attacks!	Jack	Nicholson
Mars Attacks!	Glenn	Close
Mars Attacks!	Annette	Bening
Mars Attacks!	Pierce	Brosnan
Mars Attacks!	Danny	DeVito
The Terminator	Arnold	Schwartzenegger
The Terminator	Linda	Hamilton
Terminator 2: Judgment Day	Arnold	Schwartzenegger
Terminator 2: Judgment Day	Linda	Hamilton
Terminator 2: Judgment Day	Edward	Furlong
Plan 9 from Outer Space	Gregory	Walcott
Plan 9 from Outer Space	Mona	McKinnon
Plan 9 from Outer Space	Duke	Moore
.	.	.
.	.	.
.	.	.
Lost in Space	William	Hurt
Lost in Space	Mimi	Rogers
Lost in Space	Gary	Oldman

The FOREIGN KEY constraint allows us to require that the `movie_stars` table never contain a row in which the `title` column has a value that doesn't identify a row in the `movies` table.

With that under our belts, let's look into more complex SQL queries. One of the most important ways of combining data from multiple tables is called "joining." You'd normally join rows from two tables based on the equality of values in two columns. For example, if we wanted to get a list of all movies in which Arnold Schwartzenegger has starred, we could simply execute the statement shown in Example 3.13.

EXAMPLE 3.13 SELECTING SCHWARTZENEGGER.

```
SELECT    title
FROM      movie_stars
WHERE     star_first_name = 'Arnold'
  AND     star_last_name = 'Schwartzenegger'
```

Although this method is straightforward and works well (and the result would be a virtual table somewhat similar to that illustrated in Result 3.2), what if we also wanted the names of the directors? SQL's ability to join tables would allow us to write the statement shown in Example 3.14.

EXAMPLE 3.14 SELECTING SCHWARTZENEGGER AND HIS DIRECTORS USING A JOIN.

```
SELECT    movies.title, director
FROM      movie_stars, movies
WHERE     star_first_name = 'Arnold'
  AND     star_last_name = 'Schwartzenegger'
  AND     movies.title = movie_stars.title
```

The fact that each table has a column named `title` means that we need to qualify the names of those columns with the names of the tables from which we want the value to be taken. In our select list, we arbitrarily chose `movies` as that table, but could have just as easily chosen `movie_stars` since the values are going to be equal—a consequence of the equality specified by the WHERE clause. Result 3.10 shows the results of this last SQL statement.

There are other ways of combining data from multiple tables. One popular way uses an operation called UNION. That operation requires that the two tables being combined have the same number of columns and that the data types of columns in the same position have compatible data types; the result is a table with that number of columns and rows corresponding to every row from the two tables. UNION might be used to produce a table of movies from tables of VHS movies and Betamax movies, as shown in Example 3.15.[11]

Result 3.10 The two-table query result (using a join).

title	director
The Terminator	James Cameron
Terminator 2: Judgment Day	James Cameron
Conan the Barbarian	John Milius
Conan the Destroyer	Richard Fleischer
Predator	John McTiernan
The Running Man	Paul Michael Glaser
Red Heat	Walter Hill
Total Recall	Paul Verhoeven
Kindergarten Cop	Ivan Reitman
Last Action Hero	John McTiernan
True Lies	James Cameron
Junior	Ivan Reitman
Jingle All the Way	Brian Levant
Eraser	Chuck Russell
Terminator 3	James Cameron
Twins	Ivan Reitman

As you can guess, there are a great many more facilities defined by the SQL standard (and by implementations of the language) that support "complex operations." We're not going to go through all of them in this book, but be aware that our examples may use one or more of those additional facilities without further explanation.

[11] This example does not involve syntax that isn't widely implemented, but it does use base tables that we have not defined in our schema; it is here only to illustrate the power of UNION operations.

EXAMPLE 3.15 PRODUCING A RESULT USING UNION.

```
   SELECT   title, YearToDateSales
   FROM     VHS_movies_in_stock
   WHERE    movie_title LIKE '%Terminator%'
UNION
   SELECT   title, YearToDateSales
   FROM     Betamax_movies_in_stock
   WHERE    movie_title LIKE '%Terminator%'
```

3.5 Stored Routines

Most vendors of SQL database management systems have long recognized the importance of allowing at least some components of application logic to be performed directly inside the DBMS system to minimize the amount of data that has to be transported in both directions (possibly over a network of some sort) between the DBMS and the application program. Writing such logic normally involves procedural approaches, so the DBMS vendors have provided a "stored procedures" (and functions) capability that allows (procedural) application logic to be stored in the DBMS (often inside the database itself) and executed on request. Some products (e.g., IBM's DB2) allow these stored procedures to be written only in an ordinary programming language, such as C. Others, such as Cloudscape's Cloudscape, support only Java for stored procedures (which we'll cover in Chapter 6). Still other products (e.g., Sybase's Adaptive Server Anywhere and Adaptive Server Enterprise, Oracle's ORACLE, and Informix's INFORMIX) provide a dialect of the SQL language with extensions that give procedural capabilities. The SQL standard reflects these products in a specification called Persistent Stored Modules (SQL/PSM). If you'd like to know more about procedural extensions to SQL, the publisher of this book offers *Understanding SQL's Stored Procedures: A Complete Guide to SQL/PSM* by Jim Melton. A brief introduction to the subject is in order, however.

Most commercial SQL products, as well as the SQL/PSM standard, provide the ability for applications—or at least database administrators—to store procedures (and functions) in the database for use by application code. These stored routines, to use the more generic term, can often be written in SQL itself, although various vendors of SQL DBMSs have often adopted their own dialects of SQL and have not yet implemented the standard SQL/PSM dialect. In addition, stored routines can usually be written in one of several ordinary host programming languages, such as C. Let's look at an example in Example 3.16.

EXAMPLE 3.16 EXAMPLE SQL STORED ROUTINES.

```
-- Create an SQL procedure that automatically updates
--   the database whenever we sell a movie

CREATE PROCEDURE update_inventory
                    ( movie_name   CHARACTER VARYING (100),
                      number_sold  INTEGER,
                      new_price    DECIMAL (5, 2))

   UPDATE   movies_in_stock
   SET      quantity = quantity - number_sold
   WHERE    movie_title = movie_name

-- Create an external function for a C function that
--   computes a discount based on an input percentage off

CREATE FUNCTION compute_discount ( cost REAL, percent INTEGER )
   RETURNS REAL
   LANGUAGE C
   SPECIFIC shop.movies.discount_in_c
   DETERMINISTIC
   NO SQL
   EXTERNAL NAME 'file:///F:/routines/discounter.bin'
   PARAMETER STYLE GENERAL
```

These two routines can be invoked from SQL using code like that shown in Example 3.17.

EXAMPLE 3.17 INVOKING SQL STORED ROUTINES.

```
EXEC SQL CALL update_inventory
   ( 'Terminator 2: Judgment Day', 2,
     compute_discount ( 24.98, 20 ) );
```

Code such as that shown in Example 3.17, embedded in a C program, would update the database records associated with selling the movie *Terminator 2: Judgment Day* to show that we have sold two more copies and that we brought in 24.98 (dollars, presumably) minus a 20% discount. (No, we haven't shown the C code used to implement the external routine; you'll just have to trust us that it does what we want it to do.)

3.6 Why Use SQL Instead of an OODBMS?

The SQL language can get pretty complex, as is clearly suggested by the size of most products' documentation and even by the SQL standard itself. Why on earth would you, a Java programmer, want to have to learn SQL? Wouldn't you be better off taking a different approach to storing your data, perhaps in a form more friendly to Java itself?

The first step toward answering this question lies in this (possibly obvious) fact: If your Java applications have no need to access, store, or otherwise manage persistent data, then you don't need a database at all. There are undoubtedly a great many Java applications that have this characteristic—but more complex, possibly enterprise-oriented, applications have to meet this requirement.

Let's look at the alternatives because there are several worth considering. One possibility is to manage all your own data, perhaps by writing it to an operating system file, which would work except for the minor problem that the environment in which Java applets run generally prohibits such operations. Also, managing file operations can be quite complex, time-consuming, and error-prone. Worse, it's quite difficult to ensure that your operations have *transactional semantics*—meaning that you can demarcate them so that all operations in one group are successfully performed or an error in one of them forces the rest of the group to be "undone" for consistency. Though it's possible to deal with these (and other) problems, it is at best expensive to do so. Few enterprises today have the resources to spend pursuing this alternative: not only does it consume resources at a sometimes frightening and usually unpredictable rate, it distracts from conducting the principal business of the enterprise.

Another alternative, endorsed by the Object Database Management Group,[12] is to manage your data through an object-oriented database management system (OODBMS). A number of such products are available, and many of them have Java interfaces. This option may be attractive under certain circumstances, principally because an OODBMS could have semantics that are close to those of Java, making it relatively easy to store, retrieve, and manage objects instead of rows of data. However, although the market for OODBMSs is growing (even growing rapidly, according to some sources), there are several problems with this choice.

The first problem is that, in spite of the existence of a nominal standard for OODBMSs, the reality is that the products available today implement very little of that standard, and no two products implement the same bits. Although this criticism can be leveled at many

[12] *The Object Database Standard: ODMG 2.0,* Rick Cattell et al., Morgan Kaufmann, 1997.

different standards (including SQL's!), it is especially relevant for OODBMSs because their internal models tend to be widely divergent and the lack of a common language among multiple products makes it very difficult to overlook those model differences.

This situation leads to a second problem: the ability to apply personnel trained on one OODBMS to work using another. Without a common model or a common language, knowledge gained from using one system cannot readily be applied to a different system.

In contrast, SQL (the so-called intergalactic dataspeak) allows implementations of relational database management systems to shield (largely, if incompletely) application programmers from their internal models and to provide an interface to the data they manage that is significantly like the interface provided by other SQL products. In this way, training on one product can be meaningful when working with a different product.

The third problem is perhaps more subtle. OODBMSs excel at managing *objects,* especially in environments where the operations to be performed on those objects are reasonably well known when the database is designed. They rarely perform well when called upon to deal with ad hoc query environments or applications requiring significant use of traditional data such as numbers and character strings. SQL is well designed to deal with that traditional data, and virtually all SQL products today are quite efficient when dealing with unpredictable—and unpredicted—queries and combinations of data.

This last situation brings us to a final alternative: combining an SQL product for managing traditional data and an OODBMS for managing complex, object-oriented data. Several variations on this theme come to mind, but two of them illustrate the possibilities. You could buy an SQL product and a separate OODBMS product and write your applications to use the first for traditional data and the other for objects, using a third product—a transaction monitor—to ensure that transactional semantics are applied to updates that invoke both products. Alternatively, you could acquire a product with thorough SQL support built into it that has also integrated support for object management, either through the use of specialized storage managers or through built-in object facilities. The first choice requires that your application manage the relationship between traditional data and objects, but probably allows greater flexibility in choosing the products you acquire. The second option may limit your product choices somewhat, but all of the major SQL vendors are delivering products that support one (or sometimes both) of the variations we mentioned. Among products that are SQL-based and have integrated object management support, the fastest growing approach to delivering that support is to integrate Java with the database engine in some fashion, which of course, is what this book is primarily about.

3.7 SQL and Java Together

You already know that the intent of this book is to discuss the use of SQL and Java together, but before we start discussion of that topic specifically we'd like to go over a few issues that affect the relationship between these two languages. Among these issues are the similarities and differences between their object models, the compatibilities and incompatibilities between SQL's data types and Java's types and classes, and SQL's mechanisms for interfacing with application languages.

3.8 Object Models: SQL and Java

Although we don't think this chapter is the appropriate place to discuss either the Java object model (which we assume you Java programmers already know) or the SQL object model in detail, we did think it was reasonable to at least mention in this chapter that SQL does have an object model and that it has both similarities to and differences from the Java model. The similarities will, of course, make it easier to use the two languages in harmony, whereas the differences will require application developers to pay close attention to areas where those differences may cause difficulties. Is this just another example of the infamous impedance mismatch between SQL and host languages? Perhaps so, but its nature is somewhat more subtle than the issues raised by cursors and differing data types. In any case, the SQL object model is covered more completely in Chapter 7.

3.9 Data Type Relationships

In Section 3.4, we discussed the impedance mismatch between SQL and other programming languages with which SQL is often used. It won't surprise you to know that that impedance mismatch includes the relationship between SQL's data types and Java's classes and primitive types. Ironically, although SQL and Java are designed to be as portable as possible among computing platforms, they have taken very different approaches to achieving that end. Consequently, the impedance mismatch between the two languages has not been much relieved by those efforts.

Let's start by looking at Java's primitive types and SQL's predefined data types. (The difference in terminology—"type" versus "data type"—is merely an artifact of the language chosen by each specification's authors and doesn't imply anything more sinister.) Table 3.1 shows each of SQL's predefined data types, along with the name of the corresponding Java primitive type. When two data types appear in the same cell of the table, it's because they are completely equivalent to

SQL predefined data type	Java primitive type
SMALLINT	short
INTEGER INT	int
DECIMAL(precision, scale) DEC(precision, scale)	(none)
NUMERIC(precision, scale)	(none)
FLOAT(precision)	double
REAL	float
DOUBLE PRECISION	double
CHARACTER(length) CHAR(length)	(none)
CHARACTER VARYING(maxlength) VARCHAR(maxlength)	(none)
NATIONAL CHARACTER(length) NATIONAL CHAR(length) NCHAR(length)	(none, but single-character values are supported)
NATIONAL CHARACTER VARYING(maxlength) NATIONAL CHAR VARYING(maxlength) NCHAR VARYING(maxlength)	(none)
CHARACTER LARGE OBJECT(maxlength) CHAR LARGE OBJECT(maxlength) CLOB(maxlength)	(none)
BIT(length)	(none)
BIT VARYING(maxlength)	(none)
BINARY LARGE OBJECT(maxlength) BLOB(maxlength)	(none)
BOOLEAN	boolean
DATE	(none)
TIME(precision)	(none)
TIME(precision) WITH TIME ZONE	(none)
TIMESTAMP(precision)	(none)
TIMESTAMP(precision) WITH TIME ZONE	(none)
INTERVAL(qualifier)	(none)
ROW(field, field,...)	(none)
REF(referenced type)	(none)
datatype ARRAY[size]	(arrays generated by applying dimension to type declaration)

TABLE 3.1 *SQL predefined data types and corresponding Java primitive types.*

Java primitive type	SQL predefined data type
byte	(none)*
short	SMALLINT
int	INTEGER
long	(none)†
float	REAL
double	DOUBLE PRECISION
char	NATIONAL CHARACTER(1)
boolean	BOOLEAN

* TINYINT is a frequently encountered product extension for a 1-byte integer type.

† BIGINT and LONGINT are frequently encountered product extensions for longer integer types.

TABLE 3.2 *Java primitive type and corresponding SQL predefined data types.*

one another (they are mere spelling variations). Table 3.2 illustrates the converse notion; it shows each of Java's primitive types, along with the name of the corresponding SQL predefined data type. Nonetheless, the two tables together do not fully show the relationships between the two languages' data types—they don't address the problems of mapping values of one language's types to the types of the other language. Table 3.3 goes the rest of the way, addressing the additional Java capabilities that provide support for the SQL types for which there are no Java primitive types. The most important aspects of this additional support are those related to SQL's character (string) types and SQL's null value.

From the information in Table 3.1, it's easy to conclude that SQL's type system is richer than Java's. In fact, SQL's predefined type system is richer than Java's because SQL was designed to manage very large amounts of traditional persistent data that have inherent semantics associated with them. The richness of predefined types reflects the mission for which SQL is intended. By contrast, as you probably already know, Java's mission is somewhat different—to manage objects—and it does so by providing extensibility capabilities that allow support of as many additional data types as an application requires by means of class definitions. In fact, at least some of SQL's data types that don't have corresponding Java primitive types *do* have standardized Java types in the form of Java classes supplied in standard packages.

Note that we say the SQL equivalent of Java's `char` primitive type is `NATIONAL CHARACTER(1)`. The length of 1 may be obvious because Java's `char` is inherently only a single character. However, the use of `NATIONAL CHARACTER` instead of simply `CHARACTER` deserves a bit of

SQL predefined type	Java object type
CHAR	String
VARCHAR	String
LONGVARCHAR*	String
NUMERIC	java.math.BigDecimal
DECIMAL	java.math.BigDecimal
BIT or BOOLEAN†	Boolean
TINYINT*	Integer
SMALLINT	Integer
INTEGER	Integer
BIGINT*	Long
REAL	Float
FLOAT	Double
DOUBLE	Double
BINARY	byte[]
VARBINARY*	byte[]
LONGVARBINARY*	byte[]
DATE	java.sql.Date
TIME	java.sql.Time
TIMESTAMP	java.sql.Timestamp

* LONGVARCHAR, TINYINT, BIGINT, VARBINARY, and LONGVARBINARY are not SQL standard data types, but are sometimes encountered in implementations.

† Although some database systems map Java's Boolean type to an SQL BIT type, it is becoming more common for SQL's BOOLEAN type to be used (new to SQL:1999).

TABLE 3.3 *Java object types corresponding to SQL predefined types.*

explanation. In Java, all character strings are inherently expressed in Unicode, a 16-bit character set designed specifically for worldwide use. However, SQL's design precedes Unicode's existence by many years; as a result, SQL's ordinary CHARACTER type is virtually always ASCII, Latin-1 (ISO 8859-1) or some similar 7- or 8-bit character set, simply because of common practice among all the vendors. In SQL-92, the SQL standard was enhanced to support additional character sets, which could be specified explicitly by an application designer if desired (e.g., CHARACTER(50) CHARACTER SET LATIN1). In addition, as a convenience to users, who after all often reside in a single country, the syntax NATIONAL CHARACTER was provided to imply a specific, implementation-defined (or installation-defined!) character set automatically. In SQL:1999, Unicode has been added as a character set for which specific SQL vendor support is strongly encouraged (though still not mandated). As a result, we believe that many, if not most, SQL vendors will define `NATIONAL CHARACTER(n)` to be equivalent to `CHARACTER(n) CHARACTER SET UNICODE`.

Java does not provide support per se for any data types beyond those primitive types shown in Table 3.2. However, because Java provides the ability for you to build packages of Java classes, support for virtually any data type can be added for use by applications. In fact, one of the primary resources for learning about JDBC programming[13] specifies the mapping between various JDBC types and their analogous Java object types. We have included that information in Table 3.3 for handy reference.

You should note that some SQL types have two analogous types that can be used in your Java programs—the Java primitive type and the Java object type. For example, the SQL type `INTEGER` corresponds to the Java primitive type `int` and to the Java object type `Integer`. Deciding which of these to use may not always be obvious. The most obvious criterion to use in making this decision is whether you need to represent null values. The Java primitive types do not admit the notion of nullness, whereas the Java object types do (closely aligning with SQL's inherent support for null values in each of its predefined data types). Because each of the types shown in the Java object type column of Table 3.3 are class types, instead of primitive types, they are manipulated through their (method-oriented) interface just as any other Java class.

3.10 Null Values, 3-Valued Logic, and Related Issues

If you've never really used an SQL database management system, you may not have had the chance to become familiar with null values. Though this book is not necessarily the most appropriate place to deal with this subject in detail, we do think it's important that you have at least a modest understanding of the concept so you can take advantage of the relationship between SQL's data types and their corresponding Java object types.

In SQL terms, the *null value* is a value that is associated with every data type, but it is never a value of the data type. Therefore, the null value for integers is different from 0, 1, –1, or 65,535; it's a special value that can't ever be mistaken for any other "real" integer value. Similarly,

[13] *JDBC API Tutorial and Reference, Second Edition: Universal Data Access for the Java 2 Platform,* Seth White, Maydene Fisher, Rick Cattell, Graham Hamilton, and Mark Hapner, Addison-Wesley, 1999.

the null value for character strings isn't a string with no characters (although C programmers are often heard calling such strings the "null string") or a string containing only blanks.

Null values can be used for several different purposes (such as "information not available," "to be supplied later," "not applicable," or even "we don't know and we don't care"), but the meaning is "no data here."

One of the most important aspects of null values is how they affect the results of operations in which they participate. In general, combining a null value with a non-null value through, for example, addition causes the result to be the null value, too! One way to think about this fact is to ask yourself the question, "What is the result of adding some known value, such as 5, with an unknown value?" and you're bound to come up with the answer "unknown"!

But is that first unknown value—the one you added to 5—the *same* as the unknown value that you got as a result? In other words, if `c1` and `c2` are two columns, each containing the null value for some row, what is the "answer" to the predicate shown in Example 3.18?

EXAMPLE 3.18 COMPARING TWO NULLS.

```
c1 = c2
```

Even though both `c1` and `c2` are the null value, we can't say they're equal—because that would be like saying that I don't know what value `c1` is, and I don't know what value `c2` is, but I'm sure they're equal to one another. Doesn't make much sense, does it? Instead, a better answer is that we don't know whether `c1` and `c2` are equal, so the result of the predicate above is *unknown*. That answer is unchanged whether the comparison operator is =, <, >, or any other SQL comparison operator.

SQL allows you to combine predicates in boolean expressions, using operators such as `AND`, `OR`, and `NOT`. And you won't be surprised to hear that SQL has special rules for evaluating these expressions when one of the predicate operands has the result *unknown*. Tables 3.4, 3.5, and 3.6 specify those rules. Of course, Table 3.6 leaves us with the entirely logical, though possibly amusing, result that "NOT unknown" is unknown!

3.11 SQL and Programming Languages

We've mentioned several times in this chapter and earlier in the book that SQL is rarely used alone, but is normally used in conjunction with a program written in a more traditional programming language. We

AND results	true	false	unknown
true	true	false	unknown
false	false	false	false
unknown	unknown	false	unknown

TABLE 3.4 *Three-valued logic for AND.*

OR results	true	false	unknown
true	true	true	true
false	true	false	unknown
unknown	true	unknown	unknown

TABLE 3.5 *Three-valued logic for OR.*

NOT results	true	false	unknown
	false	true	unknown

TABLE 3.6 *Three-valued logic for NOT.*

think it's worth giving you a brief look at how SQL interfaces with several other programming languages before we get into the meat of using SQL with Java.

There are essentially three mechanisms by which SQL is used (other than "standalone SQL"—which we won't bother addressing here, since it's little more than typing SQL statements into a command line processor and having the results displayed on your screen). The three mechanisms are

1. Embedded SQL and the equivalent module language,
2. Dynamic SQL,
3. Call-level, or functional, interface.

3.11.1 Embedded SQL (and Module Language)

SQL statements may be embedded directly into a host language program, distinguished by means of a prefix, such as `EXEC SQL` (which varies by host language). A preprocessor then effectively translates those SQL statements into host language "calls" that invoke special SQL-only procedures, each containing one of those SQL statements. Equivalently, some products also implement SQL's module language directly, allowing the user to write those SQL-only procedures (collected into modules) and to write the "calls" explicitly. The two approaches are isomorphic with one another. This approach is most appropriate when the SQL statements to be executed are fully known at the time the application is written, typical of most major data processing applications. To be clear: the SQL statements have to be fully known with respect to the tables and columns that are being used and the predicates that will be used. Host variables can be placed in the statements so that the application can supply values at runtime and receive values as a result of the execution of the statement. This is generally referred to as "static SQL." Languages for which the SQL standard defines this type of support are Ada, C, COBOL, Fortran, MUMPS (a.k.a. M), Pascal, and PL/I.

Example 3.19 illustrates a sample of embedded C.

EXAMPLE 3.19 EXAMPLE C APPLICATION.

```
EXEC SQL BEGIN DECLARE SECTION;
   char SQLSTATE[6];
   char title[101];
   char year[5];
EXEC SQL END DECLARE SECTION;

EXEC SQL DECLARE movie_cursor CURSOR FOR
   SELECT   title
   FROM     movies
   WHERE    year_introduced = :year;

main () {
   EXEC SQL WHENEVER SQLERROR GOTO oops;
   year = "1992";
   EXEC SQL OPEN movie_cursor;
   while (strcmp (SQLSTATE, "02000") != 0) {
      EXEC SQL FETCH movie_cursor
               INTO :title;
      printf ("%s\n", title);
   };
   return;

oops:
   printf ("An error has occurred!\n");
};
```

3.11.2 Dynamic SQL

When the SQL statements to be executed are not completely known at the time the application is written, the embedded SQL approach cannot be used. Instead, a more dynamic approach is required—one that allows SQL statements to be completed or fully constructed at runtime and then prepared for execution. The SQL standard provides special (embedded and module language) statements to accomplish these activities. The PREPARE statement accepts a character string containing an SQL statement and prepares it (e.g., compiles it or optimizes it) for execution; the EXECUTE statement takes a prepared statement and executes it. Other special statements are used to manage the data structures required by an SQL system to deal with dynamic SQL activities. This approach is most appropriate for environments in which ad hoc querying of an SQL database is a significant activity.

The following example assumes that a list of columns and a search condition are passed to this routine. From this list, an SQL statement is constructed and executed, and the resulting rows are displayed. For simplicity, we'll assume in Example 3.20 that only CHARACTER columns are selected.

EXAMPLE 3.20 EXAMPLE USE OF DYNAMIC SQL.

```
void execute (char *selectlist, char *wherecond) {
   EXEC SQL BEGIN DECLARE SECTION;
      char SQLSTATE[6];
      char source[250];
      char s[101];
      long ind;
   EXEC SQL END DECLARE SECTION;

   int n;
   int i;

   /* Create a dynamic cursor, then create the statement */

   EXEC SQL DECLARE dcursor CURSOR FOR dstmt;
   sprintf (source, "SELECT %s FROM movies WHERE %s",
            selectlist, wherecond
           );

   /* Prepare the statement for dynamic execution */

   EXEC SQL PREPARE dstmt FROM :source;
```

```
    /* Allocate an SQL dynamic descriptor area */

    EXEC SQL ALLOCATE DESCRIPTOR dparams;

    /* and describe the results of the prepared statement */

    EXEC SQL DESCRIBE OUTPUT dstmt
      INTO SQL DESCRIPTOR dparams;

    /* Find out how many values the prepared
       statement returns */

    EXEC SQL GET DESCRIPTOR dparams :n = COUNT;

    /* Open the cursor to process its rows */

    EXEC SQL OPEN dcursor;

    /* Until SQL says "end of the cursor"... */

    while (strcmp (SQLSTATE, "02000") != 0) {

       /* Retrieve the next row into the descriptor area */

       EXEC SQL FETCH FROM dcursor
                INTO SQL DESCRIPTOR dparams;

       /* Then, for each returned value, get it from the
          descriptor area */

       FOR (i = 1; i <= n; i++) {
          EXEC SQL GET DESCRIPTOR dparams
                   VALUE :i
                   :s DATA, :ind INDICATOR;
          printf ("%s", ((ind < 0) ? "NULL" : s));
          if (i == n) {
             printf ("\n");
          }
          else {
             printf (", ");
          }
       }
    }
}
```

This routine might be invoked by the following C statement:

```
execute ("title, year_introduced",
         "runs BETWEEN 120 AND 145"
        )
```

We've used SQL-92 syntax for this example to make it a bit more readable. Most products actually use an application-allocated SQLDA structure to hold dynamic parameter information, rather than the SQL-allocated and -controlled SQL DESCRIPTOR.

3.11.3 Call-Level Interfaces

In recent years, it has become more popular to invoke SQL database systems through some sort of a functional interface, or a *call-level interface,* such as that described in the standard for SQL/CLI.[14] A call-level interface offers an approach that is even more dynamic in many respects than ordinary dynamic SQL, in part because it doesn't require that any SQL statements be hard-coded, precompiled, and so forth—not even statements such as PREPARE and EXECUTE. Instead, the program invokes a series of functions defined in the API, some of which require a character string argument containing an SQL statement to be prepared and executed.

There are at least two popular call-level interfaces to SQL. One of these is called ODBC (Open DataBase Connectivity) and was specified by Microsoft Corporation. At the time we wrote this book, ODBC Version 3.0[15] was the most recent version of that interface. The other is JDBC—which does not, according to JavaSoft, the creator and owner of the specification, stand for Java DataBase Connectivity or anything else. We'll discuss JDBC in some detail in Chapter 4 (although Chapter 4 is not intended to be a complete reference to JDBC).

---

14 ISO/IEC 9075-1:1999, *Information technology—Database languages—SQL—Part 1: Framework,* ISO/IEC 9075-2:1999, *Information technology—Database languages—SQL—Part 2: Foundation,* ISO/IEC 9075-3:1999, *Information technology—Database languages—SQL—Part 3: Call-Level Interface (SQL/CLI),* International Organization for Standardization, 1999, ISO/IEC 9075-4:1999, *Information technology—Database languages—SQL—Part 4: Persistent Stored Modules,* and ISO/IEC 9075-5:1999, *Information technology—Database languages—SQL—Part 5: Host language bindings,* International Organization for Standardization, 1999.

15 *Microsoft Open Database Connectivity Software Development Kit, Version 3.00, Programmer's Reference (Volumes One and Two),* Microsoft Corporation, 19 March 1996.

EXAMPLE 3.21 ODBC PROGRAM USING C.

```
void main () {
   SQLHENV        henv;
   SQLHDBC        hdbc;
   SQLHSTMT       hstmt;
   SQLRETURN      rc;

   SQLINTEGER     runs, runs_ind, title_ind;
   SQLCHAR        title[101];

   // Allocate environment handle

   rc = SQLAllocHandle (SQL_HANDLE_ENV, SQL_NULL_HANDLE, &henv);
   if (rc != SQL_SUCCESS) {
      report_and_exit (rc, "Allocate Environment Failed");
   }

   rc = SQLSetEnvAttr(henv, SQL_ATTR_ODBC_VERSION,
                        (void*)SQL_OV_ODBC3, 0
                      );
   if (rc != SQL_SUCCESS) {
      report_and_exit (rc, "Set Environment Failed");
   }

   // Create connection

   rc = SQLAllocHandle(SQL_HANDLE_DBC, henv, &hdbc);
   if (rc != SQL_SUCCESS) {
      report_and_exit (rc, "Allocate DBC handle Failed");
   }

   rc = SQLConnect (hdbc, (SQLCHAR *) "Movies", SQL_NTS,
                          (SQLCHAR *) "dba", SQL_NTS,
                          (SQLCHAR *) "sql", SQL_NTS
                   );

   if (rc != SQL_SUCCESS) {
      report_and_exit (rc, "Allocate Environment Failed");
   }

   rc = SQLAllocHandle(SQL_HANDLE_STMT, hdbc, &hstmt);

   // execute the select statement
```

```
    rc = SQLExecDirect
            (hstmt,
             (SQLCHAR *) "SELECT   title, runs "
                         "FROM     movies "
                         "WHERE    year_introduced = '1980'",
             SQL_NTS
            );
    if (rc != SQL_SUCCESS) {
       report_and_exit (rc, "Statement Execution Failed");
    }

    // bind the result columns to variables

    SQLBindCol (hstmt, 1, SQL_C_CHAR, title, 100, &title_ind);
    SQLBindCol (hstmt, 2, SQL_C_ULONG, &runs, 0, &runs_ind);

    // get data from database

    while ((rc = SQLFetch (hstmt)) != SQL_NO_DATA) {
       if (rc != SQL_SUCCESS) {
          report_and_exit (rc, "Fetch Failed");
       }
       cout << "\"" << title << "\"";
       if (runs_ind >= 0)
          cout << ", " << runs << " minutes";
       cout << endl;
    }

    // Cleanup

    SQLFreeHandle(SQL_HANDLE_STMT, hstmt);

    SQLDisconnect (hdbc);

}
```

3.12 Result Sets

SQL-92 didn't support the notion of result sets, but SQL:1999 does (and additional support is planned for the next generation of the SQL standard). Most major SQL products have implemented the concept for several years, yet this remains one of the most poorly understood features of SQL—except, that is, by programmers who build applications using a call-level interface, where the concept is very well understood.

Because Java's use of SQL is anticipated to be highly dynamic (not a pun at all: a deliberate reference to dynamic SQL and call-level interfaces), you won't be surprised to hear that result sets play an important role in the mechanisms provided for interfacing Java and SQL. Although it's not the place of this book to teach you all about SQL's result sets, the notion is important enough—and poorly enough understood by too many programmers—to warrant a few paragraphs in this book.

Before we talk about how a result set is used, perhaps you'd like us to tell you just what a result set *is*. SQL terminology includes phrases like "the result set returned by an SQL procedure," which leads one to the impression that SQL procedures (unlike those of most programming languages) can return *sets* of data to a caller. Well, that could be true—if an SQL routine (that is, a routine written in SQL) is called from another SQL routine, using the SQL CALL statement, and one of the parameters of the routine being called is an OUT parameter whose data type is SET, then a set of data would indeed be returned to that invoking SQL routine. There are only two things wrong with this scenario. First, SQL:1999 doesn't have a SET data type (although there are tentative plans to include it in the next generation of the SQL standard), and, second, that's not what the result set is about!

One definition of result set is: An ordered transient virtual table that has [several attributes]. (We've left out the list of attributes here; not only is it irrelevant to the point we're making, it's sometimes lengthy and not all sources agree on the exact contents of the list.) It is the result table associated with, or created by, a cursor. Another definition is: The set of rows created by executing a SELECT statement.

We find both of these definitions unsatisfying—the first because it uses terminology that most programmers wouldn't find familiar, and the second because it's vague and incorrect in detail. Our definition of a result set is this: "When an SQL routine returns to its invoker, it can return one or more ordered sets of rows, called *result sets,* that are the result of cursors opened in the routine but not closed before the routine returns." We note that standard SQL:1999 requires that the SQL routine be written such that the cursors that are allowed to return result sets be coded using the syntax `WITH RETURN`; not all SQL implementations make that requirement.

Our definition emphasizes three important aspects of result sets. First, they must be created in an SQL routine that is invoked either from another SQL routine or from a client program. Second, they are nothing more than the rows of a cursor opened by the routine and not closed before the routine returns. Finally, they have all of the consequent characteristics of a cursor's rows (they may be ordered, they are transient, they collectively have a number of attributes that cursors have). What our definition fails to address clearly is the fact that the SQL routine can return result sets either through parameters that have been declared to be result set parameters or as an ad hoc result set that results directly from treating the SQL routine as a dynamic SQL statement.

If an SQL routine declares one of its parameters to be a result set parameter, then it is said to return a *preplanned result set*. Unfortunately for applications that want this facility, preplanned result sets are unavailable in SQL:1999, although support is planned for the next version of the SQL standard. Java does not address (even through JDBC) preplanned result sets, so we will not consider them further in this book.

When an SQL routine is declared to have a characteristic of returning one or more *dynamic result sets*, then that information can be discovered by a potential invoker through one of several means: an invoker using dynamic SQL can DESCRIBE the SQL routine (using the name under which it is stored, if appropriate) and learn that it returns some maximum number of dynamic result sets. Stored SQL routines (those stored in the database) are declared to return dynamic result sets by using the syntax `DYNAMIC RESULT SETS` *`max`*, where `max` is an integer specifying the largest number of result sets—not the largest number of rows in a result set!— returned by the routine.

Example 3.22 shows an Adaptive Server Anywhere procedure that returns multiple result sets.

EXAMPLE 3.22 GENERATING RESULT SETS WITH ADAPTIVE SERVER ANYWHERE.

```
CREATE PROCEDURE for_years
                  (start_year CHAR (4), end_year CHAR (4))
   BEGIN
      SELECT   title
      FROM     movies
      WHERE    year_introduced BETWEEN
               start_year AND end_year;

      SELECT   award, person, award_year
      FROM     awards
      WHERE    award_year BETWEEN start_year AND end_year
        AND    person IS NOT NULL;
   END
```

An application using SQL/CLI (or ODBC) discovers the same information by invoking `Routines()` to get detailed information about some stored SQL routine. SQL/CLI (and its product equivalent, ODBC) provides another way to get a result set: by invoking `Prepare()` and `Execute()`, providing a so-called SELECT statement as an argument.

The SELECT statement returns zero or more rows in the form of a virtual table. An application using SQL/CLI (or ODBC) discovers the information about the result sets by invoking `MoreResults()` and providing a statement handle to identify that prepared and executed SELECT statement. Rows are then retrieved from the result set(s) by use of additional functions, such as `Fetch()`.

An ODBC program to examine the results of the `for_years` procedure defined above would appear as shown in Example 3.23 (JDBC examples will appear in Chapter 4).

JDBC also supports this dynamic mechanism for creating result sets. When using JDBC, you might execute a statement like this:

```
ResultSet rs =
   stmt.executeQuery("SELECT movie_name FROM movies");
```

The result (sorry . . . this time, the pun was unintentional) of that Java statement is the creation of a new object of class `ResultSet` and its initialization with the result set caused by executing that SELECT statement. The rows belonging to the result set are then processed through the invocation of the `ResultSet`'s methods, such as `next`. We'll cover this in more detail in Chapter 4.

3.13 Data and Metadata—Relationships and Differences

Earlier in this chapter we mentioned that SQL stores its data (called SQL-data in the SQL standard) as well as the description of its data—its metadata—in the database. Metadata, at least in the SQL standard, is conceptually stored in the database in something called "schemas." A schema is a collection of tables, views, and other database objects that are all owned by a single user. We think of a schema as principally being the collection of descriptions of those database objects, not merely the collection of the data those objects contain.

In spite of the unfortunate ambiguity in the concept *schema,* you need to recognize that SQL products often, but not always (in spite of the SQL standard!), provide two mechanisms for accessing a database's metadata. The first way is through special commands or functions. SQL/CLI (and ODBC), for example, provide specialized functions, such as `Tables()` and `Columns()`, to discover the identities of tables and columns in a database and all relevant information about them. Similarly, JDBC provides methods such as `getTables()` and `getColumns()` for the same purpose. The second way (which is, in fact, the point of this paragraph!) is through the use of the ordinary SQL data retrieval statement—SELECT.

EXAMPLE 3.23 USING ODBC TO PROCESS RESULT SETS.

```
rc = SQLExecDirect
        (hstmt,
         (SQLCHAR *) "CALL for_years ('1993', '1994')",
         SQL_NTS
        );
if (rc != SQL_SUCCESS) {
   report_and_exit (hstmt, rc, "Statement Execution Failed");
}

// bind the result columns to variables

SQLBindCol (hstmt, 1, SQL_C_CHAR, title, 101, &title_ind);

// get data from database

cout << "First Result Set:" << endl;
while ((rc = SQLFetch (hstmt)) != SQL_NO_DATA) {
   if (rc != SQL_SUCCESS) {
      report_and_exit (hstmt, rc, "Fetch Failed");
   }
   cout << "  \"" << title << "\"" << endl;
}

// go to next result set

rc = SQLMoreResults (hstmt);
if (rc != SQL_SUCCESS) {
   report_and_exit (hstmt, rc, "No more result sets");
}

// bind the result columns to variables

SQLBindCol (hstmt, 1, SQL_C_CHAR, award, 21, &award_ind);
SQLBindCol (hstmt, 2, SQL_C_CHAR, person, 61, &person_ind);
SQLBindCol (hstmt, 3, SQL_C_CHAR, award_year, 5, &award_year_ind);

// get data from database

cout << "Second Result Set:" << endl;
while ((rc = SQLFetch (hstmt)) != SQL_NO_DATA) {
   if (rc != SQL_SUCCESS) {
      report_and_exit (hstmt, rc, "Fetch Failed");
   }
```

```
    cout << "   " << award;
    cout << ", " << person;
    if (person_ind >= 0)
       cout << ", " << award_year << endl;
}
```

Although not every SQL product provides the metadata tables that contain information such as that describing all tables in the database, all views, all character sets, various privileges, and so forth, SQL:1999 does (as did SQL-92), and many products do provide this capability, though not all in SQL-standard form (at least not yet). Products that define such metadata tables, as well as the SQL standard, allow application programs to retrieve information from them using an ordinary SQL SELECT statement or an ordinary SQL cursor, *just* as though they were user-defined data tables. This capability treats SQL metadata so completely like SQL data that information in those tables can be joined to application data in data tables!

The specialized-function approach also is not implemented by every SQL product, but most such products do have this capability, as does the SQL standard (through SQL/CLI). SQL/CLI functions such as `Tables()` return a result set (see Section 3.12) describing every table available to the user, including all the metadata tables, such as the `TABLES` table.

Thus, we see that SQL's metadata has many characteristics in common with SQL data, but it doesn't have all characteristics in common. In particular, you are not permitted to *update* SQL's metadata tables directly through the use of SQL INSERT, UPDATE, or DELETE statements. The only way to update metadata is through the use of SQL's schema manipulation commands, such as CREATE and DROP.

3.14 Chapter Summary

In this chapter, we've covered a lot of material about the SQL language that is likely to be unfamiliar to Java programmers unless they've had the opportunity to use SQL. We started off by explaining what SQL is and why it is important to Java programmers, then continued by giving you several examples to help you understand how SQL is used and how we will use it in this book.

After describing the concept of a result set, we concluded by briefly discussing metadata and how it relates to data in the SQL world.

Now it's time to start looking at the ways in which you and your applications can utilize SQL and Java together!

CHAPTER

4

JDBC 1.0 API

4.1 Introduction

JDBC defines an API that allows an application to access the services of a relational DBMS. The design of JDBC was strongly influenced by call-level APIs that have become widely accepted in the industry, specifically Microsoft's ODBC and SQL/CLI,[1] on which ODBC is based. Like these APIs, JDBC provides a method of connecting to a remote database, executing ad hoc SQL statements, and examining the results of those statements.

JavaSoft has provided an API that will feel natural to Java programmers. They have addressed the mapping of data types between SQL and Java, including the representation of SQL's null values. In addition, they have extended the Java exception mechanism in a way that captures SQL's SQLSTATE parameter facilities.

---

[1] ISO/IEC 9075-1:1999, *Information technology—Database languages—SQL—Part 1: Framework,* ISO/IEC 9075-2:1999, *Information technology—Database languages—SQL—Part 2: Foundation,* ISO/IEC 9075-4:1999, ISO/IEC 9075-3:1999, *Information technology—Database languages—SQL—Part 3: Call-Level Interface (SQL/CLI),* International Organization for Standardization, 1999, *Information technology—Database languages—SQL—Part 4: Persistent Stored Modules,* and ISO/IEC 9075-5:1999, *Information technology—Database languages—SQL—Part 5: Host language bindings,* International Organization for Standardization, 1999.

JDK 1.1 was the first JDK to provide the JDBC 1.0 API (JDBC 1.22 can be installed on JDK 1.0.2). This chapter discusses the JDBC 1.0 API,[2] which is widely implemented and used today. Chapter 9 will discuss the JDBC 2.0 Core API, which is provided in JDK 1.2.

JDBC provides the `java.sql.DriverManager` class, which allows the registration and use of JDBC drivers provided by DBMS and middleware vendors. These drivers provide access to a wide range of DBMSs. JDBC does not provide any data management services of its own. The JDBC API is provided by the `java.sql` package.

This chapter gives an overview of the JDBC 1.0 API. It does not discuss all of the methods provided in JDBC's classes and interfaces. For those that are discussed, they are discussed at a very high level. Readers who desire more information are encouraged to look at the JDBC home page, found at *java.sun.com/products/jdbc/index.html*. This site contains a wealth of information on JDBC, including the specifications for each version of the JDBC API. Numerous books have been written on JDBC alone, the most notable of which is part of the Java Series.[3] It's beyond the scope of this book to give a full and comprehensive presentation of all aspects of JDBC.

4.1.1 Types of JDBC Implementations

JavaSoft defines four architectures that DBMS and middleware vendors are likely to use when they implement their JDBC drivers.

Type 1—JDBC-ODBC Bridge

The Type 1 architecture shown in Figure 4.1 implements JDBC by making calls to ODBC on the client machine. It requires that ODBC drivers have been installed and configured on the client. The calls to ODBC are made outside of the Java environment.

Type 2—Native-API Partly Java Driver

The Type 2 architecture shown in Figure 4.2 implements JDBC by making calls to a DBMS native-API on the client machine. Sybase's native-API is Open Client; Oracle's native-API is OCI.

Type 3—Net-Protocol All-Java Driver

The Type 3 architecture, illustrated in Figure 4.3, implements JDBC by sending messages to a server, using a message protocol that is independent of the underlying DBMS. A process on the server machine receives

---

[2] *JDBC: A Java SQL API,* Version 1.20, Graham Hamilton and Rick Cattell, JavaSoft, 10 January 1997.

[3] *JDBC API Tutorial and Reference, Second Edition: Universal Data Access for the Java 2 Platform,* Seth White, Maydene Fisher, Rick Cattell, Graham Hamilton, and Mark Hapner, Addison-Wesley, 1999.

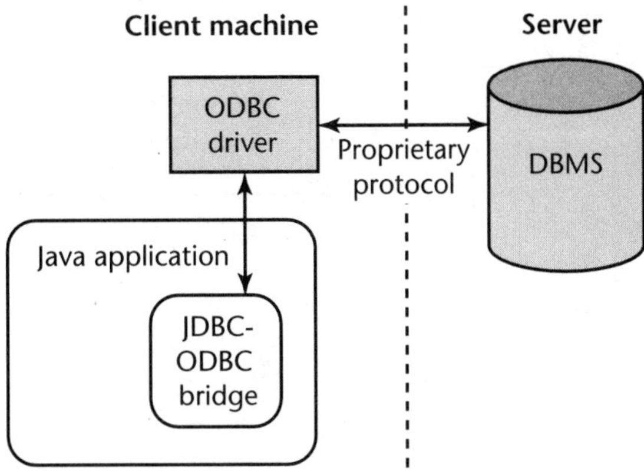

FIGURE 4.1 *Type 1 JDBC driver.*

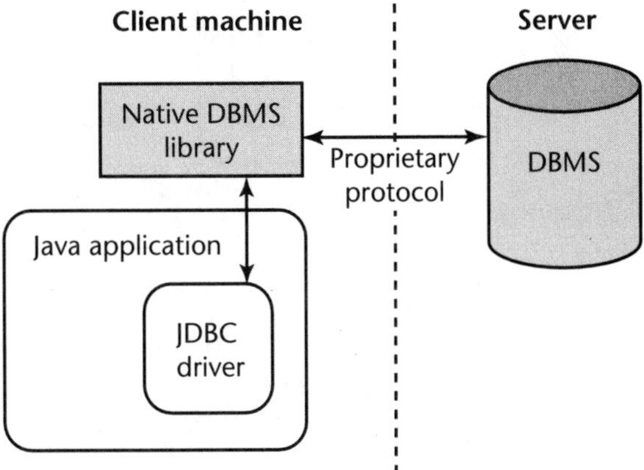

FIGURE 4.2 *Type 2 JDBC driver.*

these messages and makes calls to the DBMS. The client code is written completely in Java, so that it will run on any hardware platform that supports a JVM.

Type 4—Native-Protocol All-Java Driver

The Type 4 architecture shown in Figure 4.4 is similar to Type 3, except that the message protocol used is specific to a particular DBMS. As there is no need for intervening processes and translation, this architecture can be extremely efficient.

Type 1 and Type 2 implementations of JDBC require the use of non-Java code on the client. This condition makes them suitable for intranet

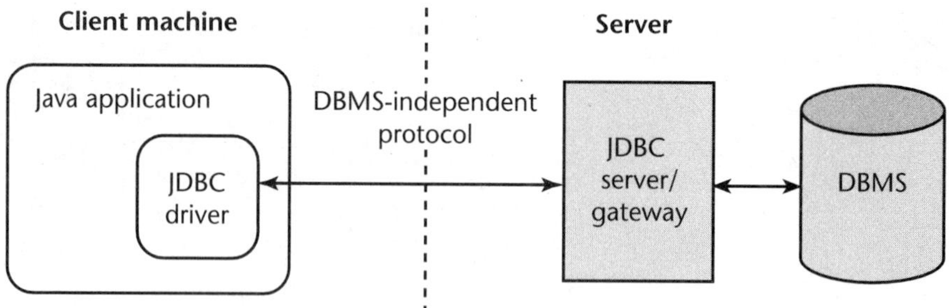

FIGURE 4.3 *Type 3 JDBC driver.*

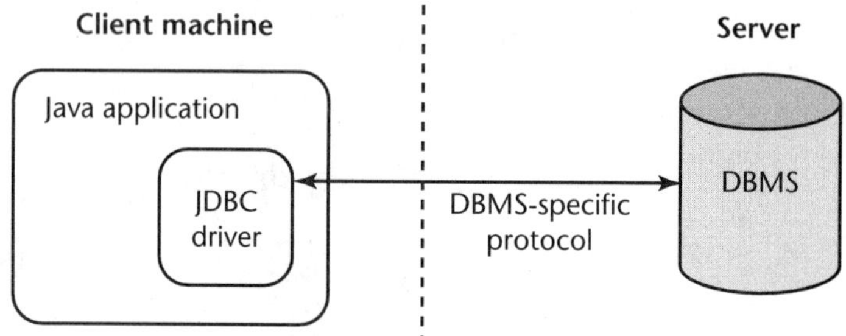

FIGURE 4.4 *Type 4 JDBC driver.*

client applications, where the client platform can be restricted and the necessary DBMS libraries can be installed and configured. An applet created using a JDBC implementation of one of these types would require special permission to run in a client's browser. These types of implementations could also be suitable for use in an application server.

Type 3 and Type 4 implementations are completely written in Java, so that they can run on any client that supports a JVM. This capability makes them suitable for both Internet and intranet applications and for use in application servers. An applet created using a JDBC implementation of one of these types will run on any client browser.

4.1.2 JDBC Implementations

Numerous JDBC implementations are available in the marketplace today. In this section, we'll mention just a few of them.

Sybase's implementation of JDBC, shown in Figure 4.5, is jConnect. It is a Type 4 JDBC implementation, written completely in Java and using Sybase's TDS (Tabular Data Stream) protocol. It is about 200KB in size, so that it can conveniently be incorporated into an applet that can be downloaded over the Internet. The use of TDS means that the driver can be used to connect to Sybase's Adaptive Server Enterprise, Adaptive Server Anywhere, or OmniConnect (which provides access to numerous enterprise and legacy databases). TDS is supported by some firewall products (products that attempt to protect an enterprise's network from access through the Internet by unauthorized persons), and—for those that do not support it—jConnect can use HTTP Tunneled TDS. A jConnect Proxy Gateway is provided to decode the tunneled TDS and pass the TDS on to the database server.

Oracle provides two JDBC drivers: JDBC/OCI and Thin JDBC. JDBC/OCI is a Type 2 JDBC implementation, invoking OCI (Oracle Call Interface), which then uses SQL*Net to communicate with Oracle7 and Oracle8 database servers. These are both shown in Figure 4.6. Like Sybase's TDS, SQL*Net is supported by some firewall products.

Thin JDBC is a Type 4 JDBC implementation, written completely in Java and using a lightweight implementation of a TCP/IP version of

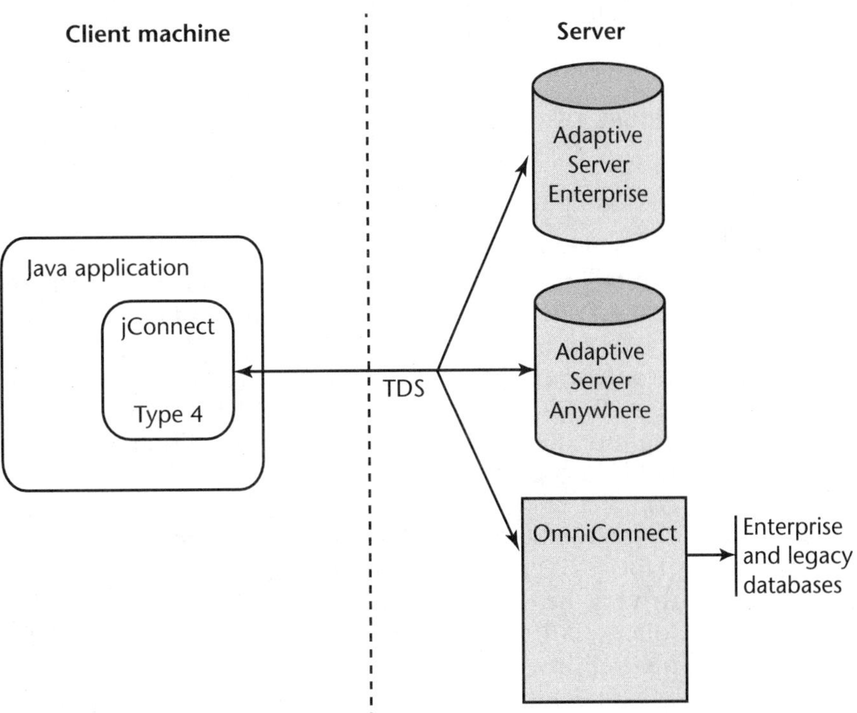

FIGURE 4.5 *Sybase's implementation of JDBC.*

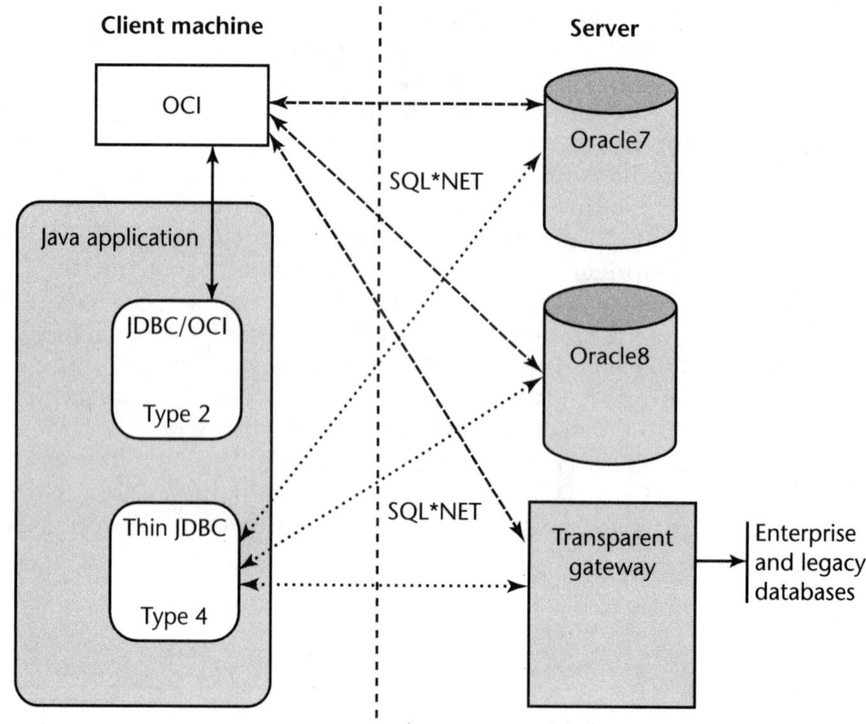

FIGURE 4.6 *Oracle's implementation of JDBC.*

the SQL*Net protocol. It is about 150KB in size (compressed) so that it can be incorporated into an applet. Oracle's Transparent Gateway products can be used to access enterprise and legacy databases.

WebLogic offers Type 2, Type 3, and Type 4 JDBC implementations as shown in Figure 4.7. jdbc Kona/Oracle, jdbc Kona/Sybase, and jdbc Kona/MSSQLServer are all Type 2 JDBC implementations that call the appropriate database vendor–supplied library. Tengah/JDBC is a Type 3 JDBC implementation. The application uses the Tengah/JDBC driver to connect to the Tengah JDBC Server, using a proprietary protocol. The Tengah JDBC Server then connects to the data source using JDBC. The JDBC driver on the server side can be one of the WebLogic JDBC drivers, or it can be any other JDBC driver. Finally, WebLogic offers jdbcKona/Informix4 and jdbcKona/MSSQLServer4 Type 4 JDBC implementations.

Cloudscape offers an embedded object/relational DBMS that is 100% pure Java. This DBMS, along with its JDBC driver, can run in the same JVM as the application program, which eliminates the need for any server process or network transport. The Cloudscape DBMS consists of class files that are about 1.5MB in size. Cloudscape can also support the familiar client/server architecture with a WebLogic server process that contains the Cloudscape DBMS and a WebLogic JDBC driver. In this case, the implementation is Type 4 JDBC. Both of these configurations are illustrated in Figure 4.8.

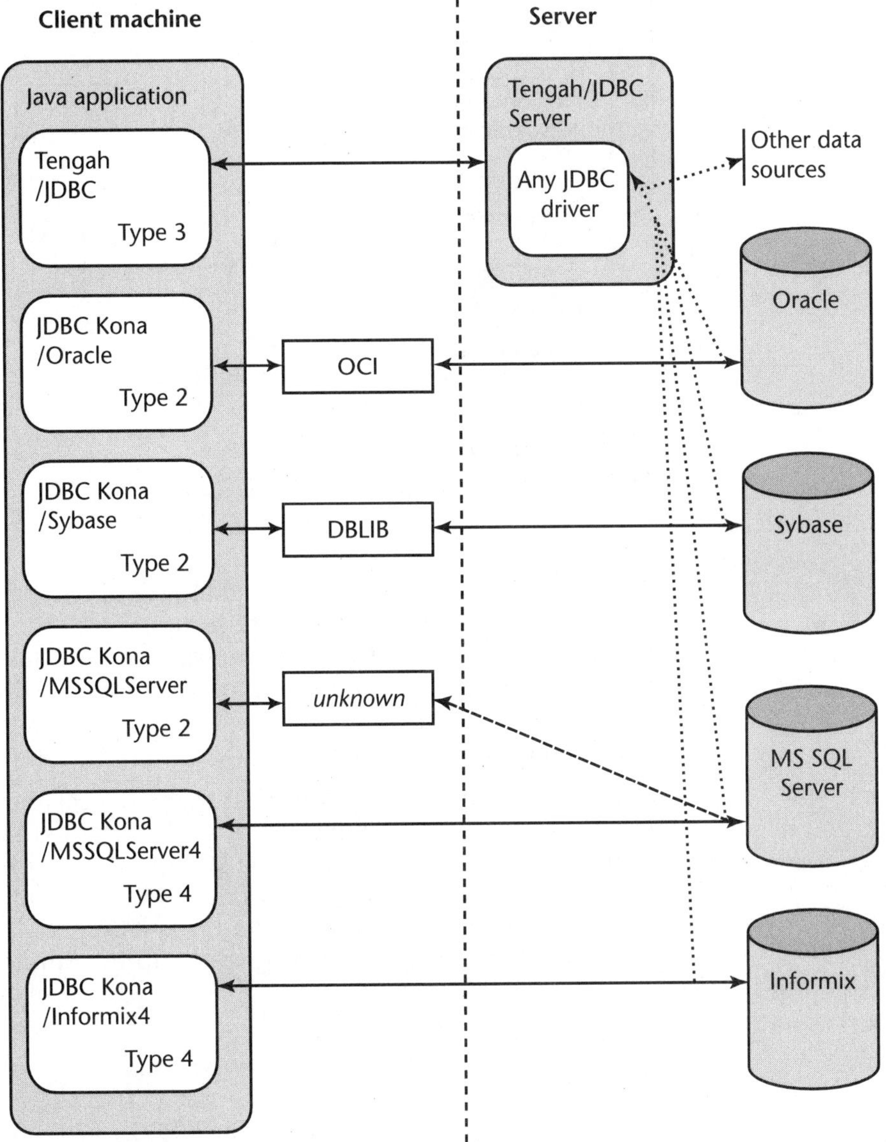

FIGURE 4.7 *WebLogic's implementation of JDBC.*

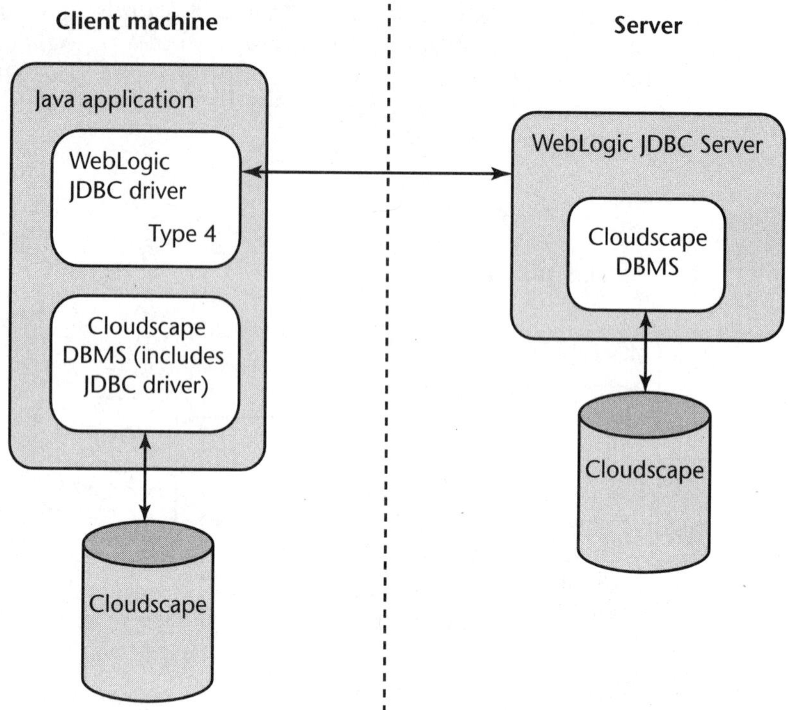

FIGURE 4.8 *Cloudscape's implementation of JDBC.*

The preceding discussion gives you a taste of the variety of offerings in the marketplace. These products compete on criteria such as code size, performance, feature set, and firewall support. JavaSoft maintains a list of vendors of JDBC implementations on their JDBC Web site.

4.1.3 SQL Statements

It is, perhaps, a sad state of affairs that many dialects of SQL exist in the world. There are the levels defined by SQL-92, called Entry, Intermediate, and Full. There is the level of SQL-92 defined by NIST in FIPS 127-2,[4] called Transitional, which falls about halfway between Entry and Intermediate. Oracle supports Entry SQL-92 with parts of the higher levels of SQL-92, and it supports features completely outside the

[4] FIPS 127-2, *Federal Information Processing Standards Publication 127-2,* National Institute of Standards and Technology, 2 June 1993.

standard. The same is true for Sybase, Informix, IBM, and all the others. In fact, most vendors that supply more than one implementation of SQL actually have more than one dialect of the language—one per product, in some cases.

Let us, for a moment, discuss the statements that are executed via the JDBC interface. Later parts of this chapter will show exactly how they are executed.

For the most part, JDBC allows any statement provided by an application to be passed to the DBMS. The statement could use one of the standard or proprietary dialects we have mentioned, or it could use some other language altogether. JavaSoft recognizes that most commercial DBMS's today support at least Entry SQL-92, so that is a requirement for a JDBC-compliant driver. A JDBC-compliant driver must also support the DROP TABLE statement, which comes from Transitional SQL-92.

If you are writing a JDBC application for a specific DBMS, then you are able to use the full range of statements provided by the DBMS.

If your application can be written using only Entry SQL-92, then it will more easily run against different DBMSs. As always, you need to be aware that SQL-92 does not specify every aspect of a DBMS's behavior. For example, SQL-92 provides syntax for sorting the results of a query in ascending or descending order; it does not, however, specify whether null values are sorted higher or lower than all non-null values.

Variations among DBMSs

If you are writing a JDBC application that can support connections to different DBMSs and the features of Entry SQL-92 are not sufficient, then your life becomes a bit more complicated. JDBC is designed to make it as easy as possible for application programmers to deal with variations among implementations of SQL. Let's take a look at how that is accomplished.

Your application might require that a specific dialect of SQL be supported. JDBC allows your application to find out (we'll see exactly how in a little while) whether specific SQL dialects, such as Intermediate SQL-92 or ODBC Core, are supported.

Your application might be able to construct different statements, depending on whether certain features are supported by a DBMS. JDBC allows your application to find out whether full outer joins are supported, whether multiple result sets are supported, or whether columns not in the select list can be used in an ORDER BY clause.

Your application might behave differently if it could determine some of the behavior that is not specified by the SQL standard. JDBC allows your application to find out whether null values are sorted higher or lower than non-null values, or whether a DDL statement forces the termination of the current transaction.

Your application might generate syntax specific to the DBMS to which it is connected. JDBC allows your application to find out what character is used to quote strings or identifiers, what keyword is used when referring to a procedure or a schema, and what keywords are supported beyond those of SQL-92.

Finally, your application can determine which DBMS and JDBC driver are being used, and—if required—generate code specific to them.

JDBC Escape Syntax

JavaSoft has recognized that some features beyond Entry SQL-92 have been widely implemented in DBMSs, but with differing syntax. Some of these were seen as valuable enough that a specific JDBC syntax was provided for them, which a JDBC driver could recognize and turn into the syntax recognized by the DBMS. Note that this type of escape syntax will work only if the DBMS supports the feature. JDBC (which adopted this capability from ODBC) uses curly braces to surround such extended syntax.

Stored procedures with and without a result parameter, respectively, can be invoked using the following syntax:

```
{ call procedure_name [(arg1, arg2, ..., argn)] }
{ ? = call procedure_name [(arg1, arg2, ..., argn)] }
```

As you no doubt deduced, the square brackets (`[ ]`) indicate that the arguments are all optional. Notations like $\texttt{arg}_{\texttt{i}}$ indicate the *i*-th argument in a list of *n* arguments. Of course, *i* (and *n*) can be 1 (meaning a single argument valid for a procedure that has only a single parameter), but the number of arguments has to match the number of parameters in the procedure being invoked.

The question mark (`?`) corresponds to SQL's (and most products') *dynamic parameter specification,* used in dynamic SQL for passing values to SQL statements executed dynamically and returning values from such statements.

DATE, TIME, and TIMESTAMP literals can be specified with the following syntax:

```
{ d 'yyyy-mm-dd' }
{ t 'hh:mm:ss' }
{ ts 'yyyy-MM-dd hh:mm:ss.ff...' }
```

The characters within those literals represent components of datetime data, such as values for the year, month, day, hour, minute, second, and fraction of second.

A number of scalar functions can be invoked with the following syntax:

```
{ fn function_name ( [arg1, arg2,..., argn] ) }
```

Some of the functions supported in this way are concatenation (`concat`), left trim (`ltrim`), and data type conversion (`convert`). It is worth mentioning that invoking a *function* requires that the parentheses be included even when there are no arguments to be supplied, whereas invoking a *procedure* allows you to omit the parentheses when there are no arguments.

The escape character to be used in a pattern in the LIKE clause can be specified with the following syntax:

```
{ escape ' character ' }
```

Left outer joins may be specified with the following syntax:

```
{ oj table LEFT OUTER JOIN
   { table | outer-join } ON search condition }
```

Unfortunately, the notation we just used is ambiguious. The outermost curly braces ({ }) are required characters when passing SQL expressions to JDBC; the inner curly braces in italics (*{ }*) as well as the vertical bar (|) are the BNF metacharacters for grouping and alternative, indicating that the user must choose to code either a `table` or an `outer-join` (nested inside the outermost outer join). All explicit joins, not just left outer joins, are coded using the `{oj...}` escape sequence syntax.

To provide a concrete example of JDBC escape clauses, let's consider the following query (we'll use a `release_date` DATE column that isn't in our sample database):

```
SELECT   *
FROM     {oj awards LEFT OUTER JOIN movies
          ON awards.title = movies.title}
WHERE    release_date > {d '1997-03-01'}
```

This query might be transformed by a JDBC driver into the following:

```
SELECT   *
FROM     awards LEFT OUTER JOIN movies
          ON awards.title = movies.title
WHERE    release_date > '1997-03-01 00:00:00'
```

An application can see the result of this transformation with the `Connection.nativeSQL` method. A string with escape syntax is provided to the method, and an equivalent SQL statement without the escape syntax is returned. This method seems most useful for the debugging of an application, rather than in its normal execution.

It's worth pointing out that a JDBC driver may not support some of these escape sequences if the DBMS does not support the corresponding feature. Not all possible escape sequences are supported by every driver, so *caveat programmer.*

4.2 Registering JDBC Drivers

The first step to using JDBC is to register one or more JDBC drivers with the JDBC driver manager (provided by the `DriverManager` class). This can be done in one of two ways.

First, when the `java.sql.DriverManager` class initializes, it looks for the `jdbc.drivers` system property. If this property exists, then its value is expected to be a colon-separated list of class names of JDBC drivers. These classes are loaded one by one.

Second, an application can explicitly load a JDBC driver with the following statement:

```
Class.forName ( driver name );
```

Loading these classes registers them with the JDBC `DriverManager`. When a connection is created, the `DriverManager` will pass the URL that has been specified to each of the registered JDBC drivers in turn until it finds one that is willing to provide the connection.

4.3 Connecting to a Database

With one or more JDBC drivers registered, the next step is to open a connection. JDBC allows multiple connections to be opened simultaneously. These connections could be to the same database, to different databases that use a single JDBC driver, or to different databases that use different JDBC drivers.

There are many reasons an application would need to connect to multiple databases. An example that comes immediately to mind is the movement of data from one database to another, possibly with some type of cleansing en route. An application might want multiple connections to the same database in order to improve concurrency. Some operations might be done with a connection that specifies SERIALIZABLE, and other operations might be done with a connection that specifies READ UNCOMMITTED.

4.3.1 JDBC URLs

All JDBC URLs have the following form:

```
jdbc:subprotocol:other-stuff
```

JavaSoft provides a service as an informal registry for all of the subprotocol names. The `other-stuff` provides naming and parameters specific to the subprotocol chosen.

Examples of JDBC URLs are the following:

```
jdbc:odbc:distribution
jdbc:sybase:TDS:www.sampleco.com:2638
jdbc:sybase:TDS:www.mco.com:2638;personnel?PACKETSIZE=512
jdbc:cloudscape:weblogic://www.anotherco.com:7005/usazips
```

As you undoubtedly inferred, the syntax of the *`other-stuff`* is completely dependent on the subprotocol chosen and is not specified by JDBC. A subprotocol could be created that would take a name and call on a specific naming service to provide the actual URL that would be used to make the connection.

4.3.2 getConnection

Once the vendor's driver is registered and has a proper URL, it is time to connect to a database. The `getConnection` method of the `DriverManager` class is used for this purpose. Three variants of `DriverManager.getConnection` exist.

java.sql.DriverManager Class

```
public static Connection getConnection (String url)
  throws SQLException
```

Connect to the specified database.

```
public static Connection getConnection (String url, Properties info)
  throws SQLException
```

Connect to the specified database. `info` contains name/value pairs, usually providing a value for "user" and "password".

```
public static Connection getConnection (String url,
                                        String user,
                                        String password)
  throws SQLException
```

Connect to the specified database, using the user and password that are provided.

A sample program that puts these steps together is shown in Example 4.1.

EXAMPLE 4.1 REGISTERING A JDBC DRIVER AND ESTABLISHING A CONNECTION.

```
Connection con = null;

String url = "jdbc:sybase:TDS:www.sampleco.com:2638";

// Attempt to load and register a specific JDBC driver
//   Failure throws ClassNotFoundException; just print a msg

try {
   Class.forName("com.sybase.jdbc.SybDriver");
}
catch (ClassNotFoundException cnf) {
   System.out.println (cnf.getMessage ());
   return;
}

// Attempt to connect to the database at the URL
//   Failure throws SQLException; just print a msg

try {
   con = DriverManager.getConnection (url, "dba", "sql");
   .
   .
   .
}
catch (SQLException sqe) {
   System.out.println (sqe.getMessage ());
   return;
}
```

We have not shown the `import java.sql.*` statement in this example, nor will we show it in future examples. We just wanted to remind you that this statement is necessary if you wish to avoid completely specifying the name of every class and interface that JDBC provides.

The `Connection` interface provides several methods to set and get properties (sometimes called *attributes*) of the connection.

java.sql.Connection Interface

`public boolean getAutoCommit () throws SQLException`

Returns the (value of the) auto commit attribute.

`public void setAutoCommit (boolean autoCommit) throws SQLException`

Sets the auto commit attribute, which indicates whether a commit is performed automatically after the execution of every SQL statement.

`public String getCatalog () throws SQLException`

Returns the current catalog name.

`public void setCatalog (String catalog) throws SQLException`

Sets the attribute that specifies the current catalog name. `setCatalog` may be silently ignored if the database does not support the operation.

`public int getTransactionIsolation () throws SQLException`

Returns the transaction isolation attribute.

```
public void setTransactionIsolation (int level)
   throws SQLException
```

Sets the transaction isolation attribute, which specifies the level of isolation for the current transaction. Values for `level` are

```
TRANSACTION_NONE
TRANSACTION_READ_UNCOMMITTED
TRANSACTION_READ_COMMITTED
TRANSACTION_REPEATABLE_READ
TRANSACTION_SERIALIZABLE
```

`public boolean getReadOnly ()throws SQLException`

Returns the read only attribute.

`public void setReadOnly (boolean readOnly) throws SQLException`

Sets the read only attribute, which specifies whether the current transaction is read only.

`public boolean isClosed () throws SQLException`

Returns an indication of whether the current connection is closed.

When a connection is first created, the `autocommit` property will be true; an application must explicitly set it to false if it wishes to control the transaction boundaries itself.

The `Connection` class provides several methods that act on the database through the connection, some of which are shown below.

java.sql.Connection Interface

`public void commit () throws SQLException`

Commits the current transaction.

`public void rollback () throws SQLException`

Rolls back the current transaction.

`public void close () throws SQLException`

Closes the connection.

`public DatabaseMetaData getMetaData () throws SQLException`

Returns an object that provides many types of information about the database.

`public Statement createStatement () throws SQLException`

Returns an object that can be used to execute SQL statements.

```
public PreparedStatement prepareStatement (String SQLStatement)
   throws SQLException
```

Returns an object that can be used to execute SQL statements.

```
public CallableStatement prepareCall (String SQLStatement)
   throws SQLException
```

Returns an object that can be used to call SQL procedures.

4.4 Examining Database Metadata

Once the `DatabaseMetaData` object has been received from the connection, through invocation of the `getMetadata` method, all kinds of information about the database are available to the application. In Example 4.2, we show how to retrieve information about the JDBC driver itself. The code fragment in Example 4.2 might produce the following output:

```
Driver:
   jConnect (TM) for JDBC (TM)
   jConnect (TM) for JDBC(TM)/4.0 ...
Database Product:
   Adaptive Server Anywhere
   6.0.2.2188
```

EXAMPLE 4.2 DISPLAY JDBC DRIVER AND DATABASE METADATA.

```
Connection con;

...

// Get a metadata object from the connection

DatabaseMetaData md = con.getMetaData();

// Driver information

System.out.println ( "Driver:" );
System.out.println ( "    " + md.getDriverName() );
System.out.println ( "    " + md.getDriverVersion() );

// Database information

System.out.println ( "Database Product:" );
System.out.println ( "    " + md.getDatabaseProductName() );
System.out.println ( "    " + md.getDatabaseProductVersion() );
```

Information about the objects in the database—such as catalogs, schemas, tables, columns, primary keys, and privileges—is readily available. Example 4.3 provides a hierarchy of catalogs, schemas, tables, and columns in the database. This type of information is quite valuable for browsers and tools that access the database in an ad hoc manner. Execution of the code fragment in Example 4.3 produces the following result:

```
Catalog Movies
   dba.awards
   dba.movies
   dba.sqlj_awards
   dba.sqlj_movies
   dba.votes
   .
   .
   .
```

This example may be a bit confusing. JavaSoft has decided to return collections of information from methods of the `DatabaseMetaData` interface as `ResultSet` objects, the same objects that are used to return the resulting rows of a query. We will discuss result sets shortly.

EXAMPLE 4.3 HIERARCHICAL DISPLAY OF DATABASE OBJECTS (CATALOGS, SCHEMAS, ETC.).

```
DatabaseMetaData md = con.getMetaData();

// Information about catalogs; this method returns a result
//   set potentially containing more than one catalog name

ResultSet catalogRs = md.getCatalogs();

// For each catalog in the result set...

while (catalogRs.next()) {

   // Print out the catalog name

   System.out.println
            ("Catalog " + catalogRs.getString(1));

   // Then, get a result set containing information about
   //   tables contained in the catalog

   ResultSet tableRs = md.getTables ( catalogRs.getString(1),
                                      "%",
                                      "%",
                                      (String []) null
                                    );

   // For each table in the result set for this catalog

   while (tableRs.next()) {

      // Print out the schema name and the table name.

      System.out.println
            ( "   "
              + tableRs.getString("TABLE_SCHEM")
              + "."
              + tableRs.getString("TABLE_NAME")
            ) ;
   }
}
```

Finally, quite a bit of information about the characteristics of the database is made available via the methods of the `DatabaseMetaData` object. Some, but only some, of these methods are listed below. You should be aware that there are many, many more methods associated with `DatabaseMetaData`—about 134 in all!

java.sql.DatabaseMetaData Interface

```
public String getDatabaseProductName() throws SQLException

public String getCatalogSeparator() throws SQLException

public int getMaxColumnsInOrderBy() throws SQLException

public int getMaxConnections() throws SQLException

public int getMaxStatementLength() throws SQLException

public boolean nullsAreSortedHigh() throws SQLException

public boolean supportsANSI92EntryLevelSQL()
  throws SQLException

public boolean supportsExpressionsInOrderBy()
  throws SQLException
```

4.5 Executing an SQL Statement Once

Once a connection has been established, an application can execute an SQL statement. This section describes how an application executes a statement a single time. Section 4.6 describes how an application can execute an SQL statement multiple times.

The first step in executing an SQL statement is for the application to get a `Statement` object from the connection, using something like this:

```
Statement stmt = con.createStatement();
```

4.5.1 SELECT Statements

If the application needs to execute a SELECT statement, then it continues by invoking the following method:

```
ResultSet rs = stmt.executeQuery (string);
```

The `ResultSet` object can be used to examine the metadata associated with the result set, such as the number of columns and their types, and it can be used to fetch the rows themselves.

Result Set Metadata

Example 4.4 shows how an application could be written to examine the metadata associated with the result set.

EXAMPLE 4.4 DISPLAY INFORMATION ABOUT THE COLUMNS IN A `ResultSet`.

```
// Allocate a new Statement variable and create a new
//   Statement object to initialize it

Statement stmt = con.createStatement ();

// Create a String to contain the text of a SELECT statement

String stmtsource = "SELECT * FROM movies";

// Invoke the executeQuery method of the Statement object,
//   with the text of the SELECT statement to be executed

ResultSet rs = stmt.executeQuery (stmtsource);

// Get a metadata object describing the executed statement

ResultSetMetaData rsm = rs.getMetaData ();

// For each column of the statement result, print selected
//   metadata information

for (int i = 1; i <= rsm.getColumnCount(); i++) {
   System.out.println ( "(" + i + ") "
                       + rsm.getColumnName (i)
                     );
   System.out.println ( "       Type = "
                       + rsm.getColumnTypeName (i)
                     );
   System.out.println ( "       Display Size = "
                       + rsm.getColumnDisplaySize (i)
                     );
}
```

The code in Example 4.4 produces the following result:

```
(1) title
       Type = varchar
       Display Size = 100
```

```
(2) director
      Type = varchar
      Display Size = 50
(3) year_introduced
      Type = char
      Display Size = 4
(4) runs
      Type = int
      Display Size = 11
```

In this example, the `for` loop iterates over all of the columns in the result set. For each column, various `ResultSetMetadata` methods are used to determine properties for each column in turn, such as the column name, column type name, and the display size.

Result Set Data

The `next` method advances our position in the `ResultSet` object from one row to the next. It returns true until it is past the last row of the result (after which it—surprise, surprise—returns false). Once an application is positioned on a row, it will want to retrieve the data values contained in one or more of the result set columns.

In a moment we will discuss some "get" methods that will be used to determine the value of a column as a specific Java data type. There are also some `getObject` methods that will return the value of a column as simply a Java `Object`. The specific class of the returned object is determined by the SQL data type of the column, as seen in Table 4.1.

Some of the SQL type names may be unfamiliar to readers familiar with the SQL standard; names such as LONGVARCHAR, VARBINARY, LONGVARBINARY, TINYINT, and BIGINT reflect JDBC's extensions to the SQL standard (these extensions have their origins in ODBC).

We will also, momentarily, discuss some set methods that provide a value for input parameters in prepared statements. The `setObject` methods accept a variety of Java data types and by default map to specific SQL data types, as seen in Table 4.2.

Some of the Java classes shown in these mappings may not be familiar to you. We discussed `java.math.BigDecimal` in Section 2.4.4. JDBC created its own classes of `java.sql.Date`, `java.sql.Time`, and `java.sql.Timestamp`. We will discuss these in the next section.

In Example 4.5, we see how an application can access the rows of the `ResultSet`.

This application might produce a result such as the following:

```
Tom Hanks in 1993 for "Philadelphia"
Al Pacino in 1992 for "Scent of a Woman"
Anthony Hopkins in 1991 for "The Silence of the Lambs"
Jeremy Irons in 1990 for "Reversal of Fortune"
```

SQL type	Java class
CHARACTER (CHAR)	String
CHARACTER VARYING (VARCHAR)	String
LONGVARCHAR	String
NUMERIC	java.math.BigDecimal
DECIMAL	java.math.BigDecimal
BIT	Boolean
TINYINT	Integer
SMALLINT	Integer
INTEGER	Integer
BIGINT	Long
REAL	Float
FLOAT	Double
DOUBLE PRECISION	Double
BINARY	byte []
VARBINARY	byte []
LONGVARBINARY	byte []
DATE	java.sql.Date
TIME	java.sql.Time
TIMESTAMP	java.sql.Timestamp

TABLE 4.1 *The SQL data type to Java class mapping used by* `getObject` *methods.*

Java class	SQL type
String	VARCHAR or LONGVARCHAR
java.math.BigDecimal	NUMERIC
Boolean	BIT
Integer	INTEGER
Long	BIGINT or LONGINT
Float	REAL
Double	DOUBLE
byte[]	VARBINARY or LONGVARBINARY
java.sql.Date	DATE
java.sql.Time	TIME
java.sql.Timestamp	TIMESTAMP

TABLE 4.2 *Default Java class to SQL data type mapping used by the* `setObject` *method.*

EXAMPLE 4.5 USING A `ResultSet` TO DISPLAY THE RESULT OF A QUERY.

```
// Build an SQL SELECT statement to retrieve awards

String stmtsource =    "SELECT * "
                     + "FROM   awards "
                     + "WHERE  award = 'Actor' "
                     + "AND    award_year BETWEEN '1990' "
                     + "                   AND '1993'";

// Allocate a Statement object variable

Statement stmt = con.createStatement ();

// Execute the statement to form a result set

ResultSet rs = stmt.executeQuery (stmtsource);


// Process the result set, retrieving columns 3 different ways

while (rs.next()) {
   // printing information about each award returned
   System.out.println ( rs.getString (2).trim()
                        + " in "
                        + rs.getString ("award_year")
                        + " for \""
                        + (String) rs.getObject ("title")
                        + "\""
                      );
}
```

The `getString(int)` method was used to get a `String` value from the second column, `person`, of the current row. The `trim` method was then used to remove leading and trailing blanks (and any other white space) from that value. The `getString(String)` method was used to get a `String` from the column named `award_year`. Finally the `getObject(String)` was used to get an `Object` from the title column. There are accessor methods for all of the Java types that correspond to SQL types, with variants for accessing columns both by using the position of the column in the select list and by using the name of the column. These methods and their return types are shown in Table 4.3.

Consider that each column of the result set has an SQL data type associated with it. When the application issues its "`getXXX`" method, it specifies the type of the result it wishes to see. The get methods will do

Accessor method	Return type
getAsciiStream	java.io.InputStream
getBigDecimal	java.math.BigDecimal
getBinaryStream	java.io.InputStream
getBoolean	boolean
getByte	byte
getBytes	byte[]
getDate	java.sql.Date
getDouble	double
getFloat	float
getInt	int
getLong	long
getObject	Object
getShort	short
getString	String
getTime	java.sql.Time
getTimeStamp	java.sql.Timestamp
getUnicodeStream	java.io.InputStream

TABLE 4.3 *`ResultSet` accessor methods.*

their best to convert values from one type to another. If the application issues `getString` for an INTEGER column, then it will almost certainly succeed. If the application invokes the `getInt` method for a CHAR (5) column, then it might succeed, or it might throw an `SQLException`. If the application issues `getTime` for a DECIMAL column, then it cannot succeed and will always throw the exception.

It is possible that any of the columns that were examined in the example above could have contained the SQL null value. The accessors that returned `String` and `Object` would then return a Java null. The `int` accessor would return 0. To differentiate between an actual value of 0 and a 0 returned because the column contained an SQL null value, the `wasNull` method can be called immediately after the accessor. The `wasNull` method returns a `boolean` value that indicates whether the last column accessed was the SQL null value or not.

Large binary columns can be retrieved in a single operation using the `getBytes` method. Due to their large size, an application will often wish to retrieve the values of these columns piecemeal. The getBinaryStream method can be used for this purpose. This method returns a Java InputStream object, upon which read methods can be invoked. The input streams will be automatically closed when a get method on another column is invoked. Example 4.6 will help to illustrate this.

EXAMPLE 4.6 RETRIEVING THE CONTENTS OF A LARGE BINARY COLUMN.

```
int size;
ResultSet rs;

byte [] buffer = new byte [1024];

// Retrieve an InputStream object from the image
//   column of the ResultSet object

java.io.InputStream is = rs.getBinaryStream ("image");

// As long as the remaining size indicates valid data ...

while ((size = is.read (buffer)) != -1) {
   // do something with the buffer
}
```

As with the other get methods, the column can be identified by its name or its position.

Large character columns can be operated upon in a similar way. Instead of getString, an application can use either getAsciiStream or getUnicodeStream. In the case of getUnicodeStream, the JDBC driver will perform the necessary character conversions.

The Date, Time, and Timestamp Classes

Java provides the java.util.Date class, which contains both date and time information, but it is not a close enough match to be used for the SQL DATE, TIME, or TIMESTAMP data types. It is closest to the TIMESTAMP data type but does not store fractions of seconds. In order to support these SQL data types, therefore, JDBC introduced the java.sql.Date, java.sql.Time, and java.sql.Timestamp classes. These classes are, in fact, extensions of the java.util.Date class. In addition to the usual constructors and get and set methods, these classes provide a toString and a valueOf method. The methods, for the Time class, are described below.

java.sql.Time Class

`public String toString()`

Return a string that represents the time value in this object. This string is in the format specified by the JDBC escape syntax for a Time literal (hh:mm:ss).

`public static Time (String s)`

Return a `Time` object that represents the time value specified by *s*, which is in the format specified by the JDBC escape syntax for a Time literal (hh:mm:ss).

The use of these classes can be seen in Example 4.7.

EXAMPLE 4.7 THE `Date`, `Time`, AND `Timestamp` CLASSES.

```
long now = System.currentTimeMillis();

Date d = new Date (now);
System.out.println ("Date:        " + d.toString());

Time t = new Time (now);
System.out.println ("Time:        " + t.toString());

Timestamp ts = new Timestamp (now);
System.out.println ("Timestamp:   " + ts.toString());

System.out.println();

Timestamp Y2K  = Timestamp.valueOf("2000-01-01 00:00:00.00");
System.out.println ("Y2K is: " + Y2K);
```

The code in Example 4.7 produces the following output:

```
Date:       1999-09-12
Time:       08:22:02
Timestamp:  1999-09-12 08:22:02.67

Y2K is: 2000-01-01 00:00:00.0
```

4.5.2 Positioned Update and Delete Statements

Your application might need to execute positioned update or delete operations while working its way through a result set. In order to do so, a cursor name must be specified before the statement is executed using the `setCursorName` method, as shown in Example 4.8.

EXAMPLE 4.8 USING A POSITIONED UPDATE STATEMENT.

```
String stmtSource =
               "SELECT  voter, title, vote "
             + "FROM    votes "
             + "WHERE   title = 'My Cousin Vinny' "
             + "  AND   voter = 'Andrew'";

String positionedStmtSource =
               "UPDATE  votes "
             + "SET     vote = 6 "
             + "WHERE CURRENT OF vote_cur";

// Associate a cursor name with the query

Statement stmt = con.createStatement();
stmt.setCursorName("vote_cur");
ResultSet rs = stmt.executeQuery (stmtSource);

// Create a positioned statement

Statement pstmt = con.createStatement();

// Display information for each result row, and
// then execute a positioned update on that row

while (rs.next()) {
   System.out.println (rs.getString(1)
                       + " voted \""
                       + rs.getString(2)
                       + "\" a "
                       + rs.getString(3)
                      );

   n = pstmt.executeUpdate (positionedStmtSource);
   System.out.println (n + " row(s) were affected");

}
```

The code in Example 4.8 produces the following output:

```
Andrew voted "My Cousin Vinny" a 7
1 row(s) were affected
```

Once the cursor name has been specified ("`vote_cur`" in the example above), positioned update and delete operations with the usual "WHERE CURRENT OF *cursor-name*" can be executed.

4.5.3 DML and DDL Statements

If the application is executing a DML statement, such as INSERT, UPDATE, or DELETE, then it can use a statement like the following to indicate the result of the statement:

```
int count = con.executeUpdate (string);
```

The variable `count` now indicates the number of rows that were modified. This statement can also be used for SQL statements that do not return anything, such as DDL statements—in which case, `count` will have the value 0.

4.5.4 Unknown Statements and Call Statements

An application may need to execute an SQL statement for which the type of SQL statement is not known, perhaps because it is supplied by another piece of code or because it is supplied by a user. An application may also wish to execute a call statement or a compound (BEGIN/END) statement, which can return multiple result sets and execute multiple DML statements. In either case, it can use the approach shown in Example 4.9.

EXAMPLE 4.9 EXECUTION WHERE THE TYPE OF SQL STATEMENT IS NOT KNOWN.

```
Statement stmt = con.createStatement();
int n;

// Execute statement; if true, it returned a result set

if (stmt.execute (stmtSource)) {
   // So display the result set and continue
   displayResultSet (stmt);
}

else {

   // get the update count

   n = stmt.getUpdateCount();

   // If update count is 0 or greater, then display
   //   the number of affected rows and continue. Otherwise
   //   just return
```

```
    if (n != -1)
        displayUpdateCount (n);
    else
        return;
}

// Continue processing as long as there are more rows in
//   the result set, indicated by returned update count -1

while (true) {
    if (stmt.getMoreResults ()) {
        displayResultSet (stmt);
    }
    else {
        if ((n = stmt.getUpdateCount()) != -1)
            displayUpdateCount (n);
        else
            return;
    }
}
```

On the initial execution of the statement, the execute method returns a boolean value, indicating whether a result set is being returned. If it is, then the application's displayResultSet method can operate on it as we discussed before. If it is not a result set, then the application looks to see whether there is an update count with the getUpdateCount method. A value of –1 is returned by this method if no update count is to be returned.

The while loop uses the getMoreResults method. This closes any result set that might be open and moves on to the next result. It returns true if this next result is a result set. When getMoreResults is false and getUpdateCount returns –1, then the statement has fully run its course.

4.5.5 SQL Exception and Warning Conditions

SQL exception conditions are turned into Java SQLException exceptions that can be thrown by almost all of the JDBC methods. SQLException exceptions are chained together, and subsequent SQLException exceptions can be accessed by the SQLException .getNextException method.

SQL warning conditions are made available by Connection, Statement, and ResultSet objects via a getWarnings method. An application can look for these warnings after it has operated on these types of objects. Warnings are chained together, and subsequent warnings can be accessed by the `SQLWarning.getNextWarning` method. Example 4.10 illustrates this characteristic.

EXAMPLE 4.10 DISPLAYING ZERO, ONE, OR MORE WARNING MESSAGES AND EXCEPTIONS.

```
try {
   Statement stmt = con.createStatement ();
   ResultSet rs = stmt.executeQuery (stmtSource);
   SQLWarning rsWarn;

   while (rs.next()) {
      System.out.println (rs.getInt (1));
      rsWarn = rs.getWarnings();

      // Display any warnings

      while (rsWarn != null) {
         System.out.println (rsWarn.getMessage());
         rsWarn = rsWarn.getNextWarning();
      }
   }
}
catch (SQLException sqe) {

   // Display all SQLExceptions

   while (sqe != null) {
      System.out.println (sqe.getMessage());
      sqe = sqe.getNextException();
   }
}
```

4.6 Executing an SQL Statement Multiple Times

If your application needs to execute the same type of statement repeatedly, but with different values in the search criteria or update values, then the use of prepared statements will likely be the most efficient way to do this. To begin with, the SQL statement is constructed with dynamic parameter markers (`?`), where a value is to be supplied or returned. Example 4.11 shows the steps that an application must go through.

EXAMPLE 4.11 PREPARING AND EXECUTING A PARAMETERIZED QUERY.

```
// Construct a SELECT statement using a ? as a
//   placeholder for the desired title value

String stmtSource =
             "SELECT   title, COUNT (DISTINCT award) "
           + "FROM     awards "
           + "WHERE    title = ? "
           + "GROUP BY title";

// Prepare the statement for execution

PreparedStatement pstmt =
           con.prepareStatement(stmtSource);

// Set the value of the parameter and execute the statement

pstmt.setString (1, "Fargo");
ResultSet rs = pstmt.executeQuery ();

// Print information for all awards for that movie

while (rs.next()) {
   System.out.println ("\"" + rs.getString(1)
                       + "\" received "
                       + rs.getInt(2) + " awards"
                      );
}

// Now, set the value of the parameter for a different
//   movie and execute the statement again

pstmt.setString (1, "The Silence of the Lambs");
rs = pstmt.executeQuery ();

// Print information for all awards for the other movie

while (rs.next()) {
   System.out.println ("\"" + rs.getString(1)
                       + "\" received "
                       + rs.getInt(2) + " awards"
                      );
}
```

The code in Example 4.11 produces the following output:

```
"Fargo" received 2 awards
"The Silence of the Lambs" received 5 awards
```

As you can see, the statement was prepared, which was followed by the setting of the input parameters. Unlike the get methods, which can identify a column by its name or position, the set methods identify parameters only by their positions. As before, there are set methods for all of the expected data types, and a `setObject` method is provided. The values placed in these parameters remain from one execution to the next, until they are explicitly changed. With the value for the ? in place, the execution proceeds as it did before—the result set is returned and is used to access the data values. An application can use the `execute` method, the `executeQuery` method, or the `executeUpdate` method, depending on the type of SQL statement that was prepared.

The value of an input parameter can be set to the null value explicitly with the `setNull` method. This method requires that the data type of the SQL null value be specified, and would appear this way:

```
pstmt.setNull (1, Types.CHAR);
```

This statement uses a manifest constant defined in the `java.sql.Types` class to indicate the SQL data type.

4.7 Executing a Call Statement

A CALL statement that does not have any OUT parameters or return value, and needs to be executed only once, can be executed just as any single SQL statement can be executed—a case we have already covered. An application must use the `prepareCall` method to deal with OUT parameters or return values, as can be seen in Example 4.12. The execution of the code in Example 4.12 produced the following output:

```
1 was voted 1 times
2 was voted 3 times
3 was voted 4 times
4 was voted 10 times
5 was voted 11 times
6 was voted 16 times
7 was voted 24 times
8 was voted 23 times
9 was voted 12 times
10 was voted 4 times

The median vote was 7.
```

EXAMPLE 4.12 PREPARING AND EXECUTING A CALL STATEMENT.

```
// Create a CALL statement with two dynamic parameters

String stmtSource =    "{CALL median_votes (?, ?)}";

// Prepare that CALL statement

CallableStatement cstmt = con.prepareCall(stmtSource);

// Fill in the first parameter
//   and indicate the second is used for returning a value

cstmt.setString (1, "Jim");
cstmt.registerOutParameter (2, Types.INTEGER);

// Execute the CALL statement
//   and access the result set created by that execution

cstmt.execute();
ResultSet rs = cstmt.getResultSet ();

// As long as there is at least one row returned,
//   get the value of the two columns in each row

while (rs.next()) {
   System.out.println (String.valueOf (rs.getInt(1))
                       + " was voted "
                       + rs.getInt(2) + " times"
                      );
}

// The value returned in the out parameter itself is the
// median of the second value in all rows of the result set

System.out.println ();
System.out.println ("The median vote was "
                    + cstmt.getInt (2) + "."
                   );
```

The procedure being called, `median_votes`, has two parameters. The first of these is an IN parameter identifying the person whose votes are to be considered, and the second is an OUT parameter that returns the median vote for that person. Before the CALL statement can be executed, two things must be done: the value of the input parameter must be set, as we saw previously, and the `registerOutParameter` method must be used to associate an SQL data type with each of the OUT parameters. Once the execution has taken place, including the traversal of any result sets that the procedure may generate, the values of the OUT parameters can be retrieved. This technique can be used whether the CALL statement is executed once or many times.

4.8 Asynchronous Execution

JDBC does not provide asynchronous execution of its methods. Instead, an application simply uses the threading capabilities inherent in Java. JDBC drivers are all required to be multithread safe (meaning that they can be used concurrently by multiple threads in the same process). While a query is executing and the rows are being retrieved in one thread, another thread can interact with the user, write to a file, or execute other statements on the database. If a database cannot support concurrent operations, then the JDBC driver will perform any necessary synchronization. A specific use of Java's multithreading is the `Statement.cancel` method, which will normally be invoked from one thread to stop the execution of a statement on another thread.

You must be careful if your application uses JDBC in multiple threads. A commit that is executed on one thread may affect other threads that are using the same connection because result sets are automatically closed when the transaction that created them ends. The occurrence of this situation can be quite subtle because the default for a connection is to have the auto commit mode turned on.

4.9 JavaSoft JDBC-ODBC Bridge

The JDBC-ODBC Bridge (see Section 4.1.1) is provided by JavaSoft with JDBC. Jointly developed by JavaSoft and Intersolv, this software allows an application using the JDBC API to access any ODBC data source. It is a Type 1 JDBC interface, as it makes calls to ODBC in non-Java code. To use this bridge, an application must load `sun.jdbc.odbc.Jdbc.OdbcDriver`. The subprotocol for this style of JDBC URL is defined as follows:

```
jdbc:odbc:data-source-name
            [;attribute-name=attribute-value]*
```

(The optional `;attribute-name=attribute-value` can be repeated as many times as required to specify all necessary attributes and their values.) Examples of these URLs are the following:

```
jdbc:odbc:distribution
jdbc:odbc:production;uid=melton;pwd=jim
```

(But don't get your hopes up. . . we *never* violate basic security protocols by using our names as our passwords!)

4.10 Chapter Summary

We have seen that the JDBC 1.0 API allows an application to access database data and metadata in a way natural for Java programmers. Different types of JDBC drivers support intranet client applications, Internet client applications and applets, and application server programs. The SQL passed in JDBC requests can be standard Entry SQL-92, standard Entry SQL-92 with Escape Syntax, or proprietary SQL.

JDBC, like SQL/CLI and ODBC, must be considered a low-level interface to a DBMS. An application writer must focus on statements, parameters, and cursors, and result set columns are accessed one at a time. Application writers can author JDBC applications directly, or JDBC can be generated by some sort of GUI application development environment such as Sybase's PowerJ, Microsoft's Visual J++, Borland's JBuilder, Symantec's VisualCafe, or IBM's Visual Age. JDBC can also be used to implement higher-level APIs.

We'll discuss Sun's most recent enhancements to the JDBC API in Chapter 9.

CHAPTER

5

SQLJ Part 0 (Embedding SQL in Java)

5.1 Introduction

We've done our preparation in the preceding chapters, so now it's time to get to the heart of our subject matter: using SQL and Java in a single application. One of the most basic ways to accomplish this task is to write a Java program that executes some SQL statements that are coded along with the Java statements—in other words, embedding SQL in Java.

SQLJ Part 0 allows SQL statements to be embedded in Java programs. We've looked at JDBC, which provides for the dynamic execution of SQL statements. The raison d'être for SQLJ Part 0 is the support of *static* SQL statements.

Before we completely focus on the details of SQLJ Part 0, we'll discuss how the group of SQLJ standards came about. We'll show a simple example of using SQLJ Part 0, followed by an in-depth discussion of each of its features. Later in the chapter, we'll discuss SQLJ Part 0 Translators in general, and we'll specifically discuss the Oracle SQLJ Part 0 reference implementation. After all of this is covered, we'll finish up by pointing out the advantages that SQLJ Part 0 brings you in the development of applications.

In this chapter, we'll provide many examples of SQLJ Part 0 and discuss its features in a high level of detail. We've included the definition of classes and interfaces provided by SQLJ Part 0 at the end of this chapter. The complete syntax of SQLJ Part 0 is presented in Appendix E. You'll need this material when you are ready to begin writing your own SQLJ Part 0 applications.

5.2 SQLJ—An Informal Group of Companies

Starting in the first half of 1997, an informal and open group of companies has been meeting to consider how the Java programming language and relational databases might be used together. Initially called JSQL and later SQLJ (because of trademark issues), the companies that have participated in the group are Cloudscape, Tandem (which has since been acquired by Compaq), IBM, Informix, Micro Focus, Microsoft, Oracle, Sun, and Sybase. The group met fairly regularly to make suggestions and review each other's ideas, to see where they agreed on syntax and semantics, and to eventually provide a basis for one or more formal standards.

The work began with a proposal, put forward by Oracle, on how SQL statements might be embedded in Java. Later, Sybase put forward proposals on how to use Java in the database to provide an implementation of stored routines and user-defined data types (UDTs). Once an initial draft of a specification was put forward, the entire group reviewed it, spotting problems and suggesting enhancements. The technology was specified in three parts, roughly described as

Part 0	Embedded SQL in Java
Part 1	SQL Routines using the Java™ Programming Language
Part 2	SQL Types using the Java™ Programming Language

These three parts have all progressed rapidly. Since work on Part 0 was started before the other parts, it was the first to be submitted to a formal standards body. SQLJ Part 0 has been adopted as Database Language SQL—Part 10: Object Language Bindings (SQL/OLB),[1] by NCITS H2, the database technical committee. The name for this part of the SQL standard implies a broad scope, with SQLJ Part 0 being the first such binding to be defined. Although there are presently no proposals to extend this sort of binding to other languages, several participants have expressed interest in supporting other object-oriented languages,

[1] ANSI X3.135.10:1998, *Information systems—Database language—SQL—Part 10: Object Language Bindings (SQL/OLB),* American National Standards Institute, New York City, 1998.

such as C++ or Smalltalk. SQLJ Part 1 was submitted to NCITS in early 1999 and was adopted in September 1999 as SQLJ—Part 1: SQL Routines using the Java™ Programming Language,[2] the first part of a new multipart standard. SQLJ Part 2 will likely be submitted to NCITS in 2000.

The SQL/OLB standard is more readable than are most standards. For one thing, it contains a well-written tutorial section. For each statement and language clause, the standard contains its syntax and description and specifies what Java statements must be generated by a SQLJ Part 0 Translator. It also contains a great deal of material that is needed only by the implementers of SQLJ Part 0 Translators and Customizers and is therefore not covered in this book.

ANSI standards have long been available for purchase in hardcopy format. Recently these standards have been made available for purchase at a reasonable price in electronic form via the World Wide Web. For more information you can look at the following page: *http://www.cssinfo.com/ncits.html*. It is possible that SQL/OLB and the two parts of the new SQLJ standard will be available for purchase at that site by the time you read this book.

5.3 Writing an SQLJ Part 0 Program

SQLJ Part 0 allows static SQL statements to be embedded in a Java program, in somewhat the same way that SQL allows SQL statements to be embedded in C, COBOL, and several other languages (we showed an example of Embedded SQL in Section 3.11.1). Dynamic SQL statements are handled just fine by JDBC, and so SQLJ Part 0 did not have to include any support for them. However, SQLJ Part 0 does support the mixing of embedded static SQL statements with JDBC statements in an application.

5.3.1 A Simple SQLJ Part 0 Program

The code fragment in Example 5.1 shows how SQLJ Part 0 can be used to access our sample database using a Sybase driver for JDBC.

Some parts of this example should be familiar to you by this time. We start the example by registering our JDBC driver with the JDBC driver manager. We then establish a connection to a database (covered in detail in the next section). Finally, we execute an SQLJ Part 0 statement.

---

[2] ANSI NCITS 331.1-1999, *SQLJ—Part 1: SQL Routines using the Java™ Programming Language,* 1999.

EXAMPLE 5.1 A SIMPLE SQLJ PART 0 PROGRAM.

```
import java.sql.*;
import sqlj.runtime.*;
import sqlj.runtime.ref.DefaultContext;

public class Simple {

  public static void main (String [] argv) {

    try {
       // register JDBC driver

       Class.forName ("com.sybase.jdbc.SybDriver");

      // Setup default context; use command line args for user id
      // and password

      String URL = "jdbc:sybase:Tds:localhost:2638";
      DefaultContext defCtxt
         = new DefaultContext (URL, argv[0], argv[1], false);
      DefaultContext.setDefaultContext (defCtxt);

      // Execute a DELETE statement

      #sql { DELETE
             FROM     awards
             WHERE    award_year = '1962'
           };
    }
    catch (SQLException sqe) {
       System.out.println (sqe.getMessage());
    }
    catch (Exception ex) {
       System.out.println (ex.getMessage());
    }
  }
}
```

The syntax "`#sql {...};`" identifies an SQLJ Part 0 executable statement. The curly braces (`{}`) have been used to delimit the SQL statement it contains and separate it from the rest of the Java program. The SQL statement will be processed according to SQL's syntactic rules and not those of Java. This means that SQL keywords can be in upper or lower case, that character string literals are enclosed in single quotes, and so forth. An SQLJ Part 0 Translator will look for these embedded statements and replace them with Java statements that cause the SQL statements to be executed. The resulting Java source program will be compiled normally.

Without the use of an SQLJ Part 0 Translator, this program is not a legal Java program, and a Java compiler will refuse to compile it. This could (obviously) be a problem if you are using one of the Java development environments or tools that is not aware of SQLJ Part 0.

Example 5.1 also shows that the JDBC model for dealing with SQL exception conditions has been used by SQLJ Part 0. In other host language bindings, the SQLSTATE variable is used to inform the application of an SQL exception condition. In SQLJ Part 0, such an exception condition will cause the SQLJ Part 0 statements to throw a Java exception, `java.sql.SQLException`.

Within embedded SQL statements, SQL-style comments may be used, but within a host expression, Java-style comments must be used. They are

SQL comments:	`/* enclosed comment */` `-- comment to end of line`
Java comments:	`/* enclosed comment */` `// comment to end of line`

Let us offer some words of caution for you when you get ready to write your own SQLJ Part 0 programs. The SQLJ Part 0 Translator will be generating some variables of its own when it runs. These will all be prefixed with the six-character sequence "`__sJT_`". It is, therefore, a good idea if you do not create fields, variables, or parameters that use this prefix. The SQLJ Part 0 Translator will also generate some internal classes and files of its own. These classes and files will be prefixed with "*`filename`*`_SJ`", where the source file being processed is *`filename`*`.sqlj`. You should avoid using this prefix for your class names and file names.

5.3.2 Connection Contexts

In Example 5.1, we established a connection to the database and then said we'd cover this concept in detail. Let's take a close look at SQLJ Part 0's database connections, how they're used, and how they're established. One of the most important aspects of connections is a connection context object, used to manage all information pertinent to a connection.

A *connection context object* is used to associate the execution of each SQL statement with a particular connection to a database. In Example 5.1, an *implicit* connection context object was used. In Example 5.2, an *explicit* connection context object will be used instead. We'll return to implicit connection contexts in a little while.

The example begins with `#sql context MoviesContext;` to declare an explicit connection context class called `MoviesContext`. The SQLJ Part 0 Translator will replace this SQLJ Part 0 declaration with a Java definition of the `MoviesContext` class. Because the SQLJ Part 0 Translator that we are using creates some static members in this class, Java requires that we put this declaration outside of the `ExplicitConnectionContext` class.

Next, a `moviesCtxt` object of this class is created. We've chosen a constructor that takes a URL, user id, password, and a boolean value (false in this case) to indicate whether auto commit should be on or off. SQLJ Part 0 provides several constructors for connection contexts, as we'll see in a moment. The connection context class also provides methods that can examine and change some of the properties of the connection.

You might be a bit confused about why the `#sql` prefix is used in some places and not in others. In both the declaration of our connection context and the execution of the DELETE statement, the SQLJ Part 0 Translator has to recognize this syntax and substitute Java declarations and statements. The creation of the `moviesCtxt` object, on the other hand, requires no action on the part of the SQLJ Part 0 Translator, so the prefix isn't used.

With the connection context object successfully created, we can now use it to execute a DELETE statement against the target database. The connection context object appears in square brackets (`[moviesCtxt]`) to indicate the target connection for the DELETE statement.

A connection context class has another use. It gives an SQLJ Part 0 Translator the ability to check the validity of executable statements at the time that translation takes place. Consider that all executable statements have an associated connection context object (explicitly or implicitly). The SQLJ Part 0 implementation can determine the connection context class for each of these objects. At translation time, a user can specify which database schema should be used to check the validity of the executable statements for each connection context class.

Explicit connection context objects allow an application to operate on multiple connections to the same database, or multiple connections to different databases.

It is also useful to know that connection contexts may be safely shared among threads in a multithreaded application.

EXAMPLE 5.2 AN EXPLICIT CONNECTION CONTEXT.

```
import java.sql.*;
import sqlj.runtime.*;

// Declare a connection context class

#sql context MoviesContext;

public class ExplicitConnectionContext {

   public static void main (String [] argv) {

      try {
         // register JDBC driver

         Class.forName("com.sybase.jdbc.SybDriver");

         // Create an explicit connection context object;
         //   use command line args for user id and password

         String URL = "jdbc:sybase:Tds:localhost:2638";

         MoviesContext moviesCtxt =
             new MoviesContext(URL, argv[0], argv[1], false);

         // Execute a DELETE statement

         #sql  [moviesCtxt] { DELETE
                              FROM     awards
                              WHERE    award_year = '1962'
                            };

      }
      catch (SQLException sqe) {
         System.out.println (sqe.getMessage());
      }
      catch (Exception ex) {
          System.out.println (ex.getMessage());
      }
   }
}
```

Connection Context Declaration

The syntax for the connection context declaration (slightly abbreviated) is the following:

```
<connection declaration clause> ::=
     [ <modifiers> ] context <java class name>
     [ <implements clause> ] [ <with clause> ]

<implements clause> ::= implements [ <interface list> ]

<interface list> ::= <interface element>, ...

<interface element> ::=
       sqlj.runtime.ForUpdate
     | <user defined interface class>

<with clause> ::= with ( <with element>, ... )

<with element> ::= <with keyword> = <with value>

<with keyword> ::=
       sensitivity
     | holdability
     | returnability
     | updateColumns
     | <user defined with keyword>

<user defined with keyword> ::= <java id>
```

We will discuss all of the predefined names above when we get to iterators; they are not used by connection contexts. The <user defined interface class> and <user defined with keyword> can be used for connection contexts. To be honest, we're not exactly sure why an application writer would take advantage of this feature, but we mention it for the sake of completeness.

The Generated Connection Context Class

When a connection context declaration appears in your program, the SQLJ Part 0 Translator will generate a class of the following form (where *ContextName* is the name specified for <java class name>).

```
<modifiers> class ContextName
    implements sqlj.runtime.ConnectionContext, <interface list> {

  static public final <with type> <with keyword> = <with value> ;

  // constructors and methods for this class

  ...

  // methods for the ConnectionContext interface

  ...

}
```

The constructors and methods for the generated class are presented below.

"ContextName" Class

`public ContextName (String url, java.util.Properties info, boolean autoCommit) throws SQLJException`

This constructor creates the connection context using a JDBC URL. The properties for the connection are determined by the URL, a `Properties` object, and a `boolean` that indicates whether the auto commit feature should be on or off. You can look at JDBC's `getConnection` method to see how the `Properties` object is used.

`public ContextName (String url, boolean autoCommit) throws SQLJException`

Constructor for a connection context without the `Properties` object.

`public ContextName (String url, String user, String password, boolean autoCommit) throws SQLJException`

Constructor for a connection context using a user name and password instead of a `Properties` object.

`public ContextName (ConnectionContext other) throws SQLJException`

This constructor creates a connection context by specifying an existing connection context object. The new connection context shares the underlying database session.

`public ContextName (java.sql.Connection conn) throws SQLJException`

This constructor creates a connection context by specifying an existing JDBC connection object. The new connection context shares the underlying database session with the JDBC connection.

`public static ContextName getDefaultContext()`

Return the default connection context object for this class. This method will return the following:

1. The value that was supplied with `setDefaultContext`, if it has been invoked.
2. The default connection context that is part of the runtime environment, if it exists.
3. Otherwise, null.

`public static void setDefaultContext (ContextName ctx)`

Set the default connection context object for this class.

There are several ways for your application to create and use a connection context object. A class in an application can declare a nonpublic connection context class and then create one or more local instances of it in the same source file (as we did in Example 5.2). Another option is to use `public` as a <modifier> in the declaration of a connection context class. Instances of such a class can then be created in application classes in several source files and shared among them.

The default connection context for a connection context class is stored in a static variable. Java applets and multithreaded applications may wish to avoid the use of static variables by using only explicit connection contexts.

Implicit Connection Contexts

SQLJ Part 0 allows an application to be written without the explicit declaration of a connection context and without the use of a connection context object in an SQLJ Part 0 statement. This was the case with the very first SQLJ Part 0 example (Example 5.1) we showed you in this chapter.

This strategy is not recommended because the name for the implicit connection context is not specified by the SQLJ Part 0 standard, but is instead chosen by the implementers of the SQLJ Part 0 Translator that you have selected (in Example 5.1 this was `sqlj.runtime.ref.DefaultContext`). This name has to be used in order to create the connection context object and invoke the `setDefaultContext` method. The use of this implicit connection context name in your programs will limit their portability.

For those of you who are curious, the following expression is generated when the implicit connection context is used, where *implicitCC* is the implicit connection context name chosen by the SQLJ Part 0 Translator:

```
implicitCC.getDefaultContext()
```

5.3.3 Execution Contexts

An *execution context* object allows some aspects of a statement's execution to be controlled, and it allows the retrieval of information about the execution after it has completed. Like a connection context, the use of an execution context can be implicit or explicit. Let's look first at explicit execution contexts, as shown in Example 5.3.

EXAMPLE 5.3 AN EXPLICIT EXECUTION CONTEXT.

```
ExecutionContext execCtxt = new ExecutionContext();

execCtxt.setQueryTimeout(30);

#sql  [moviesCtxt, execCtxt] { DELETE
                                FROM     awards
                                WHERE    award_year = '1962'
                              };

System.out.println
      ( "Deleted "
        + execCtxt.getUpdateCount()
        + " rows."
      );

if (execCtxt.getWarnings() != null) {
         System.out.println (execCtxt.getWarnings().getMessage());
}
```

In Example 5.3, we have created a new `executionContext` object, named `execCtxt`. We then set a 30-second timeout value for this object. Both an explicit connection context and execution context are associated with the DELETE statement. The execution context is the second object provided in the square brackets (`[moviesCtxt, execCtxt]`) preceding the executable SQLJ Part 0 statement. You are allowed to specify either a connection context or an execution context individually in square brackets. If you specify them together, then they must be in the order used above.

The following attributes may be set by your application for an execution context:

`MaxRows`	The maximum number of rows to be returned by a query.
`MaxFieldSize`	The maximum number of bytes to be returned for any column or output argument.
`QueryTimeout`	The number of seconds to wait for an SQL operation to complete.

In Example 5.3, we have set a value for `QueryTimeout`. If this number of seconds is exceeded, then the execution of the statement will end, and an `SQLException` will be thrown. It is also possible that setting one of these values will cause an `SQLException` to be thrown at the time an SQL statement is executed, indicating that the feature is not supported.

After the execution of the DELETE statement, the execution context holds some useful information. The `getUpdateCount` method is used by our example to print a message with the number of rows that were affected by the statement. The `getWarnings` method is used to determine whether any warnings were generated by the statement and to display the first of these warnings.

As we said, an execution context can also be implicitly specified. Each connection context has a default execution context associated with it. This default execution context is used if an explicit execution context has not been specified. The default execution context can be retrieved from the connection context using the `ConnectionContext.getExecutionContext` method. Unlike a connection context, an execution context should not be shared among threads in a multithreaded application.

5.3.4 Host Variables and Expressions

Static SQL for most programming languages allows the use of host variables within SQL expressions, in addition to literals, column references, SQL variables, and SQL parameters. Similarly, SQLJ Part 0 allows the use of Java host variables, and even host expressions, as we show in Example 5.4.

The Java host variable, `name` in this example, is used within an SQL statement to indicate that a value must be placed into a Java variable. The host variable name is identified in the SQL statement by the colon (:) that precedes it (just as it is in other embedded SQL languages). The pattern in the LIKE predicate is a host expression (preceded by a colon, just as though it were a host variable name) that concatenates an element of a `String` array with a `String` literal. It's worth repeating that a host variable name or expression is processed according to Java's syntax rules. The case of variable names, for example, is significant to Java.

EXAMPLE 5.4 USING A JAVA HOST VARIABLE AND HOST EXPRESSION.

```
String name;

#sql { SELECT   person
       INTO     :name
       FROM     awards
       WHERE    title LIKE :(argv[2] + "%")
         AND    award = 'Director'
     };

System.out.println ("The director is " + name);
```

The SQLJ Part 0 syntax for host variables and expressions is as follows:

```
<host expression> ::=
   : [ <parameter mode> ] <expression>

<parameter mode> ::= IN | OUT | INOUT

<expression> ::=
     <variable>
   | ( <complex expression> )
```

SQLJ Part 0 specifies that the <parameter mode> keywords are case-insensitive. Java variables and host expressions have a parameter mode that, if not explicitly specified, is implicitly determined by its use. In Example 5.4, the host variable `name` has mode OUT, and the host expression in the LIKE predicate has mode IN.

Side effects are a possibility when Java expressions are evaluated. For this reason SQLJ Part 0 evaluates all of the Java host expressions that appear in an SQL statement before the statement is executed. The expressions are evaluated in left-to-right order, as seen in Example 5.5.

Example 5.5 contains two Java host expressions. If the value of `i` was 3 when this statement is executed, then the patterns `pattern[3]` and `pattern[4]` will be used in the LIKE predicates. Assignment to host variables and expressions also takes place in left-to-right order of their appearance in the statement.

EXAMPLE 5.5 MULTIPLE JAVA HOST EXPRESSIONS.

```
#sql { SELECT   person
       INTO     :name
       FROM     awards
       WHERE    title LIKE :(pattern[i++])
         AND    title LIKE :(pattern[i++])
     };
```

When a host variable has a Java primitive data type and it is being used with a mode of IN, then there is no way to represent a null value to SQL. If it is necessary to represent a null value, then you must use one of the Java wrapper classes instead. When a host variable has a Java primitive data type and it is being used with a mode of OUT or INOUT, then attempting to return an SQL null value will throw an `SQLNullException` exception. You should either be prepared to catch this exception or avoid the situation by using a wrapper class instead of the primitive type.

5.3.5 Data Type Issues

SQLJ Part 0 uses the same mapping between Java data types and SQL data types that is defined by JDBC. In the examples above, the Java variables and expressions are of type `String`, and the SQL data types are VARCHAR.

The specific set of Java data types that can be used by an SQLJ Part 0 application are shown in Table 5.1.

SQLJ Part 0 does provide a set of classes to allow passing large CHARACTER or BINARY values as input arguments to an SQL statement. These classes, `AsciiStream`, `BinaryStream`, and `UnicodeStream`, all wrap a `java.io.InputStream` object that provides a stream of bytes. Instances of these classes can be used only when a length has been given to them, which can happen as part of their construction or with the `setLength` method later on. The `AsciiStream` and `UnicodeStream` can be used for CHARACTER and BINARY arguments, whereas the `BinaryStream` can be used only for BINARY arguments. Example 5.6 shows how `AsciiStream` can be used for input to a query and output from a query (it's admittedly a bit silly—after all, you don't often use a stream for only four characters).

5.3.6 Calling Stored Routines

In Examples 5.8 and 5.9, we'll illustrate the use of the stored procedure and function defined in Example 5.7.

Java data type	Corresponding `java.sql.Types` value
`boolean`	`BIT`
`byte`	`TINYINT`
`short`	`SMALLINT`
`int`	`INTEGER`
`long`	`BIGINT`
`float`	`REAL`
`double`	`DOUBLE`
`Boolean`	`BIT`
`Byte`	`TINYINT`
`Short`	`SMALLINT`
`Integer`	`INTEGER`
`Double`	`DOUBLE`
`String`	`VARCHAR`
`java.math.BigDecimal`	`NUMERIC`
`byte[]`	`VARBINARY`
`java.sql.Date`	`DATE`
`java.sql.Time`	`TIME`
`java.sql.Timestamp`	`TIMESTAMP`
`sqlj.runtime.BinaryStream`	`OTHER`
`sqlj.runtime.AsciiStream`	`OTHER`
`sqlj.runtime.UnicodeStream`	`OTHER`
any other class	`OTHER`

TABLE 5.1 *Java data types supported by SQLJ Part 0.*

Example 5.8 shows how the `award_lookup` stored procedure can be invoked using the SQLJ Part 0 CALL statement.

About the only thing that you need to be aware of in this example is that the mode of the host variables and host expressions in the CALL statement will default to IN. You must remember to mark any INOUT or OUT arguments explicitly.

Example 5.9 shows how the `count_awards` stored function can be invoked.

There's really nothing to it. Invoking SQL's stored procedures and functions is about as simple as you could hope for.

EXAMPLE 5.6 USE OF THE AsciiStream CLASS.

```
#sql iterator Awards (String award,
                       sqlj.runtime.AsciiStream title);

// Construct and use an AsciiStream input variable, as_in
// Retrieve title as using an AsciiStream output variable, as_out

StringBufferInputStream sbis
   = new StringBufferInputStream("1980");
sqlj.runtime.AsciiStream as_in
   = new sqlj.runtime.AsciiStream(sbis, 4);

Awards awards;

#sql awards =  { SELECT   award, title
                 FROM     awards
                 WHERE    award_year = :as_in
               };

while (awards.next()) {
   sqlj.runtime.AsciiStream as_out = awards.title();
   BufferedReader br
      = new BufferedReader (new InputStreamReader (as_out));
   System.out.println (awards.award() + ": " + br.readLine());
}

awards.close();
```

EXAMPLE 5.7 STORED PROCEDURE AND FUNCTION THAT WE WILL INVOKE.

```
CREATE PROCEDURE award_lookup
             (IN  lu_award VARCHAR(20), IN lu_year CHARACTER (4),
              OUT lu_person VARCHAR(60), OUT lu_title VARCHAR (100)
             )
BEGIN
   SELECT   person, title
   INTO     lu_person, lu_title
   FROM     awards
   WHERE    award = lu_award
     AND    award_year = lu_year;
END
```

```
CREATE FUNCTION count_awards (IN ca_person VARCHAR (60))
   RETURNS INTEGER
BEGIN
   DECLARE r INTEGER;

   SELECT   COUNT(*)
   INTO     r
   FROM     awards
   WHERE    person = ca_person;

   RETURN (r);
END
```

EXAMPLE 5.8 INVOKING A STORED PROCEDURE.

```
String person = null;
String title = null;

#sql { CALL award_lookup (:in (argv[2]),
                          :in (argv[3]),
                          :out person,
                          :out title
                         )
     };

System.out.println (person + " for \"" + title + "\"");
```

EXAMPLE 5.9 INVOKING A STORED FUNCTION.

```
int count = 0;

#sql count = { VALUES (count_awards (:in (argv[2]))) };

System.out.println
        (argv[2] + " received " + count + " awards.");
```

5.3.7 Result Set Iterators

By far the most often used statement in applications is the SELECT statement. A *result set iterator* is roughly comparable to an SQL cursor; it is used to access the rows of the result of a query. Because a result set iterator is a Java object in SQLJ Part 0, it can be passed as an argument in the invocation of a method. SQLJ Part 0 provides two types of result set iterators. These two types cannot be intermixed for a single result set—one or the other must be chosen.

Binding to Columns by Name

The first type of result set iterator, the *named iterator,* allows the columns of the result to be referenced by name. Example 5.10 shows how a named iterator is both declared and used.

EXAMPLE 5.10 RETRIEVING DATA USING A NAMED ITERATOR.

```
#sql iterator Awards (String award, String title);

public class IterByName {

   public static void main (String [] argv) {

         ...

         Awards awards;

         #sql awards =  { SELECT   award, title
                          FROM     awards
                          WHERE    award_year = :(argv[2])
                        };

         while (awards.next()) {
            System.out.println (awards.award() + ": " +
                                awards.title());
         }

         awards.close();

         ...

   }
}
```

The SQLJ Part 0 iterator declaration `#sql iterator...` defines an `Awards` class. It is the use of column name/data type pairs (`String award, String title`) in the iterator declaration that determines that this is a named iterator.

The `awards` object is created and is then bound to the result of the query in the statement `#sqlj awards = { SELECT...};`. This statement can contain an SQL-92 query that can be arbitrarily complex, containing GROUP BY, HAVING, and ORDER BY clauses, UNION, DISTINCT, and so forth.

The `Awards` class is generated with accessor methods for each of the columns of the query result. The methods `next` and `close` are generated as part of this class. Using these methods, the `while` loop then iterates over the rows that result from the query, printing a line for each one; finally, the result of the query is closed.

The column names in the query are matched to the iterator names in a case-insensitive way. This means that SQLJ Part 0 requires the select list column names to be unique when they are compared in this way (without regard to case).

It is good practice to explicitly close an iterator that you are no longer using. Iterators acquire database resources, and these are best freed up immediately, rather than waiting for the garbage collector to run.

The syntax for an iterator declaration (slightly abbreviated) is as follows:

```
<iterator declaration clause> ::=
     [ <modifiers> ] iterator <java class name>
     [ <implements clause> ] [ <with clause> ]
     ( <iterator spec declaration> )

<implements clause> ::= implements [ <interface list> ]

<interface list> ::= <interface element>,...

<interface element> ::=
       sqlj.runtime.ForUpdate
     | <user defined interface class>

<with clause> ::= with ( <with element>,...)

<with element> ::= <with keyword> = <with value>

<with keyword> ::=
       sensitivity
     | holdability
     | returnability
     | updateColumns
     | <user defined with keyword>

<user defined with keyword> ::= <java id>
```

We've seen some of these elements before—when we discussed connection contexts. A named iterator declaration generates a class of the following form:

```
<modifiers> class <java class name>
     implements sqlj.runtime.NamedIterator, <interface list> {

   static public final <with type> <with keyword> = <with value> ;

   // Accessor methods for each column

   public <java datatype> <accessor method>() throws SQLException {
      ...
   }

   // methods for the NamedIterator interface

   ...
}
```

The <with keyword>s can be used as shown in Table 5.2.

Keyword	Description
`sensitivity`	The value for this keyword shall be one of the following constants that are defined in the class definition `sqlj.runtime.ResultSetIterator`: `SENSITIVE`, `INSENSITIVE`, or `ASENSITIVE`. This will determine the sensitivity of the cursor underlying the iterator.
`holdability`	The value for this keyword shall be the boolean value `true` or `false`. This will determine whether the cursor underlying the iterator is a HOLD (holdable) cursor. A HOLD cursor that is open when a transaction commits will not be automatically closed, as is the case for non-HOLD cursors.
`returnability`	The value for this keyword shall be the boolean value `true` or `false`. This will determine whether the cursor underlying the iterator is a result set cursor (specified in SQL by `WITH RETURN`). A result set cursor, when left open, returns a result set to the invoker of a procedure.
`updateColumns`	This keyword may only be specified if the iterator implements `sqlj.runtime.ForUpdate`. The value for this keyword shall be a `String` literal, containing a comma-separated list of column names. These columns may be updated by a positioned UPDATE statement.

TABLE 5.2 *<with keyword>s.*

Binding to Columns by Position

The second type of result set iterator that is used to access the result of a query is the *positioned iterator.* Example 5.11 shows the definition and use of this type of iterator.

EXAMPLE 5.11 RETRIEVE DATA USING A POSITIONED ITERATOR.

```
#sql iterator Awards (String, int);

public class IterByPos {

   public static void main (String [] argv) {

         ...

         Awards awards;

         String title = null;
         int count = 0;

         #sql awards =  { SELECT   title, COUNT(*)
                          FROM     awards
                          GROUP BY title
                          HAVING   COUNT(*) > 2
                        };

         while (true) {
               #sql {FETCH :awards INTO :title, :count};

            if (awards.endFetch()) break;

            System.out.println
               ("\"" + title + "\" received " + count + " awards");
         }

         awards.close();

         ...

   }
}
```

The iterator statement in this example contains only Java data types (`String, int`), rather than column name/data type pairs, indicating that a positioned iterator has been chosen. At the time the FETCH statement is executed, the result columns are stored in the Java variables provided in the INTO clause, in the order in which they were specified. The `Awards` class includes the methods `endFetch` and `close`. The application traverses the rows of the query result with the SQLJ Part 0 FETCH statement. The `endFetch` method returns a `boolean` value that is initially `false`, but becomes `true` after a FETCH statement has been executed and finds that there are no more rows.

The choice between named iterator and the positioned iterator is entirely a stylistic one. To use the named iterator, the columns that are selected must all have unique names, or they must be given unique names using SQL's ability to rename columns with the AS clause.

A positioned iterator declaration generates a class of the following form:

```
<modifiers> class <java class name>
    implements sqlj.runtime.PositionedIterator, <interface list> {

  static public final <with type> <with keyword> = <with value> ;

  // methods for the PositionedIterator interface

  ...
}
```

Positioned Update and Delete Statements

The use of SQL's positioned UPDATE statement can be seen in Example 5.12. We've presupposed a `newValue` method in this example that queries the user for an integer value.

The use of `implements sqlj.runtime.ForUpdate` in the iterator declaration is required to indicate to SQLJ Part 0 that this is an updateable result set iterator—that without this clause, the iterator would be read-only. The SQL positioned UPDATE statement in SQLJ Part 0 has been changed slightly from the SQL-92 definition: instead of specifying a cursor name in the "`WHERE CURRENT OF`" clause, the Java iterator variable is used instead.

Multiple Result Sets

Several DBMSs allow a stored procedure to return result sets during the execution of the procedure. These are sometimes called *side-channel* result sets, reflecting the fact that they are not declared in the same explicit way that out parameters are.

EXAMPLE 5.12 MODIFYING DATA WITH SQL'S POSITIONED UPDATE STATEMENT.

```
#sql iterator Movies
        implements sqlj.runtime.ForUpdate
        (String title, Integer runs);

public class Positioned {

   public static void main (String [] argv) {

         ...

         Movies movies;

         #sql movies =  { SELECT   title, runs
                          FROM     movies
                          WHERE    runs IS NULL
                          FOR UPDATE3
                        };

         while (movies.next()) {

            // If the input is not a blank line,
            // then do the update

            int newval = newValue(movies.title());

            if (newval != -1) {
               #sql { UPDATE   movies
                      SET      runs = :newval
                      WHERE CURRENT OF :movies
                    };
            }
         }

         movies.close();

         ...

   }
}
```

[3] The FOR UPDATE clause is required by Sybase Adaptive Server Anywhere but is not required by SQLJ Part 0.

These result sets are dynamic in nature. Two invocations of the same procedure could result in the return of different numbers of result sets or the same number of result sets with different columns in each. The procedure in Example 5.13 shows how multiple result sets may be generated (this example uses a Sybase Adaptive Server Anywhere extension to SQL that is found in several products to generate the result set capability).

EXAMPLE 5.13 A PROCEDURE THAT RETURNS MULTIPLE RESULT SETS.

```
CREATE PROCEDURE picture_and_director (year_pattern VARCHAR(10))
BEGIN
   SELECT  title
   FROM    awards
   WHERE   award = 'Picture'
     AND   award_year LIKE year_pattern;

   SELECT   title
   FROM     awards
   WHERE    award = 'Director'
     AND    award_year LIKE year_pattern;
end
```

SQLJ Part 0 allows an application to deal with these result sets by "escaping" to JDBC, as can be seen in Example 5.14.

EXAMPLE 5.14 ESCAPING TO JDBC TO PROCESS MULTIPLE RESULT SETS.

```
ExecutionContext ectxt = new ExecutionContext();

#sql [ectxt] { CALL picture_and_director (:in (argv[2])) };

ResultSet rs;
while ((rs = ectxt.getNextResultSet()) != null) {
   while (rs.next()) {
      System.out.println (rs.getString(1));
   }
   System.out.println();
}
```

`ResultSet`, you may recall, is the JDBC interface that allows an application to process result sets. Once the procedure has been executed, the `getNextResultSet` method is used to navigate through them. In this example, the first column of the rows of each result set are retrieved and printed. If a result set is open when `getNextResultSet` is invoked, then it will be closed and the next result set will be returned. When there are no more result sets, `getNextResultSet` will return null.

If a stored procedure generates result sets, then you should use the `getNextResultSet` method to iterate through all of them. The execution context used to execute the procedure call cannot be used to execute another SQL statement until `getNextResultSet` has returned a null value.

5.3.8 Other SQLJ Part 0 Statements

We've shown examples of the execution of the SELECT statement, DELETE statement, positioned UPDATE statement, and of the invocation of stored procedures and functions. This is certainly not all that SQLJ Part 0 can do. All of the executable statements of Entry SQL-92 can be used in SQLJ Part 0, including the familiar DML and DDL statements and transaction management statements such as SET TRANSACTION, COMMIT, and ROLLBACK. As you probably expect by now, all SQL statements that JDBC supports can be used in SQLJ Part 0.

SQLJ Part 0 supports the SQL/PSM compound statement (BEGIN/END) and the SQL/PSM assignment statement. These statements are shown in Example 5.15 and Example 5.16.

EXAMPLE 5.15 USING SQLJ PART 0 TO EXECUTE A BEGIN/END STATEMENT.

```
#sql  { BEGIN
            DELETE   movies
            WHERE    year_introduced < '1960';

            DELETE   awards
            WHERE    award_year < '1960';
        END
      };
```

EXAMPLE 5.16 USING SQLJ PART 0 TO EXECUTE A SET STATEMENT.

```
int n = 0;

#sql  { SET :n = ( SELECT  COUNT(*)
                   FROM    movies )
      };

System.out.println (n + " total rows in the movies table.");
```

5.4 SQLJ Part 0/JDBC Interoperability

As we have stated more than once, JDBC was designed to process dynamic SQL statements, and SQLJ Part 0 was designed to process static SQL statements. Clearly, there are some applications that will need to do both types of processing. SQLJ Part 0 provides interoperability between itself and JDBC through the use of connection contexts and result set iterators.

A connection context may be created using a URL, as we showed earlier, or it may be created by specifying a JDBC connection. Going the other way, the `getConnection` method may be applied to a connection context in order to obtain the JDBC connection that it is using.

In either of these ways, you can execute static and dynamic statements in the same session and transaction context. If you are using this strategy in one of your applications, then you should be careful when you close the connection context. The `close` method allows you to keep or close the underlying JDBC connection, depending on your application's needs.

An SQLJ Part 0 iterator may be created from a JDBC result set with the SQLJ Part 0 CAST statement (be sure not to confuse this SQLJ Part 0 statement with SQL-92's CAST expression!). We show the use of this statement in Example 5.17.

Going the other way, the `getResultSet` method may be applied to an SQLJ Part 0 iterator, returning the JDBC result set associated with the iterator, as shown in Example 5.18.

In order to guarantee portability of your application, you should issue the `getResultSet` method before the first invocation of a `next` method on the iterator. All operations should then be performed on the result set, and *not* on the iterator.

If your application requires a JDBC result set from the result of a query, and it is not going to process the result of the query with either a named iterator or a positioned iterator, then it can avoid the unneeded declarations by using an *untyped iterator.* This process is shown in Example 5.19.

5.5 Using SQLJ Part 0 Inside a Database

SQLJ Part 1 and Part 2, which we'll discuss in the next several chapters, will allow Java programs to be executed within a DBMS. These Java programs can access the database that invoked them using JDBC or using SQLJ Part 0. But what connection context should the SQLJ Part 0 application use?

If the SQLJ Part 0 application establishes its own connection context (a capability that a DBMS vendor might not support), then it may operate in a session and transaction different from that of its

EXAMPLE 5.17 CREATING AN SQLJ PART 0 ITERATOR FROM A JDBC RESULT SET.

```
#sql public iterator AwardsIter (String title);

...

String query =    "SELECT DISTINCT title "
               + "FROM     awards "
               + "WHERE    award_year "
               + "             BETWEEN ? AND ?";

PreparedStatement ps
   = defCtxt.getConnection().prepareStatement(query);
ps.setString(1, argv[2]);
ps.setString(2, argv[3]);
ResultSet rs = ps.executeQuery();

AwardsIter awards;

#sql awards = { CAST :rs };

while (awards.next()) {
   System.out.println (awards.title());
}
```

EXAMPLE 5.18 CREATING A JDBC RESULT SET FROM AN SQLJ PART 0 ITERATOR.

```
#sql iterator Awards (String title);

...

Awards awards;

#sql awards = { SELECT DISTINCT title
                FROM     awards
                WHERE    award_year
                             BETWEEN :(argv[2]) AND :(argv[3])
              };

ResultSet rs = awards.getResultSet();
while (rs.next()) {
   System.out.println (rs.getString(1));
}
```

EXAMPLE 5.19 CREATING A JDBC RESULT SET FROM AN UNTYPED ITERATOR.

```
ResultSetIterator awards;

#sql awards = { SELECT DISTINCT title
                FROM     awards
                WHERE    award_year
                             BETWEEN :(argv[2]) AND :(argv[3])
              };

ResultSet rs = awards.getResultSet();
while (rs.next()) {
   System.out.println (rs.getString(1));
}
```

invoker. The SQLJ Part 0 application can use the `ConnectionContext.getDefaultContext` method to determine whether a connection context is being provided to it. If a connection context is returned, then it can be used to share the session and transaction context of its invoker. If this method returns a null value, then the application knows that it must establish its own connection context.

5.6 SQLJ Part 0 Translator

Now that we've discussed how to write SQLJ Part 0 applications, let's look at the operation of an SQLJ Translator in more detail. In this section, we'll discuss the SQLJ Part 0 Translators in the abstract. You may acquire an SQLJ Part 0 Translator from some vendor as a stand-alone tool, or you might find that an SQLJ Part 0 Translator has been included in your Java interactive development environment (IDE). You might choose to use the Oracle SQLJ Part 0 reference implementation, which we will discuss in Section 5.8.

The SQLJ Part 0 Translator takes as input your source file, which typically has a `.sqlj` extension. The SQLJ Part 0 Translator may provide *on-line checking,* which allows you to provide an *exemplar* database to be used to validate the SQL statements that are embedded in your SQLJ Part 0 source program. This exemplar database may be the target database of your application, or it may be another database with the same schema. On-line checking can notify you of several types of errors:

- whether a table or column name has been misspelled
- whether a procedure has been called with the wrong number of arguments
- whether an SQL keyword is used in the wrong place
- whether the data types of two operands of a comparison predicate are not comparable
- whether the data types of result set columns and named iterator columns are not comparable
- whether the data types of result set columns and Java variables in a FETCH statement are not comparable (this item is relevant only for positioned iterators)

The SQLJ Part 0 Translator may provide *off-line checking,* which checks the syntax of your SQL statements without actually going to a database for its metadata. This type of checking can catch the incorrectly placed SQL keyword mentioned above, but the other errors would not be caught until runtime.

An SQLJ Part 0 Translator that provides on-line checking will allow you to use any extensions that the vendor of the exemplar database provides. This use could be problematic if application portability is your goal. If your SQLJ Part 0 Translator provides off-line checking, then you should know which SQL dialect is being checked. It is possible that your SQLJ Part 0 Translator will give you a choice of which SQL dialect the off-line checking should use.

If the SQLJ Part 0 Translator runs successfully, then it produces a Java program, along with one or more additional files. The Java program can now be compiled and executed normally. This process can be seen in Figure 5.1.

Your SQLJ Part 0 Translator will provide several runtime classes that will supplement your own classes. The `sqlj.runtime` package is used by your SQLJ Part 0 program. The `sqlj.runtime.profile` package provides infrastructure for the application, but is not called directly by your SQLJ Part 0 program.

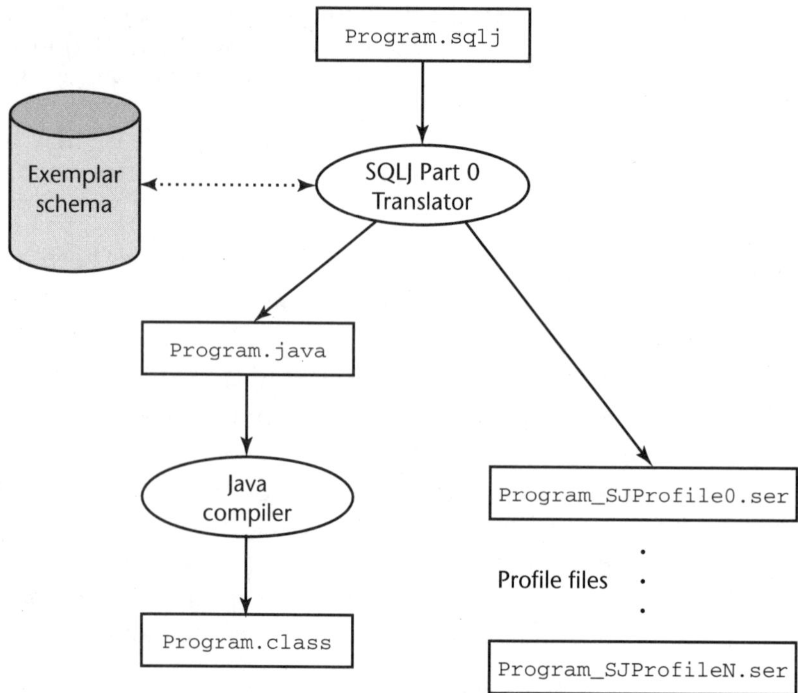

FIGURE 5.1 *SQLJ Part 0 translation process.*

5.6.1 Binary Portability

Java programs are independent of the hardware platform on which they run. The JDBC API allows applications to be written that are independent of the DBMS that will be used at execution time. With a Type 4 JDBC driver, which is written completely in Java, a Java application that executes dynamic SQL statements is extremely portable.

In comparison to JDBC, SQLJ Part 0 provides an additional level of independence from the DBMS. As SQLJ Part 0 programs are turned into pure Java, they can run anywhere that a Java Virtual Machine exists. A SQLJ Part 0 Translator generates Java code that contains invocations of a JDBC-like API for the SQL statements it contains. It also provides a default customization, which in most cases will implement calls to this JDBC-like API by directly invoking JDBC methods. This capability means that a single SQLJ Part 0 application could be run against multiple DBMSs, which provides a degree of portability equal to that of JDBC.

The SQL statements that have been processed by a SQLJ Part 0 Translator are accessible to a vendor-specific *customizer.* This customizer might, for example, implement some of the JDBC-like API method invocations with code that creates and then executes stored procedures that contain the application's original SQL statements (using a JDBC API). It could even be smart enough to install the stored procedures the first time it is run on a specific database and skip that step for subsequent sessions. This generated code will become part of the SQLJ Part 0 application. At runtime, if a customization for the connected DBMS exists, then the code generated by that customizer will be used. If no such customization is found, then the default customization will be used. This process has the happy benefit of allowing applications that are normally intended to run on one vendor's SQL implementation to run more efficiently there, without inhibiting its ability to be run on other platforms when required.

It is possible that a vendor's customizer will go even further and implement the calls to the JDBC-like API using its own API, leaving JDBC out of the picture. In this case, interoperability between SQLJ Part 0 and JDBC may be impaired. The SQLJ Part 0 specification acknowledges that some of these operations, such as the `ResultSetIterator.getResultSet` method, may raise exceptions if they are not supported. Other operations, such as creating a connection context using a JDBC connection, do not have this same type of acknowledgment. We believe that there is some room for interpretation on whether support of any of these operations is actually required. We recommend that you consult your vendor's documentation if your application requires this type of interoperability.

An SQLJ Part 0 application could be generated, customized for several popular DBMSs, and then distributed to customers. If a customer's DBMS is one of those for which the application was customized, then it may gain a performance boost. If the customer's DBMS was not one of those for which the application was customized, then it will run with the default customizer, which almost always uses JDBC. As we said, SQLJ Part 0 provides a level of portability that is greater than that of JDBC.

5.6.2 Customization of an SQLJ Part 0 Application

Let's look a bit more closely at the process of customization. We mentioned that, when the SQLJ Part 0 Translator ran successfully, it produced Java programs and one or more additional files. These additional files are called *profile files*. For each connection context within each source program, a separate profile file is produced. This profile file contains a complete description of the SQL statement within each and every executable SQLJ Part 0 statement. The profile file also contains the default JDBC customization we discussed in Section 5.6.1.

A profile file contains a number of Java instances to represent all of this information. The file itself may be a serialization of these objects, or it may be a class file that contains the objects as static variables.

Profile files are named in the following way:

```
[package].program_SJProfileN.ser
```

or

```
[package].program_SJProfileN.class
```

where *N* is an integer that begins at 0 and increments for each additional profile file.

All of the files comprising an SQLJ Part 0 application may be placed in a JAR file. The SQLJ Part 0 profile section of the manifest has the following entry:

```
Name: [path]/program_SJProfileN.ser
SQLJProfile: TRUE
```

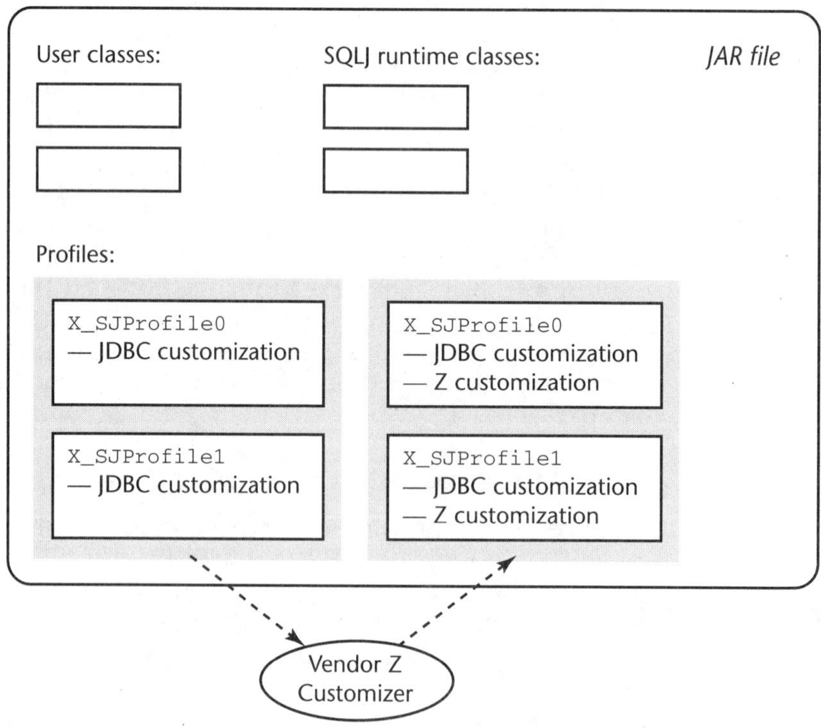

FIGURE 5.2 *SQLJ Part 0 customization process.*

or

```
Name: [path]/program_SJProfileN.class
SQLJProfile: TRUE
```

An SQLJ Part 0 Customizer is able to examine each profile in a JAR file. For each SQL statement, it can create new customization objects and add them to the profile. This process can be seen in Figure 5.2.

5.6.3 Execution of Your SQLJ Part 0 Application

Putting all of these pieces together, we have an execution environment like the one shown in Figure 5.3.

All of these pieces are Java code (actually, the JDBC driver may or may not be 100% Java, depending on which type it is). As such, the application can be run in applets, Java clients, middle-tier application servers, or, in conjunction with the other parts of SQLJ, in the database itself. The use of SQLJ Part 0 does not change the options you would have had if you had remained with JDBC.

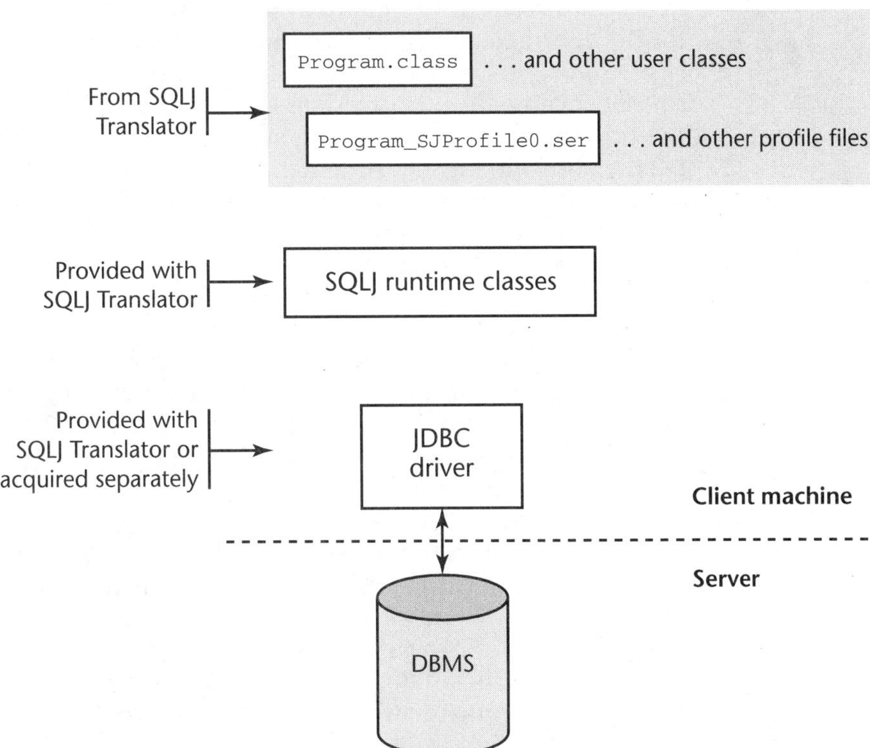

FIGURE 5.3 *SQLJ Part 0 application execution environment.*

5.7 Levels of Conformance

An SQLJ Part 0 implementation is *specification conformant* if it supports the syntax and semantics specified in SQL/OLB, supports JDBC 1.2 or higher, and supports the SQL language specified in JDBC 1.2. An SQLJ Part 0 implementation is *Core SQLJ conformant* if it meets the above requirements, with the exception of a small number of features including the following:

- calls to stored procedures and functions
- Execution context attributes (`MaxFieldSize`, `MaxRows`, and `QueryTimeout`)
- `getResultSet` and `getJDBCResultSet` methods
- SQL BEGIN/END statements

5.8 SQLJ Part 0 Reference Implementation Translator

Oracle, when it introduced SQLJ Part 0 to the SQLJ group, also made available a reference implementation of this technology, which can be found at Oracle's Web site (*www.oracle.com*) or at the SQLJ Web site (*www.sqlj.org*). This reference implementation is itself written in Java, so that it can be run on any platform that supports a JVM. It is vendor neutral. It provides an on-line syntax checker that uses a JDBC connection to validate SQL statements and an off-line checker that can be invoked if a JDBC connection is not available. The offline checker is implemented by a well-defined Java class, so that vendors of DBMSs can write an off-line checker for their own dialects of SQL.

The reference implementation is well documented and very full featured. The correspondence between connection contexts and schemas can be provided in a properties file, or on the command line. The reference implementation will translate your SQLJ Part 0 files and can automatically invoke your Java compiler on the resulting Java source files. All of the examples in this chapter have been developed using this reference implementation.

This reference implementation provides a default customization that uses JDBC. Vendors may write their own customizers to work with this SQLJ Part 0 Translator—in fact, we know of several that are doing so. Some of these will modify the SQL that is executed, while continuing to use JDBC, and others will use their own API. With the extensibility that Oracle has provided in their implementation of the SQLJ Part 0 Translator, it is unclear whether many vendors will see a need to implement their own Translator.

5.9 Products Supporting SQLJ Part 0

As this book is being written, products are just beginning to come to market that support SQLJ Part 0. Though we have not had the opportunity to try these products, we still thought them worthy of brief mention.

Oracle provides its own SQLJ Part 0 Translator. Oracle has included support for SQLJ Part 0 in its JDeveloper Java programming tool and in Oracle 8i. Java programs with SQLJ Part 0 statements can be stored in the database with the CREATE OR REPLACE JAVA SOURCE statement. The SQLJ Part 0 code included in the statement will be automatically translated and then compiled.

IBM supports SQLJ Part 0 in DB2 Universal Database (Version 5), DB2 Common Server (Version 2), and DB2 for OS/390. IBM provides its own SQLJ Part 0 Translator, a Customizer, and utilities such as a profile printer.

5.10 Advantages of SQLJ Part 0

In an earlier chapter, we discussed JDBC and indicated that it was designed to process dynamic SQL statements. What then are the advantages of using SQLJ Part 0 rather than JDBC for static SQL statements?

- SQLJ Part 0 supports translator-time validity checking. With JDBC, there is no checking of SQL statements until the application is run.
- SQLJ Part 0 statements and programs are generally shorter and more easily read (and written!) than their JDBC equivalents.
- SQLJ Part 0 allows a DBMS vendor to offer tools to customize the SQLJ Part 0 application, optimizing it in ways that would be impractical for a JDBC application.

5.11 SQLJ Part 0 Runtime Interfaces and Classes

The following interfaces and classes are defined in the `sqlj.runtime` package. This package contains some interfaces, classes, and methods that are provided for the implementers of SQLJ Part 0 Translators. We do not expect that these interfaces, classes, and methods will be used in applications, and so we have not described them in this section. The `sqlj.runtime.profile` package is defined in the SQL/OLB specification. (This package and its components are also not described in this section for the reason we just provided.)

5.11.1 `sqlj.runtime.AsciiStream`

```
public class AsciiStream
   extends StreamWrapper
```

Constructors

```
public AsciiStream (InputStream in)
```

Create an `AsciiStream` without a specified length. The `StreamWrapper.setLength` method must be invoked before this object can be used as the value of an input host variable.

```
public AsciiStream (InputStream in, int length)
```

Create an `AsciiStream` with a specified length. This object can be used as the value of an input host variable.

5.11.2 `sqlj.runtime.BinaryStream`

```
public class BinaryStream
   extends StreamWrapper
```

Constructors

```
public BinaryStream (InputStream in)
```

Create a `BinaryStream` without a specified length. The `StreamWrapper.setLength` method must be invoked before this object can be used as the value of an input host variable.

```
public BinaryStream (InputStream in, int length)
```

Create a `BinaryStream` with a specified length. This object can be used as the value of an input host variable.

5.11.3 `sqlj.runtime.ConnectionContext`

```
public interface ConnectionContext
```

The `sqlj.runtime.ConnectionContext` interface defines the following variables and methods. This interface is used when a `ConnectionContext` class is generated by an SQLJ Part 0 connection context declaration.

Variables

`public static final boolean CLOSE_CONNECTION`

`public static final boolean KEEP_CONNECTION`

Methods

`public void close () throws SQLException`

Closes all resources used by this object and closes the underlying JDBC connection.

`public void close (boolean) throws SQLException`

Closes all resources used by this object. If `CLOSE_CONNECTION` is passed as an argument, then the JDBC connection is closed. If `KEEP_CONNECTION` is passed as an argument, then the JDBC connection is not closed.

`public java.sql.Connection getConnection()`

Returns the underlying JDBC connection.

`public ExecutionContext getExecutionContext()`

Returns the default execution context for this connection.

`public boolean isClosed()`

Returns true if this connection context has been closed; returns false otherwise.

5.11.4 `sqlj.runtime.ExecutionContext`

`public class ExecutionContext`

Variables

`public static final int EXCEPTION_COUNT`

Value returned by `getUpdateCount` to indicate that there is no valid value to return. This might be because the previous statement raised an exception, or because no statement was previously executed.

`public static final int QUERY_COUNT`

Value returned by `getQueryCount` to indicate that there is no valid value to return. This might be because the last execution produced a result set or an iterator.

Constructors

`public ExecutionContext()`

Constructor for the `ExecutionContext` class.

Methods

`public cancel () throws SQLException`

Cancels an SQL operation. This method can be issued by one thread to cancel an SQL operation that is executing in another thread. An `SQLException` may be thrown if the SQL operation cannot be canceled.

`public int getMaxFieldSize()`

Returns the value of the MaxFieldSize attribute. Zero indicates that the field size is unlimited. For further information, see `setMaxFieldSize`.

`public int getMaxRows()`

Returns the value of the MaxRows attribute. Zero indicates that the maximum number of rows is unlimited. For further information, see `setMaxRows`.

`public java.sql.ResultSet getNextResultSet() throws SQLException`

The first time this method is called after the execution of an SQL statement, it returns the first result set that the statement produced. Null is returned if it did not produce any result set, or if no statement had previously been executed.

Subsequent calls to the method will close the current result set, if it is still open, and return the next result set. Null is returned if there are no more result sets to return.

The SQL statement might also be returning update counts. These are not visible from SQLJ Part 0. If the last SQL statement produced result sets, then this execution context cannot be used to execute another statement until this method has been used to traverse all of the result sets and a null is returned.

`public int getQueryTimeout()`

Returns the value of the QueryTimeout attribute. Zero indicates that the query will not timeout. For further information, see `setQueryTimeout`.

`public int getUpdateCount()`

Returns the number of rows updated by the last SQL statement executed using this context. Zero is returned if the SQL statement was not a DML statement. `QUERY_COUNT` is returned if the last SQL statement produced an iterator or a result set. `EXCEPTION_COUNT` is returned if the last SQL statement raised an exception condition, or no SQL statement has yet been executed.

`public java.sql.SQLWarning getWarnings()`

Returns the first warning reported by the last SQL statement executed using this context. If no warnings were reported, then null is returned. Subsequent warnings for this statement, if they exist, can be found with the `SQLWarning.getNextWarning` method. Note: Warnings raised during the use of an iterator are accessed from the iterator itself.

`public void setMaxFieldSize(int max)`

Sets the maximum field size (in bytes) for the amount of data returned for any column or out parameter. This method applies only to columns and parameters that are BINARY, VARBINARY, CHARACTER, VARCHAR, and LONGVARCHAR.

If a value that exceeds this limit is passed, then the excess bytes are silently discarded. Zero indicates that the maximum field size is unlimited. This value is the default for an execution context. If a DBMS does not support this feature and the maximum field size is set to a value other than its default, then at the time that an SQL statement with this context is executed an `SQLException` will be thrown.

`public void setMaxRows(int max)`

Sets the maximum number of rows that will be returned by an SQLJ Part 0 iterator or a JDBC result set. If this limit is exceeded, then any additional rows will be silently dropped. Zero indicates that the maximum number of rows is unlimited. This value is the default for an execution context. If a DBMS does not support this feature and the maximum number of rows is set to a value other than its default, then at the time that an SQL statement with this context is executed an `SQLException` will be thrown.

`public void setQueryTimeout(int seconds)`

Sets the time (in seconds) that an SQL statement is allowed to execute before it times out. Zero indicates that the time an SQL statement may execute is unlimited. This value is the default for an execution context. If a DBMS does not support this feature and the time an SQL statement may execute is set to a value other than its default, then at the time that an SQL statement with this context is executed an `SQLException` will be thrown.

5.11.5 `sqlj.runtime.ForUpdate`

```
public interface ForUpdate
```

This interface is specified by iterators that are intended to be used by positioned UPDATE or DELETE statements.

Methods

```
public String getCursorName() throws SQLException
```

Returns the name of the SQL cursor used by this iterator.

5.11.6 `sqlj.runtime.NamedIterator`

```
public interface NamedIterator
   extends ResultSetIterator
```

This interface is implemented by all named iterators.

5.11.7 `sqlj.runtime.PositionedIterator`

```
public interface PositionedIterator
   extends ResultSetIterator
```

This interface is implemented by all positioned iterators.

Methods

```
public boolean endFetch() throws SQLException
```

Returns true if the last execution of the FETCH statement had no more rows to fetch, or if FETCH has not yet been executed; otherwise false is returned.

5.11.8 `sqlj.runtime.ResultSetIterator`

```
public interface ResultSetIterator
```

The `sqlj.runtime.ResultSetIterator` interface defines the following variables and methods.

Variables

`public static final int ASENSITIVE`

Indicates that the iterator is to use an asensitive cursor. An asensitive cursor may provide sensitive behavior, insensitive behavior, or a mix of the two.

`public static final int INSENSITIVE`

Indicates that the iterator is to use an insensitive cursor. An insensitive cursor, after it has been opened, will not reflect changes that have been made to the database by other transactions or by other operations within this transaction.

`public static final int SENSITIVE`

Indicates that the iterator is to use a sensitive cursor. A sensitive cursor, after it has been opened, will reflect changes that have been made to the database by other transactions (if the isolation level of the transaction permits this) or by other operations within this transaction.

Methods

`public void clearWarnings() throws SQLException`

Discards any `SQLWarning` instances that might have been reported during the use of this iterator. Immediately after invoking this method, `getWarnings` will return null.

`public void close() throws SQLException`

Closes the iterator object and returns all of its resources. It is recommended that iterators be explicitly closed, rather than waiting for resources to be freed by the garbage collector.

`public java.sql.ResultSet getResultSet() throws SQLException`

Returns the JDBC result set associated with this iterator. An exception may be thrown if this operation is not supported (this is possible if a customization is not using JDBC in its implementation). For maximum application portability, it is recommended that this method be invoked before the `next` method is invoked and that all further access to the result set be through JDBC methods and not through the iterator.

```
public java.sql.SQLWarning getWarnings() throws SQLException
```

Returns the first warning reported by the use of the iterator. If no warnings were reported, then null is returned. Subsequent warnings for this iterator, if they exist, can be found with the `SQLWarning.getNextWarning` method. Note: Only warnings raised during the use of an iterator are reported here. Warnings associated with other parts of the statement are reported via the execution context.

```
public void isClosed() throws SQLException
```

Returns true if this iterator has already been closed; otherwise, false is returned.

```
public void next() throws SQLException
```

Advances this iterator to the next row (when it was created, the iterator was positioned before the first row). Returns true if there was a next row; otherwise, false is returned.

5.11.9 `sqlj.runtime.StreamWrapper`

```
public class StreamWrapper
   extends java.io.FilterInputStream
```

Constructors

```
public StreamWrapper (InputStream in)
```

Create a `StreamWrapper` without a specified length. The `setLength` method must be invoked before this object can be used as the value of an input host variable.

```
public StreamWrapper (InputStream in, int length)
```

Create a `StreamWrapper` with a specified length. This object can be used as the value of an input host variable.

Methods

```
public java.io.InputStream getInputStream()
```

Return the `InputStream` on which this object is based.

```
public int getLength()
```

Return the length of this object.

```
public void setLength (int length)
```

Set the length of this object.

5.11.10 `sqlj.runtime.UnicodeStream`

```
public class UnicodeStream
   extends StreamWrapper
```

Constructors

`public UnicodeStream (InputStream in)`

Create a `UnicodeStream` without a specified length. The `StreamWrapper.setLength` method must be invoked before this object can be used as the value of an input host variable.

`public UnicodeStream (InputStream in, int length)`

Create a `UnicodeStream` with a specified length. This object can be used as the value of an input host variable.

5.11.11 `sqlj.runtime.SQLNullException`

```
public class SQLNullException
   extends SQLException
```

Constructor

`public SQLNullException()`

Creates a new `SQLNullException` object. The SQLSTATE value is initialized to `'22002'`.

5.12 SQLJ Part 0 Exceptions

SQL/OLB defines some additional SQLSTATE values, in addition to those defined in SQL-92. These new SQLSTATE values are shown in Table 5.3.

Category	Condition	Class	Subcondition	Subclass
X	OLB-specific error	46	(no subclass)	000
			invalid class declaration	120
			invalid column name	121
			invalid number of columns	122
			invalid profile state	130
			unsupported feature	110

TABLE 5.3 *SQLSTATE values introduced by SQLJ Part 0.*

5.13 Chapter Summary

This has been a long chapter. We've shown you the complete SQLJ Part 0 language for embedding SQL statements in Java. We've discussed the statements that you will write and the classes that are generated on your behalf. We've covered the process of translating an SQLJ Part 0 application into Java, and we've discussed customizing an SQLJ Part 0 application for a particular vendor's DBMS.

SQLJ Part 0 provides an interesting alternative to JDBC when your application needs to execute static SQL statements. SQLJ Part 0 allows you to write less code, provides either on-line or off-line checking of your SQL statements at translation time, and allows for optimization against particular DBMSs. Perhaps the only downside to consider is that SQLJ Part 0 is still an emerging technology—support for it in Java development environments is a bit weak at present (but expected to grow quickly).

CHAPTER 6

SQLJ Part 1 (SQL Routines Using the Java™ Programming Language)

6.1 Introduction

In this chapter we're going to discuss SQLJ Part 1. SQLJ Part 1 allows you to bring Java code into the DBMS and use it to implement stored routines: procedures and functions. The naming of this part might suggest that there is some relationship with SQLJ Part 0. Other than the fact that the same group of companies worked on it, however, the two parts are quite separate.

SQLJ Part 1 was brought in to the SQLJ group of companies by Sybase, and the Sybase representative acted as its editor while the group made corrections and enhancements to it. In April 1999 it was submitted to NCITS for Fast Track processing, and in September 1999 it was adopted as NCITS 331.1-1999.[1]

Because SQLJ Part 1 enables an association to be created between Java methods and SQL routines, we will begin this chapter by reviewing SQL routines. We'll discuss how JAR files are brought into a database, how SQL routines are associated with Java methods, and how the JAR files in a database can be altered and dropped. Finally, we'll end the chapter by discussing a product that has begun to implement some of this technology.

---

1 ANSI NCITS 331.1:1999, *SQLJ—Part 1: SQL Routines Using the Java™ Programming Language*, 1999.

6.1.1 Review of SQL/PSM

This section will provide a very brief review of some of the features of SQL Part 4: Persistent Stored Modules (SQL/PSM). Jim Melton has, as you are probably aware, already written a very thorough treatment of this material.[2]

SQL-86 defined *externally-invoked procedures*—procedures that were defined in a client module and were called by a host language program. SQL/PSM:1996 introduced *SQL routines,* which are more commonly known as stored routines, or stored functions and stored procedures. A stored function, once it has been created, may be used as part of an expression in any SQL statement. The CALL statement was introduced so that stored procedures could be invoked. Example 6.1 shows a stored function that returns a string containing the number of asterisks specified by the input parameter.

EXAMPLE 6.1 AN SQL/PSM FUNCTION TO PRODUCE A RATING USING STARS.

```
CREATE FUNCTION stars (vote INTEGER) RETURNS VARCHAR(10)
   BEGIN
      DECLARE result VARCHAR(10);

      SET result = '';
      WHILE vote > 0 DO
         SET result = result || '*';
         SET vote = vote - 1;
      END WHILE;

      RETURN result;
   END
```

The `stars` function is used in Example 6.2 to more graphically see how much Jim liked certain movies. The result of Example 6.2 is shown in Result 6.1.

In the example above, we provided the body of the stored function with SQL statements, including the BEGIN/END statement and the WHILE statement. SQL/PSM also provides *external routines,* stored routines that are defined with a body that is external to SQL. Such a body

---

[2] *Understanding SQL's Stored Procedures: A Complete Guide to SQL/PSM,* Jim Melton, Morgan Kaufmann, 1998.

could be written in one of several host programming languages. Example 6.3 shows what this type of external function would look like. SQL/PSM is silent about contents of the string that is provided for the external name. In this example, the string provides an entry name within a dynamic-link library (DLL) file.

EXAMPLE 6.2 A QUERY THAT USES THE STARS FUNCTION.

```
SELECT  title, stars(vote) AS jim
FROM    votes
WHERE   voter = 'Jim'
  AND   title LIKE 'A%'
```

Result 6.1 The use of the stars function.

title	jim
A Fish Called Wanda	********
A Passage to India	********
A Room with a View	****
Amadeus	*******
An Officer and a Gentleman	********
Arthur	*****
As Good As It Gets	******

EXAMPLE 6.3 AN EXTERNAL FUNCTION THAT INVOKES A C VERSION OF STARS.

```
CREATE FUNCTION stars (vote INTEGER) RETURNS VARCHAR(10)
LANGUAGE c
EXTERNAL NAME 'stars@util.dll'
PARAMETER STYLE GENERAL
```

There is one feature in SQL/PSM that is unique to stored procedures—OUT and INOUT parameters. SQL/PSM requires stored functions to have only IN parameters. For IN and INOUT parameters, the value of the user's argument is copied into the routine's parameter when the routine is invoked. For OUT and INOUT parameters, when the procedure finishes the value of these parameters is copied into the variables and parameters that the user specified. Example 6.4 shows the use of output parameters.

We've provided the syntax for SQL:1999 Routines in Appendix D.

EXAMPLE 6.4 AN SQL/PSM PROCEDURE WITH AN OUT PARAMETER.

```
CREATE PROCEDURE stars_proc (IN rating INTEGER,
                             OUT result VARCHAR (10))
  BEGIN
    SET result = stars (rating);
  END
```

Routine Characteristics

When you create a routine, you may provide values for several characteristics of the routine's behavior. In this section, we will discuss them one by one. These characteristics may be provided for stored routines that have an SQL body and for routines that have an external body.

The author of a function may state that the function is `DETERMINISTIC` or `NOT DETERMINISTIC`. By stating that the function is deterministic, the author is saying that every time the function is called with a specific combination of input arguments, the result will be the same (for a given state of the database). This condition allows a query optimizer to cache results of the function if it is going to be called many times in the execution of a statement and reduce the number of times the function is actually executed. A function that calculates a 10% raise, given a particular salary as input, would be deterministic. A function that returns the average salary of three randomly chosen employees would be nondeterministic.

For both stored procedures and stored functions, the routine creator may specify one of the following indications of how the routine accesses SQL data:

`NO SQL`	The routine may not execute any SQL statements.
`CONTAINS SQL`	The routine may execute a limited set of SQL statements (those that do not access the database).
`READS SQL DATA`	The routine may execute SQL statements that read data (e.g., the SELECT statement or fetching data via a cursor).
`MODIFIES SQL DATA`	The routine may execute SQL statements that modify data, such as the INSERT, UPDATE, and DELETE statements.

In Example 6.5, we have modified our stored function to explicitly provide these attributes.

EXAMPLE 6.5 AN SQL/PSM PROCEDURE WITH EXPLICIT ATTRIBUTES.

```
CREATE FUNCTION stars (vote INTEGER) RETURNS VARCHAR(10)
   LANGUAGE SQL
   DETERMINISTIC
   CONTAINS SQL

   BEGIN
      ...
   END
```

SQL:1999 introduced the ability for a stored procedure to return result sets—something that relational products have long been able to do. At the time the procedure is created, the author may specify whether result sets will be returned and, if so, the maximum number of these result sets. This can be seen in Example 6.6.

EXAMPLE 6.6 AN SQL/PSM PROCEDURE WITH DYNAMIC RESULT SETS SPECIFIED.

```
CREATE PROCEDURE dynresultsets (IN person VARCHAR (10))
   DYNAMIC RESULT SETS 1
   BEGIN
      DECLARE c1 CURSOR WITH RETURN FOR
         SELECT    vote, COUNT(*) AS "COUNT"
         FROM      votes
         WHERE     voter = person
         GROUP BY  vote
         ORDER BY  vote;

      OPEN c1;
   END
```

SQL:1999 also introduced the ability for the author of a stored function to specify the behavior of the function when one or more of the arguments are the null value. The choices are as follows:

`RETURNS NULL ON NULL INPUT`	When one or more of the function arguments are the null value, the function is not executed and the null value is returned automatically.
`CALLED ON NULL INPUT`	The function is executed normally, even when one or more of the arguments is the null value. It is possible that an external function cannot be passed a null value, in which case an exception will be raised.

The `stars` function that we introduced in Example 6.3 would return an error if it was provided with a null input because `PARAMETER STYLE GENERAL` tells SQL to provide a `long` value to the C function, and there is no mechanism to pass the null value. Example 6.7 shows how `stars` could be written to return the null value in this case.

EXAMPLE 6.7 AN EXTERNAL FUNCTION THAT CAN RETURN NULL VALUES.

```
CREATE FUNCTION stars (vote INTEGER) RETURNS VARCHAR(10)
LANGUAGE c
RETURNS NULL ON NULL INPUT
EXTERNAL NAME 'stars@util.dll'
PARAMETER STYLE GENERAL
```

As an aside, `PARAMETER STYLE SQL` could be used to pass the C function additional arguments, one of which would indicate the occurrence of the null value by taking the role of an indicator parameter. This strategy would, of course, require that the C function be written to expect these additional arguments.

Now that we have reviewed this material, we can move on to our discussion of SQLJ Part 1. We'll use what we've learned here very shortly.

6.2 Installing JAR Files in SQL

In order to use SQLJ Part 1, the very first thing that we will need to do is to make our database aware of our JAR file, which contains our Java classes. We do this with the `install_jar` procedure, as follows:

```
CALL sqlj.install_jar ('file:///c:/Cinema.jar', 'cinema_jar', 0)
```

This procedure takes the JAR file specified by the URL in the first argument and gives it the SQL-style name within your database that is provided by the second argument. The final argument has to do with deployment descriptors, which we won't address until later in this chapter (Section 6.7).

The `install_jar` procedure has the following signature:

```
sqlj.install_jar (url IN VARCHAR(*), jar IN VARCHAR(*),
                  deploy IN INTEGER)
```

Although this has the form of an SQL procedure and is invoked as such, this statement is actually a DDL (data definition language) statement, just as the CREATE TABLE statement and the DROP COLUMN statement are. The purpose of this statement is to copy the JAR file into the database and to give it an SQL-style name for use in subsequent SQL statements. The form of this statement was chosen to make product implementation easier for vendors: A new schema, named `sqlj`, is required, but new keywords and statements are not required. The operation of the `install_jar` procedure can be seen in Figure 6.1.

Like some of the other DDL statements, the `install_jar` procedure will fail if the name chosen for the JAR file in SQL is already being used to name another JAR file. The JAR file name is an ordinary SQL three-part name (catalog part, schema part, and local part), and if

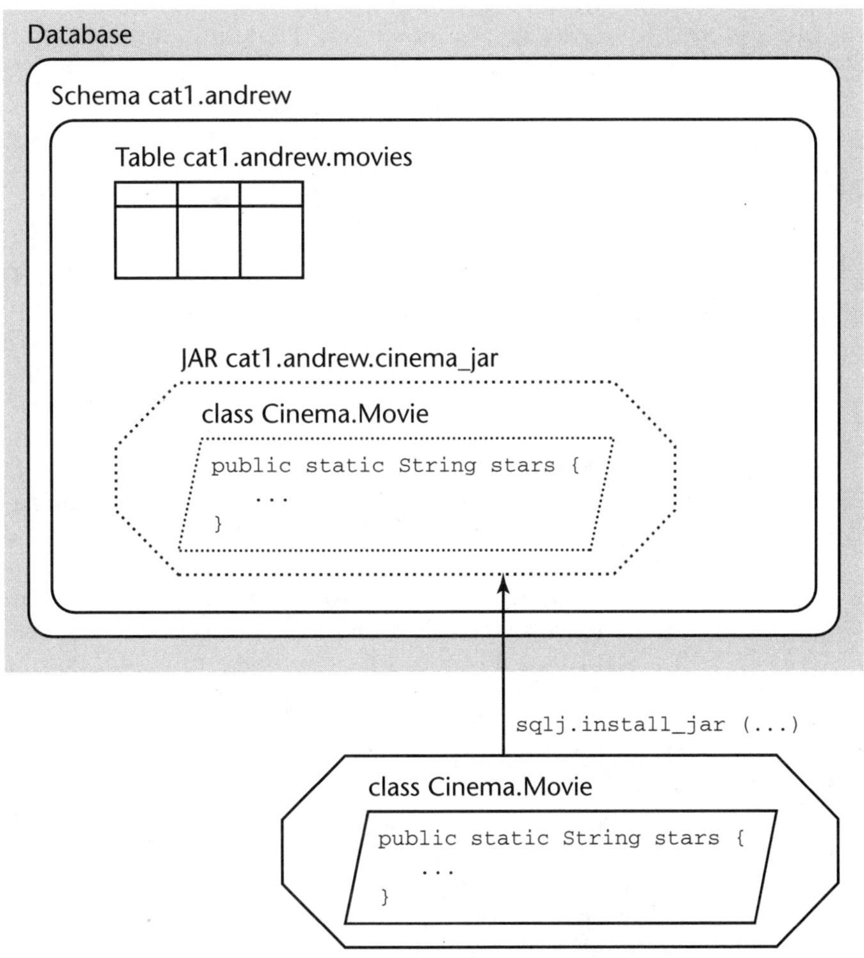

FIGURE 6.1 *JAR file installation.*

the catalog name or schema name are specified, then they must match the current catalog name or schema name. The string provided for the name of the JAR file is stripped of any leading or trailing blanks. Like all other SQL names, if the name is not a delimited identifier (in double quotes), then it is compared in a case-insensitive manner.

Also, as with other DDL statements, the current user becomes the owner of the JAR file and is given the grantable USAGE privilege on the JAR file.

There is one "gotcha" that we should mention, and this is as good a place to do so as any. The execution of the `install_jar` procedure may fail for any number of reasons, and an exception will be raised. The effect of such a statement is up to the vendor of the DBMS. It might have no effect at all, or it might complete some of its actions. This is very unlike most SQL DDL statements, which must have no effect on the database if an exception is raised. This behavior is shared by all of the DDL procedures that are introduced by SQLJ Part 1.

6.3 Creating Procedures and Functions

This is probably as good a time as any to say out loud what you've probably already surmised: to support SQLJ Part 1, a DBMS must have a Java Virtual Machine (JVM) associated with it. This JVM might be a general purpose JVM for the operating system on which the DBMS is running, or it might be a special purpose JVM provided by the DBMS vendor. This necessity certainly raises issues of performance and resource management, but these are beyond the scope of this book.

We've now reached the central design decision of SQLJ Part 1. We have SQL statements, and the DBMS runtime engine that executes them, a JVM, and classes that have been installed in a database. In SQLJ Part 1, we are concerned with static methods only; nonstatic methods are the province of SQLJ Part 2. How do we write statements that can bridge these two environments? One solution (not the solution chosen for SQLJ Part 1) would be to create new SQL syntax to allow Java methods to be directly invoked from expressions in a SELECT statement or a new form of the CALL statement that could be used in a BEGIN/END statement.

The solution that was chosen was to provide a new form of SQL's external routines, in which an SQL routine signature is defined, along with the information about which external piece of code is to be executed. New forms of the CREATE PROCEDURE and CREATE FUNCTION statements are provided, in which the usual SQL routine signature is specified, along with information on which Java method to invoke at execution time. The routines are called *Java routines*. By taking this approach, SQL's function and procedure invocation semantics are not changed. The invoker of one of these routines does not know—or does not need to know—whether the routine is an SQL routine, an external routine, or a Java routine.

6.3.1 Using a Method in an SQL Function

Example 6.8 allows us to consider the very simple case of a method in the `Cinema.Movie` class that reimplements the `stars` function that we saw in Example 6.1.

EXAMPLE 6.8 JAVA IMPLEMENTATION OF THE `stars` FUNCTION.

```
public static String stars2 (int rating) {
   String result = "";

   while (rating-- > 0) {
      result += "*";
   }

   return result;
}
```

Let us suppose that this class was placed in a JAR file, which was installed in a database with the name "`cinema_jar`". This method could be associated with an SQL function using the following statement:

```
CREATE FUNCTION stars2 (INTEGER) RETURNS VARCHAR(10)
EXTERNAL NAME 'cinema_jar:Cinema.Movie.stars2'
LANGUAGE JAVA
PARAMETER STYLE JAVA
```

The name of the Java method is specified using the *`jar name : class name`* format in the `EXTERNAL NAME` clause. This association can be seen in Figure 6.2.

Once the association is done, the function is invoked like any other function:

```
SELECT   title, stars2(vote)
FROM     votes
WHERE    voter = 'Jim'
```

This invocation could come from a JDBC statement or an SQLJ Part 0 statement in a client-side application, or it could come from a statement in a stored procedure.

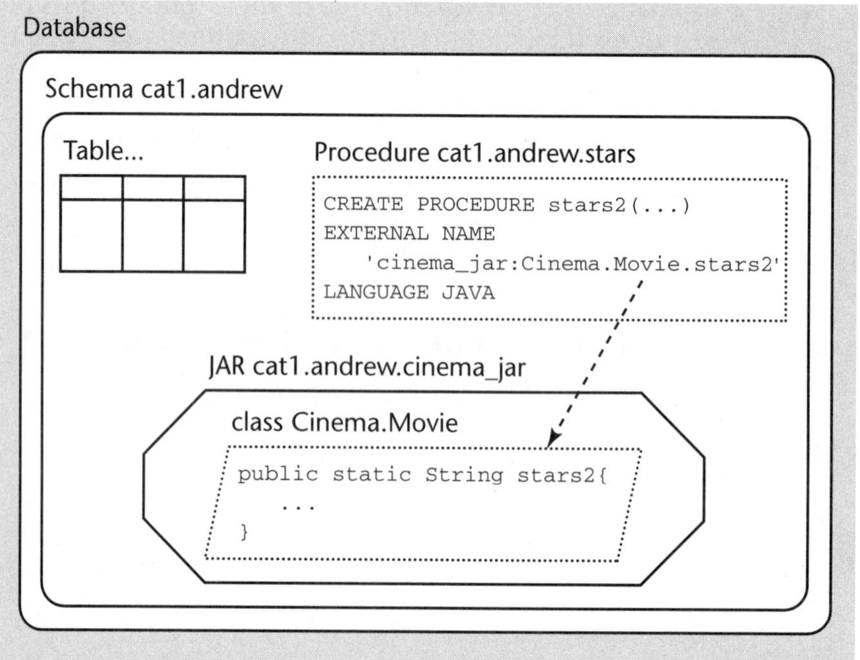

FIGURE 6.2 *Associating SQL routines with Java methods.*

Many of the characteristics that can be specified for SQL routines can also be specified for the Java routines. We have provided the complete syntax for the SQLJ Part 1 statements in Appendix F.

Not all static methods can be used as the basis for an SQL function. Since we are associating methods with SQL functions, there has to be a mapping from the return type of the SQL function to the return type of the method, and a mapping between each of the SQL function parameters and the method parameters. The specific data type mapping that is used is the one that is used by JDBC. Methods that have a return type of `void` cannot be used for SQL functions, but can be used for SQL procedures, as we'll see in the next section.

In our example, we did not specify the complete signature of the `Cinema.Movie.stars` method. Because we did not specify it, the signature was inferred from the SQL signature of the function. From the SQL INTEGER parameter, a Java `int` parameter type is inferred, so the complete Java signature that is inferred is `Cinema.Movie.stars(int)`. If we had a variant of the `stars` method that took an `Integer` parameter, then the Java signature would have to be spelled out in the CREATE FUNCTION statement. This can be seen in Example 6.9.

EXAMPLE 6.9 A JAVA FUNCTION DEFINED WITH AN EXPLICIT SIGNATURE.

```
public static String stars2 (Integer rating) {
   String result = "";
   int r;

   if (rating != null) {
      r = rating.intValue();
      while (r-- > 0) {
         result += "*";
      }
   }

   return result;
}

CREATE FUNCTION stars3 (INTEGER) RETURNS VARCHAR(10)
EXTERNAL NAME 'cinema_jar:Cinema.Movie.stars2 (Integer)'
LANGUAGE JAVA
PARAMETER STYLE JAVA
```

Mappable Data Types

Because SQLJ Part 1 (and SQLJ Part 2) relies so heavily on the mapping of SQL and Java data types, we'll take a moment to add some precision to this subject. An SQL data type and a Java data type are *mappable* if they are *simply mappable* (to a Java primitive type), *object mappable,* or *output mappable* (which will be discussed in Section 6.3.2). These mappings are shown in Table 6.1. We haven't really introduced new concepts with simply mappable or object mappable; they come to us straight from JDBC.

We can now restate the rule we gave in the last section for determining which SQL functions and Java methods may be associated. For an association to be made, each SQL parameter and its corresponding Java parameter must be mappable and the two return types must be mappable. This means that if we have defined a static method that returns `java.util.Hashtable`, then this method cannot be associated with an SQL function. No SQL return type can meet the requirement that the return types must be mappable. If a static method returns `int`, but has a parameter that is `Object[]`, then it too cannot be associated with an SQL function.

We need to be very clear on one issue here. Methods that are not suitable to be bound to an SQL routine are still available to Java methods that are Java routines. Once an SQL function call has begun the execution of a Java static method, that method has available to it

SQL data type	Simply mappable	Object mappable
CHARACTER	–	String
VARCHAR	–	String
LONGVARCHAR	–	String
NUMERIC	–	java.math.BigDecimal
DECIMAL	–	java.math.BigDecimal
BIT	boolean	Boolean
TINYINT	byte	Integer
SMALLINT	short	Integer
INTEGER	int	Integer
BIGINT	long	Long
REAL	float	Float
FLOAT	double	Double
DOUBLE PRECISION	double	Double
BINARY	–	byte[]
VARBINARY	–	byte[]
LONGVARBINARY	–	byte[]
DATE	–	java.sql.Date
TIME	–	java.sql.Time
TIMESTAMP	–	java.sql.Timestamp

TABLE 6.1 *Mappable SQL and Java data types.*

all of the richness of functionality that Java provides. The method we showed in Example 6.9 could be written to create and operate on objects of type `java.util.Hashtable`, if that is what its author wanted to do.

Executing SQL Statements

The Java methods that you define may need to execute SQL statements. An implementation of SQLJ Part 1 must support JDBC, providing the `java.sql` package. It must also support the use of the URL `jdbc:default:connection` in the `getConnection` method, which provides the *default connection.* This default connection provides access to the current session and transaction. The `AUTOCOMMIT` setting of this connection is false. Example 6.10 shows how we might determine whether a movie received any awards.

Example 6.10 uses JDBC to access the database from which the method was invoked. It is also possible to use SQLJ Part 0 to access the database (with an underlying JDBC driver), as we have shown in Example 6.11.

You might well ask, "Can I connect to a database other than the default database?" The answer we must give is that it is up to the implementor of the DBMS. The default connection is the only one that the implementor is required to support.

EXAMPLE 6.10 JAVA FUNCTION THAT RETURNS THE NUMBER OF AWARDS A MOVIE RECEIVED.

```
// Return the number of awards a movie has received

public static int countAwards (String title)
   throws SQLException {

   int n = 0;

   String stmt =    "SELECT   COUNT(*) "
                  + "FROM     awards "
                  + "WHERE    title = '" + title + "'";

   // Use the default connection

   Connection con = DriverManager.getConnection
                         ("jdbc:default:connection");

   ResultSet rs = con.createStatement().executeQuery(stmt);

   // Return the first column of the first row of the result

   rs.next();
   n = rs.getInt(1);
   rs.close();

   return n;
}


CREATE FUNCTION count_movie_awards (IN title VARCHAR (60))
   RETURNS INTEGER
EXTERNAL NAME 'cinema_jar:Cinema.Utility.countAwards'
LANGUAGE JAVA
PARAMETER STYLE JAVA
```

EXAMPLE 6.11 WRITING THE BODY OF A JAVA FUNCTION USING SQLJ PART 0.

```
import java.sql.*;
import sqlj.runtime.*;

#sql context sqlj1Context;

public class SQLJ1 {

   public static int countAwardsSqlj1 (String title)
      throws SQLException {

      // Use the default connection

      sqlj1Context ctxt
         = new sqlj1Context("jdbc:default:connection", false);

      int n = 0;

      #sql [ctxt] { SELECT   COUNT(*)
                    INTO     :n
                    FROM     awards
                    WHERE    title = :title
                  };

      return n;
   }

}
```

It is possible that you'd like to write Java methods that can operate either in an application or within a database, or both. You can do so by getting the value of the `sqlj.defaultconnection` property—if the execution is within a database, then the value will be `jdbc:default:connection`; otherwise it will be null. This test can be seen in the following code fragment:

```
String s = System.getProperty("sqlj.defaultconnection");
if (s == null) {
   s = "...";
}
```

With this same mechanism, your application can get the value of `sqlj.runtime`. This value will be the class name of an SQLJ runtime context class, which is a subclass of `sqlj.runtime.RuntimeContext`.

6.3.2 Using a Method in an SQL Procedure

We've shown how to create a correspondence between SQL input parameters and Java parameters. This is a straightforward process because Java uses a pass-by-value parameter passing mechanism. Because Java supports neither pass-by-reference parameter passing nor pointers, some amount of indirection is necessary to support SQL OUT and INOUT parameters. For an SQL OUT or INOUT parameter of some type *x*, the corresponding Java parameter must be an array of the Java type that corresponds to *x*. The first element of the array, located at array index 0, is used to pass the desired value to and from the Java method. Example 6.12 extends our `stars` example a bit further to show how this works.

EXAMPLE 6.12 A JAVA PROCEDURE WITH AN OUTPUT PARAMETER.

```
// Produce a string of stars, reflecting a 1-10 rating

public static void toStarsProc (int rating, String[] result) {
   String s = "";

   while (rating-- > 0) {
      s += "*";
   }

   result[0] = s;
}


CREATE PROCEDURE stars_proc2 (IN INTEGER, OUT VARCHAR(10))
EXTERNAL NAME 'cinema_jar:Cinema.Movie.toStarsProc'
LANGUAGE JAVA
PARAMETER STYLE JAVA
```

In this example, `toStarsProc` takes its input from the first parameter and places the result of the operation in the first element of the array that is passed in the second parameter. This second parameter is declared to be an SQL OUT parameter. We say that an SQL type is *output mappable* to an array of the Java types to which it is simply mappable or object mappable. In the example above, VARCHAR and `String[]` are output mappable.

In Example 6.13, `toStarsProc2` uses the first element of the array that is passed as input and then places the result of the operation in the same place. This single Java parameter is declared to be an SQL INOUT parameter.

EXAMPLE 6.13 A JAVA PROCEDURE WITH AN INPUT/OUTPUT PARAMETER.

```
// Produce a string of stars, reflecting a 1-10 rating.

public static void toStarsProc2 (String[] io)
   throws NumberFormatException {

   String s = "";
   int rating = Integer.parseInt(io[0]);

   while (rating-- > 0) {
      s += "*";
   }

   io[0] = s;
}
```

```
CREATE PROCEDURE stars_proc3 (INOUT VARCHAR(10))
EXTERNAL NAME 'cinema_jar:Cinema.Movie.toStarsProc2'
LANGUAGE JAVA
PARAMETER STYLE JAVA
```

In both of these examples, the OUT and INOUT parameters are treated normally by the SQL invoker of the procedures. The DBMS will automatically create the necessary array, populate the first element if it is being used as an INOUT parameter, invoke the Java method, and then use the value that is returned in the first element to set the invoker's variable or parameter. These SQL procedures can, of course, be invoked from host languages such as C or COBOL. They can also be invoked using JDBC or SQLJ Part 0. We'll use JDBC in Example 6.14.

EXAMPLE 6.14 INVOKING OUR JAVA PROCEDURE AND RETRIEVING THE VALUE IN THE OUTPUT PARAMETER.

```
String stmtSource = "{call stars_proc2 (?, ?)}";

CallableStatement cstmt = con.prepareCall(stmtSource);

cstmt.setInteger (1, 5);
cstmt.registerOutParameter (2, java.sql.Types.VARCHAR);
cstmt.execute();

System.out.println
   ("The result was \"" + cstmt.getString (2) + "\".");
```

Returning Result Sets

In our review at the beginning of this chapter, we saw that SQL stored procedures could return result sets. SQLJ Part 1 allows Java methods to return result sets as well. The Java method will return result sets that are either of class `java.sql.ResultSet` or of class `sqlj.runtime.ResultSetIterator`, generated by JDBC or SQLJ Part 0, respectively. In order to return values of these types, the same mechanism as OUT parameters is used—a one-element array. Let us look at Example 6.15, which shows a Java method that will return *two* result sets and the procedure that will use this method.

EXAMPLE 6.15 JAVA PROCEDURE THAT RETURNS TWO RESULT SETS.

```
public static void BestActorsActresses
                  (String after, ResultSet[] rs1, ResultSet[] rs2)
   throws SQLException {

   String stmt1 =    "SELECT   DISTINCT person "
                + "FROM     awards "
                + "WHERE    award = 'Actor' "
                + "  AND    award_year > '" + after + "'";

   String stmt2 =    "SELECT   DISTINCT person "
                + "FROM     awards "
                + "WHERE    award = 'Actress' "
                + "  AND    award_year > '" + after + "'";

   Connection con = DriverManager.getConnection
                      ("jdbc:default:connection");

   rs1[0] = con.createStatement().executeQuery(stmt1);
   rs2[0] = con.createStatement().executeQuery(stmt2);

}


CREATE PROCEDURE Actors_Actresses (IN after_year CHAR(4))
READS SQL DATA
DYNAMIC RESULT SETS 2
EXTERNAL NAME
'cinema_jar: Cinema.Utility.BestActorsActresses
   (String, ResultSet[], ResultSet[])'
LANGUAGE JAVA
PARAMETER STYLE JAVA
```

The Java method has two parameters that are arrays of ResultSet. These are required to be placed after all of the non–result set parameters. The SQL procedure specifies that there will be two dynamic result sets generated by the procedure. When Actors_Actresses is called, SQL will generate a one-element array containing a single null reference for each of the result set arguments. When the Java method is executed, ResultSet (or ResultSetIterator for SQLJ Part 0) instances may be placed into the arrays. When the Java method completes, SQL will look at the result set arguments that contain non-null references, and pass them to the caller one by one. If more non-null result set instances are produced by the Java method than are declared in the SQL procedure, a warning is raised and the excess result sets are not seen by the caller of the procedure—they are simply discarded. The code in Example 6.16 might be used to invoke Actors_Actresses.

EXAMPLE 6.16 RETRIEVING THE RESULT SETS PRODUCED BY THE JAVA PROCEDURE IN EXAMPLE 6.15.

```
String stmtSource =   "{call Actors_Actresses (?)}";

CallableStatement cstmt = con.prepareCall(stmtSource);

cstmt.setString (1, "1994");
System.out.println(cstmt.execute());

System.out.println("Actors:");
ResultSet rs = cstmt.getResultSet ();
while (rs.next()) {
   System.out.println ("    " + rs.getString(1));
}

System.out.println ();

System.out.println("Actresses:");
cstmt.getMoreResults();
rs = cstmt.getResultSet ();
while (rs.next()) {
   System.out.println ("    " + rs.getString(1));
}
```

6.3.3 Special Treatment for the main Method

We might wish to create an SQL procedure that will invoke a Java main method. You may recall that Java requires methods named main to have the following signature:

```
public static void main (String[])
```

If we used the correspondence we explained just a moment ago, we would have to create an SQL procedure with a single OUT or INOUT parameter. This would not match the way Java classes actually use the main method, so an exception to the rules was created for this one method.

The SQL parameters for a main method can take one of two forms. The SQL procedure can have a single CHARACTER or VARCHAR array parameter, if the DBMS supports arrays, or it can have zero or more parameters, each of which is CHARACTER or VARCHAR. These two alternatives can be seen in Example 6.17.

EXAMPLE 6.17 TWO JAVA PROCEDURES THAT SPECIFY THE main METHOD.

```
CREATE PROCEDURE main1 (VARCHAR (50) ARRAY[3])
EXTERNAL NAME 'cinema_jar:Cinema.Utility.main'
LANGUAGE JAVA
PARAMETER STYLE JAVA

CREATE PROCEDURE main2 (VARCHAR(50), VARCHAR(50), CHAR (10))
EXTERNAL NAME 'cinema_jar:Cinema.Utility.main'
LANGUAGE JAVA
PARAMETER STYLE JAVA
```

6.3.4 Null Values

The Java routines that you create will certainly be invoked with null values (whether or not you like null values, they are widely used). Let us once again use our stars Java function:

```
CREATE FUNCTION stars (INTEGER) RETURNS VARCHAR(10)
EXTERNAL NAME 'cinema_jar:Cinema.Movie.stars'
LANGUAGE JAVA
PARAMETER STYLE JAVA
```

If the `stars` function is called with a null value, then an exception will be raised. Why? Right—the Java `int` parameter has no way to represent a null value.

This exception can be avoided in one of two ways. The first is to use a Java method that accepts `Integer` instead of `int`. With `Integer`, a null reference can represent SQL's null value. The second way is to specify `RETURNS NULL ON NULL INPUT` when the function is created. These two solutions can be seen in `stars3` and `stars4`, respectively, in Example 6.18.

EXAMPLE 6.18 JAVA METHODS THAT CAN ACCEPT NULL VALUES.

```
CREATE FUNCTION stars3 (INTEGER) RETURNS VARCHAR(10)
EXTERNAL NAME 'cinema_jar:Cinema.Movie.stars2 (Integer)'
LANGUAGE JAVA
PARAMETER STYLE JAVA

CREATE FUNCTION stars4 (INTEGER) RETURNS VARCHAR(10)
RETURNS NULL ON NULL INPUT
EXTERNAL NAME 'cinema_jar:Cinema.Movie.stars2'
LANGUAGE JAVA
PARAMETER STYLE JAVA
```

When `stars3` is called with a null value, then an empty string will be returned. When `stars4` is called with a null value, then a null value will be returned (without the method being invoked).

6.3.5 Static Variables

We've seen many static methods in this chapter, but none of them have used static variables. There is, indeed, a reason for this. When you execute a Java application, static variables have a very well defined lifetime. They are created when the class that contains them is loaded and exist until the application terminates. SQLJ Part 1 gives DBMS implementors a great deal of freedom in choosing when Java Virtual Machines are started and stopped. Several alternatives spring immediately to mind:

- A JVM might be started when a database server is started and then be shared among the concurrent users of the database.
- A JVM might be started at the beginning of each SQL session.

- A JVM might be started for an SQL session the first time that a Java routine is invoked.
- The JVM might be terminated at the end of each statement or each transaction.

These alternatives expand when one considers DBMSs with implementations that can span multiple processors. Because implementors have been given this freedom, the author of a Java routine is advised not to use static variables, other than variables that are declared to be final static. Naturally, you're free to use static variables, but you must do so with the awareness that portability of your applications will be suspect—and, after all, portability is probably one reason you're using Java!

6.3.6 Privilege Checking

There is a somewhat subtle privilege checking issue, concerning the use of one user's routine by another user, that you should be aware of. Consider the situation of Jonathan invoking a Java function or procedure that is owned by Alyssa. For this to happen, Alyssa must have granted the execute privilege to Jonathan. Jonathan invokes the routine, which uses the default connection to execute an SQL statement. This SQL statement could be executed with Jonathan considered by SQL to be the current user. This is called *invoker's rights*. Alternatively, Alyssa could be considered by SQL to be the current user, which is called *definer's rights*. In the former case, Jonathan must have been granted the necessary privileges to execute the SQL statement, and in the latter case Alyssa must have these privileges. This choice of whether to provide invoker's rights or definer's rights is left to the implementor of the DBMS.

Yes, we're aware that this issue may have portability implications. However, this is one area where the SQLJ definers have been unable to reach a single conclusion for the correct default behavior. Of course, you don't face this issue in cases where the invoker and definer are the same user!

6.3.7 Exceptions

The static methods that are associated with SQL routines may have exceptions raised during their invocation. Some of these exceptions might be handled by try-catch-finally blocks, in which case SQL would never be made aware of them. A Java routine might be declared with `throws SQLException`, and the routine might test for some condition and raise such an exception, as can be seen in Example 6.19.

EXAMPLE 6.19 A JAVA METHOD THAT THROWS `SQLException`.

```
public static String starsWithException (int rating)
   throws SQLException {

   if (rating < 0 || rating > 10) {
      throw new SQLException ("Invalid rating value", "38111");
   }

   String result = "";

   while (rating-- > 0) {
      result += "*";
   }

   return result;
}
```

If a Java routine raises an `SQLException` and provides an SQLSTATE value, then the SQLSTATE class (first two characters) should be "38". If the SQLSTATE is not "38" or the subclass (the next three characters) is not supplied, then SQL will raise *external routine invocation exception,* with an SQLSTATE value of "39001". The Java routine might also raise some other exception besides `SQLException`. If it does, then SQL will raise *uncaught Java exception,* with an SQLSTATE value of "38000".

As a general rule, if your method can anticipate certain exceptions and recover from them locally, then this should be done. When the invocation of an SQL routine raises an exception condition, then any work done by the statement that contains the routine invocation is undone. The exception condition is then either handled at that level or eventually passed back to the client application and the user.

6.4 SQL-Java Paths

We've seen how Java routines have associated Java static methods, so that the SQL invocation of a function or procedure can cause a Java method to be invoked. Java statements within such a method may invoke other Java methods—we've seen this in all of the examples in this chapter. Without taking any special steps, a Java method can invoke other methods in system classes (`java.lang.*` and `java.sql.*`) and in the classes of its containing JAR file.

Let us suppose that we have installed a JAR file called `entertainment_jar` that contains a class called `entertainment` that in turn contains a method that tries to invoke `Cinema.Movies.stars`. When this method is invoked, `Cinema.Movies.stars` will not be found, and an exception will be thrown. To make this work correctly, the owner of the `entertainment_jar` JAR file would have to execute the following:

```
sqlj.alter_java_path ('entertainment_jar',
                      '(Cinema/*, cinema_jar)');
```

The first argument is the SQL name of a JAR file. It is the Java path of this JAR file that we'd like to change. The second argument is a sequence of pairs, where each pair first has a pattern and then has the SQL name for a JAR file. When a method needs to be resolved, the pairs are searched from left to right. When a pattern is matched, the JAR file that is with it is used to locate the method.

The existence of the path above will cause the JVM to look for `Cinema.Movies.stars` in the `cinema_jar` JAR file. This is not unlike the use of the classpath environment variable when Java applications are executed to determine which directory structures are to be searched when a class needs to be loaded. The path for `entertainment_jar` might be a bit more complicated, as it is in the following statement:

```
sqlj.alter_java_path
   ('entertainment_jar',
    '(Cinema/Theaters/getLocal, cinema2) (Cinema/*, cinema1)
     (*, other1) (*, other2)'
   );
```

Let's call a pattern with no "*" in it, which is the case with the first pair in this example, a *fully qualified path.* Let's call a pattern with only a "*" in it, which is the case with the last pair, an *unqualified path.* Finally, lets call a pattern with some non-"*" parts and a trailing "*", which is the case with the second pair, a *partially qualified path.*

When a class must be loaded by our method in the `entertainment_jar` that is not a system class and is not located in the `entertainment_jar`, the parts of the SQL-Java path are examined from left to right. If a fully qualified or partially qualified element matches the class to be loaded, then the JAR file in the second part of that element is used. If the class does not exist in such a JAR file, then an exception is thrown (and the rest of the path is not used). If an unqualified path is examined, and the class to be loaded exists in the JAR file in the second part of the element, then it is used. Otherwise, the remainder of the path is examined. If the entire path is examined and no class is found, then an exception is thrown.

These rules are a bit complicated. Table 6.2 shows some classes that might be used in `entertainment_jar` and the classes that would actually get loaded.

Class to be loaded	Result
Cinema.Theaters.getLocal	This class is either found in cinema2, or an exception is thrown.
Cinema.Movies.stars	This class is either found in cinema1, or an exception is thrown.
TV.favorites	If this class is found in other1, then it is used. Otherwise, if this class is found in other2, then it is used. Otherwise, an exception is thrown.

TABLE 6.2 *Loading classes referenced in* entertainment_jar.

We'll be discussing privileges in just a moment. It is important to note that the successful execution of the alter_java_path statement requires that the executor of the statement be the owner of the specified JAR file, and that the executor has the USAGE privilege for each of the JAR files in the path.

6.5 Privileges

When a user first installs a JAR file, he or she is the only one that can create functions or procedures that use the classes in the JAR file because he or she is the only one that has the USAGE privilege on the JAR file. SQLJ Part 1 extends the GRANT and REVOKE statements so that they apply to JAR files in the same way that they apply to other SQL objects. The user might invoke the following statements:

```
GRANT USAGE ON JAR cinema_jar TO nancy;
GRANT USAGE ON JAR cinema_jar TO barbara;
```

The USAGE privilege on a JAR file is required in order to create a Java routine that uses a method in the JAR file. This privilege is also required for the JAR files mentioned in an alter_java_path statement. The USAGE privilege can be revoked from a user, as seen in the next statement:

```
REVOKE USAGE ON JAR cinema_jar FROM nancy RESTRICT;
```

The REVOKE statement will fail if the user losing the privilege has created any Java routines that use methods in the JAR file, or if the user owns any JAR files that have a Java path that specifies this JAR file.

6.6 Dropping Java Routines

We've shown several instances of creating Java routines. SQLJ Part 1 also allows these Java routines to be dropped. For example:

```
DROP FUNCTION stars RESTRICT
```

This statement drops the SQL definition of the routine but does not change the associated Java method or JAR file in any way. The usual SQL rules apply to this statement, so, for example, it must be executed by the owner of the routine.

6.7 Deployment Descriptors

We've seen that, once a JAR file is installed, additional operations are necessary before the methods it contains can be used. Associations must be made between SQL functions or procedures and the methods in the JAR file, and privileges may need to be granted to the SQL functions and procedures.

Although these operations could be carried out manually, you are probably thinking, "There must be a better solution than that." Indeed there is! SQLJ Part 1 contains *deployment descriptors* for exactly this purpose. Deployment descriptors are statements that are placed in a deployment descriptor file and included in the JAR file that is to be installed. The manifest entry for a deployment descriptor file is written as follows:

```
Name: deploy.txt
SQLJDeploymentDescriptor: TRUE
```

The deployment descriptor file we identify (`deploy.txt`) might have the contents shown in Example 6.20.

The install actions can be automatically executed by the `sqlj.install_jar` statement, and the remove actions can be automatically executed by the `sqlj.remove_jar` statement. A deployment descriptor file may have at most one string for the install actions and one string for the remove actions. The install actions may contain only CREATE PROCEDURE or CREATE FUNCTION statements that associate SQL routines with Java methods, and GRANT statements that grant privileges to these new routines. Similarly, the remove actions can contain only DROP PROCEDURE, DROP FUNCTION, and REVOKE statements.

If you are reading the examples closely, then you probably noticed the use of "`thisjar`". This special name serves as a placeholder for the actual SQL name of the JAR file being installed or removed. This allows a JAR file to be installed in multiple different databases with different SQL names. Example 6.21 shows how a deployment descriptor file may be extended by DBMS vendors.

EXAMPLE 6.20 DEPLOYMENT DESCRIPTOR FILE.

```
SQLActions[] = {
   "BEGIN INSTALL

      CREATE FUNCTION stars2 (INTEGER) RETURNS VARCHAR(10)
      EXTERNAL NAME 'thisjar:Cinema.Movie.stars2'
      LANGUAGE JAVA
      PARAMETER STYLE JAVA;

      GRANT EXECUTE ON stars2 TO PUBLIC;

   END INSTALL",
   "BEGIN REMOVE

      REVOKE EXECUTE ON stars2 FROM PUBLIC RESTRICT;

      DROP FUNCTION stars2 RESTRICT;

   END REMOVE"
}
```

EXAMPLE 6.21 DEPLOYMENT DESCRIPTOR FILE EXTENDED FOR TWO VENDORS.

```
SQLActions[] = {
   "BEGIN INSTALL
       ... ;
       BEGIN SYBASE ... END SYBASE;
       BEGIN ORACLE ... END ORACLE;
       ... ;
    END INSTALL",
   "BEGIN REMOVE
       ... ;
       BEGIN SYBASE ... END SYBASE;
       BEGIN ORACLE ... END ORACLE;
       ... ;
    END REMOVE",
}
```

The SYBASE and ORACLE deployment descriptors may, for example, be defined by these two vendors. The SYBASE descriptors will be ignored if they are used in a non-Sybase database.

6.8 Operations on JAR Files

SQLJ Part 1 specifies several operations that support the use of JAR files.

6.8.1 Installing JAR Files

We've already discussed the installation of JAR files in Section 6.2. The only thing that we still need to cover in order to complete the discussion is the running of deployment descriptor files. Remember that the syntax for this statement is

```
sqlj.install_jar (url IN VARCHAR(*), jar IN VARCHAR(*),
                  deploy IN INTEGER)
```

The final argument must be non-zero to indicate that the install actions of a deployment descriptor file should be run, and 0 to indicate that these actions should not be run.

```
CALL sqlj.install_jar ('file:///c:/Cinema.jar', 'cinema_jar', 1)
```

This statement installs the Cinema.jar JAR file and then executes its install actions. What could be easier!

6.8.2 Replacing JAR Files

During the development of your application, you may wish to modify some of your methods, create a new JAR file, and replace the JAR file that you installed in the database. For this, you will use the replace_jar procedure. Let us continue with our example from the beginning of this chapter. Let us suppose that we have modified the bodies of some of our methods and added several new methods, creating the Cinema2.jar JAR file.

```
CALL sqlj.replace_jar ('file:///c:/Cinema2.jar', 'cinema_jar')
```

The signature for the replace_jar procedure is as follows:

```
sqlj.replace_jar (url IN VARCHAR(*), jar IN VARCHAR(*))
```

To begin with, the URL provided must identify a JAR file, and the second argument must be the SQL name of a JAR file already in the database. Let us call these the *new JAR file* and *old JAR file*, respectively.

There are two rules that must be satisfied for the operation to succeed. Let us consider the *dependent SQL routines* to be those procedures and functions that were created with a reference to a class in the old JAR file. The first rule to be satisfied is that all of the classes in the dependent SQL routines must exist in the new JAR file. The second rule is that the CREATE PROCEDURE and CREATE FUNCTION statements that created the dependent SQL routines (which used the old JAR file) must still be valid with the contents of the new JAR file.

Basically, these rules mean that we can add any methods we like, and we can drop or alter methods that are not being used by SQL routines. As long as the signatures of the methods are maintained, the implementations of the methods can be changed to as large a degree or as small a degree as we wish.

We did not mention the classes and methods in the old JAR file that were not directly referenced by an SQL routine. These might be dropped or altered in any way in the new JAR file, even if they are used by the methods of dependent SQL routines. If you are not careful, then runtime Java exceptions may be thrown, resulting in SQL exception conditions.

6.8.3 Removing JAR Files

The syntax for the `remove_jar` procedure is the following:

```
sqlj.remove_jar( jar IN VARCHAR(*), undeploy IN INTEGER)
```

To complete the life cycle of the JAR file we created at the beginning of this chapter, we can remove our JAR file with the following statement:

```
CALL sqlj.remove_jar ('cinema_jar', 1)
```

Let us consider the JAR file in the database identified by the first argument to be the old JAR file. If the value of the `undeploy` argument is non-zero, then the remove actions of any deployment descriptors are executed. With this done, let us once again consider the dependent SQL routines to be those procedures and functions that were created with a reference to a class in the old JAR file. If there are any dependent SQL routines, then the operation raises an SQL exception condition. Otherwise, the operation succeeds, and the old JAR file is deleted, and the usage privilege for the old JAR file is revoked from its owner.

It is possible that some of the classes in the JAR file that you are attempting to remove (or replace) are in use by someone else. It is left up to each implementation of SQLJ Part 1 to decide what it will do under this circumstance.

6.9 Optional Features in SQLJ Part 1

Some of the features that we have been describing are considered to be optional in SQLJ Part 1. Use of these features will make your applications subject to portability problems, so use them with caution! These optional features are as follows:

- Java paths
- Deployment descriptor files: An implementation must support the CREATE PROCEDURE, CREATE FUNCTION, DROP PROCEDURE, and DROP FUNCTION statements either in deployment descriptor files, or as SQL statements, but it does not have to support them both ways.
- Java procedures or functions with overloaded names
- Java procedure parameters with modes of OUT or INOUT
- Java procedures that return result sets
- Parameters with JDBC data types that do not have corresponding Entry SQL-92 data types
- The USAGE privilege for JAR files
- The SQL ARRAY data type, specifically for a parameter of a Java procedure that is mapped to a `main` method

6.10 Status Codes

Table 6.3 lists the SQLSTATE values (the combination of the Class and Subclass values) defined by SQLJ Part 1.

6.11 Products in the Marketplace

Since SQLJ Part 0's reference implementation is freely available, you might be hoping that this is the case for SQLJ Part 1 as well. Sorry! We'll have to disappoint you in this case. A reference implementation is impractical because SQLJ Part 1 extends the capabilities of the DBMS itself; that means that a reference implementation would essentially have to be a complete DBMS implementation, which very few vendors would be willing to give away.

We will mention Sybase's Adaptive Server Anywhere as an example of an implementation of SQLJ Part 1, simply because it is one of the first products to implement this technology. Undoubtedly many other products will do so as well in the near future.

Category*	Condition	Class	Subcondition	Subclass
W	warning	01	too many result sets	00E
X	uncaught Java exception	38	(no subclass)	000
			user-defined	*mmm*
X	Java execution	39	invalid SQLSTATE	001
			invalid null value	004
X	Java DDL	46	(no subclass)	000
			invalid URL	001
			invalid jar name	002
			invalid class deletion	003
			invalid jar name	004
			invalid replacement	005
			invalid grantee	006
			invalid signature	007
			invalid method specification	008
			invalid REVOKE	009
			invalid jar name in path	102
			unresolved class name	103

* W ⇒ Warning, X ⇒ Exception

TABLE 6.3 *SQLSTATE values introduced by SQLJ Part 1.*

The capabilities that we have been discussing have been provided by Adaptive Server Anywhere (ASA) 6.0, although with a somewhat different syntax than SQLJ Part 1. (This syntax variance happened because the development of ASA 6.0 began well before SQLJ Part 1 stabilized.)

ASA 6.0 ships with its own JVM. A database must be Java enabled (that is, it must have the ability to execute Java code) in order to invoke Java methods. The enabling can happen at the time the database is created, or at a later time. The JVM starts up automatically the first time a Java method is invoked. ASA 6.0 allows both JAR files and class files to be installed. The syntax it provides for this operation differs a bit from that of SQLJ Part 1:

```
INSTALL JAVA NEW JAR 'cinema_jar' FROM FILE 'Cinema.jar'
```

ASA 6.0 allows the direct reference to Java methods from within SQL. It does not require that SQL procedures or functions act as intermediaries. Because the dot "." is used by SQL to separate the catalog, schema, and local parts of a name, there is the possibility of ambiguity with Java method invocations. ASA 6.0 allows the symbol ">>" to be used in place of the dot to remove such ambiguity. The statements in Example 6.22 are supported by ASA 6.0.

EXAMPLE 6.22 METHOD INVOCATION IN ASA 6.0.

```
SELECT   title, Cinema.Movie.stars2(vote) AS jim
FROM     votes
WHERE    voter = 'Jim' AND title LIKE 'A%'

SELECT   title, Cinema>>Movie>>stars2(vote) AS jim
FROM     votes
WHERE    voter = 'Jim' AND title LIKE 'A%'

SELECT   title,
         Cinema.Movie.stars2(vote) AS jim,
         java.lang.System.currentTimeMillis()
FROM     votes
WHERE    voter = 'Jim' AND title LIKE 'A%';
```

A method in ASA 6.0 may even use `System.out.println` to send output to the system console!

The implementors of ASA have been constant participants in the activities of the SQLJ informal group and the formal standards process. We expect that future releases will provide all of the SQLJ Part 1 syntax.

6.12 The Value Proposition for SQLJ Part 1

Now that we've talked about SQLJ Part 1 at length, let's discuss the advantages that it provides over SQL/PSM. The development community is rapidly gaining expertise in Java. The expertise developed in writing Java client applications or applets can be applied to the development of Java in the database. In fact, some amount of code that is written for the client or middle-tier servers can be used "as is" in the database. We've heard that this type of reuse is somewhat possible with Oracle's PL/SQL, but not with any of the other vendor's procedural languages.

There is also the protection of your investment to consider. SQL/PSM has not been completely implemented by any DBMS vendor (and, as far as we can tell, may never be fully implemented). All of the vendors have picked and chosen among the SQL/PSM features, often adding their own syntactic twists. By contrast, SQLJ Part 1 methods can be easily ported from one vendor's DBMS to another's.

Although we were very active participants in the development of SQL/PSM, we have to admit that Java is a far more modern and rich programming language. We also recognize that several vendors provide powerful development environments for Java (such as Sybase's PowerJ, Microsoft's Visual J++, Borland's JBuilder, Oracle's JDeveloper, and Symantec's Café).

In the areas of safety and robustness, both SQL/PSM and the proprietary procedural languages fare quite well. None of them allow direct access to memory or to system services, which cannot be said for the external routines written in languages other than Java. The DBMS vendors recognized this when the external routines were first offered and often provided environments in which the external routines could run that were safer, but at a cost to their performance.

There are, however, two strengths of SQL/PSM that you do give up when you choose Java. First, SQL/PSM uses SQL data types for its variables and parameters—there is no impedance mismatch or data conversions to be concerned with. These variables and parameters can all store the null value and provide the same null value semantics as columns.

The second strength of SQL/PSM is that ordinary nonprocedural SQL statements can be freely intermixed with procedural statements. Any expression can contain a subquery. With Java, either JDBC or SQLJ Part 0 must be used to execute additional SQL statements. Example 6.23 contains an SQL/PSM program that finds the median vote for the votes of some person.

EXAMPLE 6.23 RETURN THE MEDIAN VOTE FOR A PERSON.

```
CREATE FUNCTION median_vote (person VARCHAR (20)) RETURNS INTEGER
   BEGIN
      DECLARE c1 CURSOR FOR
         SELECT   vote
         FROM     votes
         WHERE    voter = person
         ORDER BY vote;

      DECLARE i INTEGER;
      DECLARE v INTEGER;
```

```
    -- i will contain the position of the median value

    SELECT   COUNT(*) / 2
    INTO     i
    FROM     votes
    WHERE    voter = person;

    OPEN c1;

    -- Fetch until the median row is reached

    WHILE i > 0 DO
       FETCH c1 INTO v;
       SET i = i - 1;
    END WHILE;

    RETURN v;

END;
```

We can find the median vote for all voters with the query in Example 6.24 and show the result in Result 6.2.

EXAMPLE 6.24 FIND THE MEDIAN VOTE FOR ALL VOTERS.

```
SELECT   voter, median_vote(voter) AS median
FROM     (SELECT DISTINCT voter FROM votes) AS voters
```

Result 6.2 The median votes for all voters.

voter	median
Andrew	7
Jim	7

6.13 Chapter Summary

The examples that we've provided have been brief and to the point. Almost certainly, any use of SQLJ Part 1 that you are considering is going to be much more complex. Let's discuss briefly a use of Java that you really wouldn't want to consider writing in SQL alone. The method canonicCharacters that we provide in Example 6.25 transforms a string by removing any whitespace characters, replacing any uppercase characters with their lowercase equivalent, and then sorting the characters. "Jim Melton" will be transformed into "eijlmmnot" by this method.

EXAMPLE 6.25 A MORE COMPLEX JAVA FUNCTION.

```
public static String canonicCharacters (String source) {

   // make the string lower case

   StringBuffer s = new StringBuffer (source.toLowerCase());

   // remove whitespace characters

   for (int n = 0; n < s.length(); n++) {

      // if a whitespace character is found, then replace it with
      // the last character, reduce the string's length, and test
      // this position again

      if (Character.isWhitespace(s.charAt(n))) {
         s.setCharAt(n, s.charAt(s.length()-1));
         s.setLength(s.length()-1);
         n--;
      }
   }

   // sort the characters

   sortCharacters(s);

   return s.toString();
}

static void sortCharacters (StringBuffer s) {
   ...
}

CREATE FUNCTION canonic (IN s VARCHAR(60)) RETURNS VARCHAR(60)
EXTERNAL NAME 'cinema_jar:Cinema.Utility.canonicCharacters'
LANGUAGE JAVA
PARAMETER STYLE JAVA
```

The `canonic` Java function can be used to find strings that are anagrams of one another. Example 6.26 shows the query that would be used to find a movie title that is an anagram of "valid when random." The result is shown in Result 6.3.

EXAMPLE 6.26 USE `canonic` TO SEARCH FOR AN ANAGRAM.

```
SELECT    title
FROM      movies m1
WHERE     canonic (m1.title) = canonic ('valid when random')
```

Result 6.3 Anagram of "valid when random".

title
Melvin and Howard

Now, we've covered SQLJ Part 1 "from soup to nuts." We've discussed how JAR files containing classes and methods of interest can be installed in the database. We've examined the writing of deployment descriptor files to make the installation process as easy as possible for JAR files that have to be installed in many databases.

Once the methods are in the database, we've covered how Java routines are written, providing an SQL signature for Java methods that are both public and static. These methods may be computational in nature, or they may use JDBC or SQLJ Part 0 to access data in the database, or to operate on this data. We've discussed how JAR files can be maintained over time, and we finished the chapter with a discussion of the advantages that SQLJ Part 1 will provide for you, if you choose to use it.

CHAPTER

7

SQL User-Defined Types

7.1 Introduction

As we've said before, this is not a book about SQL per se, but is a book about using SQL and Java together. Why, then, should you read this chapter—a chapter that covers SQL's user-defined types with very little attention to Java? In fact, one aspect of using SQL and Java together, which you'll encounter in Chapter 8, allows application developers to use Java classes within SQL database systems and, under some circumstances, to use them just as though they were SQL's own UDTs! This facility has proven to be both powerful and popular among the users of certain products, but understanding its use and appeal depends in part on an understanding of the SQL approach to user-defined types. In addition, the new version of JDBC (JDBC 2.0), which we'll discuss in Chapter 9, provides the ability to map SQL user-defined types to Java classes. Understanding SQL's UDTs will therefore enable you to take better advantage of JDBC.

In this chapter, we'll tell you about user-defined types in general and about SQL's approach to them. We're not going to go into excruciating detail about SQL's UDT capabilities (there are other books that cover this subject comprehensively—or at least there will be shortly after publication of the book you have in your hands right now). Instead, we'll give a solid overview of the facility and the supporting technology in SQL. We expect that this will be enough to help you understand the relationship between SQL's type system and Java's, and to give you the background required to deal most effectively with Chapter 8's information.

In particular, in this chapter, we'll tell you what user-defined types are and why you might want to use them in your applications. Then we'll get more specific and show you SQL's UDT facilities, with examples of creating UDTs and manipulating instances of those UDTs. This discussion includes the creation and use of user-defined functions and methods that applications can use to invoke appropriate behaviors of those UDT instances.

We'll also let you see how SQL's UDTs can be used as the data types of columns in tables and even the types of SQL variables. In addition, you'll see how a UDT can be declared to be the "data type" of an entire table—such that the table's columns are intimately related to the UDT's attributes. Before finishing up, we'll give you an overview of the SQL object model, comparing and contrasting it (to some degree, at least) with Java's object model. Finally, we'll discuss the limitations on SQL's user-defined type facilities—both the technical limitations and the economic ones. The discussion of the technical limitations may be the most interesting to programmers, but the economic limitations are equally important and actually may have more influence on what products support. Don't neglect this section, since it has the potential to affect your organization's use of the technology.

7.2 User-Defined Types

The term "user-defined type" may seem to be pretty much self-explanatory, but we'll try to expand on it anyway. The use of "type" is meant to imply "data type," that is, a data type that can be the type of some piece of data in the environment under discussion. In an SQL environment, this would normally be the data type of a column in a table, of an SQL variable in an SQL-invoked routine written in SQL, or of a parameter to an externally invoked SQL routine (which is nothing but a fancy name for the implicit procedures generated for embedded SQL statements). The inclusion of the phrase "user-defined" suggests that the type isn't built into the database system but is defined in some other manner. Before we examine user-defined types specifically, let's look at the history that brought us to this discussion.

7.2.1 Evolution of Type Systems

SQL database systems have always had a selection of built-in data types that are available for use in applications. They range from types specified in the SQL standard (such as INTEGER and SMALLINT, CHARACTER and CHARACTER VARYING, and DATE, TIME, and TIMESTAMP) to proprietary types defined by individual database system products (such as Sybase's SMALLMONEY and IMAGE types or Oracle's NUMBER and RAW types). These built-in types served applications well for quite a few years, since SQL database systems were used principally to manage "traditional" data: data easily represented using numbers, character strings, and datetime values.

However, as time passed, users of SQL database systems began to encounter the need to represent and manage more complex data—such as very large text documents on which search operations more complex than equality (and similar comparisons) could be performed, graphics and other image data, spatial and geographic information, and so forth. At first, the vendors of SQL systems responded by supporting "large object" types (LOBs, usually BLOBs for binary data and CLOBs for character data—though the names given to these types varied from vendor to vendor). Although these types made it possible to store very large data items in a single cell (intersection of a column and a row) of a table, the database systems rarely supported any operations, including comparisons, on such data; if any operations were supported, they tended to be very simple ones such as substring, concatenation, and basic comparisons. In other words, the semantics of the data stored in such cells were not handled by the database system—they were left to the applications to tackle.

As a result of customer dissatisfaction with this state of affairs, SQL database system vendors began to explore other approaches to handling the new requirements. Some vendors responded fairly quickly by providing support for certain specific types of data—text, geospatial data, images, and time series data were among the most common—and often did so by tightly coupling their products with special-purpose modules that dealt specifically with those selected data types. This approach proved very successful because it focussed on the most popular of the complex data types for which support was being demanded by large customers.

But everybody—customers and vendors alike—recognized that this approach would satisfy requirements only for so long. For one thing, it was unlikely that this technique would continue to be successful if it were applied to dozens of specialized types. Instead, a more generalized approach was required. The answer (obvious to some, but not all, observers) was deceptively simple: build into the SQL engines the capability to allow application builders to define their own specialized data types, especially including code to provide the semantics of those types. Some vendors used a pure-SQL approach to providing this capability, while others used a hybrid approach that allowed SQL to invoke code written in another programming language (and sometimes even supported data types of that other language directly in the SQL engine).

Which brings us to "user-defined types"!

Even though they were not defined by "users" per se, one could argue that the few specialized types some vendors supported were "user-defined types" since they weren't exactly built-in from the database engine's point of view. However, we would dispute this definition, since we believe that the term should be reserved for types that can be defined flexibly enough to allow the creation of new behaviors not envisioned by the original authors of those special-purpose modules. Note, if you will, that we do not insist that end users be allowed to define either types or behaviors on them! The term "user-defined" does not have to imply end users; we are quite happy with the term applying to types defined by (or whose behaviors are defined by) system administrators, builders of commercial application packages, or authors other than end users.

In fact, we would argue that very few end users would even *want* to define their own types or behaviors! Most end users—by which we mean the armies of application developers who are responsible for the majority of corporations' data processing and information systems—are far too busy trying to respond to business requirements being thrown at them to want to spend time inventing new data types. Instead, we anticipate that information systems groups are likely to assign responsibilities for inventing these new data types to a small number of system programmers or database administrators—who will design the types and their behaviors to make available to the application programmers who will, in turn, use them to build the bread-and-butter applications needed by their organizations.

7.2.2 Introducing User-Defined Types

"Well," we can hear some of you asking, "exactly *what* is a user-defined type?" This question is not unexpected, especially since we just said that it doesn't have to be a type defined by a user at all! Here's a working definition: A user-defined type is a type not built into a database system or programming language that can be defined as part of an application development effort, often (but not always) with behaviors provided by its definition.

Hmmm . . ."Do you really mean that user-defined types don't have to have user-defined behaviors?" Right! As we'll see in the next section of this chapter, SQL's user-defined type capabilities allow an application (or a database) to define a new type that is identical in most respects to some existing, built-in type. That's a pretty limited definition of user-defined type, we admit, but it does have its uses, as we'll see in Section 7.3.1. As you'll see, these types are permitted to have user-defined behaviors, but not required to, which distinguishes them from the other category of user-defined types.

Aside from such restricted types, most of what you'll see called *user-defined types* (or *abstract data types,* which is a phrase once employed in SQL:1999 during its development period) are likely to have some structure associated with them—comparable to the C programming language's `struct`—and also to have several user-defined functions to provide behaviors of the types. This could be as simple as a type for "temperature" that stores a single value, possibly an integer, and allows its users to store and retrieve the value in their choice of degrees Fahrenheit, degrees Celsius, or kelvins. Or, it could be as complex as a type associated with spatial data having dozens or hundreds of data components and hundreds of functions to manipulate those components in various ways. It might even be a representation of a business entity, such as an employee, a department, an invoice, or a movie. (You *had* to see that coming!)

7.3 SQL:1999 User-Defined Types

As we suggested in Section 7.2.2, SQL:1999 provides more than one sort of user-defined type. While it provides a very powerful variation, called "structured types" (which we'll cover a bit more thoroughly in Section 7.4 and the rest of the chapter), it also provides a more limited variant, called "distinct types." Our discussion of distinct types is relatively short, since it has little to do with using SQLJ and Java together; in fact, we're including it only because we felt the need to complete the picture of SQL's user-defined types. We'll spend most of this chapter's space, and energy, on structured types.

7.3.1 Distinct Types

A *distinct type* is a data type that is based on a single built-in data type, such as INTEGER, but whose values cannot be directly mixed in operations with that built-in type or with other distinct types based on that built-in type. They are first-class types—meaning that they can be used to define columns, variables, and so forth, just like any SQL built-in type. They provide *strong typing* in the SQL language (in which typing is traditionally viewed as moderately strong at best, since you are allowed to mix data types in expressions within fairly generous bounds).

The best way to explain SQL's distinct types is by example. Consider an application that gathers information about people who buy music CDs and videotapes in an effort to learn how to predict—based on their demographics—what products people will be interested in hearing more about. This application, let's call it DEMOGRAPH, might gather quite a variety of data in hope that a "data mining" product could use it to uncover unexpected relationships.

DEMOGRAPH might choose to collect both a person's shoe size rounded to the nearest integer size *and* the person's IQ. (OK, shoe size is unlikely to have much correlation with taste in music, but who knows!) It seems unlikely that DEMOGRAPH would ever want to compare anybody's shoe size with their IQ (now, now. . . no jokes about which one is larger for your buddy down the hall!), nor is it likely that we'd want to add them together, multiply them, or otherwise mix them in any sort of expression. If both values were collected into columns whose data types were declared to be INTEGER, however, there would be no protection against a programmer making an error and mixing those values in a single expression.

On the other hand, in SQL:1999, if the database designer declared two distinct types as shown in Example 7.1:

EXAMPLE 7.1 DISTINCT TYPES.

```
CREATE TYPE shoe_size AS INTEGER FINAL;
CREATE TYPE iq AS INTEGER FINAL;
```

then appropriate column definitions could be created, as shown in Example 7.2:

EXAMPLE 7.2 TABLE DEFINITION USING DISTINCT TYPES.

```
CREATE TABLE demograph_people (
  name            CHARACTER VARYING(50),
  shoesize        shoe_size,
  smarts          iq,
  last_purchase   DECIMAL(5,2))
```

(Don't worry about the keyword `FINAL`; it's required by SQL:1999 for arcane reasons not relevant to this discussion.) The *source type* of the two distinct types defined above is INTEGER, but we can't blissfully use instances of the two types as though they were ordinary integer values. In fact, that table definition makes it impossible to accidentally write something like Example 7.3:

EXAMPLE 7.3 INCORRECT USE OF DISTINCT TYPES.

```
SELECT   name
FROM     demograph_people
WHERE    shoesize > smarts
```

Any such mixing of the columns shoesize and smarts in an expression (including a predicate like the one in the WHERE clause) will cause a syntax error. On the other hand, if your application really, *really* wants to do something like this, SQL:1999 provides a way to do so. . . deliberately, as shown in Example 7.4:

EXAMPLE 7.4 CORRECT (PERHAPS NONSENSICAL) USE OF DISTINCT TYPES.

```
SELECT   name
FROM     demograph_people
WHERE    CAST(shoesize TO INTEGER) > CAST(smarts TO INTEGER)
```

By coding the explicit CAST expressions, you've told SQL that you know what you're doing and it's not an accident for which a syntax error should be raised.

In SQL:1999, distinct types are made more powerful by allowing database designers to create user-defined comparisons, user-defined casts, and other sorts of user-defined functions based on the distinct types in the database. Such functions, if defined, provide at least part of the distinct type's semantics. It's beyond the scope of this book to go into that level of detail about distinct types, though. If you're interested in it, we urge you to acquire one of the SQL:1999 books that are (or soon will be) available.

By the way, if you are familiar with SQL-92, you've probably learned something about its domain capabilities. While SQL:1999 retains that capability (and makes no statement about its relationship to distinct types), we believe that distinct types provide a much better solution to the problems that domains attempted to solve. Based on this belief, we suspect that future generations of the SQL standard may delete domains entirely.

7.3.2 Introducing Structured Types

As indicated above, the other sort of user-defined type supported in SQL:1999 is called "structured type"; you should infer from its name that such types are permitted to have—and usually do have—internal structure to them. For example, a structured type named address might contain several components: number, street_name, apartment_number, city, state_or_region, country, and postal_code. Similarly, a type named movie might contain components such as title, length, and description.

In SQL:1999, users may create any number of structured types and use them as first-class types in their databases and applications. (Reminder: we use the phrase "first-class type" to indicate a data type that can be used as the data type of database columns, SQL variables, and so forth.) In addition to an internal structure, SQL's structured types can be given specific user-defined functions that are used for all comparisons of instances of the type, for casting values of the type to and from other types, and for implementing all sorts of behaviors (that is, semantics) of the type.

Example 7.5 contains the syntax of the CREATE TYPE statement (which is given in BNF in Appendix G). Please don't be too intimidated by the many different parts of this statement. We'll get to them all in due time. Our purpose in giving you the entire syntax now is so that we can refer back to it as we get to each component in our discussion of structured types throughout the rest of this chapter.

EXAMPLE 7.5 CREATE TYPE SYNTAX.

```
CREATE TYPE type-name [ UNDER supertype-name ]
    [ AS representation ]
    [ [ NOT ] INSTANTIABLE
    [ NOT ] FINAL
    [ reference-type-specification ]
    [ cast-option ]
    [ method-specification-list ]
```

7.4 Structured Types

As we just said in Section 7.3.2, SQL:1999's structured types normally have some sort of internal structure associated with them. (Of course, that's not an absolute requirement: you could define a structured type with only a single element, although the advantages of such a structured type are not always obvious when compared with defining a distinct type.) We've also said that they have behaviors, or semantics, associated with them. It's time to look much more closely at structured types and see just what they're capable of doing.

7.4.1 Major Characteristics

The two principal characteristics of structured types in SQL:1999 are these: They normally have stored data associated with them, and the operations that can be performed on them are provided by user-provided code. (Although distinct types can have operations on them enhanced by user-provided code, and they certainly have stored data associated with them, they behave much more like SQL's built-in types and thus don't really share with structured types all of the characteristics discussed in this section.) However, there are other characteristics that we'll cover, including a very important one called *encapsulation,* which we'll discuss in some detail later on, primarily in Section 7.4.3, but will introduce now because of its importance.

In SQL:1999, all structured types are *encapsulated,*[1] meaning that they are defined in a way that makes it difficult—though, as we'll see later in this chapter, not quite impossible—for applications to learn how various characteristics are actually implemented. The word "encapsulated" means that every component of the thing that is encapsulated is presented only through some interface. This interface permits the internal implementation details to be changed without affecting the use of applications (as long, of course, as the interface remains the same and any changes to the resulting behavior don't cause problems for the applications). In practice, encapsulation of structured types largely means that all access to instances of the types—including both their data and behaviors—is through the use of various sorts of functions (mostly, but not exclusively, methods; we'll discuss the differences between methods and ordinary functions in Section 7.4.3) that are associated in some way with the types. As we go through the details of structured types in the next few sections of this chapter, we'll identify the ways in which encapsulation is provided.

7.4.2 Attributes

The stored data associated with a structured type is actually stored in the various elements comprising the structure of the type. These elements are called the type's *attributes.* Each attribute has a single data type, although (as we'll see) those data types are not limited to SQL's built-in "atomic" types. The collection of attributes of a structured type is called the type's *representation.* In fact, in Example 7.5, you saw the optional clause "`AS representation`"; that is the clause in which you would specify all of the attributes of a user-defined type.

In the Java programming language, objects may have *fields* or *instance variables,* each of which has a data type. Those variables may be simple values, such as short integers (`short`) or single characters (`char`), or they may be more complex values, such as Java objects like arrays (using notations such as "`int[]`") or strings (`String`). The fields of Java's objects correspond to the attributes of SQL's structured types.

---

[1] There are several different ways to define "encapsulation." The definition we give here is consistent with the SQL:1999 standard, but is deficient according to some observers. For example, the fact that SQL:1999's object model doesn't allow for private attributes, but only public attributes, makes it impossible to completely hide the implementation details of types.

Data Types

In SQL, there are very few limitations on where a given data type can be used. In fact, the primary limitation is that certain complex data types cannot be used to exchange data with the client programs that invoke the SQL statements of an application. For example, SQL-92 provided three datetime types (DATE, TIME, and TIMESTAMP) for which there were no mappings to host language types. Similarly, SQL:1999 provides an ARRAY type and a ROW type for which the SQL standard provides no mapping to host language data types (although such mappings are possible for most host languages and some vendors are expected to provide these mappings as product extensions). You may not be surprised to learn that SQL:1999 does not provide direct mappings from structured types to host languages, either. However, as we'll see very shortly, there are straightforward ways of accessing structured types' values from client programs, as well as ways for type definers to provide user-defined routines to "map" structured type values to and from host program storage.

Each attribute of an SQL structured type can be specified to have a data type that is one of SQL's built-in scalar types, such as INTEGER, DECIMAL(7,2), CHARACTER VARYING(255), or TIMESTAMP(6). In addition, any attribute can be specified to have a data type that is one of SQL's built-in "constructed types," such as ARRAY or ROW (it's beyond the scope of this book to go into detail about those types, but we think their use will be intuitive once you see the examples that incorporate them). Finally, attributes can be specified to have a data type that is some other structured type—but, unfortunately, not the structured type in which the attribute is defined (more on this later).

There are no limits in the SQL:1999 standard on the relationships of all of these data types other than those appearing in the preceding paragraph. That is, a structured type can have attributes whose data types are ARRAYs of ROWs, some of whose fields are ARRAYs of some structured type, some of whose attributes are ROWs of ARRAYs of other types. For example, consider in Example 7.6 the type that would be reasonable for representing street addresses in the United States.

This type contains within it two attributes whose data types are not scalar types. These two ROW types happen to have two fields each, but that is of course a coincidence, as is the fact that all non-ROW attributes and all fields are some variation of the CHARACTER type.

Accessing Attributes

You would be very surprised—and disappointed—to learn that attributes of structured types couldn't be accessed fairly easily. And nobody wants to surprise or disappoint you! In fact, they can be accessed quite easily, using more than one syntax notation. (To avoid any confusion, let us

EXAMPLE 7.6 CREATE TYPE address.

```
CREATE TYPE address AS (
    number            CHARACTER(6),
    street            ROW (
       street_name       CHARACTER VARYING(35),
       street_type       CHARACTER VARYING(10) ),
    city              CHARACTER VARYING(35),
    state             CHARACTER(2),
    zip_code          ROW (
       base              CHARACTER(5),
       plus4             CHARACTER(4) ) )
    NOT FINAL
```

state clearly that "access" doesn't only mean "retrieve." It means both retrieval and modification, accessing for whatever supported purpose.)

The most intuitive notation (for most programmers, at least) is what we call *dot notation*. To access a structured type attribute using dot notation, you simply specify the name of the "site" whose data type is that structured type, followed by a period (the eponymous "dot"), followed by the name of the attribute.

Suppose we have a `customers` table with an associated correlation name `c`, one of whose columns, named `cust_addr`, has a data type of `address`—the same structured type we defined in Example 7.6. The following notation would access the `number` attribute of that column:

```
c.cust_addr.number
```

Now, we find that notation to be intuitive simply because it follows the long-standing pattern in SQL—use a period (or dot) to separate the components of the name of some datum you want to access in your application. In fact, SQL takes this still further: the dot notation is used to "reach" within a row:

```
c.cust_addr.zip_code.base
```

If, by some chance, our `customers` table had an array of addresses, perhaps to capture the fact that some customers have home addresses, vacation addresses, and business addresses, we could access the second of those using the notation:

```
c.cust_addr[2].zip_code.base
```

Like we said: intuitive!

A Note about Table Names versus Correlation Names

SQL programmers have long been accustomed to writing code like the following:

```
SELECT   name, city
FROM     customers
WHERE    cust_id = :hostvar1
```

This code, we've all learned, is equivalent to the fully qualified version:

```
SELECT   customers.name, customers.city
FROM     customers
WHERE    customers.cust_id = :hostvar1
```

And, in turn, that is equivalent to the alternative that defines a *correlation name* to use in place of the table name:

```
SELECT   c.name, c.city
FROM     customers AS c
WHERE    c.cust_id = :hostvar1
```

When SQL:1999 added structured types to the data type mix, it would have been "obvious" to allow references to attributes of columns whose data type is some structured type by allowing a statement like this:

```
SELECT   name, city, address.street_name
FROM     customers
WHERE    cust_id = :hostvar1
```

or the expected equivalent:

```
SELECT   customers.name, customers.city,
         customers.address.street_name
FROM     customers
WHERE    customers.cust_id = :hostvar1
```

Unfortunately, the possibility of syntax ambiguities raised its ugly head. Consider that you might happen to have in your database a catalog named `customers` that holds a table named `address` that, in turn, has a column named `street_name`. How, then, should an expression like `customers.address.street_name` be resolved: as `schema.table.column`, or as `table.column.attribute`? (Whether this is likely or not is irrelevant to a language specification—the very possibility has to be taken into account and the possible ambiguity resolved.)

The solution chosen for SQL:1999 was to prohibit references to attributes that are qualified with table names and column names (or, for that matter, with column names alone). Instead, applications are required to create and use a correlation name in such instances.

Therefore, we could write either

```
SELECT   name, city, c.address.street_name
FROM     customers AS c
WHERE    cust_id = :hostvar1
```

or

```
SELECT   c.name, c.city, c.address.street_name
FROM     customers AS c
WHERE    c.cust_id = :hostvar1
```

But we cannot use either `address.street_name` or `customers.address.street_name` as an expression. Any attempt to do so will cause a syntax error. *Caveat programmer*!

Attribute Characteristics

Attributes, naturally, are where structured types store their data. Naturally, attributes have various characteristics, the most evident of which are their names and their data types. (In case we didn't make it clear, *every* attribute of SQL:1999's user-defined types has a name and a data type.) But attributes have characteristics other than name and data type as well. For example, attributes can be given a specified default value—like the default for `street_type` in the structured type definition shown in Example 7.7.

EXAMPLE 7.7 CREATE TYPE WITH DEFAULT VALUES.

```
CREATE TYPE address AS (
    number            CHARACTER(6),
    street            ROW (
       street_name       CHARACTER VARYING(35),
       street_type       CHARACTER VARYING(10)
                           DEFAULT ( 'No', 'Street' ),
    city              CHARACTER VARYING(35),
    state             CHARACTER(2),
    zip_code          ROW (
       base              CHARACTER(5),
       plus4             CHARACTER(4) ) )
    NOT FINAL
```

Like columns in SQL's tables, attributes have a "default default" value—the null value—that is used whenever the application designer doesn't provide a different default value. And, perhaps obviously, you can explicitly make the null value an attribute's default value by using the keyword `NULL`, just as you can do for a column.

In addition, character string attributes, like character string columns, always have a known character set (that's a characteristic of the CHARACTER data type variations) and a known default collation, which you can either provide explicitly or permit to default to the character set's default collation.

However, unlike columns in tables, you cannot specify *constraints* on the attributes of a structured type—not even a `NOT NULL` constraint! When SQL:1999's definers were developing the structured type specifications, the ability to specify at least some sorts of constraints on attributes was considered. However, SQL has always distinguished between data stored in its tables and data in other, more transient, locations, such as in host variables, SQL variables, and the parameters to SQL routines. Only data stored in tables are affected by SQL's transaction semantics and by its constraints; variables, arguments, and other transient sites are outside the scope of those mechanisms.

Structured types can be used as the data types of variables, arguments and parameters, and so forth, so permitting constraints to be put on their attributes would violate that aspect of SQL's design. Instead, the designers concluded that constraints on some column whose data type is some structured type could be used to control the values allowed in the type's attributes, but only for instances stored in that column.

Attributes have an additional characteristic, called a "reference scope check," that we won't cover right now. It's premature to address that here, but you can be sure we'll get to it later. (We mention it here only for completeness.)

In Section 7.4.1, you learned that all aspects of structured types are encapsulated; naturally, that includes their attributes. Every attribute of an SQL:1999 structured type has two built-in, system-defined methods associated with it (although the SQL standard calls them "functions," they are actually methods—see Section 7.4.3 for details about methods and their invocation syntax). One of these methods is called an *observer function* and the other a *mutator function*. The observer function returns the value of its associated attribute of a structured type instance to its caller, whereas the mutator function allows the value of its associated attribute to be changed. In fact, these pairs of functions are automatically created by the database system when the structured type is created; you don't have to explicitly create them in any way other than defining the attributes of the type. In spite of the fact that these two methods encapsulate the attribute for which they're defined, you *always* use dot notation for invoking them—functional notation is reserved for (all) functions that are not methods.

The name of the observer function (*ahem*—observer method) for an attribute is identical to the name of the attribute itself. The observer function takes a single argument: the name of some site (e.g., a column, parameter, or variable) whose data type is the structured type; this argument is always provided implicitly, by using it to "qualify" the attribute (or method) name. You always use the observer function to get the value of an attribute of a structured type instance. Using the `address` example from earlier in this section, you could write the following:

```
customers.cust_addr.number
```

or perhaps this:

```
customers.cust_addr[2].zip_code.base
```

or even the following:

```
customers.cust_addr[2].zip_code.base()
```

Invocation of one of those function invocations *must be written* using the dot notation we showed you earlier in this section (note, however, that an empty pair of parentheses are permitted to indicate that the invocation has no arguments other than the implicit one). The data type returned by the observer function is the data type of the attribute, which is of course the data type of the "dot notation expression" that you wrote.

The mutator function for an attribute isn't very different in appearance from the observer function—and, in fact, it has exactly the same name as the observer function (we'll see in Section 7.4.3 how this *overloading* works). The principal differences are these: First, the mutator function takes two arguments—the first argument is the name of some site whose data type is the structured type, and the second argument is an expression whose data type is the data type of the associated attribute and whose value is the value to which you want that attribute set. The second difference is perhaps unexpected: The data type returned by a mutator function has nothing to do with the data type of the attribute, but is the structured type itself! The reason for this is a little subtle and a complete discussion will have to wait until Section 7.4.4, but for now we'll just say that the mutator function actually returns a new instance of the type whose attribute is being changed.

The observer function and the mutator function together *encapsulate* the attribute completely. If some future enhancement to the type changed the internal representation (that is, the data type) of the `number` attribute from CHARACTER(6) to INTEGER, it would be possible to write a new method that contained a statement to CAST the INTEGER value retrieved to a CHARACTER(6) value before returning it to the invoker, thus protecting application programs from that change in the structured type's definition.

Unlike Java, SQL does not permit you to "protect" your types' observer and mutator methods. Java permits you to leave some observers and mutators `public`, and to limit others' uses only to subtypes (`protected`) and still others' uses only to the type being defined (`private`). SQL has no analog to this capability (though it may be added in a future version of the standard); all methods in SQL are effectively public methods. You can prevent their access by unauthorized users through the use of SQL's privilege mechanisms, such as denying EXECUTE privilege to some users of the methods.

At this point, let's stop talking about attributes and their pairs of methods. We'll want to say more (quite a lot more, in fact) about methods later in the next section, and we'll have to address the issue of using these two methods to encapsulate attributes one more time (in subsection Polymorphism and Overloading). But, for now, you've got the basics of attributes and are ready to tackle structured types' semantics.

7.4.3 Behaviors and Semantics

The other important characteristic of SQL:1999 structured types is their semantics, or behaviors. As in other object-oriented systems, the semantics/behavior of these types is provided through *routines* (including methods, of course, as well as functions and procedures). Unlike many other such systems, however, SQL:1999 allows type designers to provide the behaviors of its user-defined types through routines written in any of several languages, not only in SQL. (As you have undoubtedly figured out—because you're reading this book, if for no other reason—Java is one of those languages . . . but we'll cover that in Chapter 8.)

Now, you've probably noticed that we've been fairly vague about this subject so far: we've talked about behavior and semantics as though they're the same thing. Well, if truth be told, that's not quite right.

The "semantics" of a type have to do with the *meaning* of the type—what it's used for, what it can represent and do, and so forth. By contrast, the "behavior" of a type is simply those actions that can be performed by, or on behalf of, an instance of the type. The terminology gets a bit confusing at times, largely because of the use of different vocabularies to describe different object models. For example, some object models talk about objects as though they were independent entities that respond to external stimuli on their own (e.g., an application "sends a message" to an object and the object acts on that message), whereas other object models, including SQL:1999's, describe the same situation by saying that an application "invokes a routine" and specifies the target object's identity as part of that invocation, in which case it's the routine that is active and the object passive.

Whichever way you like to think about these things, let's agree to use the terminology that SQL:1999 uses (in no small part because it's compatible with Java's terminology). Therefore, a type's behaviors are supplied by the invocation of one or more routines, either directly by an application program or indirectly by some other routine, which may or may not be associated with some type. Now, by "behaviors," we mean actions that are performed by the system (in the case of SQL:1999 types, this will naturally be the SQL system) that either change the state of some type instance, return some value derived from the state of some type instance, or perform some other action, usually one related to some type or type instance.

Some examples will help illustrate: A type that represents rational numbers (numbers representable by fractions in which both the numerator and denominator are integers) might have actions such as "add two rational values together" or "return the value of the numerator" or "send an email message containing the real number resulting from the division of the numerator by the denominator and then turn on the lights at the Eiffel Tower." There are no limits to what these behaviors can be, other than those set by the environment in which you're operating. A type designer typically determines the behaviors supported by, or available to, the types being defined, but some systems permit applications to add new behaviors to existing types.

Encapsulation

You already know that the behaviors of structured types are encapsulated. They are encapsulated by the routines that implement those behaviors. Your applications won't be affected in any way if some routine implementing some behavior of a structured type is rewritten in a more efficient way, or even in another programming language, as long as the calling interface remains the same and the results of calling it remain the same.

As will become more apparent when we get to the subsection Polymorphism and Overloading, the value of encapsulation is enhanced by other facilities provided by SQL:1999's structured types. For now, it's sufficient to emphasize that encapsulation of structured type behaviors protects your applications from changes in the internal implementations—the code—that provides those behaviors.

Methods

SQL/PSM-96[2,3] standardized for the first time the ability for SQL programmers to write functions and procedures ("SQL-invoked routines") for use in their SQL code. Those functions and procedures could be written in SQL or in any of several supported programming languages. SQL:1999 adds a third sort of routine to the mix: *methods*. Before we get into the details of methods, let's briefly review the broader subject of routines. (Although some of this material was introduced in Chapter 6, our orientation here is somewhat different, so don't skim it too quickly.)

In the SQL world (and, with few exceptions, in most programming languages), the word "routine" generically applies to a variety of types of subprograms, including both functions and procedures. A function is a routine that "has a value"—in other words, that returns a value without using a parameter to do so. Functions are typically used in contexts such as value expressions. In SQL, functions have only input parameters; therefore, you cannot return more than a single value from a function. By contrast, procedures are routines that return values only through parameters. Procedures are typically invoked using some form of "CALL" statement. In SQL, procedures can have both input parameters and output parameters (and parameters that are both at once).

In SQL:1999, a method is a special type of function. The most important differences between SQL's functions and its methods are summarized in Table 7.1.

In other words, an SQL:1999 method is a function that is associated with a single structured type and is defined in the same schema as that type, that must be invoked using dot notation, and whose invocations may not be fully resolved when the containing program is compiled. Later in this section, we'll cover the invocation syntax and schema of residence issues (see the subsection Method Definition) and

---

[2] ISO/IEC 9075-1:1999, *Information technology—Database languages—SQL—Part 1: Framework,* ISO/IEC 9075-2:1999, *Information technology—Database languages—SQL—Part 2: Foundation,* ISO/IEC 9075-3:1999, *Information technology—Database languages—SQL—Part 3: Call-Level Interface,* ISO/IEC 9075-4:1999, *Information technology—Database languages—SQL—Part 4: Persistent Stored Modules,* and ISO/IEC 9075-5:1999, *Information technology—Database languages—SQL—Part 5: Host language bindings,* International Organization for Standardization, 1999.

[3] ISO/IEC 9075-4:1996, *Information technology—Database languages—SQL—Part 4: Persistent Stored Modules (SQL/PSM),* International Organization for Standardization, 1996.

Characteristic	Functions	Methods
Attached to a specific type?	No	Yes—tightly bound to exactly one type
Invocation syntax	Functional notation	Dot notation
Schema of residence	Any schema	Schema of its associated type
Routine resolution	Fully resolved at compilation time	Compilation resolves to set of candidate methods, final resolution at runtime

TABLE 7.1 *Differences between functions and methods.*

the routine resolution situation (see the subsection Method Invocation); however, the notion of associated type is very central to understanding methods, and we'll address it right now.

SQL:1999 supports two types of method: *static methods* and *instance methods*. We're not going to cover static SQL methods in this book, except to mention their existence and say that they behave rather more like functions than like instance methods. A static method operates on the user-defined type itself, whereas an instance method operates on an instance of the type. That distinction has implications on the method's parameter declarations and invocations. For the rest of this chapter, when we use the word "method," we will mean "instance method" unless we explicitly say otherwise. (By the way, we recognize that you sometimes might not know exactly what we mean when we use the word "invocation" of a function or a method. That's because we often—perhaps even usually—mean the source code that specifies the routine's name, uses functional notation or dot notation, and supplies any required arguments; in a few other situations, though, the word refers to the actual process of causing the code in the routine to be executed. We hope that the meaning in each case is clear from the context!)

Associated Type In SQL:1999, an ordinary *function* (although methods are functions, too, we'll reserve use of the word "function" for those functions that are not methods) is not associated with, or bound to, a specific user-defined type. Instead, it may have one or more parameters whose data types are one or more user-defined types; alternatively, many functions in your database might have no user-defined type parameters at all—that is, all of their parameters are of built-in types.

By contrast, an SQL *method* is closely associated with—tightly bound to—exactly one user-defined type. The method might have several parameters whose data types are some structured type (even the same type as its associated type!), but only one of those parameters is treated specially. All methods that are closely associated with a given structured type are declared along with the type itself (well, to be thorough, their *signatures* are declared as part of the structured type's definition, whereas their *implementations* appear elsewhere). This process is done as part of the CREATE TYPE statement. (In Example 7.5, this appears as the `method-specification-list`. Feel free to go back to that syntax definition and check it out now; we'll wait until you get back.) SQL:1999 allows type definers to add to the set of methods associated with a given type, and also allows them to disassociate existing associated methods from the type, through the ALTER TYPE statement.

The associated type of a method has several significant effects on the method's definition and invocation. Arguably, the most surprising effect to some is that the method's declaration does not specify an explicit parameter corresponding to the associated type! (Similarly, the method's invocations don't use an explicit argument corresponding to that associated type.) However, the SQL system effectively creates an implicit parameter for methods that precede the first declared parameter. This implicit parameter is always named `SELF`, and its data type is always the associated user-defined type of the method. Within those methods, you reference the instance of the structured type for which the invocation was intended by using the name `SELF`, just as though it were a user-assigned parameter name. (An obvious implication of this arrangement is that no explicit parameter can be named `SELF`.)

But we're getting a little ahead of ourselves. We'll cover this implicit parameter thoroughly in the subsections Method Definition and Method Invocation. Before we do that, though, we thought you might like a very brief comparison of SQL:1999's methods with Java's.

Comparison with Java Methods We're not going to devote space in this book to the syntax of declaring methods in Java; there are any number of books on Java that do an excellent job of that. Instead, we'll take just a couple of paragraphs to highlight similarities and differences between Java methods and SQL methods.

Java methods, like SQL methods, are closely associated with a specific type (called a "class"). Java methods return a single value whose data type is the return type of the method, as do SQL methods. Java methods, however, can be declared as `void` methods, meaning that they do not return a value. By contrast, SQL methods always return a value—the nearest analog in SQL to a `void` method in Java is a procedure. SQL can make reference to the instance of the structured type that it is operating on with `SELF`, whereas Java uses the keyword `this` for the same purpose. You can define multiple methods in Java that have the same name (these are said to exhibit *name overloading*); SQL offers a similar capability, as we'll see in subsection Polymorphism and Overloading. Overloaded SQL methods and overloaded Java methods both resolve to a single specific method at runtime, based in part on the exact ("most-specific") type of a particular distinguished argument.

Java methods can be instance methods (that is, they operate on instances of the class with which they are associated) or class methods (meaning that they don't operate on specific objects, but on the class itself, indicated by the keyword `static`). SQL methods have a similar distinction—they can be instance methods (specified using the keyword `INSTANCE`) or static methods (keyword `STATIC`). If you don't specify either `STATIC` or `INSTANCE`, then the method will be an instance method by default.

Java methods can be given any of several optional characteristics. SQL methods can be given some of these same characteristics (perhaps using different keywords, though) but not all of them. For example, Java methods can be specified to be `public`, `private`, `protected`, or `package`; there is no analogous facility for SQL methods (although the ability to declare SQL methods to be `public`, `private`, or `protected` is anticipated in a future revision of the SQL standard). Java allows you to declare methods as `native`, but SQL has very different ways of distinguishing between methods written in SQL and those written in another programming language. Finally, Java methods can be declared as `synchronized`, whereas there is no corresponding requirement for SQL methods.

One last thing: Java methods' signatures include a little bit more information than do SQL methods' signatures—in Java, a method signature includes all of the exceptions that the method can raise, whereas SQL method signatures do not include information about conditions that can be raised by the method.

Method Definition Methods in SQL are defined in two ways and in two places—and both are required. First, every method is declared as part of the definition of its associated structured type. That is, the method *signature* is coded within the structured type definition. (Well, although that's true of methods known at the time the structured type is defined, you can also use the ALTER TYPE statement to add the signatures of additional methods to the type definition later on, as well as removing methods—that is, their signatures—from type definitions.) It is because of this relationship (between the type definition that lists all its associated methods and the method definitions that identify the associated type) that the "association" between type and method comes into existence.

The second way, and place, in which methods are defined is independent of the structured type definition, although the end result must be that the method resides in the same schema as its associated type. This second way is the actual method declaration, including its *implementation,* either the SQL code comprising the method or the appropriate identification (e.g., filespec or URL) of some code written in a different programming language.

To illustrate this, consider the structured type definition shown in Example 7.8.

EXAMPLE 7.8 STRUCTURED TYPE DEFINITION.

```
CREATE TYPE movie (
  title              CHARACTER VARYING (100),
  description        CHARACTER VARYING (500),
  runs               INTEGER )
  NOT FINAL
```

This very simple structured type allows us to capture certain critical information about movies: the name of the movie, a description of it, and the length in minutes. (Incidentally, the `NOT FINAL` is required syntax without an alternative; future editions of the SQL standard may change this situation.) But, suppose we really wanted to retrieve the length as an SQL INTERVAL type rather than as an INTEGER? We can build a method to perform this calculation for us, and the result would be as shown in Example 7.9.

EXAMPLE 7.9 STRUCTURED TYPE DEFINITION WITH METHOD SIGNATURE.

```
CREATE TYPE movie (
  title              CHARACTER VARYING (100),
  description        CHARACTER VARYING (500),
  runs               INTEGER )
  NOT FINAL
  METHOD length_interval ( )
    RETURNS INTERVAL HOUR(2) TO MINUTE
```

The last two lines constitute the signature of our new method; it takes no parameters beyond the implicit parameter that we briefly mentioned earlier, and it returns an SQL INTERVAL (whose precision must be specified). Next, let's see the actual method definition, as shown in Example 7.10. Of course, you'll notice right away that the relationship is bidirectional: the type definition identifies the method by name, and the method definition identifies the name of the associated type.

Now, let's examine this example a little more closely. Recall from our earlier discussion of methods that both the signature and the actual definition of the method specify that the method has no parameters.

EXAMPLE 7.10 METHOD DEFINITION ASSOCIATED WITH METHOD SIGNATURE.

```
CREATE INSTANCE METHOD length_interval ( )
    RETURNS INTERVAL HOUR(2) TO MINUTE
    FOR movie

  /* Allow for movies as long as 99 hours and 59 minutes */

  RETURN CAST ( CAST ( SELF.runs AS INTERVAL MINUTE(4) )
         AS INTERVAL HOUR(2) TO MINUTE )
```

Furthermore, every method *always* has at least one parameter, whose data type is the associated type. Since that parameter is never absent and is always the first parameter, and since its data type is always known very precisely, and since it must (by definition) always be "the" instance of that type for which the method was invoked, it need not be explicitly declared. You see from the body (that is, the implementation) of the method above that we use the keyword SELF within the method to identify the instance for which the method is invoked.

The *unaugmented parameter list* of this method, therefore, has zero parameters. But SQL builds an *augmented parameter list* for the method, which naturally has to be used by the underlying function invocation mechanisms on any hardware/software platform. That augmented parameter list has one parameter. If we were allowed (we're not!) to specify that implicit parameter explicitly, the method declaration might look something like this:

```
CREATE INSTANCE METHOD length_interval ( SELF movie )...
```

Now, if a method has more than one parameter, then there are a few rules that have to be satisfied. Most importantly, the data type of the parameter declared in the method signature must be compatible with the data type of the parameter declared in the method definition. ("Compatible" means that the data types are essentially the same, even when considering things like length or precision.) The same goes for the data type specified as the RETURNS data type, by the way! Furthermore, if any parameter declaration in either the method signature or the method definition is given a name, then its corresponding parameter declaration must have the same name.

Method signatures—but not method definitions—can also contain a number of optional clauses that specify additional information about the method. The method definitions themselves are simply assigned the same characteristics that were specified with their corresponding signatures. These optional characteristics may be written in any sequence and are the following:

- The name of the programming language in which the method is written; the default is SQL.
- If the programming language is not SQL, then the style of parameter list used for the method (an SQL-style list, in which indicator parameters and SQLSTATE parameters are implicit, or a "general" style, in which all parameters, and arguments, are explicit); the default is `PARAMETER STYLE SQL`.
- Whether the method does not contain SQL statements (`NO SQL`), may contain SQL statements but does not access the database (`CONTAINS SQL`), may retrieve data from the database but may not update the database (`READS SQL DATA`), or is permitted to update the database (`MODIFIES SQL DATA`); the default is `CONTAINS SQL`.
- Whether the method is deterministic (that is, whether it returns the same result in response to a specific set of argument values for a given state of the database) or not; the fault is `DETERMINISTIC`.
- Whether the method always returns the null value when any of its arguments is null and thus need not be called in that situation; the default is `CALLED ON NULL INPUT`.

Methods written in some programming language other than SQL have one additional characteristic that participates in the signature:

- The name of the default transform group (a pair of functions used to transform instances of structured types to or from some host language representation; these are implicitly used whenever transferring a structured type instance between SQL and a host routine, such as an external method); there is no default. (A discussion of transform groups is beyond the scope of this book; we mention them here only for completeness.)

Method Invocation A method invocation is, naturally, the mechanism by which a method is called, or invoked. While method definitions (and signatures) have *parameters,* method invocations have *arguments*. The number of arguments in a method invocation must be equal to the number of parameters in the definition of the method, and the data type of each argument must be compatible with the data type of its corresponding parameter (or there must be a conversion from the data type of the argument to the data type of the parameter that SQL can perform without the aid of a CAST expression).

Let's set up an example. First, we'll assume we've defined the movie type as we did a few paragraphs earlier, including the length_interval method. Next, we need a table that has a column whose data type is movie, as shown in Example 7.11.

EXAMPLE 7.11 movie_table DEFINITION.

```
CREATE TABLE movie_table (
    stock_number          CHARACTER(8),
    movie_info            movie,
    rental_quantity       INTEGER,
    rental_cost           DECIMAL(5,2) )
```

If we wanted to retrieve the length, in hours and minutes, of a particular film, we could write an SQL statement like the one in Example 7.12.

EXAMPLE 7.12 RETRIEVING FROM movie_table.

```
SELECT   mt.movie_info.length_interval
FROM     movie_table AS mt
WHERE    mt.movie_info.title = 'The Matrix'
```

In this example, we use dot notation, as required, to reference the title attribute (or, equivalently, to invoke the title observer function) in the WHERE clause, and SQL:1999 requires that we use dot notation to invoke the length_interval method.

Note that the length_interval method invocation didn't even bother with the parentheses! If the only argument to a method invocation is the implicit argument—corresponding to the implicit SELF parameter—then you can't code an argument, and you don't have to code the parentheses surrounding that nonexistent implicit argument. However, if you prefer to code the empty parentheses, you're allowed to do so, as we see in Example 7.13.

EXAMPLE 7.13 USING EMPTY ARGUMENT LISTS.

```
SELECT   mt.movie_info.length_interval()
FROM     movie_table AS mt
WHERE    mt.movie_info.title = 'The Matrix'
```

Functions

Functions have a lot in common with methods, as you will be aware from earlier statements we've made in this chapter, but there are a number of differences as well. The most important differences were outlined in Table 7.1 and discussed fairly early in the previous subsection. Let's take a look at the other differences.

The most obvious "other" difference is that you're allowed to specify those additional characteristics (take a look at the bulleted list at the end of the subsection Method Definition, above) when you define SQL functions—logical, since there's no concept of function signatures! That list of additional characteristics is lengthened by one for functions, too, and this one can only come at the end of the list: `STATIC DISPATCH`. (A future version of the SQL standard is expected to add `DYNAMIC DISPATCH` as an alternative.) This clause, which is the default even if you don't code it explicitly, means that function invocations are fully resolved at compile time—without regard to subtypes of any arguments (see Section 7.6 for information about subtypes).

Function Definition During the course of our movie rental business, we may decide that it's important to easily discover whether there's a relationship between the length of a movie's title and the running time of the movie. In pursuit of this information, we first might want to know the ratio of title length (in characters, of course) and running time (in minutes). We could write a method to accomplish this, since it involves only a single instance of a single structured type, but we choose to write a function instead (well, that *is* what we're discussing right now!), as shown in Example 7.14.

EXAMPLE 7.14 DEFINING A FUNCTION.

```
CREATE FUNCTION another_schema.ratio (movie_param movie)
    RETURNS REAL
  RETURN CHAR_LENGTH(movie_param.title)/movie_param.length
```

In this case, as you'd expect, we declared an explicit parameter, because functions don't have the implicit parameter that methods do. Since functions are not tightly bound to any associated structured type, this function could well have been defined in a different schema than the schema containing the `movie` type definition.

Function Invocation Function invocations have no surprises, now that you understand method invocation and the differences between functions and methods. To use that function we just defined, we could write a statement like the one in Example 7.15.

EXAMPLE 7.15 INVOKING A FUNCTION.

```
SELECT   mt.movie_info.title, mt.movie_info.length,
         another_schema.ratio(movie_info)
FROM     movie_table AS mt
WHERE    mt.movie_info.title = 'Titanic'
```

Note particularly that we used *functional notation* when we invoked the `ratio` function; by contrast, we used dot notation when we invoked the `title` observer function (that is, the `title` observer method).

SQL-Paths

In many programming languages, all subprograms invoked from a given chunk of code are located in some well-defined repository, such as an object code library or a predefined file system directory. Java differs somewhat in how it locates its closest analog to "subprograms"—class definitions and the methods they contain. Java uses the concept of a *class path* that is used in locating class definitions required by a Java program. A class path is a list of "places" where the Java runtime system might find a class definition when it requires one—typically a list of file system directory names. When the Java runtime system encounters a command to use a class definition of which it is not yet aware (including an invocation of a method in such a class definition), it searches the file system directories in the order they appear in the class path. The first directory in that list that contains a class of the required name is then used as the source of the class definition being sought.

SQL's analog to a class path is called the *SQL-path*. An SQL-path is a list of database schemas in which functions may be located. In SQL:1999, an SQL-path is associated with each routine, which the routine inherits from the schema in which it is defined. (Each session also has a default SQL-path that is used when executing dynamic SQL statements.) Example 7.16 shows how an SQL-path is specified.

When SQL encounters a function invocation, it searches the schemas in the SQL-path (in the order they appear in the SQL-path, of course) for a function with the required name and parameter list. (As we'll see later in this section, functions are not uniquely identified by their names in SQL, but by a combination of their names and their parameter lists.)

SQL metadata can continue to change long after SQL programs using that metadata have been compiled. In an environment this dynamic, it is quite possible to have many functions with the same name and parameter list (but no such duplication can occur within a single schema). If this should occur, the fact that schemas are searched in the

EXAMPLE 7.16 SPECIFYING AN SQL-PATH.

```
CREATE SCHEMA movie_db
  PATH movie_db, music_db, extra_routines

  CREATE TABLE ...
```

order their names appear in the SQL-path means that a single schema can be unambiguously selected: the one in the schema appearing earlier in the SQL-path than any of the other competing functions.

Procedures

SQL:1999's procedures, we've already mentioned, are routines that do not return a value in any way other than through an explicit parameter; Java's closest analog is its `void` methods. Procedures, therefore, are permitted to have parameters that are used for output as well as parameters that are used for input (and, for that matter, parameters that are used for both).

Although procedures' parameters can have structured types as their data types, there is no special treatment of this, either in terms of notation or in terms of the handling of the parameter list. Consequently, procedures really don't affect the SQL object model very much, and we won't discuss them further in this chapter. (We included this section only for completeness!)

Effects of Null Parameters

The bulleted list at the end of the subsection Method Definition, above, included the following item:

- Whether the method always returns the null value when any of its arguments is null and thus need not be called in that situation; the default is `CALLED ON NULL INPUT`.

When you write a method (or a function or procedure), you have many choices regarding its behaviors. One choice that you might make—probably in the name of runtime efficiency—is to choose whether the method should actually be invoked in the case that any of the arguments of a method invocation have the null value. For instance, a method that returns the title of a movie concatenated with a string indicating its running time in hours and minutes would never return a meaningful value if the column containing the movie's data was missing. As a result, we might choose to bypass the otherwise-inevitable runtime costs associated with that method invocation whenever the value of the `movie_table.movie_info` column is null. To implement this decision, we would revise the function definition to look like the one in Example 7.17.

EXAMPLE 7.17 DEFINING A METHOD WITH NULL ON NULL INPUT.

```
CREATE METHOD another_schema.title_and_length
                  (movie_param movie)
    RETURNS REAL
    RETURNS NULL ON NULL INPUT
  RETURN...
```

On the other hand, we might choose to return some actual value—perhaps some numeric value such as zero—in this situation. If we wanted to do that, then we could revise the function to look like the one in Example 7.18.

EXAMPLE 7.18 DEFINING A METHOD WITH CALLED ON NULL INPUT.

```
CREATE METHOD another_schema.title_and_length
                    (movie_param movie)
    RETURNS REAL
    CALLED ON NULL INPUT

  IF movie_param.title IS NULL OR
     movie_param.runs IS NULL
    THEN RETURN 0
    ELSE RETURN...
  END IF
```

Now, there's an important exception to the rule about null values we quoted at the start of this section. The exception occurs only if the routine being invoked is a method and that method is actually a mutator for some attribute of a structured type. Even in this case, the exception is only relevant to the first, implicit parameter of the method. If the implicit argument of an invocation of a mutator is the null value, then the mutator doesn't *return* a null value—instead, you'll get a runtime exception indicating that the operation you attempted is prohibited.

Polymorphism and Overloading

Several times so far in this chapter, we've referred you forward to this section. At this point, we introduce the concept of *overloading* as it applies to SQL's methods and functions. (SQL's procedures can be overloaded only using the number of parameters; a future edition of the SQL standard might enhance that capability.)

In SQL, as in Java and other programming languages with this capability, the word "overload" means to create multiple routines that have the same name. Now, obviously, there has to be some way for any system—whether it's a compiler, a linker, or a runtime system—to choose exactly one routine to invoke in response to a given routine invocation. In SQL, one could argue that routines with the same name that are stored in different schemas can be distinguished by using the schema name. Well, that's true, but irrelevant, since SQL considers the routine name to include the schema name (and, where supported, the catalog name as well).

Well, then, you might well ask: How can there be more than one routine with the same name, since SQL doesn't permit us to store multiple objects (of the same type) with the same name into a single schema? The answer is that SQL's routines all have two names! One of these names, called the "specific name," is an ordinary schema-qualified name; this name is used to ensure that we don't store two routines with the same identifier into a given schema, and it is thus always completely unique in a database.

The other name of a routine is just called its "routine name," but we like to think of it as the "invocable name." This second name is the one that you will normally use when you want to invoke a method or function (or call a procedure), and it is the name that can be duplicated among many routines in the database. Now, it's relevant to explore just how SQL decides which routine to actually invoke among those having the same invocable name. As we suggested earlier, the argument list of the routine invocation is used (along with the SQL-path, in the case of functions, but not methods).

You can read the specific algorithm in exhaustive detail in a book that specifically addresses the SQL/PSM-96 standard (such as Jim's book that we mentioned in Chapter 6), so we won't repeat it here. However, a short review would be helpful for those of you who don't want to get into it too deeply.

The algorithm in the SQL/PSM-96 book is affected by SQL:1999's introduction of UDTs and methods, so we will briefly summarize the routine resolution differences between methods and other functions—they are few and straightforward. The only significant difference appears in how the system determines exactly which routine will be executed for a given function or method invocation.

Methods and ordinary functions in SQL:1999 are *polymorphic* (a fancy name for *overloadable*[4]), and all routines with the same invocable name are candidates for execution of some particular function or method invocation using that name—as long as there are sufficient differences in the parameter declarations to allow the system to resolve that function or method invocation to a single specific routine with the specified name. In the absence of a type hierarchy (see Section 7.6), functions and methods are resolved using almost the same algorithm—invocations of ordinary functions have an additional factor: the SQL-path (a list of schema names) can be used to resolve them.

When you write an invocation for a method or for an ordinary function, the system resolves that invocation to a single routine at the time the code containing the invocation is compiled. The number of arguments in the routine invocation is used to limit the routines examined—only those routines declared with the same number of parameters are considered. After that, the *declared type* of each argument, including the first implicit argument of methods, is used by the system to discover the specific routine with the best match between each argument and the corresponding declared parameter of the various possible functions or methods. If the invocation being resolved is for an ordinary function, then the function contained in the schema whose name appears first in the SQL-path is chosen; if the invocation is for a method, then the selection of a single routine is deferred until runtime, when the actual most-specific runtime type of the distinguished argument can be used to make the proper selection choice.

This means that the system can either find a single best-match routine to execute for the routine invocation, or else it will determine that there are two or more routines with equivalent matches of arguments and parameters, in which case a syntax error will be given at compile time.

To illustrate this, we'll invent a new kind of ratio that we'd like to investigate. This ratio, however, isn't limited to just the `movie` structured type; it is the ratio between the length of a movie (in minutes) and its rental cost (in whatever currency units we're using). The function we'll write has two parameters, as shown in Example 7.19.

Note that we've added a new clause to specify the "specific name" of this function; the default specific name of the original function is implementation-defined, but we always prefer to assign a specific name that helps us identify the routine when we need to get to *that* specific

---

[4] In recent years, it has become common to reserve the word "polymorphic" for identifying routines whose invocations' behaviors can change at runtime based solely on the most specific runtime type of one (or more) arguments. We use the more traditional (original) definition of the word here.

EXAMPLE 7.19 OVERLOADING A FUNCTION NAME.

```
CREATE FUNCTION
            another_schema.ratio (movie_param movie,
                                  cost_param  DECIMAL(5,2))
    RETURNS REAL
    SPECIFIC another_schema.ratio_2

  RETURN movie_param.runs/cost_param
```

routine. In this new function, the first parameter has the same data type (movie) that our original ratio function's first parameter has. However, the fact that it has a second parameter means that the SQL system can distinguish between invocations of the two functions, as we see in Example 7.20.

EXAMPLE 7.20 USING OVERLOADED FUNCTIONS.

```
SELECT   movie_info.title, movie_info.runs,
         another_schema.ratio(movie_info),
         another_schema.ratio(movie_info, rental_cost)
FROM     movie_table
WHERE    title(movie_info) = 'Titanic'
```

As you'll see in Section 7.6, the existence of a type hierarchy makes this slightly—but only slightly—more complex.

7.4.4 Creating Instances of Structured Types

By now, you should have a reasonable start on understanding SQL:1999's structured types, including how they are declared, how the data they contain is represented, and how their semantics are provided. But you still haven't seen how instances of these types are created. Before we can discuss the use of structured types in the database in any detail, we must first go over some important issues related to their nature and instantiation.

Instances Are Values

The most important characteristic of structured types that we have not yet mentioned is this: their instances are *values,* not objects. Some readers—especially those of you with a strong Java background—are undoubtedly raising your eyebrows about now. After all, we've been giving the impression that the purpose of this chapter on SQL user-defined types had some relationship to Java classes, and we've even used the term "SQL object model." Furthermore, we've compared structured types to Java classes and we've compared SQL's methods to Java methods. Why are we now saying that structured type instances are not objects?

Well, the fact is that instances of SQL's structured types have no object identity. There is no concept of some "other" value that uniquely identifies any structured type instance. The only "identity" that a structured type value has in SQL is its own value—just like an integer or character string value.

Still, don't despair! Structured type instances in SQL have many characteristics that would be considered "object-like" by many observers, including encapsulation (which we've already discussed) and even the ability to participate in type hierarchies (still to come in Section 7.6). Even better, when we get to Section 7.7, we'll show you exactly how SQL:1999 really does provide the remaining aspects of object orientation. But until we do, let's focus on just how structured type *values* come into being and how they are used in the database.

A Little Philosophy of Mathematics

Programmers in object-oriented programming languages use the term *constructor* to mean a routine that creates a new instance of an object class or type. As we'll see, the term has a slightly different meaning in SQL:1999. The difference is modest, and we'll let you judge for yourselves whether it's an important one or not.

Mathematical purists will argue that nobody can ever "create" a value—all values simply *exist* and the most that can be done with them is to represent them at some location. For example, the number eight exists; there's nothing you or I can do that will make it "go away" or that will change anything at all about it. We can, of course, write it down on a piece of paper in any of several notations ("Eight," "ocho," "huit," "8," "viii," "VIII," "||||||||," "(2*3)+2," and so forth). No matter what notation we use, no matter what language, national script, or font we use, the result is still the number of fingers (excluding thumbs) on most peoples' two hands.

So what?

Well, when you create a variable in some program you're writing, and you store into that variable a bit sequence that represents the number eight, you aren't "creating" the number eight, you're merely manifesting a representation of it in memory. By contrast, a great many programmers use different terminology when they manifest a representation of a more complex value, such as a structure or an array. The word "construct" appears fairly often, as does the word "create," as in "create an array with 3 elements in which the first element contains 1, the second 10, and the third 100." Of course, that array is a value, too, and already existed in the same sense that the number eight exists; but many (perhaps most!) of us think about it a little differently. So does SQL:1999, which uses the term "construct" to describe the process of manifesting a structured type value.

Constructors and the NEW Expression

An SQL:1999 constructor is a function that your applications use whenever a new value of a structured type is required. A constructor function returns a value of its associated structured type in which every attribute has its default value. (Incidentally, a structured type instance in which every attribute has the null value is *not* the same as a null structured type instance! Think about it and compare with the notion of a "null integer.")

Constructors always have the same name as the structured type with which they're associated, in much the same way—and for much the same reason—that observer and mutator functions have the same name as the attributes with which they are associated. And, like observer and mutator functions, constructor functions are really methods. Constructors have no parameters (we call them *niladic* functions). The SQL system always provides a default constructor function for you whenever you create a structured type.

Naturally, since the constructor function returns a value and not an object, you can do it as many times as you'd like and get a new instance of that value over and over. You can do what you wish with the value returned: you can store it into an SQL variable, put it into a column in a table, or simply "throw it away," just as you can with the number eight. But, just how often will your application be satisfied with a "default" instance of a structured type? We believe that applications will often, perhaps usually, want to produce structured type instances in which some or all attributes have values other than their default values.

SQL:1999 responds to this requirement by providing *initializer methods*. An initializer method is one that takes a newly constructed instance of a structured type in which all attributes have their default values and replaces it with an instance in which some or all attributes have been given different values—based entirely on the semantics of the initializer method, which is written by the application builder or the type designer. You can build as many initializer methods as you wish for a given structured type. They are (normally) not niladic methods but have whatever parameters you decide to be appropriate.

Suppose we want to create a new instance of our `movie` structured type. We know that the system has provided us with a niladic constructor method, also named `movie`. The method invocation shown in Example 7.21 will construct a new, default instance of the `movie` type, which we might visualize as shown in Table 7.2.

EXAMPLE 7.21 INVOKING A NILADIC CONSTRUCTOR.

```
MOVIE()
```

Of course, we probably don't need to represent very many movies with those characteristics, so we'll need an initializer method that we can use to put more reasonable values into our new `movie` instance. Such a method might be written something like Example 7.22.

EXAMPLE 7.22 NONDEFAULT INITIALIZER METHOD.

```
CREATE METHOD movie ( name        CHARACTER VARYING (50),
                      descr       CHARACTER VARYING (500),
                      len         INTEGER )
    RETURNS movie

  BEGIN
    SET SELF.title = name;
    SET SELF.description = descr;
    SET SELF.runs = len;
    RETURN SELF;
  END
```

This method will take the (presumably default) `movie` instance provided to it as its implicit parameter (remember: this is called `SELF` internally) and set its attributes to values passed into it as explicit parameters. In this case, we've chosen to set all of the type instance's attributes, but we could have chosen as easily to set only some of them.

When we put all this together in an application that uses this type, we might write code like that shown in Example 7.23.

Attribute name	Value
TITLE	*(null)*
DESCRIPTION	*(null)*
RUNS	*(null)*

TABLE 7.2 *Default `MOVIE` instance.*

EXAMPLE 7.23 SAMPLE APPLICATION USING NONDEFAULT INITIALIZER.

```
BEGIN            -- Some new block of code
  DECLARE film     movie;
  SET film =
     NEW movie(
       'The Game',
       'A chilling thriller in which Michael Douglas' ||
       'plays a man given a "gift" by his younger' ||
       'brother...a gift that threatens his life' ||
       'and his sanity.',
       128 );
  ...
END
```

Now, that NEW expression is syntactically transformed to the expression shown in Example 7.24.

EXAMPLE 7.24 TRANSFORMATION OF THE NEW EXPRESSION.

```
movie().movie(
       'The Game',
       'A chilling thriller in which Michael Douglas' ||
       'plays a man given a "gift" by his younger' ||
       'brother...a gift that threatens his life' ||
       'and his sanity.',
       128 )
```

In other words, the keyword NEW specifies that the constructor function, whose name is movie, is invoked, producing a new default value of the movie structured type, after which the initializer method, also named movie, is invoked—it receives the just-constructed default value as its implicit parameter and populates it with some new values. As we saw a few lines earlier, the initializer then returns the populated value to its caller, the SET statement, at which time it is assigned to the SQL variable film. One thing we don't want to forget is this: All methods that are defined with names that are the same as the name of their associated structured type are presumed to be initializers for that type. This means that you can invoke those methods *only* in the context of the NEW expression or the context of its syntactic transformation that we just showed you.

Now, if you prefer to populate your type instances "manually", you can always use the default constructor and then write statements that invoke mutator methods on the default instance that it returns, as we see in Example 7.25:

EXAMPLE 7.25 AN ALTERNATIVE TO USER-DEFINED INITIALIZERS.

```
BEGIN
  DECLARE film    movie;
  SET film = movie();    -- Invoke the default constructor
  SET film.title = 'The Game';
  SET film.runs = 128;
END                      -- The description is still null!
```

7.5 Using Structured Types

Of course, creating and giving values to structured type instances is not nearly as interesting if you're not able to store them in your database, get them back out, and modify them.

7.5.1 Storing in the Database

If you want to store a structured type instance into a column of a table—let's use that `movie_table` we declared earlier—then you'll naturally use SQL's INSERT statement, as shown in Example 7.26.

EXAMPLE 7.26 INSERTING A NEW MOVIE INSTANCE USING A CONSTRUCTOR.

```
INSERT INTO movie_table
  VALUES ( '152208-A'  -- STOCK_NUMBER
           NEW movie(
           'The Game',
           'A chilling thriller in which Michael Douglas' ||
           'plays a man given a "gift" by his younger' ||
           'brother...a gift that threatens his life' ||
           'and his sanity.',
           128 ),                -- new MOVIE instance
           23                    -- RENTAL_QUANTITY in stock
           2.99 )                -- RENTAL_COST
```

Yup . . . it's that easy. We just created—and populated—a new `movie` instance right in the middle of the VALUES clause of an INSERT statement. Of course, if we already had an SQL variable—perhaps the variable named `film` that we defined above—we could have used that in the INSERT statement, as shown in Example 7.27.

EXAMPLE 7.27 INSERTING A NEW MOVIE INSTANCE USING AN INITIALIZED VARIABLE.

```
INSERT INTO movie_table
  VALUES ( '152208-A',    -- STOCK_NUMBER
           film,          -- just a MOVIE instance
           23,            -- RENTAL_QUANTITY in stock
           2.99 )         -- RENTAL_COST
```

7.5.2 Updating in the Database

Updating structured type instances in the database isn't much more complicated. The additional complexity comes in because you're dealing with an existing value of which you often want to update only a part—not the entire value.

As shown in Example 7.28, we would correctly expect that the value of the `rental_cost` column in the row for the specified film to be set to 1.99, regardless of what the cost was previously.

EXAMPLE 7.28 UPDATING THE PRICE OF A MOVIE.

```
UPDATE   movie_table
SET      rental_cost = 1.99
WHERE    stock_number = '152208-A'
```

Similarly, as shown in Example 7.29, we shouldn't be at all surprised when the entire `movie` value is replaced with something not terribly interesting—a film with no name or description, but we *do* know that it's a really long movie! How, then, can we change just the `length` of a `movie`, without messing with the `title` or `description`? Well, we simply have to remember that all values we don't want to be affected must either be untouched or set to their original values. One way to do that is shown in Example 7.30.

EXAMPLE 7.29 CREATING AN UNINTERESTING, BUT LENGTHY, MOVIE.

```
UPDATE   movie_table
SET      movie = NEW movie('', '', 228 )
WHERE    stock_number = '152208-A'
```

EXAMPLE 7.30 UPDATING THE LENGTH OF A MOVIE.

```
UPDATE   movie_table
SET      movie = NEW movie(movie.title,
                           movie.description,
                           113 )
WHERE    stock_number = '152208-A'
```

We find that approach awkward: If we need to replace only one or two attributes of a type that has dozens of attributes, we must remember to "copy" every one of the attributes we don't want to change. That is certainly tedious and probably very prone to error. (Worse, using this approach requires that the user have been granted appropriate privileges on the observer functions, which can be even more tedious in large enterprises.) Instead, we prefer a solution that uses a mutator function, as shown in Example 7.31:

EXAMPLE 7.31 A BETTER WAY TO UPDATE THE LENGTH OF A MOVIE.

```
UPDATE   movie_table
SET      movie = movie.length( 113 )
WHERE    stock_number = '152208-A'
```

You'll recall from reading Section 7.4.3 that the mutator function for some attribute of a structured type has the name of the attribute (`length` in this case) and takes two parameters—but the first parameter is an implicit parameter that is represented by specifying the name of some site containing an instance of the type to the left of the "dot" (`movie` in this case). You may also recall that the mutator function returns a new instance of the type that is identical in all attributes to the "input" type *except* for the eponymous attribute, whose value is set to the value of the second parameter (that is, the only explicit parameter). Whew!

That's a long-winded way to say that the SET clause

```
SET movie = movie.runs ( 113 )
```

sets the value of the `movie` column to a new `movie` value in which the `title` and `description` are unchanged, but the `length` value is now 113 minutes. If we wished to change two or more of the attributes for our movie instance, we could do so by stringing multiple mutator methods together:

```
SET movie = movie.runs ( 113 ).description( '...')
```

An even more convenient way of (implicitly) invoking that mutator function is shown in Example 7.32:

EXAMPLE 7.32 AN EVEN BETTER WAY TO UPDATE THE LENGTH OF A MOVIE.

```
UPDATE   movie_table
SET      movie.length = 113
WHERE    stock_number = '152208-A'
```

This last alternative is certainly the most intuitive of the various choices! It's nothing more than a syntactic shorthand for the variation in Example 7.31, but it's surely a lot more comfortable for most programmers, including us.

7.5.3 Retrieving from the Database

We've already introduced you (throughout various sections of this chapter) to the idea of retrieving structured type values—or parts of them—from the database, so this will be quite painless.

If you wish to retrieve just the length of a movie, you might write something like Example 7.33.

EXAMPLE 7.33 RETRIEVAL INTO A HOST VARIABLE.

```
SELECT   movie.runs
INTO     :length_var
FROM     movie_table
WHERE    stock_number = '152208-A'
```

You can, of course, execute that statement (in Example 7.33) from your application program written in C or COBOL.

What you cannot do in a program written in a conventional programming language is to retrieve—without a little assistance—an entire structured type value at one time. In other words, the statement in Example 7.34, though perfectly valid if executed in an SQL/PSM stored routine, would be, well, not exactly invalid in a COBOL program, but not very useful without that assistance we just suggested.

EXAMPLE 7.34 INVALID RETRIEVAL INTO A HOST VARIABLE.

```
SELECT   movie
INTO     :movie_var
FROM     movie_table
WHERE    stock_number = '152208-A'
```

Can you quickly tell why that statement wouldn't normally be very useful in COBOL? Right—there's no way in COBOL to *meaningfully* declare a COBOL variable whose data type is an SQL structured type! Of course, you can imagine that you would be able to declare a COBOL structure as shown in Example 7.35, and that would probably work just fine if it were supported by SQL:1999. But it's very easy to define more complex structured types where the COBOL equivalent isn't as obvious, so the ability to retrieve structured type instances directly into host programs was deferred to a future edition of the SQL standard.

EXAMPLE 7.35 POSSIBLE, BUT USELESS, COBOL DECLARATION.

```
01 movie-var.
02   title           PIC X(50).
02   description     PIC X(500).
02   runs            PIC S9(9).
```

On the other hand, if you've declared an SQL variable whose data type is your structured type, you're readily able to retrieve into it, as shown in Example 7.36:

EXAMPLE 7.36 STRUCTURED TYPE RETRIEVAL INTO AN SQL VARIABLE.

```
BEGIN
  DECLARE film    movie;
  SELECT   movie
  INTO     film
  FROM     movie_table
  WHERE    stock_number = '152208-A';
END
```

The difference, of course, is that it *is* possible to declare SQL variables whose data type is a structured type.

SQL:1999 does provide a facility called *transforms* that allows type definers to provide functions that map structured types to host language structures and vice versa. Be patient—Section 7.5.7 covers this issue.

7.5.4 Deleting from the Database

You *delete* a structured type instance from the database no differently than you delete a scalar value from the database. You can UPDATE the table and set the appropriate column to a null value, or you can DELETE the entire row containing the value from the table! Those of you that are approaching this material from a Java background may be wondering whether any sort of cleanup behavior can be built into structured types, similar to Java's `finalize` method. The answer is no—an instance value is simply destroyed. Of course, SQL's triggers may be useful for cleaning up after structured types that are stored in columns.

7.5.5 Copying an Instance from One Site to Another

We've already talked about the fact that SQL variables and parameters of SQL routines can have a data type that is a structured type. But there's one additional point we want to emphasize related to using those variables and parameters. Remember that instances of structured types are *values* and not objects! Therefore, when you assign an instance of a structured type to an SQL variable, it has a life of its own. Changing the value of some attribute of the instance in that SQL variable has no effect at all on the instance stored in the location from which you made the assignment.

Consider the code snippet in Example 7.37.

EXAMPLE 7.37 SET STATEMENT EXAMPLE.

```
BEGIN
  DECLARE v1, v2   movie;
  SET v1 = NEW movie('The Game',
      'A chilling thriller in which Michael Douglas' ||
      'plays a man given a "gift" by his younger' ||
      'brother...a gift that threatens his life' ||
      'and his sanity.',
      128 );
  SET v2 = v1;
  SET v1 = v1.runs ( 139 );
END
```

The first SET statement, of course, creates a new instance of `movie` and assigns it to SQL variable `v1`. The second statement *copies* that `movie` value into SQL variable `v2`. The last SET statement changes the value of `movie.length` in the value stored in `v1`, but that has *no effect at all* on the value stored in `v2`, which will still indicate the original movie length of 128 minutes. The same phenomenon holds when you pass a structured type value through an argument of a routine invocation.

7.5.6 User-Defined Type Locators

Although we don't want to spend too much time and energy on the more arcane aspects of structured types in this book, for completeness's sake, we will just briefly mention that SQL:1999 provides a facility called a *locator* that can be used to provide the application program code written in an ordinary programming language with a way to "get at" structured type values in the database. (Locators can be used to get at certain other values, including array instances and LOB instances.)

A locator is a value that is meaningful only on the application program side of the database system interface—it's meaningless in SQL/PSM routines, for example. But when passed to a host program, it can "represent" a structured type instance without actually having to move the value across the boundary. One use might be to INSERT a new row into some table in which one column of that row has a structured type value retrieved from some other table, as shown in Example 7.38:

EXAMPLE 7.38 USING UDT LOCATORS.

```
main() {
EXEC SQL BEGIN SQL DECLARE SECTION
  SQL TYPE IS film AS LOCATOR movie_loc;
END SQL DECLARE SECTION

EXEC SQL SELECT   movie
         INTO     :movie_loc
         FROM     movie_table
         WHERE    stock_number = '152208-A';
EXEC SQL INSERT INTO other_table
         VALUES (..., :movie_loc, ...);
}
```

You can readily see that we were able to *reference* the value of the `movie` instance without actually having to retrieve it across the application/database interface and then use it to create a new row for insertion into another table.

These locators have a relatively short lifetime—they are usable until either the current transaction or session ends (each implementation decides which to use). Furthermore, they cannot be shared among different users or sessions.

7.5.7 Transforms and Transform Groups

Now that we've said—several times—that you cannot transfer instances of structured types across the application/database interface, we'll admit that our statement's not entirely true.

SQL:1999 provides the ability to create sets of functions that permit transferring *representations* of structured type instances across that interface, but the type designer (or application builder) has to provide those functions. Pairs of such functions, called *transform functions,* are called *transform groups*. One of the two functions in a transform group, called a *to-sql function,* is invoked when transferring a structured type instance from the host language side of the interface to the SQL side. The other, called a *from-sql function,* is used for transferring from the SQL side to the host language side. (Note that "host language side" does not necessarily mean "application program side," since user-defined functions—in the form of external functions—can be written in host programming languages.) No structured type can have more than one transform group of the same name associated with it.

Although the application builder or type designer frequently has to provide the transform functions and specify that they belong to the appropriate transform group, you don't have to invoke them explicitly—they are implicitly invoked whenever needed. . . as long as they have been defined and specified properly.

Let's take another look at the statement in Section 7.5.3 that you'll need a little assistance to meaningfully declare a host language variable whose type is a structured type. SQL:1999 also permits you to define a COBOL variable whose data type is an SQL structured type and specify that it is "represented" by some built-in SQL type, such as CHARACTER VARYING, as illustrated in Example 7.39.

EXAMPLE 7.39 USEFUL COBOL DECLARATION.

```
01 movie-var USAGE IS SQL
    TYPE IS movie AS CHARACTER VARYING(604).
```

That declaration states that our new COBOL variable, `movie_var`, has the `movie` data type, but that its representation for purposes of transferring to and from our application program is CHARACTER VARYING(604). (In Example 7.8, we defined the `movie` type to have three attributes; the first was up to 100 characters in length, the second up to 500, and the third was an INTEGER, which we will predict to be no larger than the size of four characters.)

With no more definition than that, we can't retrieve a `movie` instance into our host variable because the database system has no way of knowing *how* we'd like the three-attribute `movie` instance to be mapped onto a CHARACTER VARYING (even though we humans might think it's fairly obvious). And that's where transforms come into play!

Briefly, a transform is an SQL-invoked function (possibly written by an application designer or a type designer, possibly provided by the database vendor) whose job it is to map a structured type to and from the "representation" type (or, indeed, types). The application program's responsibility is to instruct the database system to use a specific *transform group* (which may comprise as many as two transform functions, one for converting from the host language environment into an SQL structured type and the other for converting in the other direction).

Transforms are created with (no surprises here) a CREATE TRANSFORM statement, in which you specify the name of the user-defined type (which can be either a structured type or a distinct type!) and one or more transform group definitions. Each transform group definition names the transform group and then names either the to-sql transform function, the from-sql transform function, or both. The functions themselves must already exist, of course, before you can create a transform group naming them.

It is the job of the from-sql function to transform an SQL user-defined type instance into some other, host language–friendly form. In particular, we'd probably want to define a from-sql function, in a transform group that we might name something like `cobol_varchar_transforms`, to extract the values of each attribute of a `movie` instance and "cast" it into the "right format," placed in the "right place" in a CHARACTER VARYING(604). We'd also probably want a to-sql function in the same transform group that populates a `movie` instance from a CHARACTER VARYING(604). The declarations of methods associated with the user-defined type would also have to specify the transform group or groups with which each such method is associated. Our application would have to specify that the appropriate transform group to use is the `cobol_varchar_transforms` group. This is done by syntax in our embedded SQL COBOL program, specifying the name of the transform group to be used for each different user-defined type used in each such COBOL variable declaration. (Naturally, if you don't specify the transform groups, SQL provides defaults for you.)

Now, in order to actually make this information *useful* to your COBOL program, you've got to take one additional step: causing two COBOL names to refer to the same piece of storage. The first name is the one we declared in Example 7.39: `movie-var`. But that's going to "look like" a CHARACTER VARYING(604), and we don't really want to have to unpack the data it contains. Instead, we have to know (by reading the documentation) what corresponding COBOL structure the from-sql function assumes, as shown in Example 7.40.

EXAMPLE 7.40 COMPLETE COBOL DECLARATIONS.

```
01 movie-var USAGE IS SQL
     TYPE IS movie AS CHARACTER VARYING(604).
01 movie-structure REDEFINES movie-var.
   02 title              PIC X(100).
   02 description        PIC X(500).
   02 length             PIC S9(9).
```

Assuming that we correctly read the documentation of the appropriate from-sql function in the `cobol_varchar_transforms` group, every time we retrieve an instance of the `movie` type into our `movie-var` variable, the fields of `movie-structure` will be populated with the attributes of that `movie` instance! (In Fortran, you'd use the `EQUIVALENCE` facility, and in C, you'd use the `union` capability; most programming languages allow this sort of duality of storage.)

This requirement is especially relevant when you want to use Java and SQL together (we'll bet you saw that coming, didn't you?). As you'll see in Chapter 9, JDBC 2.0 provides the ability for mapping tables to be defined that correlate Java classes with SQL's structured types—and this automatically selects the appropriate transform group and invokes the transform functions when you use the JDBC methods to retrieve SQL structured type instances from the database or send Java class instances to the database. That is, this capability transforms Java objects into SQL values and vice versa! (Ain't technology grand?) If you need to know more about transforms, you should consult a resource that covers SQL:1999 in more detail.

7.5.8 The Type Predicate

We'll also mention only briefly the fact that SQL:1999 provides a predicate—called a "type predicate"—that can be used to test a structured type instance to determine its exact type. You can learn the syntax and precise semantics of this predicate by referring to an SQL:1999–specific resource, but we thought it interesting enough to mention in this chapter.

7.6 Type Hierarchies

Significantly, structured types can participate in *type hierarchies;* that is, an SQL structured type can be a *subtype* of another structured type, called its *supertype.* Although many readers of this book (after all, many of you are Java programmers or otherwise familiar with Java) already understand type hierarchies, we'll take a few minutes to outline the meaning and importance of the concept. If you're already familiar with the idea, feel free to take a short break—we'll try to be done with this section before you get back.

7.6.1 What Is a Type Hierarchy?

A type hierarchy in SQL is a collection of user-defined types, some of which are "specializations" of other types. Again, this may best be illustrated by example. In our music and video store example, we need to model a number of real-life objects, such as music (CDs, cassettes, vinyl LPs, and MiniDiscs) and movies. Movies are available as VHS tapes, laserdiscs, and DVDs, which now come with Dolby Digital 5.1 sound (sometimes called AC-3) and DTS 5.1 sound. (However, we have chosen not to stock Divx products!) In designing our applications and database, we observed that all of the movie formats we handle have a lot in common but a few differences as well. For example, all movie formats include the title of the movie, the description, the studio, the director, the producer, and so forth. However, VHS tapes and DVDs have different stock numbers and quite often have different contents (DVDs usually have additional features, such as soundtracks in multiple languages, or even "featurettes" about the making of the movie). Therefore, we found it desirable to model "movie" as one concept and "DVD" as a different, but very closely related, concept. Figure 7.1 illustrates one possible relationship among the formats we handle in our store.

In this figure, the box labeled "Movie" represents a structured type whose components capture information common to all movie formats that we stock (e.g., title, description, running time), while the boxes labeled "VHS tape," "DVD," and "Laserdisc" represent structured types whose components capture—*in addition to common information*—information specific to individual formats stocked. A specific instance of the VHS tape type would contain components that identify the title of the movie on the tape, the description of the movie, the running time, the stock number of the VHS tape, the rental price, and the number of tapes we have for rental. Similarly, a specific instance of the

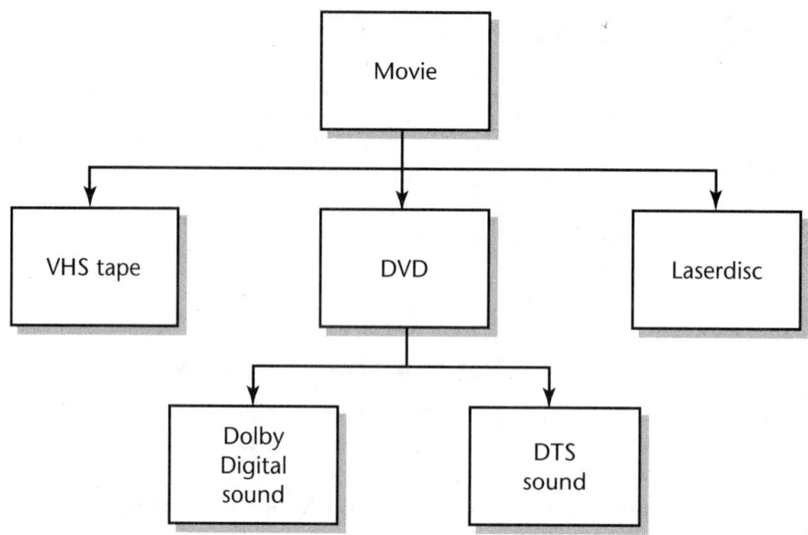

FIGURE 7.1 *Our type hierarchy.*

laserdisc type for the same movie would contain components that identify the title of the movie, the description of the movie, the running time, the stock number of the laserdisc, the rental price, the number of discs we have for rental, and whether or not it was recorded in CLV (constant linear velocity) or CAV (constant angular velocity) mode.

7.6.2 Subtypes and Supertypes

The VHS tape, DVD, and laserdisc types are called *subtypes* of the Movie type; similarly, the Movie type is a *supertype* of each of those three other types. Type hierarchies can be as deep as desired. That is, the DVD type can have its own subtypes to represent, say, DVDs recorded with Dolby Digital sound and DVDs recorded with the somewhat less common DTS sound.

Of course, attentive readers—like you—will immediately recognize that VHS tapes, DVDs, laserdiscs, and so forth, all will have a stock number, a sales price, and a list of stars—therefore, these attributes could (and probably *should*) be specified in the supertype Movie. The fact that the *values* of those attributes will differ, perhaps significantly, in various subtypes doesn't imply at all that they should be defined in the subtypes. Only attributes that appear in one subtype alone should be defined in that subtype—such as whether CLV mode or CAV mode was used for a laserdisc: since DVDs and VHS tapes don't have those characteristics, that attribute wouldn't be specified for those subtypes.

However, let's avoid passionate and opinionated discussions like data modeling for the moment; we're trying to illustrate a point here, not fully design a system!

The idea of subtypes has to be distinguished from another sort of hierarchy involving structured types. Any structured type can have attributes whose data type is another structured type (or, at least theoretically—though not in SQL:1999—the same structured type!). Although that might seem to create a "type hierarchy," the term is not applied here—it's reserved for supertype/subtype relationships.

We showed you the SQL syntax for defining structured types in Example 7.5. Because the scope of this book does not extend to teaching you all about SQL structured types, Example 7.5 is incomplete, so don't be concerned that you can't follow all of the details—they're not there. In particular, the optional `reference-type-specification`, `cast-option`, and `method-specification-list` items are irrelevant to the present discussion and won't be covered in detail in this book. However, in Chapter 8, you will see more about the `method-specification-list`, since it does have relevance to the subject of that chapter.

Perhaps obviously, if the UNDER clause is specified, the type being defined is a subtype of the type indicated by the `supertype-name`. This is how type hierarchies are formed.

A brief explanation of FINAL and NOT FINAL, as well as of INSTANTIABLE and NOT INSTANTIABLE, is in order. A user-defined type defined as FINAL cannot have subtypes defined on it—that is, it can never be a supertype of another type; in SQL:1999, this limitation is available only for distinct types. Type designers might occasionally want to ensure that no application creates a more specialized type (again, discussion of why this might be so is beyond the scope of this book; interested readers should turn to one of the many books available on data modeling to explore that subject) and would thus specify the type to be FINAL. If FINAL isn't specified, then NOT FINAL (meaning that creation of subtypes is permitted) is the default; in SQL:1999, this is available only for structured types. This arrangement pretty closely matches Java's use of `final` for methods and classes.

A structured type declared to be INSTANTIABLE is one for which instances can be created—that is, values in your applications can have that type as their data type. Once in a while, though, a type designer may decide that she's creating a specific type for which values must never be created; instead, one or more (usually more!) subtypes of that type are defined and all values in the system have to be of one of those subtypes. This requirement is enforced by making the supertype NOT INSTANTIABLE. An `abstract` class in Java is analogous to a NOT INSTANTIABLE structured type in SQL.

Now, let's consider the `AS representation` clause. This clause is optional, so you can define a new type to be a subtype of an existing type without being required to specify any additional attributes of the type. You might use that option, for example, to create a subtype with some new behaviors but without any additional stored data. On the other hand, if you're creating a structured type without any supertypes, then you *must* specify the `AS representation` clause—otherwise, the type won't have any attributes at all!

Inclusion of the `AS representation` clause allows you to specify (enclosed in parentheses) a comma-separated list of type attributes that look a lot like column definitions inside a table definition—the principal difference being that attribute definitions can't contain constraints, whereas column definitions can. Attribute definitions are composed primarily of an attribute name and a data type, and the data type can be either a built-in type, a distinct type, or a structured type. (Attributes have other characteristics, as well, but they're not relevant to this discussion.)

A definition of our Movie type from Figure 7.1 might look like Example 7.41:

EXAMPLE 7.41 A SUPERTYPE DEFINITION.

```
CREATE TYPE movie AS (
  title          CHARACTER VARYING(100),
  description    CHARACTER VARYING(500),
  runs           INTEGER )
  NOT INSTANTIABLE
  NOT FINAL
```

We made this type NOT INSTANTIABLE because we don't stock any product that is just "Movie"; we only stock VHS tapes, DVDs, and so forth. Of course, it would be meaningless to make a NOT INSTANTIABLE type FINAL as well, so SQL:1999 prohibits that combination!

Next, let's look at Example 7.42, a type definition for the DVD type:

EXAMPLE 7.42 A SUBTYPE DEFINITION.

```
CREATE TYPE dvd UNDER movie AS (
  stock_number   INTEGER,
  rental_price   DECIMAL(5,2),
  extra_features feature_desc ARRAY[10] )
  INSTANTIABLE
  NOT FINAL
```

The dvd type, being a subtype of the movie type, contains all of the attributes that the movie type has, but it has three additional attributes: the stock number, the rental price, and an array of feature_desc values. We may guess that the feature_desc type is another structured type that we use to describe the extra features that DVDs often have. We allow a maximum of 10 extra features on a single DVD (though we hasten to note that we rarely get that many features for our money!). Since DVDs have variations—Dolby Digital DVDs and DTS DVDs—we would probably create a couple of additional subtypes to deal with that, but the information particular to each would probably be somewhat esoteric; for example, a Dolby Digital DVD is very likely to have an alternate sound track encoded in Dolby Surround, but that information might not be required on a DTS DVD.

It's important to note that the feature_desc type is *not* likely to be a subtype of the movie type. In fact, it's unlikely that it's part of the same type hierarchy at all; it's more likely that it belongs to a different type hierarchy, possibly one with only a single type. In fact, SQL:1999 doesn't allow you to define any structured type as "based on" itself, directly or indirectly. This means, that it would be invalid in SQL:1999 to define, say, a "tree" type recursively. In other words, the structure shown in Figure 7.2 would not be permitted.

It's true that there are other programming languages that allow type definers to define a type in terms of itself—to define types recursively. However, those languages don't have to deal with some of the concepts that SQL does, such as persistent storage of data, including type instances, and tables defined to be "of" a given type (see Section 7.8 for more information on this subject). Those problems make it somewhat

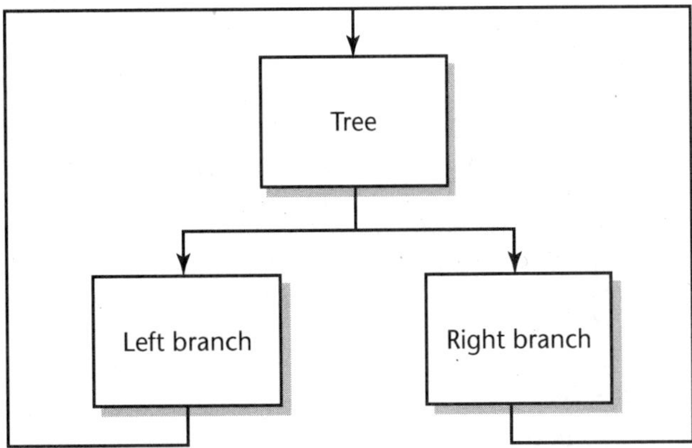

FIGURE 7.2 *Invalid SQL:1999 type structure.*

more difficult—though probably not impossible—to define SQL:1999's structured types recursively. Perhaps some future revision of the SQL standard will offer that capability.

7.6.3 Single Inheritance

Some programming languages, C++, for example, support a form of type hierarchy in which subtypes are allowed to inherit characteristics (that is, stored data and behaviors) from multiple supertypes. Although this capability offers tremendous power for modeling some types of applications, it also introduces some extremely difficult implementation problems, particularly in systems offering persistent storage of data (as opposed to memory-resident storage only) and distributed systems.

SQL:1999 made the choice to eschew multiple inheritance in favor of a model supporting only single inheritance. (If you're mathematically inclined, you'll recognize that this means that SQL:1999 type hierarchies can represent tree structures, but not network structures, whether acyclic or cyclic.) Although this may seem to have been an undesirable choice, we must point out that the same choice was made by Java, which doesn't appear to have hurt its popularity any!

It's true that Java offers single inheritance of *implementation,* but multiple inheritance of *interface*. You Java programmers know what this means, but let us spend a sentence or two for the non-Java folks in the audience. In Java terms, an interface is the definitions of signatures for a collection of methods. Java permits a subclass to inherit its implementation (that is, the code for the methods and the variables for data) from only one supertype, thus avoiding those sticky multiple inheritance implementation issues. However, it allows a class to inherit as many interfaces as needed, meaning that it gets the benefits of all of those method signatures for which the class writer then needs to add code to implement the methods. We find this a very neat compromise that avoids some very expensive implementation problems, while allowing applications that really *need* multiple inheritance to get many of the benefits. We expect this capability to eventually show up in SQL too.

7.6.4 Most Specific Type

Looking back at our Movie hierarchy, you will readily see that a movie distributed on a VHS tape is, at one time, a Movie *and* a VHS tape; similarly, one distributed on a Dolby Digital DVD is at once a Movie, a DVD, and a Dolby Digital DVD. This is, in fact, the essence of a subtype—that its instances are simultaneously of their own type as well as all of their supertypes. This condition leads to a terminology problem: If a specific structured type instance is a `dolby_dvd`, a `dvd`, and a `movie`, then what type is it really?

To resolve this modest dilemma, SQL:1999 has chosen the term "most specific type" to mean "the structured type closest to the leaves of the type hierarchy of which the instance is a member." This is also the constructor type that was used when the instance was created. Therefore, if we have a structured type value whose data type is `dvd`, but was neither a `dolby_dvd` nor a `dts_dvd`, then its most specific type is `dvd`. Of course, one of its types (though not its most specific type) is `movie`. But none of its types is `dolby_dvd` or `dts_dvd`.

7.6.5 Substitutability

The reason that the concept of "most specific type" is especially interesting is this: If you have some location whose data type is a structured type, you can store into that location any value whose most specific type is that type or any of its subtypes! For example, if you declare a variable whose type is `movie`:

```
DECLARE film movie;
```

you can store into that variable an instance that is a `movie`, a `dvd`, or a `dolby_dvd`:

```
SET film = NEW dolby_dvd(...);
```

The *declared type* of `film` is, of course, `movie`—you can see it right there on the page (that's a result of its being the declared type!). But, after executing that `SET` statement, the most specific type of the value stored in `film` is `dolby_dvd`.

The ability to use a subtype at any location where a supertype is expected is called *substitutability*—that is, you can substitute a subtype for a supertype. The reverse, which may be surprising to some, is not true. Let's look very briefly at the reason why. Recall that all attributes of structured types are encapsulated by means of the pair of methods we described earlier (the observer and the mutator). If we wanted to assign the value that contains the title of a movie stored in our `film` variable to some other variable, we might write something like this:

```
SET newvar = film.title;
```

If there's a `movie`—that is, a value whose most specific type is movie—stored in `film`, then that statement will extract the value of the `title` attribute and store it into the variable named `newvar`. However, suppose that `film` actually has a `dolby_dvd` stored in it. Since `dolby_dvd` instances are also, at the same time, `movie` instances, they have a `title` attribute, too. Therefore, the SET statement works as expected, assigning the value of the `title` attribute to `newvar`.

But what about doing things the other way around? Suppose we declared a variable:

```
DECLARE cinema dvd;
```

As you will recall, `dvd`s have a `stock_number` attribute, but `movies` do not. If we store a `dvd` instance into that variable:

```
SET cinema = NEW dvd(...);
```

then we have a value stored there in which we can use six attributes: `title`, `description`, `length`, `stock_number`, `rental_price`, and `extra_features`. However, suppose we decided to store a `movie` instance—not a `vhs_tape` or a `dvd`, just a `movie`—into that variable. The `movie` instance simply doesn't have a `stock_number` attribute, even though the variable inherently does. We can't just make up a value to put into that attribute, not even null! The only solution is to prohibit storing a `movie` instance into a location declared as one of its subtypes. As a result, substitutability works only in one direction!

7.6.6 Polymorphism and Overloading (Redux)

Now that you understand that SQL:1999's structured types can participate in type hierarchies, and the fact that they support only single inheritance, we need to slightly modify our description of method overloading from Section 7.4.3.

Recall from our earlier discussion of this subject that you are allowed to have more than one method or function (or, in a more limited way, procedures) in your database with the same invocable name—they are distinguished by having unique specific names, as well as in having distinct parameter lists. Such routines with the same invocable name are said to be overloaded, or polymorphic. The SQL environment identifies exactly one routine for each routine invocation based on the number of arguments provided and (except for procedures) their data types.

Once we add subtypes to the mix, the situation gets a little more complicated, but only a little. Adding support for type hierarchies means that we now have to distinguish between the sort of overloading we've already described and a new type of overloading—specifying a method in a subtype that has the same name and same parameter list as a method in one of its supertypes. Java programmers will know this phenomenon as *overriding,* and SQL:1999 makes the same terminological distinction.

Method Overriding

The principal new complication arises with overriding methods. As you will quickly appreciate, once you spend a few minutes thinking about it, there is a high probability that you'll want methods defined on some subtype to be different—if only slightly—from the methods of the same name (and the same conceptual functionality) defined on its supertypes. An SQL:1999 enhancement to method overloading is the key to taking care of this requirement. But let's be clear: The availability of subtypes has no effect on *function* overloading, only method overloading, and the new term (*overriding*) is used to emphasize the capability.

Method Resolution Let's look at a typical situation: You've defined a type hierarchy like the one we've been using in this chapter, including a `movie` type, its three subtypes (`vhs_tape`, `dvd`, and `laser_disc`), and the two `dvd` subtypes (`dolby_dvd` and `dts_dvd`). Now, you want to have methods that will format the attributes of instances of these types in preparation for displaying them on users' screens; let's call this method `display`.

To nobody's surprise, because `vhs_tape` instances have different attributes than `dolby_dvd` instances, the formatting won't be identical for all types in the type hierarchy. Now, you *could* define several methods, such as `display_vhs_tapes` and `display_dolby_dvds`, but that loses some of the advantages of having subtypes—including the use of substitution. Happily, SQL:1999 lets you use overriding methods to resolve this problem.

In SQL:1999, method invocations (but not invocations of ordinary functions) are *not* completely resolved at compile time—in spite of the impression you may have gotten in Section 7.4.3. Instead, at compile time, method invocations are narrowed down to just those methods for which all parameters other than the implicit parameter are an appropriate match, and for which the implicit parameters' specified data types are all in the same type hierarchy.

Therefore, you might define six methods named `display`, each having only the implicit parameter. The data type of the implicit parameter for one of these `display` methods would be `movie`; for another one, it would be `vhs_tape`; and for yet another it would be `dolby_dvd`. All six of these methods would be candidates for resolving a routine resolution like

```
...movie_info.display...
```

At runtime, the *most specific type* of the `movie` instance passed to that method invocation would be used to determine which of the six methods named `display` is actually invoked.

Overriding Methods The `display` method defined on the movie type is called an *original method*, and the "overloaded" methods defined on the subtypes are called *overriding methods*. (Henceforward, we will use the term "overload" to apply to functions or methods in which the parameter list differs in some way—other than with respect to methods' implicit, distinguished, parameter. By contrast, we'll use "override" to apply to methods within a type hierarchy in which the parameter lists differ only in the declared type of the implicit, distinguished, parameter.) SQL:1999 does not permit overloading (or overriding) the observer and mutator methods associated with a type's attributes, so there can never be overriding methods with the same names as the attributes of any type in the type hierarchy. However, any other method defined on a supertype can be overridden in any (or all!) of its subtypes, as we illustrate in Example 7.43. (The original method definition for `length_interval` can be found in Example 7.10.)

This new method, with the same name as a method of one of its supertypes (`movie`), has the same signature, and thus overrides that other method, but has somewhat different behavior.

EXAMPLE 7.43 OVERRIDING A METHOD IN A SUBTYPE.

```
CREATE TYPE dvd UNDER movie AS (
   stock_number   INTEGER,
   rental_price   DECIMAL(5,2),
   extra_features feature_desc ARRAY[5] )
   INSTANTIABLE
   NOT FINAL;

CREATE TYPE dolby_dvd UNDER dvd AS (
   alt_language   BOOLEAN )
   INSTANTIABLE
   NOT FINAL

   OVERRIDING METHOD length_interval ( )
      RETURNS INTERVAL HOUR(2) TO MINUTE;


CREATE INSTANCE METHOD length_interval ( )
  RETURNS INTERVAL HOUR(2) TO MINUTE
  FOR dolby_dvd

  /* Allow for movies as long as 99 hours and 59 minutes */
  /* Estimate 10 minutes additional for alt language */

  RETURN CAST ( CAST ( SELF.runs AS INTERVAL MINUTE(4) )
                   + INTERVAL '10' MINUTE(4)
                AS INTERVAL HOUR(2) TO MINUTE );
```

Direct Invocation and General Invocation Now, the designers of SQL:1999 recognized that there are exceptions to just about every rule. If you've built a type hierarchy and provided some overriding methods defined on subtypes in that hierarchy, there may still be times when you *really* want to invoke the original method defined on the supertype, even when a subtype instance is provided to the method invocation.

Case in point: You're likely to encounter the need to display only `dvd` attributes, even if you happen to retrieve a `dolby_dvd` from the database. If you've defined an overriding `display` method associated with the most specific type `dolby_dvd`, you normally would find that the overriding method is the one that's invoked, regardless of your needs. SQL:1999 calls this *direct invocation*. However, SQL:1999 provides us with a slightly different facility, called *general invocation*, that allows us to tell SQL that we want to use the `dvd` version of the `display` method instead:

```
...(movie_info AS dvd).display...
```

Although that might seem like a strange notation, all you have to do to analyze it is recall that the text to the left of `.display` is an expression whose type is some type in the appropriate type hierarchy. The expression `(movie_info AS dvd)` is such an expression; its type is `dvd`, even if the value returned in the `movie_info` column happens to be a `dolby_dvd`. But this approach isn't a cure-all for everything: Remember that this syntax only lets you do this for *subtypes* of the specified type—that is, the declared type of `movie_info` has to be `dvd` or some proper subtype of `dvd` (naturally, if it's `dvd`, then the syntax won't be very useful). Note that this does *not* convert or cast the `movie_info` value into a `dvd` value; it merely instructs the system to use the `display` method that is closely associated with the `dvd` type.

SQL:1999 provides a different facility that (temporarily) converts instances of one type to an instance of a specified *sub*type:

```
TREAT(movie_info AS dvd).display
```

When this `TREAT` expression is evaluated, the value retrieved from `movie_info` is actually converted into a new value whose most-specific (runtime) type is `dvd`, which would also force the use of the `display` method defined for the `dvd` type. However, in this case, it's possible that you might get, at runtime, a subtype of the declared type of `movie_info` that isn't a subtype of `dvd`, such as `vhs_tape`, in which case you'll get a runtime exception. Use with caution!

Static Method Invocation Since you're going to ask the question anyway—at least you will if you're familiar with Java—we're going to answer it, although very briefly.

Java has the notion of static methods, methods that are defined to operate on a class itself, rather than on instances of the class. SQL:1999 has a similar notion, also called *static methods*. SQL:1999's static methods do not have an implicit parameter, simply because they don't operate on (implicit) instances of the associated structured type. Instead, all their parameters must be explicit. For example, if you wanted to compare the lengths of two movies available on laserdisc, you could provide a static method on that subtype with two parameters, each of that type. Such a method might be invoked like this:

```
...laser_disc::length(v1.movie_info, v2.movie_info)...
```

The "double-colon" notation (`::`) is used to specify that a static method associated with the `laser_disc` structured type is being invoked.

We won't go into more details about static methods in this book, but those of you who are interested in the subject should consult an SQL:1999–specific reference.

Casting and Comparison

SQL:1999 naturally permits you to compare instances of structured types—certainly, you can compare `dvd` instances with other `dvd` instances, and you can even compare instances of multiple types in a type hierarchy under some circumstances. One reason that the comparison limitations are rather few is that comparisons are done through user-defined functions, so you (as a type designer) can supply whatever semantics you need to your comparisons. Of course, SQL:1999 provides a default comparison function that will be invoked for comparing instances of a given structured type. The default comparison function compares the type instances based on comparing each of their attributes, working from the first attribute to the last one ("left to right" is perhaps the best way to visualize it). Most comparison and casting functions can be ordinary functions or methods; the exception to that rule is that "relative comparisons" (which are discussed a few paragraphs below) can be done only using ordinary functions—not methods. Not to worry, though, the semantics of using a function or a method for the other forms of comparisons are identical, so the choice is up to you. (Actually, there's a single exception of which we're aware: If you choose to use a method for mapping comparisons, discussed below, it's possible to override the method, which can affect the semantics. This result can cause problems, but at least it's under your control!)

You can define other comparison mechanisms for yourself. Among the variations supported are the ability to limit comparisons strictly to equality and inequality or to enable full comparisons including equality and inequality as well as less than and greater than comparisons. Furthermore, you can do comparisons based on the values of the attributes, in which case it is called a *state* comparison. A state comparison always implies that the SQL environment creates an equality comparison function that returns a boolean value indicating whether or not the value of the first structured type instance is equal to the value of the second instance: This comparison is based on the values of the attributes alone (this is the default comparison mechanism we mentioned a couple of paragraphs above). You can specify the state comparison approach only in the type definition for a maximal supertype (that is, a type that has no supertypes itself—a type whose definition does not have an UNDER clause), in which case, this comparison mechanism is used for instances of the specified type and all of its subtypes. (What's more: you cannot specify a different sort of comparison for any subtypes—the decision to use state comparison for a maximal supertype applies to all subtypes of that supertype.)

You can also choose to compare two structured type instances by *mapping* them to some SQL built-in type and then comparing those two values. The conversion to the built-in types is performed by a *map* function, which returns a value of the selected built-in type. That function is implicitly invoked twice when constructing the comparison—you just write your normal comparison expression (`leftside > rightside`, for example), and SQL invokes the map functions for you. The comparison of the two built-in type values that result from invoking the map function is performed using ordinary SQL comparisons. You can specify mapping comparison for any type in a type hierarchy, but only if all other types in the hierarchy also use mapping comparison; however, different types in the hierarchy can use different mapping functions. A mapping function is associated with a structured type as shown in Example 7.44. (Note, however, that this association is not done as part of the structured type definition; it's a separate statement.)

EXAMPLE 7.44 SPECIFYING A MAPPING FUNCTION.

```
CREATE ORDERING FOR movie
   ORDER FULL BY MAP WITH
      FUNCTION movie_mapping (movie_type);
```

Then, we could create the mapping function as shown in Example 7.45.

EXAMPLE 7.45 DEFINING A MAPPING FUNCTION.

```
CREATE FUNCTION movie_mapping (mv movie_type)
     RETURNS INTEGER
     STATIC DISPATCH
   RETURN length(mv.title)+mv.runs;
```

The function in Example 7.45 supports the comparison of movies by adding their length in minutes to the length (in characters) of their titles. (Whether this is a reasonable way to compare movies or not is an application decision!) In case you've forgotten what STATIC DISPATCH does, you may wish to review Section 7.4.3, the subsection Functions.

Finally, you can do the comparison by using the result returned by a *relative* function. A relative function returns an integer value in which –1 implies that the first structured type instance is less than the second, 0 implies that the two instances are equal, and +1 implies that the first instance is greater than the second. As with the state comparison, you can specify this only for a maximal supertype and the relative ordering will be used for all subtypes as well. (And, as with state comparisons, you cannot specify a different comparison capability for any subtypes.)

With all three approaches, you write the function that determines the actual semantics used. If you're writing a state comparison function or a relative comparison function, you can apply any criteria you want to those comparisons. If you're writing a map function, then you can map the structured type instances to built-in types (such as INTEGER or CHARACTER) using whatever mechanisms you find appropriate. A relative function is associated with a structured type like the one in Example 7.46.

EXAMPLE 7.46 SPECIFYING A RELATIVE FUNCTION.

```
CREATE ORDERING FOR movie
  ORDER FULL BY RELATIVE WITH
    FUNCTION movie_comp (movie_type, movie_type);
```

Then, we could create the relative function like the one shown in Example 7.47.

Example 7.47's function compares movies according to criteria that you decide and then returns –1 to indicate that the first movie is less than the second, 0 to indicate that they're equal, and +1 to indicate that the first is greater than the second.

EXAMPLE 7.47 DEFINING A RELATIVE FUNCTION.

```
CREATE FUNCTION movie_comp (mv1 movie_type, mv2 movie_type)
      RETURNS INTEGER
      STATIC DISPATCH

   IF (...)          /*Some application-relevant condition */
      THEN RETURN -1
      ELSEIF (...)    /*Some application-relevant condition */
      THEN RETURN 0
      ELSE RETURN 1
    END IF;
```

Once the comparison semantics of the structured types are defined, you actually compare instances using ordinary SQL comparison operators, such as = or >. These comparison semantics are also used by SQL's ORDER BY, GROUP BY, and DISTINCT. By contrast, you normally use method invocations explicitly in Java for comparing class instances. For those of you who are curious about the complete BNF for specifying user-defined ordering, we've provided Example 7.48.

EXAMPLE 7.48 SYNTAX TO SPECIFY USER-DEFINED ORDERING.

```
<user-defined ordering definition> ::=
  CREATE ORDERING FOR <user-defined type>
      <ordering form>

<ordering form> ::=
    <equals ordering form>
  | <full ordering form>

<equals ordering form> ::=
  EQUALS ONLY BY <ordering category>

<full ordering form> ::=
  ORDER FULL BY <ordering category>

<ordering category> ::=
    <relative category>
  | <map category>
  | <state category>
```

```
<relative category> ::=
  RELATIVE WITH <relative function specification>

<map category> ::=
  MAP WITH <map function specification>

<state category> ::=
  STATE [ <specific name> ]

<relative function specification> ::=
  <specific routine designator>

<map function specification> ::=
  <specific routine designator>
```

7.7 Typed Tables

In addition to declaring some user-defined type to be the data type of a site (such as a column, a parameter, an SQL variable, a field of a row type, or an attribute of another user-defined type), SQL:1999 also allows you to declare that a user-defined type is the type of an entire table! For example, you could define a table corresponding to the `movies_type` type by writing a table definition that looks like the one shown in Example 7.49.

EXAMPLE 7.49 CREATING A TYPED TABLE.

```
CREATE TABLE movies OF movie_type
   ( REF IS OID SYSTEM GENERATED );
```

This table definition creates a new table, but it doesn't follow the usual practice of specifying a list of column definitions enclosed in parentheses (there is that "`REF IS`" business, but we'll get to that in Section 7.7.2). Instead, it says that the table is a *typed table* (sometimes called a *table of type*). In this table, each row is an instance of the type that we've called `movie_type`. Compare that table definition with the alternative approach shown in Example 7.50. This second table definition creates an ordinary table that has a single column whose data type is our UDT `movie_type`; in this case, each row contains an instance (possibly null) of `movie_type` in that single column. (By the way, in the typed table approach, there can never be a null instance of the type because SQL doesn't have the notion of "null rows" in tables. Of course, there might be one or more rows all of whose columns/attributes are null, but that's not at all the same thing.)

EXAMPLE 7.50 CREATING AN ORDINARY TABLE WITH A STRUCTURED TYPE COLUMN.

```
CREATE TABLE movies (
    movie     movie_type );
```

You create a new instance of a type as a row in a typed table through the normal SQL INSERT statement, as Example 7.51 demonstrates:

EXAMPLE 7.51 NEW ROW ≡ NEW TYPE INSTANCE.

```
INSERT INTO movies
  VALUES ('The Game',
      'A chilling thriller in which Michael Douglas' ||
      'plays a man given a "gift" by his younger' ||
      'brother...a gift that threatens his life' ||
      'and his sanity.',
      128 )
```

The statement in Example 7.51 inserts a new row into the `movies` table and, in doing so, creates a new instance of the `movie_type` type.

7.7.1 Relationship to Structured Types

The difference between these two approaches may seem subtle, but there are significant differences, philosophically as well as practically. It's beyond the scope of this book to debate the merits and difficulties of the two alternatives—or to give you a complete tutorial on the implications of choosing one or the other (such as the syntax notation used to access attributes of the values stored in the tables). Instead, we suggest that you use an SQL:1999 reference to pursue more information in this area.

We do, however, want to explain more explicitly what it means to create a typed table. In such a table, each attribute of the type is transformed into a column of the table. The methods associated with the type are then effectively associated with the table, since invoking the methods on instances of the type is exactly the same as invoking them on rows of the table; as we see in Example 7.52.

The rows of the table *are* the instances of the type; therefore, the function (`ratio`) operates on the row, indicated by use of the name of that mysterious column that appeared in the `REF IS` clause. (By contrast, in the second approach above, the rows of the table *contain* the instances of the type in a column.) SQL:1999 allows you to create as many typed tables as you'd like for any structured type. Of course, no given table can have more than one structured type!

EXAMPLE 7.52 USING A TYPED TABLE.

```
CREATE TABLE movies OF movie_type;

SELECT   mv.title, ratio(mv.oid)
FROM     movies mv
WHERE    title = 'Shakespeare in Love'
```

7.7.2 REF Types and REF Values

There is great value in the fact that attributes of a structured type are in fact columns of the table. This condition allows you to run ordinary SQL programs that only manipulate data in columns of tables and simultaneously run newer SQL programs that manipulate the same data through the method interface! We believe that many application environments can gradually migrate from a more traditional approach to database management to a more object-oriented approach by taking advantage of this capability. However, the principal value of typed tables lies in the fact that a row of the table *is* an instance of the table's type. Rows are SQL's most basic unit of data retrieval and manipulation, which makes it very easy to use rows as the fundamental unit of *referencing* data.

Every SQL:1999 typed table can have one column in addition to those provided by the table's type. This additional column is called a *self-referencing column* because the value stored in that column in a given row of the table is a value that uniquely identifies that row in the entire database—it's a sort of primary key for the table. Of course, you have to declare that self-referencing column in your table definition, as shown in Example 7.53.

EXAMPLE 7.53 CREATING A SELF-REFERENCING COLUMN.

```
CREATE TABLE movies OF movie_type
   (REF IS movie_id SYSTEM GENERATED);
```

Such tables are called *referenceable tables*. (Specification of a self-referencing column is optional in SQL:1999's syntax, but omitting it makes the table unreferenceable and makes it impossible to apply the underlying user-defined type's methods to rows of the table. In short, the table isn't much of a typed table!) The values of that self-referencing column can be system-generated (that is, neither application actions nor data stored in the row are required to generate the unique value), user-generated (meaning that the value is actually computed from some value provided by the user), or derived from data stored in some attribute or attributes of the type instance that is the row itself. In this last case, the attribute or attributes have to participate in a unique constraint for the table.

The value stored in the self-referencing column is called a *REF value* because that value can be used to uniquely reference the row in which it is stored. SQL:1999 provides a special data type, called a *REF type,* whose values are all (potential) REF values. A specific REF type is associated with exactly one structured type and is often (but not necessarily) associated with one referenceable table of that type. In fact, every value of a REF type is either a REF value associated with the referenceable table of the appropriate type or else it identifies no row at all. If you think this sounds a lot like an object identifier, well, let's just say that we wouldn't say you're wrong. But, to be truthful, SQL:1999 does not use that terminology at all. By the way, REF values are long-lived (unlike locators) and (except for user-generated REF values, over which the system has no control) are never reused in a database throughout its lifetime.

7.7.3 Scope

Sites (such as columns or SQL variables) whose data type is some REF type normally have a *scope* specified as part of their definition. The scope of a REF type is the referenceable table whose rows are referenced by values stored in that site. We believe that some future version of the SQL standard will support multitable scopes, but SQL:1999 doesn't go that far.

7.7.4 Dereferencing REF Values

Naturally, merely *having* a REF value doesn't do you much good if you can't resolve that reference into the data that it identifies. SQL:1999 provides several ways for you to "dereference" a REF value—by which we mean that you can supply a REF value and in return operate on the structured type instance that occupies the row identified by that REF value.

The most direct way of dereferencing a REF value is to use SQL's *dereference operator,* which looks something like:

```
ref value -> method name
```

The dereference operator "->" requires two operands; the first operand (the one on the left) is an expression whose data type is some specific REF type, and the second operator (on the right) is the name of some method associated with the structured type that is in turn associated with the REF type. For example, consider the two structured type definitions presented in Example 7.54.

EXAMPLE 7.54 TWO REFERENCEABLE TYPES.

```
CREATE TYPE actor AS
   ( name              CHARACTER VARYING (50),
     year_born         INTEGER,
     real_name         CHARACTER VARYING (50)
   )
   NOT FINAL
   REF IS SYSTEM GENERATED;

CREATE TYPE best_actor AS (
   year              INTEGER,
   picture           REF(actor) )
   NOT FINAL
   REF IS SYSTEM GENERATED;
```

REF IS SYSTEM GENERATED means that the DBMS is required to generate any unique REF values associated with any instances of the type for which that syntax is specified. All table definitions using such a type as its table type that also specify a self-referencing column (one containing the REF values of the rows) must specify the same syntax. Other alternatives exist to let you specify that a combination of attributes is used to create the REF values or that the application program will provide them.

In addition, we'll have to have two tables in which to store instances of these types, as illustrated in Example 7.55.

EXAMPLE 7.55 TYPED TABLES FOR REFERENCEABLE TYPES.

```
CREATE TABLE actors OF actor (
   REF IS aref SYSTEM GENERATED );

CREATE TABLE best_actors (
   best_actor   best_actor,
   picture      WITH OPTIONS SCOPE actors );
```

The rows in the actors table have, as you can readily determine, three columns (one for each of the attributes name, year_born, and real_name); it also has one additional column, named aref, that contains in each row the REF value of that row.

The rows in the best_actors table have only a single column:

- The column (best_actor) is of a structured type (also named best_actor) that has two attributes (year and picture).
- What appears to be a second column definition (picture WITH OPTIONS SCOPE actors) is actually syntax that provides a reference scope to the picture attribute of the best_actor column—a REF type whose values reference instances of the actor type but only those in the actors table.

In order to discover the name of the actor who won the Best Actor award in 1995, we could write the following:

```
SELECT   ba.best_actor.picture->name
FROM     best_actors ba
WHERE    ba.best_actors.year = 1995
```

In this example, when we find a best_actors row (presumably only one row, since only a single Best Actor award is given in a specific year), we use its picture column/attribute value to "point to" (hence the pointer symbol [->]) a row in the actors table on which we invoke the name observer function.

Other notations are used in relationship to dereferencing REF values, but this notation is the most important. You can learn about the other ways from an SQL:1999 resource.

7.7.5 Invoking Methods on Rows of Typed Tables

That last example illustrates the fact that you can reference columns of a typed table—even the ones that come from the associated type—using SQL's normal syntax. But you can go further than that: You can invoke any methods associated with the table's type on the rows of the table! Naturally, that's because the table's rows *are* the instances of the type.

Because all methods (well, all of them other than static methods!) are invoked using dot notation, just as in the observer methods we illustrated in the preceding example, it's unnecessary to present another example of invoking a method.

7.7.6 Data Modeling Decisions

Before moving to the final sections of this chapter and then getting into the use of Java types and routines in your database, we want to point out that there are no clear guidelines of which we're aware to help you choose whether to model your data using (1) ordinary SQL tables and columns of built-in types, (2) ordinary SQL tables, some of whose columns are of built-in types and some of user-defined types, (3) ordinary SQL tables with one column whose data type is some user-defined type, or (4) typed tables. Application requirements will vary greatly and choosing how to combine the power of SQL and its tables with the power of user-defined types is going to present your application writers with some interesting decisions to make! We expect that individual database vendors will make broad recommendations for their customers, while their (and other) consulting organizations will develop expertise in one approach or another.

7.8 Table Hierarchies

SQL:1999 has a second sort of hierarchy—a table hierarchy. At first, this might seem like overkill, but we think it's completely justified.

7.8.1 Relationship to Type Hierarchies

By now, many of you have absorbed the fact that SQL:1999 has both type hierarchies and typed tables and have begun to wonder how the language allows applications to handle combinations of the two features. The answer is that SQL:1999 also supports table hierarchies! That is, you can define one table to be a *subtable* of another, called its *supertable*. You can only declare table hierarchies of typed tables, though, and all of the tables in a given table hierarchy must have corresponding types in the same type hierarchy. Further, the tables in the table hierarchy must be in the same relative positions as the types in that type hierarchy. But—and this is a little tricky—the relationships of the table hierarchy and the type hierarchy do not have to be one-to-one. Recall our example type hierarchy from Figure 7.1. We could define a table hierarchy like that shown in Figure 7.3.

Note that our table hierarchy doesn't have a table corresponding to the `dvd` type in the type hierarchy! This isn't a problem—it merely means that we can't store (in this table hierarchy, at least) instances strictly of the `dvd` type, only those that are also instances of the `dolby_dvd` or `dts_dvd` types.

7.8.2 Table Hierarchy Model

There are several (we've uncovered at least four or five) *mental models* that one can develop for the relationships between the tables in a table hierarchy and the rows in those tables. We recognize that the model we describe in this section might not be in full agreement with SQL:1999's model, but we're confident that this model accurately

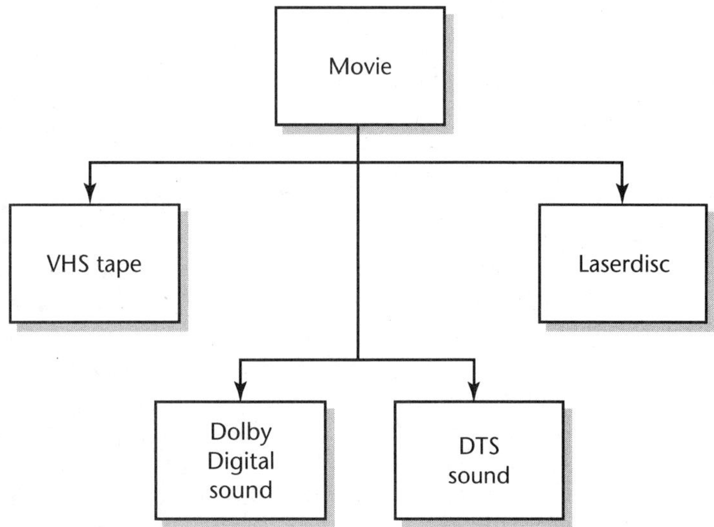

FIGURE 7.3 *A table hierarchy.*

describes the behavior of SQL:1999. Unfortunately, adherents to the various different models sometimes exhibit an almost religious fervor toward their preferred way of describing the language's behavior, so we won't be surprised if we're criticized for selecting this model—indeed, we would expect criticism and disagreement with any model that we selected!

Using the table hierarchy shown in Figure 7.3, consider the actions taken when you create a new instance of the `dolby_dvd` type—that is, when you insert a new row into the `dolby_dvd` table. A row is inserted into the table. Similarly, when you insert a row into the `MOVIE` table, a row is inserted into that table. Simple and obvious—and incomplete. It's incomplete because we must also describe the effect that the insertions have on future retrievals of data from tables in the table hierarchy.

Suppose we inserted a row into the `dolby_dvd` table for director David Lynch's *tour de confusion, Eraserhead.* When we retrieve rows from that table, we expect to see *Eraserhead* among the movies retrieved (subject to restrictions such as those in a WHERE clause). What might surprise you is that retrieving rows from the `movie` table will also result in *Eraserhead* being retrieved!

Well, perhaps you shouldn't be surprised, because *Eraserhead* is an instance of the `dolby_dvd` type and, because `dolby_dvd` is a subtype of the `movie` type, is simultaneously an instance of the `movie` type. So, you might ask, does the row for *Eraserhead* appear simultaneously in both tables? And that's where the fervor over the model comes into play: we assert that the retrieval operation effectively does a *union* of the table from which you're retrieving and all of its subtables (see Section 7.8.3 for the exception to this rule). That way, the insert, update, and delete operations don't have to run around updating multiple tables in your database every time you perform one of those operations on some subtable.

Now, adherents to a different model description might argue that the effect is the same as if the insert, update, and delete operations did manipulate rows in all supertables of the subtable on which the operation is specified, and retrieval operations could retrieve only from the single table specified. We wouldn't argue (well, not *too* much!) with that view, since it also describes the behavior of SQL:1999. But that model is, in our viewpoint, needlessly complex and doesn't reflect the actual implementation of products of which we're aware. (To be fair, adherents of this more complex model can point to the text in SQL:1999 for justification, which does describe this sort of multitable behavior for insert, update, and delete, in spite of the fact that implementations using a simpler, more direct model get the same behavior in a different manner.)

7.8.3 Syntax Enhancements

We're not going to spend a lot of space describing the syntax changes SQL:1999 has incurred to accommodate table hierarchies. The most important change is the addition of an optional keyword—`ONLY`—to the DELETE and UPDATE statements, as well as to the table references in a FROM clause (of a query expression). Let's look briefly at why.

Because every instance of a subtype is simultaneously an instance of all of its supertypes, a row in a typed table that is a subtable must be returned when retrievals (with appropriate criteria) are performed on any of its supertables. There are a number of ways to design the manner in which this relationship is specified, but our view of SQL:1999's design uses the mental model that the supertable and its subtables are truly separate tables. This requires that the retrievals (effectively) perform a union of the specified table and all of its proper subtables before applying the other retrieval criteria. When we INSERT a row into the `dolby_dvd` table, creating an instance of the `dolby_dvd` type, SQL merely inserts a row into the `dolby_dvd` table that is available whenever we retrieve rows from the `dolby_dvd`, `dvd`, or `movie` tables.

What action is taken when we delete a row from the `dolby_dvd` table? Well, that normally involves nothing more than deleting the row from the dolby_dvd table, making it disappear from retrievals from the dvd and movie tables (because performing a union between those tables and the dolby_dvd can't include the row not in any of those tables).

But what if we only discovered that *Eraserhead* isn't available in Dolby Digital sound at all, although it is available on DVD? In this case, we want to specifically delete the instance of that movie in the dolby_dvd table, but would want to continue to find the movie in the dvd table and the movie table. That's where the new keyword comes in. If we were to write the statement shown in Example 7.56, then we'd delete all movies longer than three hours that were distributed on Dolby-encoded DVDs, but not such lengthy films distributed on any other medium—that is, the row in the dolby_dvd table is deleted, but the database system would insert a corresponding row into the dvd table (containing, obviously, only the columns relevant to that table).

EXAMPLE 7.56 DELETING ONLY FROM A SUBTABLE.

```
DELETE FROM ONLY dolby_dvd
WHERE length > 180
```

On the other hand, if we were to write the statement shown in Example 7.57, then we'd delete all Dolby-encoded DVD movies longer than 180 minutes, without inserting any corresponding rows into the dvd table (or any other table)!

EXAMPLE 7.57 DELETING FROM A SUBTABLE FAMILY.

```
DELETE FROM dolby_dvd
WHERE length > 180
```

7.9 Implementation Issues

Although only a few readers of this book are likely to be database system implementors, we thought that many of you might be interested in a paragraph or two about some of the challenges that vendors face in building the SQL:1999 structured type features. Undoubtedly, the most complex part of the specification is the routine invocation algorithm; it goes on for several pages of the standard and is extremely dense. However, it is really rather simple and elegant when one pushes through the turgid prose and intricate rules. As a result, it should prove relatively easy to implement and quite stable once done.

By contrast, the concept of subtypes being "specializations" of their supertypes, simply containing a bit more data, seems awfully straightforward. But this may end up being the most difficult aspect of implementing this feature. The problem is caused in part by the very nature of a database management system and in part by the meaning of "subtype."

As you are quite aware, a database system is used for *persistent* storage of data. The nearly three decades of implementation experience that SQL vendors have accrued in developing their products has largely dealt with tables whose rows were (fairly predictably) all the same length. Of course, there were some minor exceptions, such as very long character string columns, that received special treatment—often by means of storing such data in a separate location and then "pointing" to it from the original row value. But, in general, rows in a table were usually approximately the same size.

However, if one or more columns of some table are of a structured type, and if that type participates in a type hierarchy, then different rows of the table may have values in those columns whose most specific type (that is, their actual runtime types, as opposed to the columns' declared types) varies widely in size! This problem poses some very interesting storage management challenges for SQL implementors. The problems escalate significantly when you consider the possibility of UPDATEing a row and replacing the value of some structured type column with a new value of a subtype that has significantly more data associated with it; the implementation can no longer be assured of updating a row "in place," but must be prepared to move the row to a new location that has adequate room.

Though that is not terribly difficult, it becomes more complex if the row in question is actually a row of a typed table—with an associated REF value. REF values associated with specific rows are never allowed to change, *even if the location of the row must change!* If you're familiar with SQL implementations that use something like a database key, which is often generated from a hardware-associated value such as a disk address, you shouldn't expect REF values to be the same thing. Rows are often relocated for various implementation reasons, which might (or might not) change the database key value, but the REF value will not change. We'll just leave the rest to your imaginations (and perhaps you'll appreciate the efforts that database systems implementors have to put into building the products we take for granted).

7.10 SQL Object Model

If you've been around the computer software business long enough, you've heard lots of buzzwords and phrases. One of the hottest such phrases in recent years is "data model." Regrettably, because of the confusion that it often causes, the phrase applies to a rather wide variety of concepts, ranging from a description of the data elements required by a specific application to techniques and methodologies used to design very large systems. In the context of database systems, the phrase is often intended to identify the underlying concepts supported by those systems.

7.10.1 Why Does SQL Have an Object Model?

In 1989, we heard Dr. E. F. Codd tell a seminar that object-oriented *approaches* are not needed in the database environment. He suggested that they're OK for programming languages, which don't "have the power to express complex ideas," but "the relational model is more than adequate for data storage." Dr. Codd went on to acknowledge that the relational model is not necessarily appropriate for "*all* masses of data: for example, image data and voice- or finger-printing, where the sequence of bits is important." Codd's rationale for this rejection of a need for object orientation in the database environment was straightforward: The relational model is a true model because it is based on a solid mathematical foundation and its principles are provable mathematically. By contrast, there are many different "approaches" that are called object models, and none of them have mathematical foundations. Their principles are entirely ad hoc and cannot be proven mathematically. In other words, Codd rejected the entire concept of "object model."

Although we find the plethora of object models confusing and in many ways regrettable, we disagree entirely with Codd's rejection of the need for object orientation in the database environment. We have encountered a great many application problems that are difficult or impossible to solve *effectively* with the strict use of relational model principles, but that are addressed quite nicely using certain principles of object orientation. As object orientation has proved its worth in programming languages, we find it ever more attractive to give access to those capabilities in the database environment, thus reducing the impedance mismatch between programming language concepts and database concepts. After all, any reduction of that impedance mismatch offers the promise of reducing semantic errors in applications and of reducing programming efforts—both very worthy goals.

The problem, of course, is recognizing that different programming languages have different object models—indeed, "object-oriented" is another one of those overused and inconsistent industry buzzwords—and deciding how to resolve those differences at points where they interface. Since SQL was designed to be used with several programming languages, it's unlikely in the extreme that any object model designed in SQL would map without difficulty to object models of multiple programming languages. Indeed, the designers of SQL's object model encountered numerous difficulties in their efforts to minimize the impedance mismatch between SQL and several popular object-oriented programming languages.

As we wrap up this chapter, we'd like to outline what we consider the most important aspects of the SQL object model. As a Java programmer, you probably know that language's object model fairly well, so we're not going to present it here. If you want more information on the Java object model, then we encourage you to turn to other resources (one good source is the Java language specification itself[5]). We'd like to emphasize that, in the later stages of SQL:1999 development, concerted efforts were made to "tweak" the SQL object model to more closely align with Java's, even at the potential expense of alignment with other languages, such as C++ or Smalltalk. The reason for that effort was blindingly simple: Market economics demonstrated higher and faster-growing demand for Java than for those other languages.

The rest of this section is a summary of the SQL object model. Many, even most, of the concepts and terms given here repeat material from earlier in the chapter; still, a concise summary may be useful.

7.10.2 SQL Object Model Summary

SQL's object model is at once simpler than and more complex than Java's. The reasons for the greater complexity deal entirely with the difficulties caused by the fact that SQL manages *persistent data* that is described by equally persistent *metadata*. The ability for applications to modify SQL's metadata—the data that describes the data under SQL's control—means that great care must be taken that such modifications neither impede correct and accurate access to the data itself nor create enormous performance problems by requiring immediate and time-consuming restructuring of the data. The relative simplicity of SQL's object model when compared to Java's results principally from the observation that not all of Java's facilities are necessarily required in—nor even applicable to—a database environment.

---

[5] *The Java Programming Language, 2nd edition,* Ken Arnold and James Gosling, Addison-Wesley, 1997.

SQL (perhaps obviously) does not believe that "everything is an object." In fact, the great majority, at least today, of data managed by SQL is nonobject data. Even after the addition of object-oriented capabilities to SQL, the language retains and enhances all of its "relational" capabilities, particularly the central design principle that all data is stored in tables—even object data! In fact, as will shortly become clear, it's somewhat unclear in the SQL standard exactly what *is* an object; we'll try to make it clear in this section, though.

As you've seen in this chapter, SQL provides two sorts of data in support of object orientation. The first is something called *user-defined types*. In fact, user-defined types come in two flavors, only one of which is relevant to this discussion. One flavor is the *distinct type,* which merely allows applications to give a new name to SQL's built-in primitive types while prohibiting indiscriminate mixing of the distinct type and its base type in expressions. The other is called the *structured type,* and it is the variant that relates most closely to object orientation. SQL's structured type is its closest analog to Java's classes. The other sort of data is SQL's *reference type,* whose summary discussion we'll defer for a few paragraphs.

SQL's structured types are fully encapsulated in the sense that *all* access to them is through a functional (or method) interface. That is, there is no access permitted to the components—called *attributes* in SQL—of a value of a structured type except through system-provided observer functions (to retrieve the values of the attributes) and mutator functions (to change their values). Although this would appear to imply that SQL's structured types are "more encapsulated" than Java's classes, the truth is a little more complicated. As the author of an SQL structured type, you are allowed to overload any user-defined functions that exist for the type, but you are not allowed to overload the two system-provided observer and mutator functions for any of the type's attributes.

SQL's structured types are permitted to contain primitive types (in SQL, called *predefined data types* or *built-in data types*), constructed types, other structured types, and references to tables whose rows are actually values of structured types (called *typed tables*). A *constructed type* is a type that must be defined in terms of other types; the two primary examples are arrays and row types. A row type is very much like a `struct` in the C language because it allows nesting of values within other values. SQL's *reference type* (providing the ability to reference rows in tables of some structured type) is also a constructed type, though obviously less structured than arrays or row types.

SQL's structured types can participate in a type hierarchy. SQL supports only single inheritance, meaning that no type can have more than a single supertype. A subtype's attributes are therefore inherited only from a single supertype; the same is true of its methods. SQL does not currently support any notion of inheritance of interface from any source other than its supertype; in this respect, it is more limited than Java. (A future revision of the SQL standard may add this capability.) We must note, however, that SQL:1999 does not have an abstract, non-instantiable maximal supertype like Java does (in Java, all classes are defined to be subclasses of an abstract class named `object`).

SQL allows you to specify that a structured type is FINAL, meaning that no subtypes of the type can be defined. It also permits structured types to be declared NOT INSTANTIABLE, which means that applications cannot create values of the type. These two characteristics correspond with Java's `final` and `abstract` class characteristics.

SQL distinguishes between procedures, functions, and methods. Procedures are routines that are invoked by means of an SQL CALL statement and return values, if at all, through output parameters; they do not return a value as such. By contrast, functions are invoked as a function invocation in a value expression, have only input parameters, and return a single value (not necessarily an atomic value, like an integer, though) as the value of the function invocation.

Methods are special cases of functions that have several restrictions when compared to their more general-purpose origins:

1. A method is associated with a specific structured type by including in the type's definition the signature of the method. (Note: The SQL standard uses the term "specification" in place of "signature" for obscure reasons; we stick to "signature" in this book because it is the more widely used term for the intended concept.)
2. A method signature can be an *original method signature,* meaning that the method declared in "this type" does not override a method defined in some supertype; alternatively, it can be an *overriding method signature,* meaning that it does override some method inherited from a supertype. Original method signatures contain somewhat more information than overriding method signatures, because overriding methods are required to share certain characteristics with the methods they override. Those shared characteristics are not respecified in overriding method signatures.
3. Although functions are allowed to be associated with any number of structured types, the association is loose because all arguments of that function's invocations are used equally to determine which of possibly several functions of the same name will be chosen for invocation. For any arguments whose *declared* type is a structured type, only that declared type is

used to choose the specific function to be invoked. By contrast, methods are closely associated with a specific structured type. They have a *distinguished parameter,* always the first parameter, whose type is always the associated structured type, for which the most specific type of the invocation's corresponding argument is used; all other arguments of a method invocation are resolved using only their declared types.

4. Finally, the functions associated with various structured types may be defined anywhere in an SQL database—in any *schema,* to use the proper term. Methods, on the other hand, must be defined in the schema in which their associated structured type is defined.

In SQL, the functions and methods associated with a structured type are not written as part of the type definition, but are instead created separately (don't forget, though, that methods *are* declared as part of a type's definition). Like the structured type definitions, along with all persistent values of the types, the functions and methods are stored in the database itself—the type definitions, functions, and methods are stored in the database's metadata and the values of the types are naturally stored in the database's actual data (called *SQL-data* in the SQL standard).

It has been argued that, in SQL, all arguments are passed by value. The SQL standard does not itself say anything explicit about the argument passing mechanism, but there is evidence to support this assertion: Arguments to invocations of SQL routines are permitted to be literals. If the code in an SQL routine were allowed to change the value of the argument, then that would have the effect of changing the value of the literal—for example, 3 could become 5, which is nonsense. However, SQL procedures can have output parameters, which cannot realistically be handled with arguments passed by value, in the ordinary sense of that phrase. Of course, SQL procedures also have input parameters—and SQL functions and methods have *only* input parameters—so pass-by-value works fine with them. Now, it would be confusing to have some parameters passed by reference and others by value, so it's reasonable to conclude that SQL routines use something else for their argument passing semantics. The mechanism that we conclude is used (from a very careful reading of SQL/PSM and SQL:1999) is that SQL's procedures—which are the only sort of SQL-invoked routine that can have output parameters—use "pass-by-value, copy-in and copy-out" semantics. This means that the values of input (and input-output) arguments are copied into the SQL routine from its invocation and the value of output (and input-output) arguments are set by copying the returned values out from the SQL routine. (Obviously, only "settable" arguments, such as host parameters or SQL variables, will be "set by copying," thus preserving literals.) SQL-invoked functions and methods, which do not have output parameters, can operate just fine with pure pass-by-value semantics.

SQL permits you to write procedures, functions, and methods associated with a structured type in several different languages—including SQL itself, as well as one of several more conventional programming languages (such as C or even COBOL and Fortran). Yes, of course Java is one of these, otherwise, this book would be awfully short!

Whereas Java programs reference objects (instances of classes) by means of handles, which are really pointers to the storage occupied by those instances, SQL programs can only reference rows in tables. SQL originally allowed you to define a table and explicitly specify the columns of that table, giving their name and data type. When structured types were added to SQL's repertoire, the ability to define a table based on a structured type was also added. In order to reference specific rows in such a table, called a "typed table," you use SQL's reference type. A given column (or variable or parameter) whose data type is a reference type is restricted to reference only rows of typed tables whose type is a specified structured type. There may be many such tables and a given declaration of a reference type must specify a specific table to which its values refer. In this respect, we see that references are not free to reference just any value of any structured type, nor even any arbitrary value of a given structured type—but only those values of a specific structured type that are represented as rows in a specified table. That excludes not only values of that structured type that are rows in other tables of that type, but also values of that type that are stored in columns of tables or in SQL variables or parameters. Though this might appear limiting, in practice it seems to be sufficient for a great many applications.

7.11 A Java-SQL Translation Dictionary

Earlier in this chapter, we promised you a dictionary that provides a correlation between the terms used in the Java object model and those used in the SQL object model. Table 7.3 contains the manifestation of that promise.

7.12 Limitations: Technical and Economic

Even though you're reading this book because you're interested in using SQL and Java together, you may be wondering—given the capabilities of SQL:1999's user-defined types as we've described them in this chapter—why we don't recommend that you choose pure-SQL solutions for most of your applications.

Java term	SQL term
Class	Type (especially structured type)
Superclass	Supertype
Subclass	Subtype
Instance	Value
Object	Row in a table of a structured type
Primitive type	Predefined or built-in data type
Method	Method (also function and procedure)
Constructor	Initializer

TABLE 7.3 *A Java-SQL translation glossary.*

The fact is that we sometimes do make such recommendations. Your application needs have to be the determining factors when choosing an implementation approach. If you are in a situation where you have plenty of COBOL- and SQL-trained programmers at your disposal, but Java resources are few and far between, you might indeed choose to take advantage of the benefits that object orientation can add to your environment by designing around SQL:1999's "object in the server" features, such as UDTs, type hierarchies, methods, polymorphism, and so forth.

On the other hand, if you have a staff with (or able to get) training and experience using Java, especially if your environment demands that you be able to build software that can be "moved around" from the server to the client to middleware layers and back again, then a solution using Java classes and methods may be your best choice. SQL, after all, pretty much runs only inside the database server (at least we're not aware of SQL implementations that run anywhere else!), whereas Java is intended to run "anywhere" (at least anywhere a Java Virtual Machine has been provided).

Another determining factor will be the choice of database product and vendor you've made. Some vendors, notably IBM and Oracle, have been relatively aggressive about implementing certain components of SQL:1999 user-defined types, whereas other vendors have made different choices. For example, Sybase decided fairly early that SQL:1999's UDT capabilities, though obviously useful, were less flexible for many application requirements than Java's classes would be; they chose to focus on providing Java support first, with SQL:1999 UDT support following some time afterward. Sybase's approach means that Java objects are stored in the database as opaque types from SQL's point of view (but they are accessible as Java objects when Java routines are used in SQL operations). JDBC 2.0 and SQLJ part 2 (both discussed in later chapters) allow you to treat Java objects as ordinary structured types—though in rather different ways.

If you've chosen to build your application environment around a vendor who provides Java support and not SQL UDT support, then realistic economics will almost certainly dictate that you tilt toward the use of Java for your applications using object technology; similarly, if you currently use a vendor whose products support SQL user-defined types and do not have strong Java support, then you should probably lean toward a pure SQL–based architecture.

7.13 Chapter Summary

Now, before we finish this subject, we want to emphasize that SQL:1999's user-defined type capabilities are more complex than we've shown here. If you're interested in pursuing this in more detail, we suggest that you avail yourself of one of the SQL:1999 books on the market. Our purpose here has been merely to outline the SQL:1999 facilities and prepare you for our presentation in the next two chapters on using Java in SQL.

In this chapter, we've given you a brief introduction to the origins of user-defined types in SQL and outlined one variation of them—distinct types—quite briefly. We discussed SQL's structured types at greater length, including a summary of the syntax used to create them. As part of that discussion, we distinguished between attributes and behaviors of UDTs and their instances, and talked about the differences between SQL:1999's ordinary functions and its methods.

Nearly done, we presented the various ways in which UDTs could be used in SQL:1999—as the data types of various types of sites where data appears, such as columns, parameters to routines, and SQL variables, and as the foundation for typed tables, in which attributes of a UDT become the columns of a table while retaining the ability to use methods to specify behavior. And, finally, we suggested a few considerations to keep in mind when deciding whether to pursue a pure-SQL application environment or a mixed Java-and-SQL approach.

CHAPTER

8

SQLJ Part 2 (SQL Types Using the Java™ Programming Language)

8.1 Introduction

In Chapter 6 we showed you how Java classes (in JAR files) can be installed in a database. Some of the static methods in these classes can be associated with SQL routines (functions and procedures), and then invoked in the same manner that all SQL routines can be invoked. Well, that feels like a good start, but what about the constructors and all of the other methods in these classes? Are they to be treated as second-class citizens, available only by first going through some static method? Certainly not! In this chapter we will show you how SQLJ Part 2 allows you to associate Java classes with SQL structured types. Once this type of association has been made, these structured types are used in the same manner that all structured types are used. Since the previous chapter covered structured types quite thoroughly, we will concentrate in this chapter on how these associations are made.

Like SQLJ Part 1, SQLJ Part 2[1] was brought to the SQLJ group of companies by Sybase, and the Sybase representative has acted as the editor of this specification. At the time we are writing this book, SQLJ Part 2

[1] *SQLJ—Part 2: SQL Types Using the Java™ Programming Language, www.sqlj.org,* March 17, 1999.

has not yet been submitted to NCITS. When this submission happens, we are hopeful that its adoption will be as quick and uneventful as that of SQLJ Part 1.

8.2 Associating a Class and a Structured Type

Let us begin by looking at a very simple Java class in Example 8.1 and how it can be associated with an SQL structured type. In the next several sections, we'll make both our class and the structured type more complicated, in order to show you the full set of features provided by SQLJ Part 2. We've provided the complete definition of our example classes in Appendix C.

Let us suppose that the `Movie` class in Example 8.1 exists in a JAR file that has been installed into a database with the name `cinema_jar`, as we did in Chapter 6. We will associate this class with an SQL structured type using the statement in Example 8.2.

The very first thing we see in this statement is that we are creating a structured type and associating it with a Java class, which includes in its identification the SQL name of the JAR file that contains it. Following this, we see the definition of three SQL attributes. Each of these definitions specifies the name of the Java field with which it is associated. Finally, we see the definition of an SQL initializer method, which is associated with a Java constructor method for this Java class. We'll call this type of structured type an *external Java datatype.*

Structured type to class, attribute to field, initializer to constructor—it's all very tidy. There are a couple of rules that you must be aware of, of course. In order to associate an SQL structured type with a Java class, the class must implement `java.io.Serializable`, `java.sql.SQLData`, or both of these interfaces. The reason for this will become clear in just a little while. The class `java.sql.SQLData` was introduced in JDBC 2.0. We will be discussing it in Chapter 9—for the moment, just think of it as another way of serializing a Java object.

In order to associate an attribute with a Java field, the field must be declared as `public`, and the SQL type and Java type must be mappable (this term was introduced in Section 6.3.1 and is extended in Section 8.2.10). This last rule gives us two reasons why we could not associate an SQL attribute with the `votes` field; the field is `private`, and there is no SQL data type that is mappable to `Hashtable`. Because `votes` is a private field, we expect that some methods in the `Movie` class will change its value and read its value. We might choose to associate SQL methods with them. The association to a structured type will respect the encapsulation that was chosen for the Java class.

In order to associate an SQL initializer method with a Java constructor, the constructor must be declared as `public`, the initializer method

EXAMPLE 8.1 THE `Movie` CLASS.

```
package Cinema;

import java.util.*;
import java.io.*;
import java.sql.*;

/**
 * This class represents a movie object
 */

public class Movie implements java.io.Serializable {

   public String                          title;
   public int                             length;
   public String                          description;

   private Hashtable                      votes = new Hashtable ();

   /**
    * Constructor for a Movie
    *
    * @param  title        The title of the movie.
    * @param  length       The length of the movie in minutes.
    * @param  description  A brief description of the movie.
    */

   public Movie (String title, int length, String description) {
      this.title = title;
      this.length = length;
      this.description = description;
   }
}
```

must have the name of the type being created, the return type must be the structured type that is being created, and the name of the Java method must be the same as the name of the Java class that was specified. A rule for all SQL methods that are associated with Java methods is that the number of SQL parameters and Java parameters must be the same and the types of corresponding parameters must be mappable.

In this section, we've shown how Java classes can be associated with SQL structured types with a CREATE TYPE statement, which is not, strictly speaking, accurate. SQLJ Part 2 allows the use of this statement

EXAMPLE 8.2 ASSOCIATING A STRUCTURED TYPE WITH THE Movie CLASS.

```
CREATE TYPE sqlj_movie
   EXTERNAL NAME 'cinema_jar:Cinema.Movie'
   LANGUAGE JAVA
   ( title       VARCHAR (60) EXTERNAL NAME 'title',
     length      INTEGER      EXTERNAL NAME 'length',
     descr       VARCHAR (60) EXTERNAL NAME 'description',

     METHOD sqlj_movie (p1 VARCHAR (60),
                        p2 INTEGER, p3 VARCHAR (60))
        RETURNS sqlj_movie
        EXTERNAL NAME 'Movie'
   )
```

only in a *deployment descriptor,* and not as an independent DDL statement. We've provided the complete syntax for the SQLJ Part 2 statements in Appendix H.

8.2.1 Creating Instances of External Java Datatypes

Our external Java datatype can be used in the same manner as any structured type. We can use it in the definition of a table, and we can use its initializer method to help populate such a table. We show these uses in Example 8.3.

EXAMPLE 8.3 USING THE sqlj_movie STRUCTURED TYPE.

```
CREATE TABLE sqlj_movies
   (id       INTEGER PRIMARY KEY,
    movie    sqlj_movie
   )

INSERT INTO sqlj_movies
   VALUES (1001,
           NEW sqlj_movie ('Colossus',
                           100,
                           'A machine is given control of Earth''s '
                              || 'weapons, with unexpected results.'
                          )
          )
```

We call the `sqlj_movie` column, which uses an external Java datatype, an *SQLJ column*.

You may want to take a moment and think about exactly what is happening in this example. There is a little bit of magic going on. The SQL initializer method causes the associated Java constructor to be invoked. The resulting `Movie` object is transient, as all Java objects are. It can live only as long as the Java Virtual Machine is running. But an insert into a SQL table creates a row that persists across SQL sessions and across the stopping and starting of the database, once the transaction containing the insert is committed.

It is the bridging of this gap that lead to the requirement that we stated earlier—in order to be associated with an SQL structured type, a Java class must implement either `java.io.Serializable` or `java.sql.SQLData`. When the DBMS performs the insert, it automatically uses one of these methods to create a serial form of the object—a byte string—and it is this serial form that is stored in the column (we discussed Java serialization in Section 2.9.1). Later, when the value of the column is needed, the DBMS can deserialize that stored representation and recreate the object.

If you looked carefully at the example, you saw that the `Movie` class contained the `vote` private field. When a `Movie` object is created, a `Hashtable` object is created as well, and its reference is stored in `vote`. The serialization mechanism follows this reference and serializes both of these objects. You can override this behavior by declaring the field as `transient`. This process is something for you to be aware of when you create SQLJ Part 2 applications.

"Is It Live or Is It Memorex?"

In Example 8.4, we create a new table and copy some of the movies in our `sqlj_movies` table.

EXAMPLE 8.4 COPYING AN INSTANCE OF AN SQLJ COLUMN.

```
CREATE TABLE favorite_movies
   (movie   sqlj_movie
   )

INSERT INTO favorite_movies
   SELECT   movie
   FROM     sqlj_movies
   WHERE    movie.title = 'Colossus'
```

Now there is a row in both tables that describes *Colossus*. Each row contains a serialized form of a `Movie` object, and the two are quite independent of one another. A change to one will not affect the other at all.

Because structured types, and by extension SQLJ types, have expanded SQL's type system in an orthogonal way, these types can be used in the definition of variables and parameters. In Example 8.5, we have copied an instance in an SQLJ column into a variable.

EXAMPLE 8.5 COPYING AN INSTANCE OF AN SQLJ COLUMN INTO A VARIABLE.

```
BEGIN
   DECLARE m sqlj_movie;

   SELECT   movie
   INTO     m
   FROM     sqlj_movies
   WHERE    movie.title = 'Colossus';

   INSERT INTO favorite_movies
   VALUES (m);
END
```

Between the time that we move *Colossus* into our variable and the time that it is stored in the `favorite_movies` table, we might wish to operate on it, either by reading or altering some of its state. Is the representation of the movie in variable `m` a reference to an object, or is it a serialized byte string?

The group of SQLJ companies is still discussing this. One can argue that it is far more efficient to deserialize the object once if it is going to be operated on repeatedly, and then reserialize it as part of the insert statement. On the other hand, SQL's structured types are values, and SQL contains no equivalent to Java's object references.

This issue is certainly something for you to be aware of when you begin writing your applications. If you copied the contents of variable `m` into another variable, `m2`, then you might have a shared reference to a single object, or you might have two independent objects. At this point all we can do is recommend that you look at the SQLJ Part 2 standard when it is published and that you consult the documentation of the specific DBMS that you are using.

8.2.2 Referencing the Fields of External Java Datatypes

The fields that have been associated with SQL attributes are referenced in exactly the same way as all other SQL attributes, as we see in Example 8.6.

EXAMPLE 8.6 REFERENCING THE FIELDS OF EXTERNAL JAVA DATATYPES.

```
SELECT    movie.length
FROM      sqlj_movies
WHERE     movie.title = 'The Fugitive'


UPDATE    sqlj_movies
SET       movie.length = 127,
          movie.descr
              = 'Dr. Richard Kimble is falsely accused'
                || 'of the murder of his wife.'
WHERE     movie.title = 'The Fugitive'
```

In the SELECT statement, we are accessing two of the attributes of our SQLJ column (`length` and `title`), and in the UPDATE statement we are updating the values of some of these attributes (`length` and `descr`).

It is possible that an application will try to set the `length` attribute to be the null value. This is problematic because the Java field that corresponds to `length` uses the `int` data type, which cannot represent the null value. Although the SQLJ Part 2 specification doesn't currently state that an exception shall be raised under these circumstances, we expect that it will before it is adopted.

8.2.3 Using Java Methods in SQL

Both SQL structured types and Java classes would be uninteresting without the use of their methods. Just as we have associated a Java constructor with an SQL initializer, we can easily associate a Java method with an SQL method. Let us consider the `toString` method of the `Movie` class seen in Example 8.7.

EXAMPLE 8.7 DEFINE THE `toString` METHOD FOR THE `Movie` CLASS.

```
public class Movie implements java.io.Serializable {

   ...

   public String toString () {
      return "\"" + title + "\""
             + ((length == 0) ? "" : (", " + length + " minutes"));
   }

}
```

We create an association between the SQL method to_string and this Java method in Example 8.8.

EXAMPLE 8.8 ASSOCIATING THE SQL to_string METHOD WITH THE toString METHOD IN THE Movie CLASS.

```
CREATE TYPE sqlj_movie
   EXTERNAL NAME 'cinema_jar:Cinema.Movie'
   LANGUAGE JAVA
   (...

     METHOD to_string ()
        RETURNS VARCHAR (100)
        EXTERNAL NAME 'toString'
   )
```

Example 8.9 shows how the to_string method may be used in a query whose output is shown in Result 8.1.

EXAMPLE 8.9 RETRIEVING THE "B" MOVIE SUMMARIES.

```
SELECT  movie.to_string() AS "Movie Summary"
FROM    sqlj_movies
WHERE   movie.title LIKE 'B%'
```

Result 8.1 "B" movie summaries.

Movie Summary
"Braveheart", 177 minutes
"Blue Sky", 101 minutes
"Bullets over Broadway", 98 minutes
"Belle époque", 109 minutes
"Born on the Fourth of July", 145 minutes
"Babettes gæstebud", 102 minutes
"Blazing Stewardesses", 80 minutes

In Section 6.1.1 we discussed the characteristics that can be specified for an SQL routine. Just as these characteristics can be used when you define a Java routine, they can be used when you define an SQL method in an external Java datatype. Example 8.10 shows how the method above could be written to state explicitly that it is deterministic and does not execute any SQL statements.

EXAMPLE 8.10 EXPLICIT SPECIFICATION OF METHOD CHARACTERISTICS.

```
CREATE TYPE sqlj_movie
   EXTERNAL NAME 'cinema_jar:Cinema.Movie'
   LANGUAGE JAVA
   (...

     METHOD to_string ()
        RETURNS VARCHAR (100)
        NO SQL
        DETERMINISTIC
        EXTERNAL NAME 'toString'
   )
```

Our `toString` method did not modify the objects that it operated on. Let's suppose, for a moment, that it had. For each row that satisfies the query above, the byte string stored in the column is deserialized, the method acts on the object, and then the reference to the object is lost. The objects are very shortly available for garbage collection. Let us be absolutely clear about this: The objects are not reserialized and returned to the column, so any change that is made to them is lost. It's easy to overlook this rather important consideration, so be sure you keep it in mind when writing code of this sort.

If our modified `toString` method acted upon an `sqlj_movie` instance in a variable, then it is unclear whether another operation on the instance would see this change. As we said just a little while ago, it is not yet specified whether the variable holds an object reference or a serialized byte string. (But it will be specified by the time SQLJ Part 2 is finalized and published.)

8.2.4 Using Java Methods That Modify an Object

Very often, a Java class contains several `void` methods, whose purpose is to change the state of an object in some way. Example 8.11 shows the `clearVotes` method. This method clears the votes that have been stored in the `votes` field.

In order for this method to be useful to SQL, the changed object must be explicitly returned to the invoker of the method, which is done as shown in Example 8.12.

EXAMPLE 8.11 `clearVotes` AS A `void` METHOD.

```
public class Movie implements java.io.Serializable {

   private Hashtable                    votes = new Hashtable ();

   ...

   /**
    * Clear the votes that have been cast for a movie.
    *
    */

   public void clearVotes() {
      votes.clear();
   }

}
```

EXAMPLE 8.12 ASSOCIATING THE SQL `clear_votes` METHOD WITH THE JAVA `clearVotes` METHOD.

```
CREATE TYPE sqlj_movie
   EXTERNAL NAME 'cinema_jar:Cinema.Movie'
   LANGUAGE JAVA
   (...

     METHOD clear_votes ()
        RETURNS sqlj_movie SELF AS RESULT
        EXTERNAL NAME 'clearVotes'
   )
```

The phrase "`RETURNS` *`datatype`* `SELF AS RESULT`" indicates that the external Java datatype instance, after it is modified, is to be returned to the caller of the SQL method. Example 8.13 shows how this type of method can be used.

EXAMPLE 8.13 USING THE `clear_votes` METHOD.

```
UPDATE   sqlj_movies
SET      movie = movie.clear_votes()
WHERE    movie.title = 'Fargo'
```

This mechanism is not limited to `void` methods. You may have a Java method that modifies an object and returns some value related to the modification that has been made. In Example 8.14, we see a modified form of the `clearVotes` method that returns the average of the votes that are stored before it clears them.

EXAMPLE 8.14 A MODIFIED `clearVotes` METHOD THAT RETURNS A VALUE.

```
public class Movie implements java.io.Serializable {

   ...

   /**
    * Clear the votes that have been cast for a movie.
    *
    * @return   The average of the votes received, 0 if no votes
    *           have been received.
    */

   public int clearVotes2() {
      int r;

      r = this.tallyVote();
      this.clearVotes();

      return r;
   }

}

CREATE TYPE sqlj_movie
   EXTERNAL NAME 'cinema_jar:Cinema.Movie'
   LANGUAGE JAVA
   (...

     METHOD clear_votes2 ()
        RETURNS sqlj_movie SELF AS RESULT
        EXTERNAL NAME 'clearVotes2'
   )
```

By using `RETURNS sqlj_movie SELF AS RESULT` we are explicitly throwing away the integer value that has been returned in order to get a guarantee that the change this method makes is captured. Let us be really clear about this. The behavior of the Java method has not changed at all. Our DBMS will execute the `clearVotes` method and ignore the integer value that Java returns. The DBMS will then make sure that the invoker of the SQL method receives a representation of the modified object.

8.2.5 Static Methods

SQLJ Part 2 allows us to associate a Java static method with an SQL static method, in exactly the way that you would expect. Example 8.15 defines the `stars2` method for our `Movie` class.

EXAMPLE 8.15 `stars2` AS A STATIC METHOD.

```
public class Movie implements java.io.Serializable {

   ...

   public static String stars2 (int rating) {
      String result = "";

      while (rating-- > 0) {
         result += "*";
      }

      return result;
   }

}
```

Example 8.16 shows how the `stars2` method can be used in our SQL type.

EXAMPLE 8.16 ASSOCIATING THE `stars2` JAVA METHOD WITH THE `stars` SQL METHOD.

```
CREATE TYPE sqlj_movie
   EXTERNAL NAME 'cinema_jar:Cinema.Movie'
   LANGUAGE JAVA
   (...

     STATIC METHOD stars (INTEGER)
        RETURNS VARCHAR (10)
        EXTERNAL NAME 'stars2'
   )
```

This method can now be invoked from SQL as follows:

```
SET best = sqlj_movie::stars (10);
```

If you remember Section 6.3.1, then you might have noticed that we created an SQL function that was based on this same method (in Example 6.8). The two parts of SQLJ do, indeed, provide two different ways to associate SQL constructs with the method, and two different ways to invoke these constructs. The same Java method is executed either way, so the choice is yours.

8.2.6 Static Fields

The Java classes that we are using will probably contain static fields, some of them final and some of them not. In Section 6.3.5, we cautioned you about the use of nonfinal static fields from SQL. You might want to review this section before we go on. We'll wait . . .

SQLJ Part 2 provides a mechanism for accessing the value of a final static field. We are allowed to use this mechanism for nonfinal static fields, but only to read their contents. Example 8.17 shows us some static fields in the `Vote` class.

EXAMPLE 8.17 SOME STATIC FIELDS OF THE `Vote` CLASS.

```
public class Vote {

   int                          value;
   public final static int      minVote = 1;
   public final static int      maxVote = 10;


   /**
    * Constructor for a Vote.
    *
    * @param        voteValue        Value of the Vote.
    * @exception    VoteOutOfRange   Vote outside of the range of
    *                                1 to 10.
    */

   public Vote (int voteValue) throws VoteOutOfRange {
      if (voteValue < minVote || voteValue > maxVote)
         throw new VoteOutOfRange ();
      value = voteValue;
   }
}
```

SQLJ Part 2 allows us to create an SQL method that is an accessor for this field. In Example 8.18, we have created the SQL `max_vote` method that gives us access to the `maxVote` field.

EXAMPLE 8.18 PROVIDING ACCESS TO THE maxVote STATIC FIELD WITH THE max_vote METHOD.

```
CREATE TYPE sql_vote
   EXTERNAL NAME 'cinema_jar:Cinema.Vote'
   LANGUAGE JAVA
   ( METHOD sql_vote (INTEGER)
        RETURNS sql_vote
        EXTERNAL NAME 'Vote'


     STATIC METHOD max_vote ()
        RETURNS INTEGER
        EXTERNAL VARIABLE NAME 'maxVote'
   )
```

As you can see, `max_vote` is a static method that uses "`EXTERNAL VARIABLE NAME`" to indicate that it is providing the value of the `maxVote` field. In order to find illegal values in the `votes` table, we could issue the query shown in Example 8.19.

EXAMPLE 8.19 FINDING ILLEGAL VOTES.

```
SELECT   *
FROM     votes
WHERE    vote > sql_vote::max_vote()
```

8.2.7 Null Values

We've shown how the attributes of external Java datatypes can be read and modified and how methods can be invoked on external Java datatypes. Because we are bringing Java classes into SQL, we must consider the places that null values can occur.

Let's look again at the UPDATE statement in Example 8.6, which we saw earlier in this chapter.

```
UPDATE   sqlj_movies
SET      movie.length = 127,
         movie.descr
```

```
              = 'Dr. Richard Kimble is falsely accused '
                || 'of the murder of his wife.'
WHERE     movie.title = 'The Fugitive'
```

When we evaluate this statement, we might find a row in which the `movie` column contained the null value. The rule in SQL:1999 for trying to access an attribute of a structured type instance that is null is quite simple—just return the null value. This means that this row will not meet the condition specified in the WHERE clause, so it will not be updated.

This rule is probably a bit jarring to those of you who are approaching this material from a Java or C/C++ background because you are expecting an exception to be thrown. This rule was put into SQL so that an application programmer could avoid having to write lots of additional predicates to detect and avoid such rows (after all, the occurrence of null values in SQL is quite common). Also, you should remember that when SQL raises an exception condition that is not handled, then the work of the entire statement (in this case an UPDATE statement) is undone.

Now, let us suppose that the WHERE condition were different, and this row *did* meet the qualification in the WHERE clause. We are now attempting to set the length attribute of a null instance, and here SQL:1999 specifies that an exception condition will be raised.

There is one more case to consider. We might be invoking a method on an external SQLJ datatype, and one of the arguments to the method could be the null value. If the method specifies `RETURNS NULL ON NULL INPUT`, then the method will not be executed.

In all of these cases, the external Java datatypes are treated in exactly the same way that SQL structured types are treated.

8.2.8 Ordering

When an external Java datatype is first created, none of the features of SQL that depend on ordering may be used. These include DISTINCT, GROUP BY, ORDER BY, and comparison predicates.

We saw in Section 7.6.6 that SQL:1999 allows us to specify what type of ordering operations may be used (`EQUALS ONLY` or `ORDER FULL`) and the name of the function that provides this behavior. SQLJ Part 2 extends this part of SQL:1999 in two ways.

In the first of these extensions, a user may specify a method that provides the comparison behavior, as an alternative to specifying a function. We could, for example, use the `Movie.toString` method as the basis for our ordering.

```
CREATE ORDERING FOR sqlj_movie
   EQUALS ONLY BY MAP WITH METHOD to_string
```

When this type of ordering method is used, a method must be defined for the SQL structured type that returns a predefined SQL data type. SQL applies the mapping method to the instances that are being compared and uses the result of the comparison of these two mapped values as the result of the comparison of the two instances. In the case of a relative comparison, the method must have two parameters and must return an INTEGER value of –1, 0, or +1 to indicate less than, equal to, or greater than, respectively.

The second of these extensions recognizes that Java has provided the `java.lang.Comparable` interface for the same purpose and allows the implementation of this interface to be used by SQL. This interface defines the `compareTo` method:

```
public int compareTo (object)
```

The value returned by this method is less than 0, equal to 0, or greater than 0, to indicate that the object argument is less than, equal to, or greater than the object on which the method is being invoked, respectively. We would use the `Movie.compareTo` method by specifying the following:

```
CREATE ORDERING FOR sqlj_movie
   ORDER FULL BY RELATIVE WITH COMPARABLE INTERFACE
```

This usage requires that `sqlj_movie` implement `java.lang.Comparable`. Our `Movie` class uses the tally of the votes to compare two movies, and—where the tally is equal—it uses the number of votes that have been cast (this is admittedly a bit contrived; our liking two movies to the same degree doesn't mean that they are interchangeable). The `compareTo` method is shown in Example 8.20.

We could now pose the query in Example 8.21. The result of that query can be seen in Result 8.2. The use of the `movie` column in the ORDER BY clause automatically invoked the `compareTo` method we specified.

EXAMPLE 8.20 ADDING A `compareTo` METHOD TO THE `Movie` CLASS.

```
public class Movie implements java.io.Serializable {

   ...

   public int compareTo (Movie comparand) {
      int tally1 = this.tallyVote ();
      int tally2 = comparand.tallyVote ();
```

```
        if (tally1 < tally2)
           return -1;
        else if (tally1 > tally2)
           return 1;
        else if (this.votes.size () < comparand.votes.size ())
           return -1;
        else if (this.votes.size () > comparand.votes.size ())
           return 1;
        else return 0;
    }

}
```

EXAMPLE 8.21 FINDING MOVIES WITH SHORT TITLES, ORDERED FROM BEST TO WORST.

```
SELECT    movie.to_string() AS "Movie Summary",
          movie.tally_vote() AS Tally
FROM      sqlj_movies
WHERE     CHAR_LENGTH (movie.title) < 6
ORDER BY movie DESC;
```

Result 8.2 Movies with short titles, ordered from best to worst.

Movie Summary	TALLY
"Fargo", 98 minutes	8
"Reds", 194 minutes	7
"Ghost", 128 minutes	6
"Kolya", 105 minutes	6
"Glory", 122 minutes	5
"Twins", 105 minutes	5
"Shine", 105 minutes	4

8.2.9 Subtypes

Java provides the ability for us to create a new class that extends an existing class. Similarly, SQL provides the ability for us to create a structured type that is a subtype of an existing structured type. Even though SQL uses UNDER and Java uses extends, the two concepts are very similar.

Recognizing this, SQLJ Part 2 provides the ability to associate several Java classes that are in a type hierarchy to several SQL structured types that are in a type hierarchy. In Example 8.22, we extend the `Movie` class to represent DVDs.

EXAMPLE 8.22 EXTENDING THE DVD CLASS TO THE `Movie` CLASS.

```
public class DVD extends Movie implements java.io.Serializable {

   public int                         stock_number;
   public BigDecimal                  price;
   public String                      features;

   /**
    * Constructor for a DVD
    *
    * @param  title         The title of the movie.
    * @param  length        The length of the movie in minutes.
    * @param  description   A brief description of the movie.
    * @param  stock_number  Unique identifier for the DVD.
    * @param  price         The price of the DVD, in $US.
    * @param  features      Any special features supported by
    *                       the DVD.
    */

   public DVD (String title, int length, String description,
               int stock_number, BigDecimal price,
               String features) {
      super (title, length, description);
      this.stock_number = stock_number;
      this.price = price;
      this.features = features;
   }

}
```

Now that we've extended the class, we create an association between the `DVD` class and the `sqlj_dvd` structured type, as shown in Example 8.23.

Only the fields and methods specified in the `DVD` class can be included in this definition because we have created this external Java type under `sqlj_movie`, and any fields and methods that belong to the `Movie` class can be specified in `sqlj_movie`. These fields and methods will then be inherited by `sqlj_dvd`.

EXAMPLE 8.23 ASSOCIATING THE `sqlj_dvd` STRUCTURED TYPE AND THE DVD CLASS.

```
CREATE TYPE sqlj_dvd UNDER sqlj_movie
   EXTERNAL NAME 'cinema_jar:Cinema.DVD'
   LANGUAGE JAVA
   ( stock      INTEGER       EXTERNAL NAME 'stock_number',
     price      DECIMAL (5,2) EXTERNAL NAME 'price',
     features   VARCHAR (60)  EXTERNAL NAME 'features',

     METHOD sqlj_dvd (p1 VARCHAR(60), p2 INTEGER, p3 VARCHAR(60),
                      p4 INTEGER, p5 DECIMAL(5,2), p6 VARCHAR(60))
        RETURNS sqlj_dvd
        EXTERNAL NAME 'DVD'
   )
```

Collapsing Subclasses

The ability to create an association between a hierarchy of SQL structured types and Java classes is rather straightforward and might be exactly what you want for some applications. You might, however, wish to associate only *some* of the classes to structured types. A simple example of this possibility is that you might wish to create a structured type for DVD, but you might have no interest in creating instances of the parent class, `Movie`. You would make this association as we have shown in Example 8.24. Because we did not declare `sqlj_dvd` to be under some parent type, we are allowed to include attributes and methods from `Movie`, the parent class of DVD.

With a type hierarchy of more than two types, there is a restriction that you should be aware of. Let us consider some additional classes; `DTSDVD` will extend `DVD`, and `DamagedDTSDVD` will extend `DTSDVD`. We can certainly create a structured type for each of these classes and subclasses, keeping the two hierarchies completely parallel to one another. We can also create a single structured type that corresponds to any one of these classes. Let us suppose, however, that we wish to create fewer SQL types than Java classes, but more than one.

The hierarchy of structured types that we create in SQL must correspond to a *contiguous subset* of the classes in Java. Let's take this a step at a time. We've already said that an SQL structured type that does not have a supertype can be associated with any Java class. Now, let us consider an SQL structured type *y* that has a supertype *x* that is associated with a Java class. The structured type *y* must be associated with a class that extends the class that is associated with *x*. This type of restriction can be seen in Figure 8.1.

EXAMPLE 8.24 DIRECTLY ASSOCIATING THE `sqlj_dvd` STRUCTURED TYPE WITH THE DVD CLASS.

```
CREATE TYPE sqlj_dvd
   EXTERNAL NAME 'cinema_jar:Cinema.DVD'
   LANGUAGE JAVA
   ( title      VARCHAR(60)  EXTERNAL NAME 'title',
     length     INTEGER      EXTERNAL NAME 'length',
     descr      VARCHAR(60)  EXTERNAL NAME 'description',
     stock      INTEGER      EXTERNAL NAME 'stock_number',
     price      DECIMAL(5,2) EXTERNAL NAME 'price',
     features   VARCHAR(60)  EXTERNAL NAME 'features',

     METHOD sqlj_dvd (p1 VARCHAR(60), p2 INTEGER, p3 VARCHAR(60),
                      p4 INTEGER, p5 DECIMAL(5,2), p6 VARCHAR(60))
        RETURNS sqlj_dvd
        EXTERNAL NAME 'DVD'

     METHOD to_string ()
        RETURNS VARCHAR(100)
        EXTERNAL NAME 'toString'

     ...

   )
```

This restriction is not absolutely necessary, but when the SQLJ group of companies considered it, they decided that there was little to be gained by allowing there to be gaps in the associations. Perhaps this restriction will be lifted at some point in the future if customers demand it.

8.2.10 Extending the Mappable Types

We've seen several examples of SQLJ Part 2 associating a Java class with an SQL structured type. This association extends the set of mappable data types that were first introduced in SQLJ Part 1. Example 8.25 adds the `addVote` method to our `Movie` class.

The second parameter uses the Java class `Vote` (the fully qualified name of this class is `Cinema.Vote`), which initially was not a mappable data type. Once the SQL type `sqlj_vote` has been associated with `Vote`, we can associate the `add_vote` SQL method with `addVote` as shown in Example 8.26.

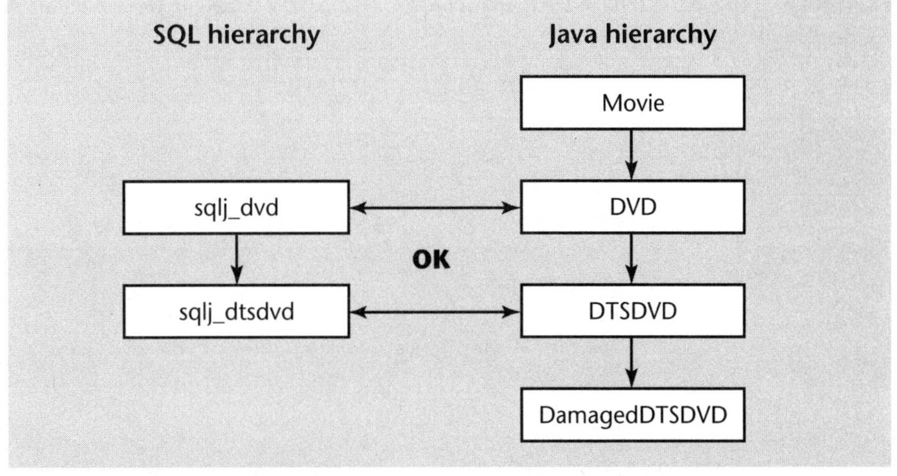

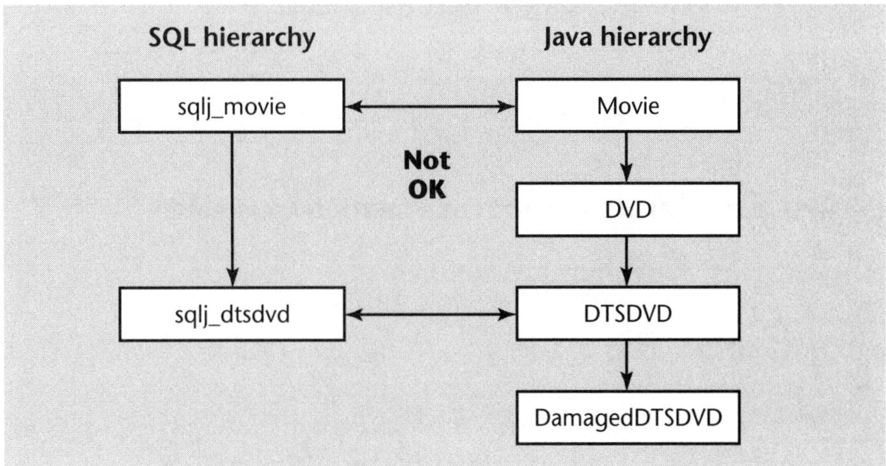

FIGURE 8.1 *Associating type hierarchies.*

This is a good time to point out that if the implicit signature of the Java method is not what you intend it to be, then you are able to specify exactly the signature that you desire. An explicit signature for Example 8.26 would be the following:

```
METHOD add_vote (VARCHAR (20), sqlj_vote)
       RETURNS sqlj_movie SELF AS RESULT
       EXTERNAL NAME 'addVote(String, Vote)'
```

EXAMPLE 8.25 MAKING A PARAMETER IN THE addVote METHOD MAPPABLE.

```
public class Movie implements java.io.Serializable {

   ...

   /**
    * Register a vote for a movie.
    * A voter may vote more than once, but only the most recent
    * vote counts.
    *
    * @param   whoVotes    The name of the voter.
    * @param   vote        The vote itself.
    */

   public void addVote (String whoVotes, Vote vote) {
      votes.put (whoVotes, vote);
   }

}
```

EXAMPLE 8.26 MAKING THE addVote METHOD MAPPABLE.

```
CREATE TYPE sqlj_movie
   EXTERNAL NAME 'cinema_jar:Cinema.Movie'
   LANGUAGE JAVA
   (...

     METHOD add_vote (VARCHAR (20), sqlj_vote)
        RETURNS sqlj_movie SELF AS RESULT
        EXTERNAL NAME 'addVote'
   )
```

8.3 Deployment Descriptors

We introduced deployment descriptors in our discussion of SQLJ Part 1 (Section 6.7). In SQLJ Part 2, the SQL definition of external Java datatypes, which we have been showing as independent DDL statements, must actually be specified in a deployment descriptor. A deployment descriptor, executed as part of an `install_jar` procedure, may contain both SQLJ Part 1 and SQLJ Part 2 entries.

We might wish to create a deployment descriptor file, `deploy2.txt`, to help us install the `Movie` class and the `sqlj_movie` external Java datatype. The manifest file for the JAR file will contain the following:

```
Name: deploy2.txt
SQLJDeploymentDescriptor: TRUE
```

Example 8.27 shows the contents of the file `deploy2.txt`.

EXAMPLE 8.27 DEPLOYMENT DESCRIPTOR FILE.

```
SQLActions[] = {
   "BEGIN INSTALL

       CREATE TYPE sqlj_movie
       EXTERNAL NAME 'cinema_jar:Cinema.Movie'
       LANGUAGE JAVA
       ( title      VARCHAR (60) EXTERNAL NAME 'title',
         length     INTEGER      EXTERNAL NAME 'length',
         descr      VARCHAR (60) EXTERNAL NAME 'description',

         METHOD sqlj_movie (...)
            RETURNS sqlj_movie
            EXTERNAL NAME 'Movie',

         METHOD to_string ()
            RETURNS VARCHAR (100)
            EXTERNAL NAME 'toString',

         METHOD clear_votes ()
            RETURNS sqlj_movie SELF AS RESULT
            EXTERNAL NAME 'clearVotes',

         METHOD clear_votes2 ()
            RETURNS sqlj_movie SELF AS RESULT
            EXTERNAL NAME 'clearVotes2',

         STATIC METHOD stars (INTEGER)
            RETURNS VARCHAR (10)
            EXTERNAL NAME 'stars2'
       );

       GRANT USAGE ON TYPE sqlj_movie TO PUBLIC;
```

```
   END INSTALL",
   "BEGIN REMOVE

       REVOKE USAGE ON TYPE sqlj_movie FROM PUBLIC;

       DROP TYPE sqlj_movie RESTRICT;

   END REMOVE"
}
```

8.4 Products in the Marketplace

As we stated in Chapter 6, we know of no freely available implementation of SQLJ Part 1; similarly, we know of no freely available implementation of SQLJ Part 2 either. We will briefly discuss Sybase's Adaptive Server Anywhere and Cloudscape because they have both implemented parts of both SQLJ Part 1 and SQLJ Part 2.

8.4.1 Sybase Adaptive Server Anywhere

In Chapter 6, we discussed the parts of SQLJ Part 1 that were implemented by Adaptive Server Anywhere (ASA) 6.0. We showed how JAR files and class files are installed in a database. ASA 6.0 does not support SQL structured types, so it could not support the type of association we have shown you throughout this chapter. Instead, Java classes and methods can be directly referred to within SQL statements. Once a class is installed in the database, its constructors and methods are immediately available for use in queries and stored procedures. The statement in Example 8.28 shows how we could populate the `sqlj_movies` table.

EXAMPLE 8.28 POPULATING THE `sqlj_movies` TABLE.

```
INSERT INTO sqlj_movies (movie)
   SELECT   NEW Cinema.Movie
                   (title, COALESCE (runs, 0), 'No Description')
   FROM     movies;
```

We can apply all of the votes that exist in our `votes` table to these movies with the compound statement shown in Example 8.29.

This operation would look significantly different with the FOR statement (a SQL/PSM statement that ASA does not yet support) and SQLJ Part 2 constructs. SQL's FOR statement makes the action within the loop much clearer. The sequence of extract, update, and replace for each of the `sqlj_movie` instances can be replaced by just an UPDATE statement that uses a method to change a `Movie` object.

```
BEGIN
  DECLARE m Cinema.Movie;

  FOR v AS CURSOR FOR SELECT * FROM votes D

    UPDATE  sqlj_movies
    SET     movie = movie.addVote (v.voter, NEW sqlj_vote (v.vote))
    WHERE   movie.title = v.title;

  END FOR;
END
```

EXAMPLE 8.29 APPLYING EACH VOTE RECORDED IN THE `votes` TABLE.

```
BEGIN
  DECLARE  c1 CURSOR FOR SELECT * FROM votes;

  DECLARE m Cinema.Movie;
  DECLARE vtitle CHAR VARYING (100);
  DECLARE voter CHAR VARYING (10);
  DECLARE vote INT;

  OPEN c1;

  c1_loop:
  LOOP
     FETCH NEXT c1 INTO vtitle, voter, vote;
     IF SQLSTATE = '02000'
        THEN LEAVE c1_loop;
     END IF;

     SELECT   movie
     INTO     m
     FROM     sqlj_movies
     WHERE    movie.title = vtitle;

     CALL m.addVote (voter, NEW Cinema.Vote (vote));

     UPDATE   sqlj_movies
     SET      movie = m
     WHERE    movie.title = vtitle;
  END LOOP c1_loop;
END
```

We expect that future releases of ASA will implement still more of the SQLJ Part 2 specification.

8.4.2 Cloudscape

Cloudscape has also implemented parts of SQLJ Part 1 and Part 2. They have done so in a manner fairly similar to that of ASA, except that no actions are necessary to load Java classes into the database; they can be used directly from the Java classpath. Method aliases in Cloudscape align the method invocation with SQLJ Part 1.

Let us consider the operations we showed for Adative Server Anywhere. We could populate the `sqlj_movies` table with the following statement:

```
INSERT INTO sqlj_movies (movie)
   SELECT   NEW Cinema.Movie ( title,
                               runs IS NULL ? 0 : runs,
                               'No Description'
                             )
   FROM     movies;
```

Cloudscape uses Java as its stored procedure language. We can apply all of the votes that exist in our `votes` table to these movies with the following Java code (within a Java method):

```
ResultSet rs = stmt.execute("SELECT * FROM votes");

PreparedStatement updatestmt
  = conn.prepareStmt(  "UPDATE sqlj_movies "
                     + "SET  movie = movie.addVote(?, NEW
                                                  sqlj_vote(?)) "
                     + "WHERE movie.title=?"
                    );

while (rs.next()) {
  updatestmt.setString(1,rs.getString(2));
  updatestmt.setInt(2,rs.getInt(3));
  updatestmt.setString(3,rs.getString(1));
  updatestmt.executeUpdate();
}

updatestmt.close();
```

8.5 Chapter Summary

We have shown how Java classes can be associated with SQL structured types and then used as the data type for SQL columns, variables, and parameters. We have also discussed how Java fields can be associated with SQL attributes, Java constructors can be associated with SQL initializers, and Java methods can be associated with SQL methods. It is your choice whether to make all of your fields, constructors, and methods available to SQL, or only some subset of them. The CREATE TYPE statement for a large and complex class could be somewhat painful to generate by hand. Perhaps tools or wizards will be written to take the drudgery out of this task.

We have presented fairly simple examples throughout the chapter, using the `Movie` and `Vote` classes. Let us now consider the "value proposition" for SQLJ Part 2. You may already have written classes to model parts of your business or organization. They might have been created for client, middle-tier, or server-side applications. These classes can now be used within your DBMS. We were going to say "used as is," but that is not quite correct. SQLJ Part 2 does require that a class implement either `java.io.Serializable` or `java.sql.SQLData` in order to associate a structured type with it. This process is trivial, but it could well require modification of the Java source file and recompilation. Even if you have not already written such classes, Java's expressive power and library classes allow you to create very powerful classes for your SQLJ columns. These classes can be written and tested using any of the popular Java IDEs available in the marketplace.

We'll leave you with one final thought—the SQLJ Part 2 specification does not specifically mention SQL:1999's typed tables, but it is very possible, maybe even likely, that vendors will support typed tables that use an external Java datatype as their basis.

CHAPTER

9

JDBC 2.0 API

9.1 Introduction

In June 1998, Javasoft released the specification for the JDBC 2.0 Core API. This specification extends the JDBC 1.0 API in a number of interesting ways. The impetus for these changes came from several directions:

- Some valuable capabilities of relational DBMSs were not available using the JDBC 1.0 API.
- SQL:1999 (which was then called SQL3) was in the final stages of its adoption as a formal standard. SQL:1999 provides many new features, including new primitive data types and user-defined types (UDTs).
- SQLJ Part 2 allows the definition of SQL columns with Java classes as their basis.

The JDBC 2.0 API is actually made up of two parts, the JDBC 2.0 Core API[1] and the JDBC 2.0 Standard Extensions API[2] (which is now being called the Optional Package API by Sun). The JDBC 2.0 Core API is a superset of the JDBC 1.0 API. Implementations of JDBC 2.0 will provide

---

1 *JDBC 2.0 API,* Version 1.0, Seth White and Mark Hapner, Sun Microsystems, 30 May 1998.

2 *JDBC 2.0 Standard Extension API,* Version 1.0, Seth White and Mark Hapner, Sun Microsystems, 7 December 1998.

backward compatibility for applications that were written against the JDBC 1.0 API. It is the JDBC 2.0 Core API that we primarily discuss in this chapter.

This split reflects a general decision by Sun to provide a Java 2 Platform core that is reasonably small and then define a series of separately loadable extensions that support particular types of applications. Along with size differentiation, this split allows the extensions to be developed after the core has been completed.

The JDBC 2.0 Core API is provided by the updated `java.sql` package contained in the Java 2 Platform, Standard Edition (provided by the SDK 1.2). The JDBC 2.0 Standard Extensions API is provided by the new `javax.sql` package that is included in the Java 2 Platform, Enterprise Edition.

In this chapter, we discuss the major features of the JDBC 2.0 Core API: scrollable and updatable cursors, batches of statements, support for SQL:1999 data types, support for Java objects in the database, and the customizing of SQL user-defined types (mapping them to Java classes).

9.2 Scrollable Result Sets

Scrollable cursors were introduced in SQL-92. This feature provides the ability to move either forward or backward through the resulting rows of a query. The feature allows `NEXT`, `PREVIOUS`, `FIRST`, `LAST`, `ABSOLUTE`, and `RELATIVE` to be specified in a FETCH statement.

In JDBC 2.0, an application may state—at the time a result set is created—whether it is to be *forward-only, scroll-sensitive,* or *scroll-insensitive.* At the same time, the application can declare whether the result set is to be read-only or updatable. The JDBC 1.0 result sets that we have discussed so far are forward-only and read-only in nature. You may be a bit confused by this statement. After all, in Section 4.5.2 we saw how to use SQL's positioned UPDATE and DELETE statements after we have fetched a row from a result set. We are, nonetheless, going to call these JDBC 1.0 result sets read-only because the result set methods did not directly change the values of the rows. In Section 9.3, we will see new JDBC 2.0 result set methods that do change the rows in the database.

A scrollable and updatable result set can be created in the following way:

```
Statement stmt = con.createStatement
                    ( ResultSet.TYPE_SCROLL_SENSITIVE,
                      ResultSet.CONCUR_UPDATABLE
                    );
ResultSet rs = stmt.executeQuery (...);
```

These same parameters can be used in the new versions of the `Connection.prepareStatement` and `Connection.prepareCall` methods. In this section, we discuss the operations that can be performed on a scrollable result set. The next section covers the operations that may be performed on updatable result sets, and the section after that discusses the two types of scrollable result sets.

An application can use the

```
DatabaseMetaData.supportsResultSetType
```

method to find out what result set types are supported by the current JDBC driver. The application can use the

```
DatabaseMetaData.supportsResultSetConcurrency
```

method to find out if updatable result sets are supported. If the application asks for a result set type or concurrency that is not supported, then an SQL warning is issued, and the driver uses values that are supported. If an `executeQuery` method specifies an SQL statement that is not updatable, such as a query based on a join, then (again) an SQL warning is issued and the concurrency value is changed. Appropriate "get" methods have been provided to return the actual values for result set type and concurrency.

The position within a scrollable result set (`rs`) can be changed by the following statements:

```
rs.first();
rs.last();
rs.beforeFirst();
rs.afterLast();
rs.next();
rs.previous();
rs.relative(3);
rs.absolute(-2);
```

Each of these methods returns a boolean value indicating whether the new position of the cursor is on a valid row. The `absolute(-2)` method changes the position to two rows before the end of the result set.

The position of the current row of the result set can be tested with the following statements:

```
if (rs.isFirst()) ... ;
if (rs.isLast()) ... ;
if (rs.isBeforeFirst()) ... ;
if (rs.isAfterLast()) ... ;
```

9.2.1 Hints for the JDBC Driver

Two types of performance hints may be provided by an application as it traverses result sets. A JDBC driver may use these hints, or it may ignore them completely. For each of these hints there is a "set" and "get" method, which are provided both for the `Statement` class and `ResultSet` class. When a result set is created, it takes as its initial value for the hint the value associated with the statement that created it. The values for these hints may be changed at any time. To be more specific, one type of hint indicates the direction in which rows will be processed, and the other indicates how many rows should be fetched from the database each time additional rows are needed. Example 9.1 shows the use of both types of hints.

EXAMPLE 9.1 PROVIDING HINTS TO THE JDBC DRIVER.

```
Statement stmt = con.createStatement ();
stmt.setFetchDirection (ResultSet.FETCH_FORWARD);
stmt.setFetchSize (10);

ResultSet rs = stmt.executeQuery (...);
while (rs.next()) {
   // operate on each row
}

rs.setFetchDirection (ResultSet.FETCH_REVERSE);

while (rs.previous()) {
   // operate on each row
}

rs.setFetchDirection (ResultSet.FETCH_UNKNOWN);
```

9.3 Updatable Result Sets

An updatable result set is one that has been created with the specification of `CONCUR_UPDATABLE`. Insert, update, and delete operations can be applied to result set rows and then propagated to the underlying rows in the database. Delete is the simplest of these operations, so let's take care of it first: When an application is positioned on a result set row, it simply invokes the `ResultSet.deleteRow` method. Updates to the current row are made by an application in two steps. First, the application must invoke one of the `ResultSet` update methods (updateString, updateInt, etc.). As with the get and set methods, the column can be identified by position or by name. These methods do not change the row in the database—if the application moves to another row at this point, then the updates will be lost. To propagate the updates to the database, the application must invoke the updateRow method. These two steps are shown in Example 9.2.

EXAMPLE 9.2 UPDATING THE ROW OF A RESULT SET.

```
ResultSet rs = stmt.executeQuery (    "SELECT    * "
                                    + "FROM      movies "
                                    + "WHERE     title = 'Fargo'"
                                   );
rs.next();

rs.updateInt ("movie_length",
              rs.getInt ("movie_length") + 5
             );
rs.updateRow();
```

If an application has issued some number of update methods before issuing the updateRow and decides that the changes should not be applied to the database, then it can invoke the cancelRowUpdates method.

Inserting a new row operates rather differently than it does in traditional embedded (static) SQL. An application begins the process of inserting a new row into the result set and the database by invoking the moveToInsertRow method. The position within the result set is remembered, and the current row of the result set is now a buffer area where a new row can be constructed. The application can invoke the update methods we discussed a moment ago to specify values for result set columns. Once a value has been specified, it can be retrieved with a get method. Result set columns for which values are not specified will get the null value. When the application is ready, it invokes the insertRow method to actually create the row in the result set and the database. Finally, the moveToCurrentRow method can be used to return the result set to its remembered position. These operations can all be seen in Example 9.3.

In JDBC 1.0, such updates and deletes could only have been performed by executing positioned UPDATE and DELETE statements, but these operations are much more cumbersome to write. You can see this for yourself by looking at the example we provided in Section 4.5.2. The inserts would have to be performed by executing an SQL INSERT statement.

EXAMPLE 9.3 INSERTING A ROW INTO A RESULT SET.

```
ResultSet rs = stmt.executeQuery (    "SELECT     * "
                                    + "FROM      movies "
                                 );

while (...) {
    ...
}

// Insert a new row

rs.moveToInsertRow ();
rs.updateString ("title",
                  "Butch Cassidy and the Sundance Kid"
                );
rs.updateInt ("movie_length", 110);
rs.insertRow ();

// Return to original position in the result set

rs.moveToCurrentRow ();
```

9.4 Result Set Sensitivity

Let us start the discussion of this topic with a bit of SQL-92 and SQL:1999 history. SQL-92 introduced the transaction isolation levels of READ UNCOMMITTED, READ COMMITTED, REPEATABLE READ, and SERIALIZABLE. These isolation levels determine the degree to which one transaction is able to "see" the changes made by other transactions that are running concurrently. READ UNCOMMITTED indicates that changes made by a concurrent transaction will be visible immediately, whereas SERIALIZABLE means that changes made by concurrent transactions will not be visible at all.

SQL-92 also began to address the topic of concurrent operations within a single transaction. A cursor could be declared INSENSITIVE, indicating that changes made within the transaction—but outside of the cursor's control—should not change the rows associated with the cursor once it has been opened. SQL:1999 allows SENSITIVE and ASENSITIVE to be specified in a cursor declaration. SENSITIVE, as the name implies, means that changes made within the transaction (again, outside of the cursor's control) must be visible through an open cursor.

ASENSITIVE (a word that is not found in any dictionary) means that it is up to the implementation whether to provide SENSITIVE or INSENSITIVE behavior—or even some arbitrary mix of those behaviors. This behavior is provided if neither SENSITIVE nor INSENSITIVE is specified.

In specifying that a result set is scrollable, the application must choose between TYPE_SCROLL_SENSITIVE and TYPE_SCROLL_INSENSITIVE. A result set that has been created with TYPE_SCROLL_INSENSITIVE will not see changes made by other transactions or by other operations in the same transaction. A result set that has been created with TYPE_SCROLL_SENSITIVE will see some or all of the changes that have been made by other transactions or by other operations in the same transaction. Rows that have been inserted since the result set was opened (and qualify to be in the result set) might be seen in the result set. A row that has been deleted since the result set was opened might not show up in the result set, or it might show up as a deleted row in the result set.

For update, there are three cases to consider: a row that qualifies for the result set might no longer qualify, a row that didn't qualify for the result set might now qualify, and a row that qualifies may still qualify but belong in a different position. In a result set of TYPE_SCROLL_SENSITIVE, the row leaving the result set may still remain visible, the row entering the result set may become visible, and the row that is moving may be seen in its new position, or not. One thing that is certain is that the new column values will be visible.

JDBC 2.0 provides new methods in the DatabaseMetaData interface to determine the type of behavior that the application will see:

```
othersInsertsAreVisible,
othersUpatesAreVisible,
```

and

```
othersDeletesAreVisible.
```

Now, let's consider the use of the new updatable result sets. An insert, update, or delete may be performed directly on a result set. The changes made to the result set may or may not be visible with subsequent position and get methods on the result set. Again, JDBC 2.0 provides methods to allow the application to determine what behavior will seen: ownInsertsAreVisible, ownUpdatesAreVisible, and ownDeletesAreVisible.

A result set of a particular type may have the ability to detect rows that have been modified by one of the three DML operations, as can be seen in Example 9.4.

EXAMPLE 9.4 DETECTING AN UPDATED ROW.

```
DatabaseMetaData dmd = con.getMetaData();
if (dmd.updatesAreDetected
      (ResultSet.TYPE_SCROLL_SENSITIVE)
   ) {
   while (rs.next ()) {
      if (rs.rowUpdated()) {
      // do something
      }
   }
}
```

Since a JDBC driver may be prefetching and caching rows, even a `TYPE_SCROLL_SENSITIVE` cursor may not reflect very recent changes. The `ResultSet.refreshRow` method is provided to allow an application to see the very latest changes that have been made to a row.

9.5 Execution of Batches

The execution of batches feature allows groups of statements to be accumulated in a batch and then executed with a single method invocation. Batches can contain DDL statements and DML statements that return an update count, but not statements that return a result set. Several methods have been added to the `Statement` interface to provide this feature.

java.sql.Statement Interface

`public void addBatch (String sql) throws SQLException`

Adds an SQL statement to the batch of statements that are awaiting execution.

`public void clearBatch () throws SQLException`

Empties the batch of statements that are awaiting execution.

`public int[] executeBatch () throws SQLException`

Executes the batch of statements that have been added. This method returns an array of the update counts, one for each statement in the batch.

Example 9.5 shows the execution of two simple statements.

EXAMPLE 9.5 EXECUTION OF A SMALL BATCH OF STATEMENTS.

```
Statement stmt = con.createStatement ();

stmt.addBatch ("INSERT INTO movie_lengths"
               + "VALUES ('Being There', 130)"
               );
stmt.addBatch ("INSERT INTO awards"
               + "VALUES ('Supporting Actor', "
               + "'Melvyn Douglas', 'Being There', "
               + "'1979', '1979')"
               );
int [] results = stmt.executeBatch();
```

If one of the statements in the batch does not execute correctly, then a `BatchUpdateException` is thrown (a subtype of `SQLException`), and methods are provided to allow the application to determine how many statements executed successfully and what the value of their update counts were.

This capability is also available to prepared statements and callable statements. In Example 9.6, we see the creation of a prepared statement and the addition of two executions of the statement to the batch. Each of the executions has been provided with its own arguments. A batch of callable statements can be created and executed in exactly the same way. These callable statements may not, however, contain either OUT or INOUT parameters.

EXAMPLE 9.6 EXECUTION OF A SMALL BATCH OF PREPARED STATEMENTS.

```
PreparedStatement pstmt =
      con.prepareStatement
          (  "INSERT INTO movie_lengths "
           + "VALUES (?, ?)"
          );

pstmt.setString (1, "Kramer vs. Kramer");
pstmt.setInt (2, 105);
pstmt.addBatch ();

pstmt.setString (1, "Breaking Away");
pstmt.setInt (2, 100);
pstmt.addBatch ();

int [] results = pstmt.executeBatch();
```

9.6 SQL:1999 Data Types

SQL:1999 adds several predefined data types to the data types that were defined in SQL-92. We've already discussed distinct types, structured types, and REF types in Chapter 7. SQL:1999 has added two flavors of the large object, or LOB, data type. The CHARACTER LARGE OBJECT, or CLOB, data type behaves a lot like SQL's character data types. The BINARY LARGE OBJECT, or BLOB, data type is a sequence of octets. As such, it does not have either a character set or a collation associated with it. Columns of these large object types may not be used in primary keys or uniqueness constraints, nor may they be used in the GROUP BY or ORDER BY clauses. SQL:1999 has also added the composite data type ARRAY. An ARRAY may be constructed from any SQL data type, other than another ARRAY. These data types can be used to construct columns in the following way:

```
ALTER TABLE movies
   ADD COLUMN commentary CHARACTER LARGE OBJECT (1M);

ALTER TABLE movies
   ADD COLUMN spoken_commentary BINARY LARGE OBJECT (1G);

ALTER TABLE movies
   ADD COLUMN producers CHAR VARYING (30) ARRAY [5];
```

JDBC 2.0 has added support for each of these new data types, and so we'll discuss each of them in turn. To begin with, JDBC 2.0 has added `java.sql.Types` variables that identify each of these data types as shown in Table 9.1. These variables allow the metadata methods of JDBC 2.0 to more accurately reflect the columns that are defined using these new SQL:1999 data types.

SQL data type	Variable in `java.sql.Types`
BLOB	BLOB
CLOB	CLOB
ARRAY	ARRAY
REF	REF
Distinct type	DISTINCT
Structured type	STRUCT

TABLE 9.1 *New variables in `java.sql.Types`.*

9.6.1 BLOBs and CLOBs

The `java.sql.Blob` and `java.sql.Clob` interfaces have been added to JDBC 2.0. Values of these types are provided by the `ResultSet.getBlob` and `ResultSet.getClob` methods, respectively. Let's first look at the methods provided by these interfaces and then we'll discuss them.

`java.sql.Blob` Interface

`public InputStream getBinaryStream() throws SQLException`

Returns the BLOB as a stream.

`public byte[] getBytes(long pos, int length) throws SQLException`

Returns a portion of the BLOB as an array of bytes.

`public long length() throws SQLException`

Returns the number of bytes contained in this BLOB.

`public long position(Blob pattern, long start) throws SQLException`

Returns the position at which the pattern begins in this BLOB. The first position in a BLOB is 1; –1 is returned if the pattern does not appear in this BLOB.

```
public long position(byte[] pattern, long start)
    throws SQLException
```

Returns the position at which the pattern begins in this BLOB. The first position in a BLOB is 1; –1 is returned if the pattern does not appear in this BLOB.

`java.sql.Clob` Interface

`public InputStream getAsciiStream() throws SQLException`

Returns the CLOB as a stream of ASCII bytes.

`public Reader getCharacterStream() throws SQLException`

Returns the CLOB as a stream of Unicode characters.

```
public String getSubString(long pos, int length)
    throws SQLException
```

Returns a portion of the CLOB as a string.

`public long length() throws SQLException`

Returns the number of characters contained in this CLOB.

`public long position(Clob pattern, long start) throws SQLException`

Returns the position at which the pattern begins in this CLOB. The first position in a CLOB is 1; –1 is returned if the pattern does not appear in this CLOB.

`public long position(String pattern, long start)`
`throws SQLException`

Returns the position at which the pattern begins in this CLOB. The first position in a CLOB is 1; –1 is returned if the pattern does not appear in this CLOB.

There's not a lot to say about these methods. They allow you to pick apart BLOBs and CLOBs just about the way you would expect them to. BLOB and CLOB locators are not directly exposed by these parts of the JDBC API. Instead, it is expected that implementations will use BLOB and CLOB locators to implement these interfaces.

A method that displays a specific column of the current row of a result set is shown in Example 9.7. The `displayHexRow` method, which is not shown, produces a `String` value, suitable for printing, from a `byte` array. The `Blob` and `Clob` objects will be valid during the transaction in which they are created. A JDBC 2.0 driver may provide a mechanism to provide a longer lifetime, such as for the session, as an extension to the JDBC 2.0 API.

9.6.2 Arrays

JDBC 2.0 returns a `java.sql.Array` object from the `ResultSet.getArray` methods (identifying the column either by name or by position) for columns of SQL's ARRAY type. The methods of this interface provide access to its individual elements.

`java.sql.Array` *Interface*

`public Object getArray() throws SQLException`

Returns a Java array that contains the elements of this SQL array.

`public Object getArray(long index, int count) throws SQLException`

Returns an array that contains a portion of the elements of this SQL array. The first element of the SQL array is designated as 1.

`public int getBaseType() throws SQLException`

Returns a value from `java.sql.Types` that indicates the type of the elements that are contained in this SQL array.

EXAMPLE 9.7 DISPLAYING THE DATA IN A BLOB COLUMN OF A RESULT SET ROW.

```
static void displayColumn (ResultSet rs, int column)
      throws SQLException {

   switch (rs.getMetaData().getColumnType(column)) {

      case java.sql.Types.CHAR:
         ...
         break;

      case java.sql.Types.BLOB:

         // Print a line for each 16 bytes in the column

         Blob thisCol = rs.getBlob (column);
         long colLength = thisCol.length();

         for (int i = 0; i < colLength; i += 16) {
            int lineLength = (int) ((colLength - i  < 16)
                                       ? colLength - i : 16);
            byte [] b = thisCol.getBytes (i, lineLength);
            System.out.println(displayHexRow(b));
         }
      break;
   }
}
```

`public String getBaseTypeName() throws SQLException`

Returns a string that contains the SQL name of the type of the elements that are contained in this SQL array.

`public ResultSet getResultSet() throws SQLException`

Returns a result set that contains a row for each element that is contained in this SQL array. The first column contains the index (starting at 1) of this element of the array, and the second column contains the element's value.

`public ResultSet getResultSet(long index, int count) throws SQLException`

Just like `getResultSet`, except that only a slice of the SQL array is represented in the result set.

Example 9.8 shows how these methods could be used to display the values in a column of a result set that contains an SQL array.

EXAMPLE 9.8 DISPLAYING THE DATA IN AN ARRAY COLUMN.

```
static void displayColumn (ResultSet rs, int column) throws
   SQLException {

   switch (rs.getMetaData().getColumnType(column)) {

      case java.sql.Types.CHAR:
         ...
         break;

      case java.sql.Types.BLOB:
         ...
         break;

      case java.sql.Types.ARRAY:
         Array thisArray = rs.getArray (column);

         switch (thisArray.getBaseType()) {
            case java.sql.Types.CHAR:
               String [] sArray = (String[]) thisArray.getArray();
               System.out.print ("[");
               for (int i = 0; i < sArray.length; i++) {
                  System.out.print (sArray[i]);
                  if (i != sArray.length - 1) {
                     System.out.print (", ");
                  }
               }
               System.out.println ("]");
               break;

            case java.sql.Types.INTEGER:
               ...
               break;
         }
         break;
   }
}
```

JDBC 2.0 specifies that a driver should implement this interface with an SQL array locator (we discussed a different type of locator, a user-defined type locator, in Section 7.5.6). JDBC 2.0 also specifies that an `Array` object remains valid only during the transaction in which it is created. The vendor of a JDBC 2.0 driver may provide some mechanism to change these two behaviors (the use of a locator and the period of validity), but JDBC 2.0 is silent on exactly what the mechanism should be.

9.6.3 REF Type

JDBC 2.0 returns a `java.sql.Ref` object from the `ResultSet.getRef` methods for columns of SQL REF Type. The `Ref` object remains valid for the lifetime of the connection in which it was obtained. As always, JDBC provides corresponding `setRef` methods.

There is a single method that can be used with `Ref` objects. This should not be too surprising, as an SQL REF is nothing more than a long-lived identifier that has meaning only within a DBMS.

java.sql.Ref Interface

```
public String getBaseTypeName() throws SQLException
```

Returns the name of the SQL structured type to which this REF type refers.

9.6.4 Distinct User-Defined Data Types

Distinct types are the first of two flavors of user-defined types that we'll be discussing (we discussed these in Section 7.3.1). Let us imagine that we have defined a distinct type, `genre`, and used it to add a column to the `movies` table.

```
CREATE TYPE genre AS CHAR VARYING (30);

ALTER TABLE movies ADD COLUMN movie_genre genre;
```

No additional interface is necessary for this SQL data type. We can retrieve this column using the get method that is appropriate for the SQL data type on which the distinct type is based.

```
String genre = rs.getString("movie_genre");
```

We might wish to query this table, examine the result set metadata, and then retrieve some of its rows. The JDBC 2.0 `ResultSetMetaData`

Method	JDBC 1.0 result	JDBC 2.0 result
getColumnType	Types.OTHER	Types.DISTINCT
getColumnTypeName	unknown	"cat1.schema1.genre"
getColumnClassName	n/a	"java.lang.String"

TABLE 9.2 *Information returned by* `ResultSetMetaData` *methods for a distinct type.*

Column	Description
TYPE_CAT	The type's catalog name.
TYPE_SCHEM	The type's schema name.
TYPE_NAME	The type's name.
CLASS_NAME	The name of the Java class that will describe all of the objects that are returned when the getObject method is applied to a column of this type.
DATA_TYPE	One of the following values defined in java.sql.Types: DISTINCT, STRUCT, or JAVA_OBJECT.
REMARKS	Explanatory comment.

TABLE 9.3 *Columns in the* `ResultSet` *returned by the* `getUDTs` *method.*

methods (see Table 9.2) will provide more information to an application than they would in JDBC 1.0. Some methods provide better information, and the `getColumnClassName` method is new. The `getColumnClassName` method returns the type of objects that will be returned by invoking the `getObject` method on this column.

The metadata for all distinct types and structured types can be found with the `getUDTs` method that has been added to `DatabaseMetaData` in JDBC 2.0. Like the `getSchemas` and `getTables` methods, this method returns a result set. The columns that are included in the result set that is returned by this method are shown in Table 9.3.

9.6.5 Structured User-Defined Data Types

We've arrived at the last of our SQL:1999 data types, the structured type (we discussed these in Section 7.4). All of the metadata methods that we just described will return `Types.STRUCT` for a column that has been created using a structured type.

JDBC 2.0 introduces the `Struct` interface, to allow an application to retrieve the data contained in a structured UDT column. We created a structured type for movies in Chapter 7, which we'll reproduce here.

```
CREATE TYPE movie (
   title          CHARACTER VARYING (100),
   description    CHARACTER VARYING (500),
   runs           INTEGER)
   NOT FINAL
   ...
   )
```

The `ResultSetMetaData` methods will provide the information shown in Table 9.4 to an application for a column of type `movie`.

The `Struct` interface is very simple. The following description of this interface contains almost all of the methods that it defines.

`java.sql.Struct` *Interface*

`public Object[] getAttributes ()`

> This method returns an array of objects that has been generated by applying the `getObject` method to the attributes of this structured type.

`public String getSQLTypeName ()`

> Returns the name of the SQL structured type that produced this object.

Let us suppose that we are positioned on a row, and that the fifth column has been defined using the `movie` data type. The code fragment in Example 9.9 would display all of the attributes of this column.

EXAMPLE 9.9 DISPLAYING THE ATTRIBUTES OF AN INSTANCE OF A STRUCTURED TYPE.

```
Struct column = (Struct)rs.getObject(5);
System.out.println(column.getSQLTypeName() + ":");

Object[] attrib = column.getAttributes();

for (int i = 0; i < attrib.length; i++) {
   System.out.println (attrib[i]);
}
```

Method	JDBC 1.0 result	JDBC 2.0 result
getColumnType	Types.OTHER	Types.STRUCT
getColumnTypeName	unknown	"cat1.schema1.movie"
getColumnClassName	n/a	"java.sql.Struct"

TABLE 9.4 *Information returned by* `ResultSetMetaData` *methods for a structured type.*

9.7 Java Objects in the Database

JDBC 1.0 provided the `getObject` and `setObject` methods to get and set values from result sets and parameters. These methods allow an application to get or set a value without having to use a more type-specific form of these methods, such as `getString` or `getInt`. Although JDBC 1.0 did not state it explicitly, the expectation was that these methods were being used to access values of traditional SQL data types.

With the increasing popularity of Java, some DBMSs have allowed Java data types to be used in the database, in addition to the traditional SQL data types. Although we expect many DBMSs to implement the SQLJ Part 2 specification to provide this feature, not all will do so (certainly not immediately). The JDBC 1.0 `getObject` and `setObject` methods are sufficient to pass Java objects to and from the database. The following statement will retrieve from a result set the value of a column that is based on a Java type `X.Y.Z`.

```
X.Y.Z z = (X.Y.Z)rs.getObject(nthColumn);
```

Though the JDBC 1.0 methods are sufficient to operate on the data contained in Java columns, the description of these columns obtained by invoking methods in the `DatabaseMetaData` and `ResultSetMetaData` classes would be unhelpful. Table 9.5 shows how this has been improved in JDBC 2.0. The value that would be returned by the `getColumnTypeName` method for this column is not precisely defined by JDBC 1.0. Values of "Java," "Serialized," the Java class name, or null are all allowed.

It is possible that an application will be looking at column or procedure metadata by invoking the `getColumns` or `getProcedureColumns` methods of the `DatabaseMetaData` interface. JDBC 2.0 will identify the columns or parameters that are Java objects as being of type `JAVA`

Method	JDBC 1.0 result	JDBC 2.0 result
`getColumnType`	`Types.OTHER`	`Types.JAVA_OBJECT`
`getColumnTypeName`	unspecified	`"X.Y.Z"`
`getColumnClassName`	n/a	`"X.Y.Z"`

TABLE 9.5 *Information returned by `ResultSetMetaData` methods for Java columns.*

_OBJECT. Now, of what classes are these objects instances? To find this out, the application must invoke the getUDTs method, looking in the CLASS_NAME column of the result set that it produces. This column will contain a string with the name of the class that underlies this UDT.

9.8 Customizing SQL Types

In the preceding sections, we've seen how an application can retrieve the data that is contained in instances of SQL's distinct types and structured types. For some types of applications, such as report generators, dealing with the individual attributes of a structured type may be appropriate. Other types of applications will want to deal with objects of a Java class that have been constructed from SQL structured type instances. JDBC 2.0 provides a framework to do this—*SQL type customization.*

To see how SQL type customization works, we'll start with the SQL structured type movie that we looked at just a moment ago. In order to create a Java class to represent movie instances, we must implement the java.sql.SQLData interface. This interface is somewhat analogous to java.io.Serializable, which we discussed in Section 2.9.

java.sql.SQLData Interface

`public String getSQLTypeName ()`

Returns the SQL type name that this object represents.

`public void readSQL (SQLInput stream, String typeName)`

Populates this object from the values obtained from the SQLInput stream.

`public void writeSQL (SQLOutput stream)`

Sends values obtained from this object to the SQLOutput stream.

The SQLInput interface provides many types of "read" methods. When an item of an SQL structured type is being retrieved and mapped to a Java object, the JDBC driver creates an object that can provide the attributes of the structured type, one at a time, via the SQLInput interface. These attributes are provided in the order that they appear in the SQL structured type declaration. If structured types are nested, one inside another, then the attributes are provided with a depth-first traversal of the types. Attributes that are inherited from a supertype appear before the attributes of the (sub)type itself.

With all of this in mind, Example 9.10 shows how we can write a jmovie class to represent a movie instance.

EXAMPLE 9.10 A `jmovie` CLASS THAT REPRESENTS THE `movie` STRUCTURED TYPE.

```
public class jmovie implements java.sql.SQLData {
   private String sqlType;
   String title;
   String description;
   int length;

   public String getSQLTypeName() {
      return sqlType;
   }

   public void readSQL (SQLInput stream, String sqlType) {
      this.sqlType = sqlType;

      title       = stream.readString();
      description = stream.readString();
      length      = stream.readInt();
   }

   public void writeSQL (SQLOutput stream) {
      stream.writeString(title);
      stream.writeString(description);
      stream.writeInt(length);
   }
}
```

Now that we know that the `movie` type maps to the `jmovie` class, we must tell JDBC to use this mapping, as you can see in Example 9.11. JDBC allows this information to be provided at different levels of granularity. At the coarsest level, we can specify mapping information that is to be used for an entire JDBC connection. JDBC uses the new `java.util.Map` class to specify the association between the name of the SQL type and the Java class that will be used to represent it. Although we have shown the mapping of just one class and structured type, the map we create could contain many such mappings.

Once this association has been added to the connection's type map, it will be used automatically whenever a `getObject` method is used. The value of a column of SQL structured type `movie` will be seen as a `jmovie` object, almost as if the column was a Java column defined with the `jmovie` class.

EXAMPLE 9.11 CREATING AND USING A MAPPING BETWEEN jmovie AND movie.

```
Connection con = ...;
java.util.Map map = con.getTypeMap();
map.put ("cat1.schema1.movie", Class.forName("jmovie"));

ResultSet rs = ... ;
jmovie jm = (jmovie)rs.getObject(i);
```

JDBC 2.0 allows type maps to be used at a finer level of granularity. Let us say that we defined a second class that is associated with the `movie` type, which we'll call `jmovie2`. This could be used for a specific `getObject` invocation as shown in Example 9.12.

EXAMPLE 9.12 APPLYING A TYPE MAP TO A SPECIFIC METHOD.

```
java.util.TreeMap tmap = new java.util.TreeMap();
tmap.put("cat1.schema1.movie", Class.forName("jmovie2"));
jmovie2 jm = (jmovie2)rs.getObject(i, tmap);
```

9.9 JDBC 2.0 Optional Package API

Though the JDBC 2.0 Optional Package API (initially called the Standard Extensions API) is beyond the scope of this book, we thought that you'd at least want us to mention the features that it provides. These features include the following:

- **Rowsets:** JavaBeans components that encapsulate a set of rows that is retrieved from a JDBC or non-JDBC data source.
- **JNDI for naming databases:** This feature allows the use of JNDI (Java naming and directory interface) to provide connection information and the JDBC driver for an application. The `DataSource` facility provides an alternative to the JDBC `DriverManager`.
- **Connection pooling:** This feature provides a cache of connections for application servers.
- **Distributed transaction support:** This item allows a JDBC driver to support the two-phase commit protocol used by Java Transaction API (JTA).

9.10 Implementation of the JDBC 2.0 API

About all that we can say about implementation is that vendors are adding support for the features we've discussed to their products at a rapid rate. They are doing so in a piecemeal way, based on the usual factors of customer demand, implementation cost, and release schedule. Some vendors will begin to implement features from the JDBC 2.0 Optional Package API even before they have implemented all of the features of the JDBC 2.0 Core API. You'll have to check your vendors' Web pages and product literature to see just what parts of JDBC 2.0 are and are not supported.

9.11 Chapter Summary

The JDBC 2.0 Core API provides useful capabilities in three broad areas. The relational capabilities include scrollable and updatable result sets and the execution of statement batches. The SQL:1999 capabilities provide interfaces that allow access to SQL's new data types—BLOB, CLOB, REF, distinct types, and structured types. The Java object capabilities provide additional metadata to support the retrieval of Java objects from an SQL DBMS and allow customized mappings between SQL structured types and Java objects. The JDBC 2.0 API allows vendors that are beginning to implement the SQL:1999 data types to provide JDBC drivers that make these types available to Java applications.

Customization bridges a part of the impedance mismatch for which SQL DBMSs have become known. Once the mapping between an SQL UDT and a Java class has been written (and associated with a connection) it need be thought about no further. An application programmer stores and retrieves the Java objects with which he or she is familiar. We'll see this impedance mismatch reduced still further in Sun's Java Blend product, which is the subject of our next chapter.

CHAPTER

10

Java Blend

10.1 Introduction

Java Blend, a product of Sun Microsystems, is representative of a class of systems that provide object/relational mapping. In these systems, an application writer creates and operates on Java objects that can be identified as persistent. The Java classes that support persistent objects are mapped to SQL tables, so that a persistent object is actually stored in one or more rows. When an application operates upon a persistent Java object, SQL statements are automatically executed to reflect any changes to the corresponding rows.

Java Blend 1.0 was released by Sun in June 1998. Java Blend provides a mapping tool that allows a user to begin with a database schema and generate Java classes. The classes that Java Blend generates may be augmented by additional methods, turning them into useful business objects. The user may also begin with Java classes and generate a database schema.

Java Blend allows an application to retrieve persistent objects in a nonprocedural way by supporting OQL (Object Query Language), which has been defined by the Object Data Management Group (ODMG).[1] OQL bears some similarity to SQL, but we'll see that it provides specific capabilities that are matched to the ODMG and Java data models.

---

[1] *The Object Database Standard: ODMG 2.0,* Rick Cattell et al., Morgan Kaufmann, 1997.

Most of this chapter is devoted to describing Java Blend—first, its underlying concepts and then the specific process of building a Java Blend application. Once we've completed this description, we will spend a little while discussing ODMG 2.0. Java Blend is one of several products on the market that supports the ODMG 2.0 specification.

10.2 Java Blend Architecture

Java Blend allows us to create Java classes and SQL tables that are mapped to one another. The Java classes are *persistence-capable,* meaning that objects of these classes may be either persistent or transient. The persistent objects have rows in SQL tables associated with them, allowing them to exist beyond the end of the Java application that created them. Transient objects exist only in memory and cease to exist at the end of the Java application.

Once this class-to-table mapping has been established, the writer of an application operates entirely on Java objects via method invocations. OQL queries may be executed to find persistent objects with specific characteristics. The result of an OQL query is a collection of persistent objects. These objects provide methods for observing or changing their state, and for navigating to other objects to which they are related. The changes to persistent objects made by these methods will automatically be propagated to their associated rows (via SQL statements). Neither Java Blend nor OQL provides insert, update, or delete operations—they are simply not needed.

Java Blend uses JDBC to access data and metadata in the SQL database, but the JDBC operations are completely hidden from the writer of an application. The Java Blend architecture can be seen in Figure 10.1. We have shown the use of Java Blend in a two-tier style of computing. Java Blend can be used equally well to support the three-tier model of computing.

10.3 Mapping between the Models

Before we delve into the specifics of the Java Blend mapping tool and the writing of Java Blend applications, let us consider in the abstract how tables and classes can be associated with each other to represent certain types of information and relationships.

10.3.1 Simple Tables

A table can be associated with a Java class. Let's consider a *simple table* to be one without any foreign key columns. The associated class for such a table can have a field for each of the table's columns. In order

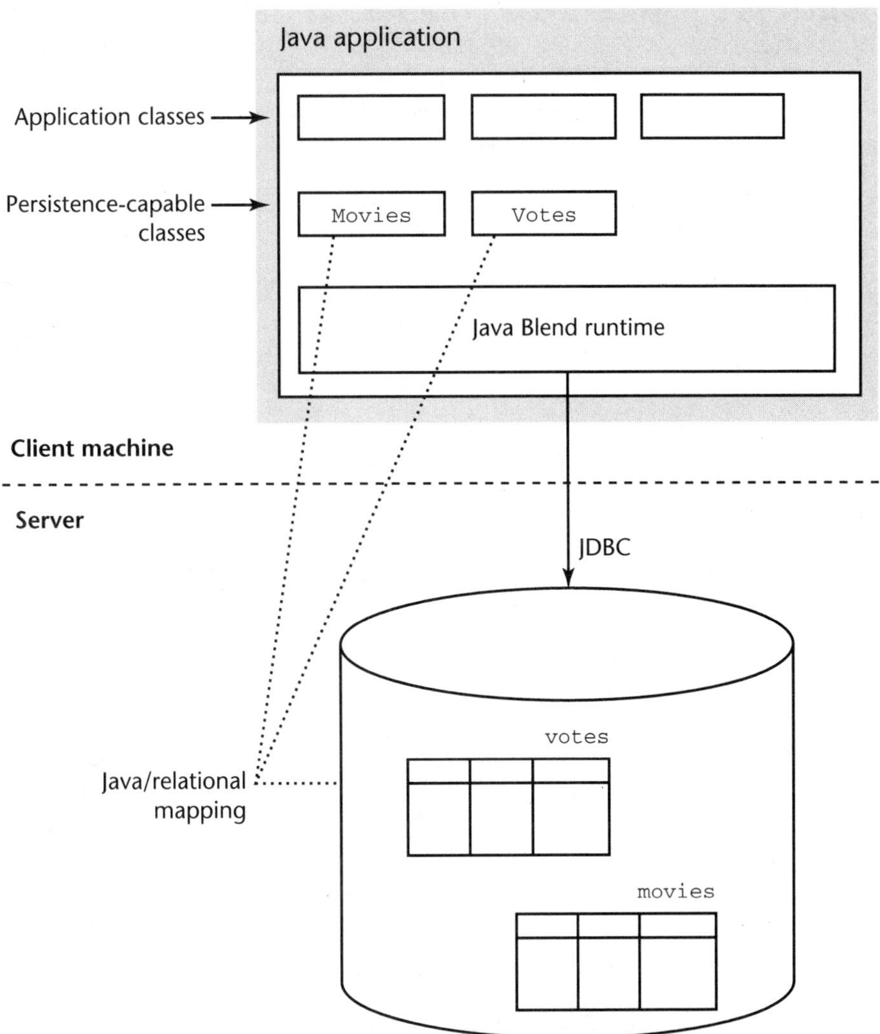

FIGURE 10.1 *Java Blend architecture.*

to establish this type of association, Java Blend imposes some requirements: The table must have a primary key, the class must implement the `PersistenceCapable` interface, and the fields must be defined as `private`. Because the fields are private, the related class has an observer, or get, method and possibly a mutator, or set, method for each field.

The Academy Award shows that are aired each year can be represented by the table and class in Example 10.1.

EXAMPLE 10.1 TABLE AND CLASS TO REPRESENT THE ACADEMY AWARDS.

```
CREATE TABLE shows
   ( year_shown  CHAR(4) NOT NULL PRIMARY KEY,
     host        CHAR VARYING (60)
   )


public class Shows implements PersistenceCapable {
             private String year_shown;
             private String host;

             // Accessor methods

             public String getYear_shown() {
                    return year_shown;
             }
             public void setYear_shown(String year_shown) {
                    this.year_shown = year_shown;
             }

             public String getHost() {
                    return host;
             }
             public void setHost(String host) {
                    this.host = host;
             }

}
```

10.3.2 One-to-Many Relationships

A table that contains a foreign key defines a many-to-one relationship between its rows and the rows of the table to which it refers. SQL users navigate this type of relationship using either a join or a subquery. Example 10.2 shows two tables that have this type of one-to-many relationship.

These tables can be individually associated with Java classes, as we have just seen, but how should the one-to-many relationship be reflected in the Java classes? That's easy—the `Votes` class will contain a method that returns the `Movies` object to which a `Votes` object is related. Java Blend implements this with a private field of type `Movies`, rather than a field of type `String`. This field and method allow us to follow the relationship in one direction.

EXAMPLE 10.2 TABLES THAT REPRESENT A ONE-TO-MANY RELATIONSHIP.

```
CREATE TABLE movies
   ( title            CHAR VARYING (100) PRIMARY KEY,
     year_introduced  CHAR (4),
     runs             INTEGER CHECK (runs BETWEEN 0 AND 480)
   )

CREATE TABLE votes
   ( id               NUMERIC (5,0) NOT NULL PRIMARY KEY,
     title            CHAR VARYING (100) REFERENCES movies,
     voter            CHAR VARYING (10),
     vote             INTEGER
   )
```

Now let's consider how we can follow the relationship in the other direction. A movie may have several votes that reference it. The `Movies` class will contain a method returning an iterator that provides access to these `Votes` objects. Java Blend implements this with a private field of type `DCollection`.

On both sides of the relationship, methods will be provided in order to change the relationships between objects. Example 10.3 shows the Java classes that correspond to the `movies` and `votes` tables above.

You might have noticed the reference to the `test3.Movies` class. We happened to be using the `test3` package while we were experimenting with Java Blend. You'll see this in several of our examples in this chapter.

10.3.3 Many-to-Many Relationships

When a many-to-many relationship must be represented in a relational database, a *linking table* is created. In Example 10.4, a many-to-many relationship between actors and movies has been created.

The `actors` and `movies` tables will each have a class associated with them, but the `appeared_in` table will not have a class associated with it. Instead, both the `Actors` and `Movies` classes will have methods to retrieve and change the objects on the other side of the relationship (see Example 10.5).

10.3.4 Subtypes

It's likely that you are already familiar with the ways of representing the relationships that we've just shown you. Perhaps this final type of relationship will be a bit more novel.

EXAMPLE 10.3 CLASSES THAT REPRESENT A ONE-TO-MANY RELATIONSHIP.

```
public class Votes implements PersistenceCapable {
   ...
   private test3.Movies moviesForVotes;
   ...

   public Movies getMoviesForVotes() {...}

   public void setMoviesForVotes(Movies moviesForVotes) {...}

}

public class Movies implements PersistenceCapable {
   ...
   private DCollection votesForMovies;
   ...

   public Iterator getVotesForMovies() {...}

   public void addVotesForMovies(Votes votesForMovies) {...}

   public void removeVotesForMovies(Votes votesForMovies) {...}

}
```

EXAMPLE 10.4 TABLES THAT REPRESENT A MANY-TO-MANY RELATIONSHIP.

```
CREATE TABLE actors
   ( fullname    CHAR VARYING (60) PRIMARY KEY,
     gender      CHAR(1),
     birth       DATE
   )

CREATE TABLE appeared_in
   ( actor       CHAR VARYING (60) NOT NULL REFERENCES actors,
     movie       CHAR VARYING (100) NOT NULL REFERENCES movies
   )
```

EXAMPLE 10.5 CLASSES THAT REPRESENT A MANY-TO-MANY RELATIONSHIP.

```
public class Movies implements PersistenceCapable {
   ...
   private DCollection actorsForMovies;
   ...

   public Iterator getActorsForMovies() {...}

   public void addActorsForMovies(Actors actorsForMovies) {...}

   public void removeActorsForMovies(Actors actorsForMovies) {...}

}

public class Actors implements PersistenceCapable {
   ...
   private DCollection moviesForActors;
   ...

   public Iterator getMoviesForActors() {...}

   public void addMoviesForActors(Movies moviesForActors) {...}

   public void removeMoviesForActors(Movies moviesForActors) {...}

}
```

A *subtype relationship* can be represented in the relational world in several ways. One of these is to use a single table to represent the supertype and its subtypes. Columns can be defined for the attributes of all of these types. The table can have an additional column to represent the specific type of the row. Certain columns will be null when the row is being used to represent an element of a supertype and non-null when the row is used to represent a subtype. As the number of subtypes grows, the table becomes "wider and wider," with more and more null values. Example 10.6 shows a table that is being used to represent instances of both the Movies type and its Dvd subtype. Java Blend does *not* support this style of representing inheritance. (Neither does SQL:1999!)

EXAMPLE 10.6 REPRESENTING SUPERTYPES AND SUBTYPES IN A SINGLE TABLE.

```
CREATE TABLE movies
   ( title              CHAR VARYING (100) PRIMARY KEY,
     specific_type      CHAR VARYING (10) NOT NULL,
     year_introduced    CHAR (4),
     runs               INTEGER CHECK (runs BETWEEN 0 AND 480),
     features           CHAR VARYING (60),

     CHECK (specific_type IN ('Movies', 'Dvd')),
     CHECK (specific_type = 'Movies' AND features IS NULL)
   )
```

Another way of representing this type of relationship—the way that Java Blend has chosen—is for the subtype to be implemented by a table separate from that of the parent type, a table that represents the additional information contained in the subtype. This table has the same primary key columns as that of its parent, and these columns are also a foreign key that references the parent table. This practice assures us that the subtype information for an object is unique, that the parent information and subtype information for an object can both be found, and that the subtype information cannot exist without its parent information. This convention can be seen in the creation of `Dvd` as a subtype of `Movies` as shown in Example 10.7.

EXAMPLE 10.7 TABLE AND CLASS TO REPRESENT A SUBTYPE RELATIONSHIP.

```
CREATE TABLE dvd
   ( title     CHAR VARYING (100) PRIMARY KEY REFERENCES movies,
     features  CHAR VARYING (60)
   )

public class Dvd extends Movies implements PersistenceCapable {
   private String features;

   public String getFeatures() {...}

   public void setFeatures(String features) {...}

}
```

10.4 Building a Java Blend Application

In this section, we get down to the specifics of Java Blend by creating some sample applications. We're not going to cover all aspects of Java Blend in these sections—this product is far too feature rich for us to be able to do it full justice. However, the process that we show in developing these applications is representative of the process that you would go through if you decide to use Java Blend in your own applications.

10.4.1 Creating the Mapping: Database to Java

We will start with an existing database and use Java Blend to create a set of corresponding classes. Java Blend calls this a *database to Java* mapping. The schema of this database, shown in Figure 10.2, has been built from the tables we were just looking at.

We start the Java Blend mapping tool and use the Import Schema operation to read in the schema of our database. To do so, we must supply the usual JDBC connection information, as shown in Figure 10.3.

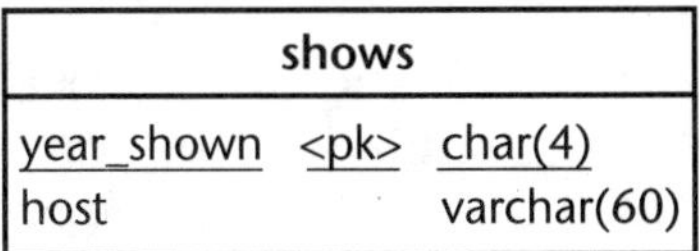

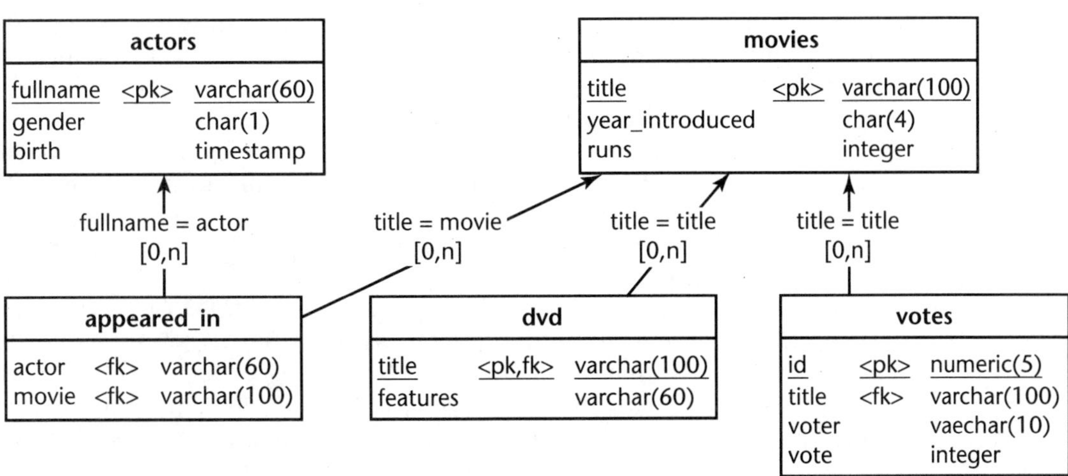

FIGURE 10.2 *Sample database schema.*

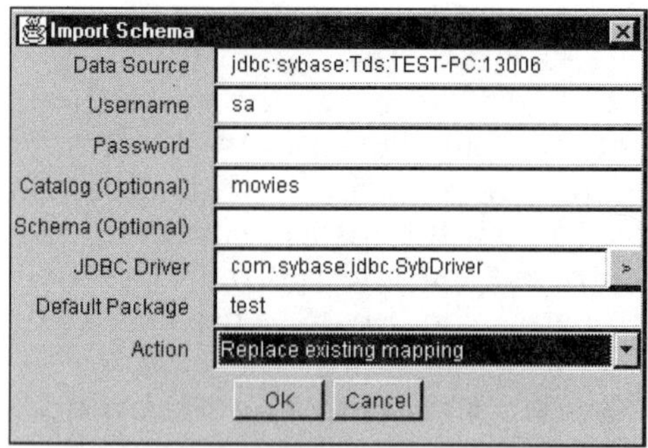

FIGURE 10.3 *Java Blend Import Schema dialog box.*

Java Blend keeps us informed of its progress once we have started this operation. Java Blend looks at the database's tables, columns, primary keys and foreign keys, and constraints. When this operation has completed, we are presented with Java Blend's default mapping, which is shown in Figure 10.4.

Specifically, we see that the `votes` table is mapped to the `Votes` Java class and that Java Blend has recognized the foreign key that relates the `votes` table to the `movies` table. The field `moviesForVotes`, of type `Movies`, is included in the `Votes` class.

Java Blend allows us to look at both the database and Java sides of the mapping at both coarser and finer levels of granularity. The result of selecting the Show Java Info button is shown in Figure 10.5. We see that this relationship is defined as two way, causing a field that reflects the inverse of this relationship to be generated in the `Movies` class.

We can change the default mapping in a variety of ways. We could, for instance, drop the mapping of some of the tables, if they are not of interest to us. The names of the Java classes can be changed, or some of the relationships can be modified.

The columns that are mapped have Java data types that correspond to the SQL data type of the column. Columns that do not allow null values can be mapped using Java's primitive types, whereas columns that do allow nulls must be mapped to a class (usually one of the familiar wrapper classes).

Java Blend provides three special classes for SQL's DATE, TIME, and TIMESTAMP data types, which are shown in Table 10.1. These classes differ from the similar types that exist in the `java.util` package and the `java.sql` package in that they are immutable. The designers of Java Blend were concerned that an application would use a method to alter an instance of one of these classes after it was retrieved from a database and expect that this change would be propagated back to the

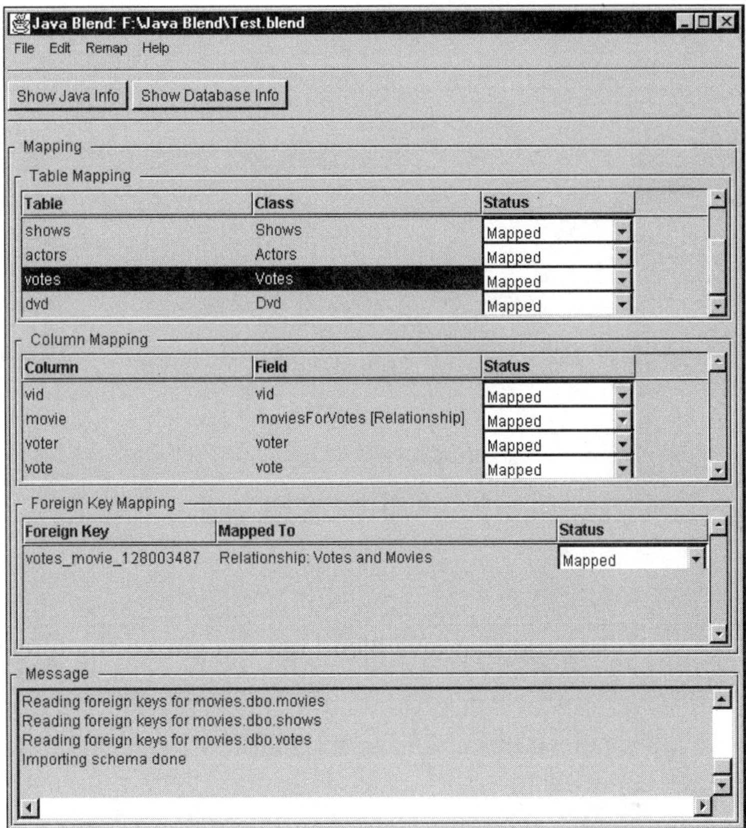

FIGURE 10.4 *Java Blend mapping tool.*

database. Java Blend cannot support this capability. With these immutable classes, an application must create a new object of the appropriate type and then invoke a set method to change the field of a class that is mapped to a table.

When we are satisfied with the mapping we have created, we can then have Java Blend create the Java classes and supporting files that we will use to create our applications. Java Blend creates two types of files that are of immediate interest to us.

Java Blend generates files with the `.xjava` extension for each of the mapped classes. These files will later be turned into actual Java source files with the Java Blend `preprocess` command. Users will add their business logic to these `.xjava` files. Let's look quickly at the `Votes.xjava` file, shown in Example 10.8.

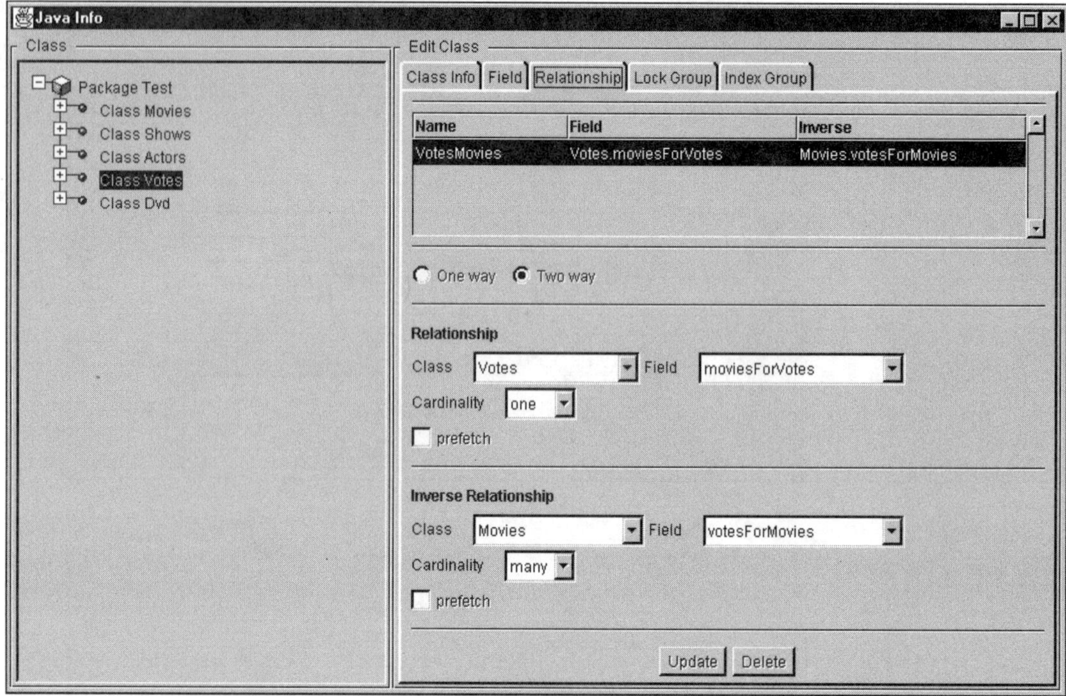

FIGURE 10.5 *Java Blend Java Info screen.*

SQL data type	Java class
DATE	javablend.types.Date
TIME	javablend.types.Time
TIMESTAMP	javablend.types.Timestamp

TABLE 10.1 *Date/time classes provided by Java Blend.*

We see that the fields that have been created are private, and that get and set methods are provided for each of these fields. Example 10.9 shows us the `votesForMovies` field in the `Movies.xjava` file and its associated methods.

The `votesForMovies` field must represent a collection of votes—after all, this is a one-to-many relationship. The `DCollection` class is specified for this field. The get method returns an `Iterator`, so that we may

EXAMPLE 10.8 THE CONTENTS OF THE `Votes.xjava` FILE.

```
package test3;

// Import Java Blend packages
import com.sun.javablend.*;
import com.sun.javablend.types.*;
// Import Collections
import com.sun.java.util.collections.*;

public class Votes implements PersistenceCapable {
        private long vid;
        private String voter;
        private int vote;
        private test3.Movies moviesForVotes;
                                // inverse: Movies.votesForMovies

        // Accessor methods
        public long getVid() {
                return vid;}
        }
        public void setVid(long vid) {
                this.vid = vid;
        }

        ...

        public Movies getMoviesForVotes() {
                return moviesForVotes;
        }
        public void setMoviesForVotes(Movies moviesForVotes) {
                this.moviesForVotes = moviesForVotes;
        }


        /* sample constructor template
        public Votes(Database db, ...) {
                // make sure all key fields are set
                db.makePersistent(this);
        }
        */

}
```

EXAMPLE 10.9 THE votesForMovies FIELD AND ITS ASSOCIATED METHODS.

```
public class Movies implements PersistenceCapable {

        ...

        private DCollection votesForMovies;
                                // inverse: Votes.moviesForVotes

                ...

        public Iterator getVotesForMovies() {
                return votesForMovies.iterator();
        }
        public void addVotesForMovies(Votes votesForMovies) {
                this.votesForMovies.add(votesForMovies);
        }
        public void removeVotesForMovies(Votes votesForMovies) {
                this.votesForMovies.remove(votesForMovies);
        }

}
```

look at each of the values in the collection. Instead of the set method that we have for scalar fields, we now have add and remove methods to allow us to change the relationship between actors and movies.

The `DCollection` and `Iterator` interfaces may not be familiar to you. Java Blend took these interfaces from a prerelease version of the JDK 1.2 Collection interfaces. The `DCollection` interface is in many ways similar to the `java.util.Vector` interface, and the `Iterator` interface is similar to the `java.util.Enumeration` interface that you are more likely to have encountered. We will not provide detailed information on these interfaces—you'll understand them well enough from seeing them in examples.

Java Blend also generates `.oql` files for each of the classes that allow an application to access all of the instances of that class—we'll talk more about these OQL files in just a moment. Java Blend's generation of these files is something of a courtesy for the user. They could easily enough be written by hand if Java Blend did not generate them.

When you instruct Java Blend to generate these classes and files, you have the option of generating stored procedures for your database that help Java Blend implement its Java to relational mapping. In Java Blend 1.0, these stored procedures are required for the DBMSs of some vendors (Sybase and Microsoft) and are not allowed for the DBMSs of other vendors (Oracle). These stored procedures are invisible to the Java programmer once they have been installed in the database.

Mapping the Other Way, Java to Database

Although we have not shown it, Java Blend can provide the reverse of the mapping that we used. We could begin with a set of classes and have Java Blend generate the schema definitions for creating corresponding database tables.

There are some requirements for the Java classes that you start with: Each class must have a package declaration and must implement the `PersistenceCapable` interface. Each of the fields that you wish to map must specify `private`. To create the mapping from the class source files, you would rename them to have the `.xjava` extension and then use the Java->DB files mapping choice. As before, Java Blend will show you its default mapping, which you can then modify.

In fact, you will definitely want to examine and modify the SQL data types that Java Blend generates. A `String` class can be mapped to either the CHARACTER or CHARACTER VARYING data type, and Java Blend has no special knowledge to use to determine what lengths should be specified for these types. The same issue applies to the numeric data types and the values of their precisions and scales.

Java Blend recognizes relationships between the classes by looking at the types of the private fields. If Java Blend finds a field that has a persistence-capable Java class as its type, then the default mapping will contain a one-to-many relationship in that field's class. If Java Blend finds a field that has `DCollection` as its type, then the default mapping will contain a many-to-one relationship in that field's class. The target of the many-to-one relationship must be filled in by the user, as Java Blend cannot determine what type of objects will be contained in the `DCollection` at runtime. The Java Blend mapping tool also allows you to specify index groups. These are collections of columns upon which indices will be defined in order to improve performance.

Once you have tailored the mapping to your satisfaction, Java Blend will generate a script containing the commands that are required to create your database schema. You will run the `preprocess` command to generate new Java source files. These Java source files will contain all of the classes and methods that you started with, but now they will also implement Java Blend's Java/relational mapping.

Because most DBMSs conform only loosely to the SQL standard with respect to schema definition language and schema manipulation language, Java Blend requires that we tell it which DBMS we are using when we are ready to have it generate a script that will create the database schema. Java Blend currently supports Oracle 7.x, Sybase Adaptive Server Enterprise 10 and 11, and Microsoft SQL Server 6.5.

When you are mapping in this direction, Java Blend does not allow you to specify which of your fields will be used to create primary key columns in the associated tables. Instead, Java Blend creates its own primary key and foreign key columns in the database that are hidden from the Java user.

Viewed Tables

Our discussion of mapping in Java Blend has so far mentioned only base tables. The mapping of viewed tables (views) is supported as well, but is a bit more complicated than that of base tables. We'll spend only a moment on this topic. Java Blend allows you to choose whether to map all tables, only base tables, only viewed tables, or only those tables on which there are no dependencies. This last alternative can be thought of as leaving out the intermediate table definitions that may not be of interest.

A view may be defined using one or several underlying tables. If the primary key columns from all of these tables are contained in the view, then Java Blend can use them all as the primary key for the view; otherwise, Java Blend must make up its own primary key for the view.

You must be careful when mapping views to classes with Java Blend. A view and a base table, or even two views, may involve the same data values in the database. The persistence-capable Java classes that are mapped to these views and tables may each store their own copies of some of the data, and updates to objects of the two classes may conflict with one another.

Changing the Mapping between Tables and Classes

The creators of Java Blend recognized that the type of mapping process we described is not a one-time activity. As your application evolves, it is often necessary to change some aspects of the mapping. Java Blend saves information about the mapping that has been used, so that you can go back to it and make appropriate changes.

If you used the database to Java mapping, then you may wish to alter some of your tables, or you may need to create new tables. Java Blend allows you to *remap* your tables. It recognizes what changes have taken place and generates new classes and new methods. You can then merge the new source code with your existing code. Java Blend preserves the customizations that you may have made to the classes it generated previously.

If you have used the Java to database mapping, then you may also wish to augment your persistent classes and create new persistent classes. When you remap your classes, Java Blend generates a script that creates the entire schema corresponding to these classes. You then have two options: You can unload and then reload your data to populate a new database, or you can edit the script to create the necessary ALTER statements for your existing database.

10.4.2 Writing OQL Queries

OQL itself is really beyond the scope of this book, but we will use some simple OQL queries that are almost indistinguishable from SQL in this chapter. Both the ODMG 2.0 specification and the Java Blend documentation provide all that you need to know to write more interesting OQL queries.

The file `OQLGetAllVotes.oql`, which was automatically generated by Java Blend, contains the following:

```
import test3.Votes;
select   o
from     Votes o;
```

This query selects all of the `Votes` objects that are stored in the database. The query is almost an SQL query, except that instead of selecting "*", indicating all of the column values, the correlation name "`o`" is used, indicating that the objects themselves are desired as the result of the query.

An OQL query can use the fields of your persistence-capable classes (including private fields) and it can use their methods. The user is encouraged to use a private field, rather than its associated get method, whenever possible, because all methods must be evaluated after retrieving data into the Java Blend runtime environment. It is true that many get methods do nothing more than return the value of their associated private fields. Java Blend cannot optimize these cases, even if it was to do further analysis of the contents of the methods, because the `.xjava` files and OQL queries can be preprocessed independently of one another. Predicates that directly reference the class's fields can be executed by the DBMS, resulting in much better performance. Java Blend allows the keyword `NULL` to be used, as a synonym for the OQL keyword `NIL`.

OQL queries can be parameterized. In Example 10.10 we see an OQL query that selects a particular `Movies` object, based on the value of its `mid` field. This query defines a `midval` parameter of the Java type `long`.

EXAMPLE 10.10 A PARAMETERIZED OQL QUERY.

```
import test3.Movies;
select   o
from     Movies o
where    o.mid = $(long)midval;
```

OQL allows a query to return several types of results. A result can be a single value or it can be a collection of values. The values returned can be scalar values, objects, or structures that contain other values. That said, we'll only be discussing queries that return collections of objects.

With Java Blend 1.0, OQL queries must be defined at the time that the application is written. The Java `preprocess` command compiles these queries and produces a serialized representation of the result of the compilation in `.ser` files. These `.ser` files will be used when we are ready to execute the OQL queries in our applications.

10.4.3 The `preprocess` Command

We've mentioned the `preprocess` command twice. This command takes existing `.xjava` and `.oql` files and produces `.java` and `.ser` files from them, respectively. This process is shown in Figure 10.6.

The `preprocess` command will alert the user to any errors that exist in the two types of source files. In the case of the `.xjava` to `.java` transformation, Java Blend adds executable code that works with its runtime environment to make the object/relational mapping work. The generated Java source files are compiled in the usual manner.

The development process is often iterative in nature. You may find from time to time that you want to add methods to your persistence-capable classes, or that you wish to write some new OQL queries. To do this, you will modify the appropriate source file and then run the `preprocess` command once again.

10.4.4 The Database Class

Now that we've created the Java classes that are mapped to our database tables and compiled the OQL queries that we will need, we are finally ready to begin constructing our applications. The Java Blend API is provided by the `com.sun.javablend` package. This package contains the `Database`, `Transaction`, and `OQLQuery` classes that we will be discussing. It also contains the `PersistenceCapable` interface we have repeatedly mentioned.

We will start by creating an instance of the `Database` class that Java Blend has supplied. Some of the most useful methods provided by the `Database` class are shown below.

com.sun.javablend.Database Class

Constructors

```
public static Database open (String url, String user,
                             String password)
  throws DatabaseNotFoundException, DatabaseOpenException
```

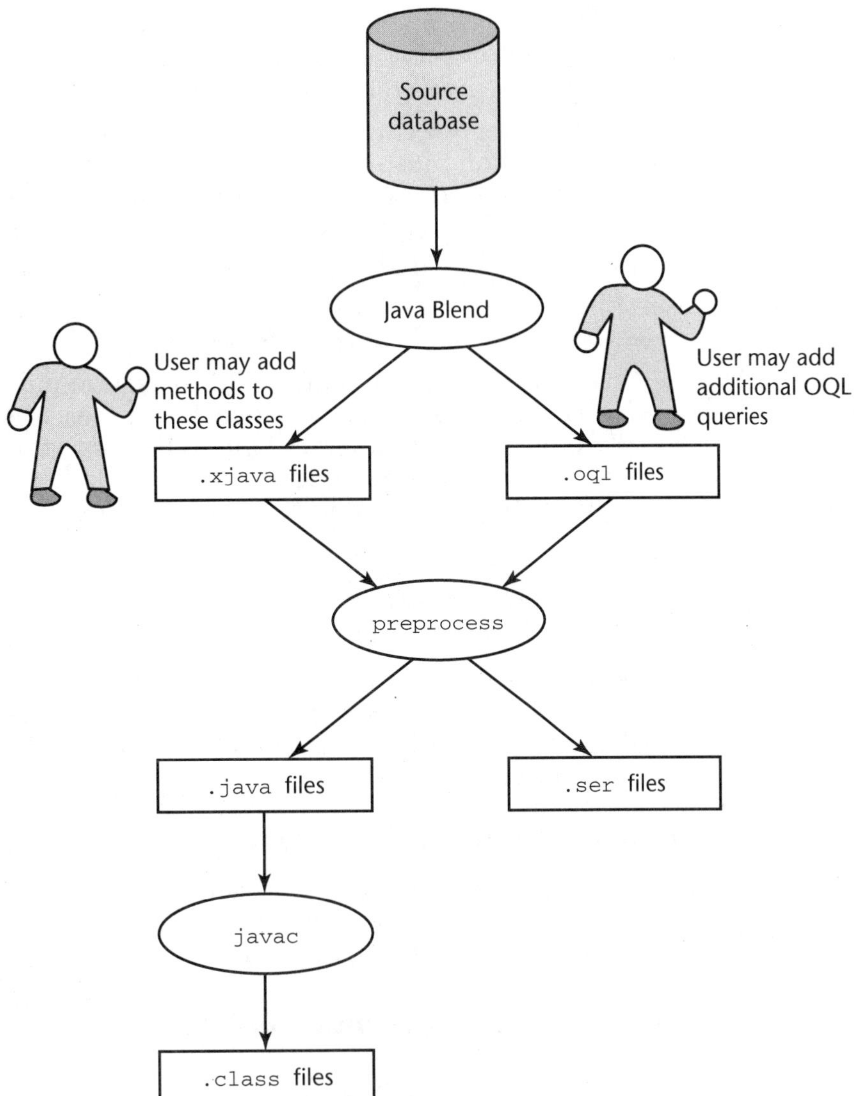

FIGURE 10.6 *Using the `preprocess` command.*

Construct a database object that contains persistent objects. The `url`, `user`, and `password` parameters are used to establish a JDBC connection to a database.

Methods

```
public void makePersistent (PersistenceCapable o)
  throws TransactionNotInProgressException
```

Make an object that is capable of persistence be persistent. This operation must be done in the context of a transaction. If a database to Java mapping was used, then the fields of the object that correspond to the primary key columns must be set for this operation to succeed.

```
public void deletePersistentObject (PersistenceCapable o)
  throws TransactionNotInProgressException
```

Delete a persistent object. This operation must be done in the context of a transaction, which will cause the row or rows in the database that correspond to this object to be deleted. The object itself remains accessible to the Java application until it is garbage collected in the usual manner.

```
public void close ()
```

Close the database.

The beginning of our application is shown in Example 10.11. We start the application by registering our JDBC driver. We then create our `Database` object, supplying the usual information that is required for a JDBC connection.

10.4.5 The Transaction Class

All of our operations on persistent data must occur in the context of a transaction. Java Blend supplies the `Transaction` class for this purpose. Some of the methods that this class provides are shown below.

com.sun.javablend.Transaction Class

Variables

```
public static final int OPTIMISTIC
```

Optimistic concurrency control.

```
public static final int PESSIMISTIC
```

Pessimistic concurrency control.

EXAMPLE 10.11 THE BEGINNING OF A JAVA BLEND APPLICATION.

```
package test3;

import com.sun.javablend.*;
import com.sun.java.util.collections.*;

public class IUD {

   public static void main (String argv[]) {

      // Load JDBC driver

      try {
          Class.forName("com.sybase.jdbc.SybDriver");
      } catch (Exception ex) {
          System.out.println ( "Couldn't add Jconnect driver!" );
      }

      try {

         // Open the database

         moviesdb = Database.open
                    ("jdbc:sybase:Tds:TEST-PC:13006/movies",
                     "sa",
                     ""
                    );

         ...

      }
      catch (Exception e) {
         System.out.println(e.getMessage());
      }

      moviesdb.close();
   }

}
```

Constructors

`public Transaction ()`

Construct a `Transaction` object that is initially closed (meaning that no transaction has been started).

Methods

`public void begin ()`

Begin a PESSIMISTIC transaction.

`public void begin(int mode)`

Begin a transaction that is either OPTIMISTIC or PESSIMISTIC.

`public void commit () throws TransactionNotInProgressException, TransactionAbortedException, TransactionAbortedCanRetryException`

Commit and close the transaction.

`public void abort () throws TransactionNotInProgressException`

Roll back and close the transaction.

`public void boolean isOpen ()`

Indicates whether a transaction is open.

`public void join () throws TransactionInProgressException`

Causes a thread to become associated with a transaction that was started by another thread.

`public void leave () throws TransactionNotInProgressException`

Causes the current thread to lose its association with a transaction.

As we said, all operations on persistent data must happen in the context of a transaction. The following fragment of code will be seen in your application quite frequently:

```
Transaction txn = new Transaction();

txn.begin();

...

txn.commit();
```

An attempt to invoke a method that requires a transaction context when a transaction is not active will result in the throwing of the `TransactionNotInProgressException` exception. A persistent object can be cloned, producing a transient object that can be used outside of a transaction context.

The `abort` method is provided in order to roll back any changes that might have been made to persistent objects. Whenever a transaction is rolled back, both the state of the database and the state of the persistent objects are returned to the state they had when the transaction was started.

You may have noticed that the `commit` method may throw the `TransactionAbortedCanRetryException` exception. When multiple users are concurrently accessing a database, it is always possible that they will conflict with each other in this way. You will often wish to place a unit of work inside a loop, so that a failure of this type will immediately try the unit of work again.

A transaction is initially associated only with the thread that created it. The `Transaction` class provides methods that allow other threads to join in this association or to leave it. Just so you don't think that we've forgotten, the two types of transactions—optimistic and pessimistic—will be discussed shortly.

10.4.6 Writing Our Applications

We'll show three brief sample applications that will give you an idea of how more complex Java Blend applications could be written.

Creating, Modifying, and Destroying Persistent Data

In Example 10.12, we show how to create a new persistent object, modify it, and then destroy it, all in rapid succession. To create our movie, we invoke the `Movies` constructor, set each of the fields, and then use the `Database.makePersistent` method to tell Java Blend that this object is persistent. When the transaction is committed, Java Blend will then take care of inserting a row in the `movies` table. We then increment (by one minute) the running time of the movie with the get and set methods for the `runs` field. Committing this action causes an update to the row in the database that we created. Finally, we see that, to remove a persistent object from the database, we must invoke the `Database.deletePersistentObject` method.

In this example, we showed an explicit use of the `makePersistent` method. In actual applications, it is more likely that this method would be hidden in the constructors for a persistence-capable class.

You can also see that our `Movies` object does not participate in a relationship with any other persistence-capable object. If it did, then we would have to invoke the `makePersistent` method on this other object (assuming that it, too, is newly created) before creating the relationship.

EXAMPLE 10.12 CREATING, MODIFYING, AND THEN DESTROYING A PERSISTENT OBJECT.

```
// Create a Movie

txn.begin();

Movies newMovie = new Movies();

newMovie.setMid(10011);
newMovie.setTitle("Colossus");
newMovie.setYear_introduced("1972");
newMovie.setRuns(100);

moviesdb.makePersistent(newMovie);
txn.commit();

// Update the Movie

txn.begin();
newMovie.setRuns(newMovie.getRuns() + 1);
txn.commit();

// Delete the Movie

txn.begin();
moviesdb.deletePersistentObject(newMovie);
txn.commit();
```

Listing All Instances of a Persistence-Capable Class

Let us say that we want to be sure that the code we have just seen is doing the right thing. We'll create a method that will take a movie ID as an argument and display any movies that it finds with that ID. To write this method, we'll need to execute an OQL query. `OQLQuery` is the final Java Blend class that we will need to understand.

com.sun.javablend.OQLQuery Class

Constructors

```
public OQLQuery (InputStream anInputStream)
  throws IOException, QueryInvalidException
```

Construct an `OQLQuery` object from an input stream (this is where we use those `.ser` files created by the `preprocess` command).

Methods

```
public void bind (String name, Object value)
  throws IllegalStateException, QueryParameterTypeInvalidException,
        QueryParameterNameInvalidException
```

Bind a value to a query parameter.

```
public Object execute ()
  throws QueryRuntimeException, IllegalStateException
```

Execute the query and return its resulting object.

```
public Iterator iterator ()
  throws QueryRuntimeException, IllegalStateException
```

Execute the query and return an iterator for the collection that is returned.

Now that we've seen the methods the `OQLQuery` class provides, let's look at Example 10.13, which shows a method that uses them.

This method creates the `OQLQuery` object we showed in Example 10.10 by loading the compiled version of the parameterized OQL query that we discussed earlier. We use the `bind` method to provide a value for that parameter and then use the `iterator` method to execute the query and create an `Iterator` for the collection of movies that the query returns. The `bind` method expects parameter values to be passed as objects, so we have passed our `midval` parameter, which was declared as `long`, as a `Long` object. From there it is pretty familiar—we loop over each instance in the collection and use the get methods to get field values that we can print.

With the insertion of some `println` statements and calls to this `displayMovies` method, our application generates the following:

```
Opening Database
Movie 1001 contains:
   Movie not found!

Create a Movie
Movie 1001 contains:
   Colossus, 1972, 100

Update the Movie
Movie 1001 contains:
   Colossus, 1972, 101

Delete the Movie
Movie 1001 contains:
   Movie not found!
```

EXAMPLE 10.13 EXECUTING AN OQL QUERY.

```
public static void displayMovies(long movieId)
   throws Exception {

   int count = 0;

      System.out.println("Movie " + movieId + " contains:");

      OQLQuery qry
         = new OQLQuery
               (Movies.class.getResourceAsStream("MoviesByMid.ser"));

      qry.bind("midval",new Long(movieId));

      Iterator i = qry.iterator();

      while (i.hasNext()) {
         Movies m = (Movies) i.next();
         System.out.println ("    "
                              + m.getTitle()
                              + ", "
                              + m.getYear_introduced()
                              + ", "
                              + m.getRuns()
                             );
         count++;
      }

      if (count == 0) {
         System.out.println("   Movie not found!");
      }
}
```

In this application, we could have used the `execute` method instead of the `iterator` method. The `execute` method returns a single object, which could be a single persistence-capable object, or it could be a `DCollection` holding a collection of such objects.

Java Blend 1.0 supports only static OQL queries. The Java Blend documentation describes the methods that will be used for executing dynamic OQL queries but then states that these methods are not yet implemented. There's nothing like a bit of foreshadowing by a vendor!

Tallying the Votes

Now that we've covered the basics, we'll show one final example that will give you an idea of the benefit that Java Blend provides. Back when we were discussing SQLJ Part 2, we created a `Movies` class and used it in the database. One of the methods that we included in our class produced a tally of the votes that had been cast for the movie. Example 10.14 shows how we have added the same capability to the `Movies` class that Java Blend generated.

EXAMPLE 10.14 DEFINING THE `tallyVotes` METHOD IN THE `Movies` CLASS.

```
public class Movies implements PersistenceCapable {

   ...

   public int tallyVotes() {
      int              valuesTotal = 0;
      int              valuesCount = 0;

      Iterator i = this.getVotesForMovies();
      while (i.hasNext()) {
         Votes v = (Votes) i.next();
         valuesTotal += v.getVote ();
         valuesCount++;
      }

      if (valuesCount == 0)
         return 0;
      else
         return (int) (valuesTotal / valuesCount);

   }

}
```

The code fragment in Example 10.15 makes use of the `tallyVote` method.

Although we've showed the addition of the `tallyVotes` method here at the end of our examples, this step will generally be performed just after database to Java mapping. This is your chance to define behavior for your persistence-capable classes, in effect turning them into

EXAMPLE 10.15 FRAGMENT OF CODE THAT USES THE `tallyVote` METHOD.

```
System.out.println ("Display Movies");

OQLQuery qry =
   new OQLQuery(
      Movies.class.getResourceAsStream("OQLGetAllMovies.ser"));

Iterator i = qry.iterator();

while (i.hasNext()) {
   Movies m = (Movies) i.next();
   System.out.println ("    " + m.getTitle());
   System.out.println ("       " + m.tallyVotes());
}
```

The fragment of code in Example 10.15 might produce the following result:

```
Display Movies
   Titanic
      0
   As Good As It Gets
      6
   Good Will Hunting
      7
   L.A. Confidential

      .
      .
      .
```

useful business objects. If they are properly written, then several applications will be able to use these business objects.

10.5 Additional Java Blend Features

Java Blend offers a few more features that we'd like to cover briefly.

10.5.1 Optimistic Concurrency Control

Most DBMSs and DBMS APIs provide *pessimistic concurrency control.* This type of concurrency control protects a user's reads and updates as soon as they are issued by acquiring locks on rows (or possibly database pages, depending on the implementation). These locks may cause other users to wait if they try to access the locked items. The user that received the locks will usually complete his or her work, commit the transaction, and give up these locks so that other users can proceed.

Java Blend, at the time that a transaction is started, gives a user the option of using *optimistic concurrency control*. This type of concurrency control does not acquire locks, but instead keeps a local copy of the rows that have been read. When a transaction that has performed updates issues its commit method, the optimistic concurrency control mechanism checks the database before propagating the updates, to see whether the rows of interest have been modified (by some other user) since the data was first read. If such modifications are detected, then the transaction is aborted, and the commit fails. The failure of the commit causes the persistent objects to be changed back to the state they were in when the transaction began. Any changes made to the database will also be undone. It is quite possible that no such changes will yet have been made by Java Blend—it is the nature of optimistic concurrency control to put the database changes off for as long as possible.

Because optimistic concurrency control does not rely upon locks, a greater degree of concurrency is provided. The downside to this, however, is that an optimistic transaction only finds out at commit time that it cannot succeed. Generally an application will try to run the transaction again, hoping that this time it will have better luck when it tries to commit.

Optimistic concurrency control may be a better choice when your application is supporting multiple concurrent updaters, but you should consider the overhead that is present when the commit finally takes place. Pessimistic concurrency control might be a better choice if there are fewer updaters and fewer actual collisions taking place.

Lock Groups

The description of Java Blend's implementation of optimistic concurrency control that we have just given is actually a little bit of an oversimplification. Java Blend allows *lock groups* to be defined at the time the Java/relational mapping takes place. A lock group is a set of fields of a persistent class that are of interest when Java Blend checks for a collision with other users. A persistent class can have multiple lock groups defined, and the fields of these lock groups are allowed to overlap. If no lock groups are defined for a persistent class, then Java Blend considers all of the fields to be part of an implicit lock group.

When a commit method is issued and Java Blend detects that a row has changed since it was initially read, Java Blend then checks to see if the change you are making and the changes of other users fall within the same lock group. If the changes are in the same lock group, then the transaction must be aborted. If the changes are in different lock groups, then the changes can be made and the commit can succeed.

Lock groups allow for the definition of groups of related fields and allow concurrent changes to fields that are not related to the fields changed by your transaction. We could, for example, define separate lock groups for the `title` and `runs` fields of our `Movies` class. One user could update a movie's title and another user could update the same movie's running time without conflicting with each other. The use of lock groups increases the degree of concurrency for applications.

10.5.2 Prefetch

During the mapping process, the user may designate for each relationship whether prefetch is enabled. Actually, the user designates this for *each direction* of each relationship. Enabling prefetch for a relationship means that, when an object is retrieved, the objects on the other side of the relationship are retrieved as well. This enabling could allow Java Blend to use a database join to fetch both sides of the relationship with a single SQL query. The use or non-use of prefetch does not change the way that an application is written in any way.

10.5.3 Object Caching

Java Blend automatically creates a cache that contains the objects that have been retrieved during a transaction. The cache provides *read consistency* by satisfying the second and subsequent reference to an object during a transaction by going to the cache, rather than retrieving the information from the database again and creating a new object. This condition means that only one copy of an object will be created, even if an application encounters the object multiple times through the navigation of relationships or the issuance of OQL queries. When a transaction is committed, any changes that have been made to persistent objects are pushed out to the database. The cached objects are then discarded.

10.6 ODMG

ODMG is a consortium that began life in 1991 as the Object Database Management Group. The purpose of this group was to define a common set of language bindings for object-oriented database management systems (OODBMSs). The group recently changed its name to the Object Data Management Group, retaining the ODMG acronym, in order to reflect a broadening of the group's scope. The ODMG specification can be applied to systems where persistence is provided by an OODBMS, a relational DBMS, an object/relational DBMS, or a product that provides object/relational mapping. It is the latter of these categories that covers Java Blend. Sun, in the person of Rick Cattell, has been a strong participant in ODMG. In fact, the group began with an invitation by Rick to interested parties in the summer of 1991.

ODMG defines an object model, which is based on the object model of the Object Management Group (OMG). It is impossible to describe an object model in the space we have available, so we'll have to settle for a brief list of some of its more interesting features.

- A type definition is made up of both a type specification and implementations. There may be more than one implementation of a given type.
- The state of an object is defined by a set of values for each of its properties. The properties consist of both attributes and relationships.
- Multiple inheritance of behavior and single inheritance of state are supported, just as they are for Java.
- *Extents,* the set of all instances of a type in a particular database, may be defined.
- The lifetime of objects may be "transient" or "persistent."
- The supported data types consist of primitive types and the collection types of Set, Bag, List, Array, and Dictionary.

ODMG defines some language-independent specifications, and then it defines bindings to these specifications from C++, Smalltalk, and Java. The creators of ODMG have worked hard to allow programmers to write applications that manipulate persistent data in the language of their choice, keeping to a minimum the need to learn new languages, models, and concepts. This state is in stark contrast to SQL, which has its own query language, data types, DDL, and DML, along with an embedding for many programming languages. The creators of SQL felt that is was more important to design the database constructs in a neutral way, accessible to applications written in multiple languages.

10.6.1 Language-Independent Specifications

Object Definition Language (ODL) is a language for defining objects. It is based on OMG's Interface Definition Language (IDL). ODL provides concrete syntax for the concepts described in the object model. In Example 10.16, we provide an ODL definition for our `Votes` class. Perhaps the most unfamiliar part of this definition is the declaration of the extent `OurVotes`. This extent can be used in an application to retrieve a collection of all of the instances of the `Votes` class.

Object Interchange Format (OIF) defines an external format that can be used to represent all of the data contained in an object database. The `odbdump` command can be used to generate an OIF representation for a database, and the `odbload` command can be used to load an object database from an OIF representation.

EXAMPLE 10.16 AN ODL CLASS DEFINITION FOR `Votes`.

```
class Votes (extent OurVotes) {
   attribute string title;
   attribute string year_introduced;
   attribute long runs;

   relationship set<Votes> VotesForMovies
      inverse Votes::MoviesForVotes;

   long tallyVotes ();
}
```

Object Query Language (OQL) is a nonprocedural query language that allows the retrieval of information from an object database. It is based on SQL-92 but modified to use the ODMG object model. It is somewhat more regular than SQL, imposing fewer restrictions on where specific language constructs can be used.

An OQL query may return a primitive value, such as an integer, a structure, an object, or a set of any of these data types. When a set of objects is expected, such as in a FROM clause, any expression that returns a set of objects can be used. This expression could be as simple as a named extent, or it could be a much more complicated expression. OQL allows the use of methods in any of its expressions. Given the limited space that we have for this topic, let's just look at Examples 10.17 through 10.20.

EXAMPLE 10.17 MOVIES WITH A TALLY GREATER THAN 8.

```
SELECT   m
FROM     Movies m
WHERE    COUNT (m.VotesForMovies) > 1
  AND    m->tallyVotes() > 8
```

The query in Example 10.17 returns the set of movies that have a tally greater than 8, with more than one voter casting a vote. Notice that the `COUNT` aggregate function operates directly on a set expression and the invocation of a method uses "->".

EXAMPLE 10.18 MOVIE TITLES AND THE LOWEST VOTE THEY RECEIVED.

```
SELECT   low_votes (title:          m.title,
                    smallest_vote:  MIN (m.VotesForMovies))
FROM     Movies m
```

The query in Example 10.18 returns a set of structures (of type `low_votes`), containing a movie title and the lowest vote that the movie received, for all movies.

The query in Example 10.19 returns a set of titles for movies that have a voter whose name matches that of the movie. Notice that in the FROM clause we are matching up each movie with its associated votes.

EXAMPLE 10.19 MOVIES WITH A TITLE AND VOTER THAT ARE THE SAME.

```
SELECT   m.title
FROM     Movies m, m.VotesForMovies v
WHERE    m.title = v.name
```

EXAMPLE 10.20 THE NUMBER OF VOTES THAT *UNFORGIVEN* RECEIVED.

```
Count ( (element (SELECT m FROM Movies m
                  WHERE title ='Unforgiven'))
         .VotesForMovies
      )
```

The query in Example 10.20 identifies the movie *Unforgiven* and returns the number of votes that it received. The use of `element` allows us to refer to just the single movie object, rather than a set of movies with one member. The query itself returns an integer, rather than a set of integers with a single member.

ODMG does not provide a language-independent *Object Manipulation Language (OML)*. The specific language being used to write an application serves as the basis for the OML.

10.6.2 The Java Binding for ODMG

Previous versions of the ODMG specification contained bindings for C++ and Smalltalk. The Java binding is new to the ODMG 2.0 specification. The Java binding provides Java ODL, Java OML, and Java OQL.

The Java binding specifies two ways for persistence-capable Java classes to be defined. Existing classes can somehow be made persistence-capable, or these classes can be generated from ODL using some type of utility. Java ODL specifies the mapping between object model data types and those of Java.

Java OML has as one of its goals orthogonality based on persistence, meaning that the same operations should apply whether an object is persistent or transient. Persistence is determined, for objects of a persistence-capable class, based on *reachability*. Methods are provided in the `Database` class to allow the association of objects and names. There may also be a set of root objects supported by an implementation. These two types of objects are persistent, and all objects reachable from these objects are persistent. These is no need for a delete operation; an object is implicitly deleted when a user makes an object unreachable from the root persistent objects. Changes to the state of a persistent object are made via methods, and the changes become permanent when the transaction containing the changes is committed.

The Java OML defines the `DCollection`, `DSet`, `DBag`, `DList`, and `DArray` interfaces. It also defines the `Database`, `Transaction`, and `OQLQuery` classes.

10.6.3 How Java Blend Relates to ODMG 2.0

Java Blend somewhat loosely implements the ODMG 2.0 specification. We say this not as criticism, because we do not know how faithfully others have implemented the specification, nor do we know how many users desire the ability to move an application from one vendor's implementation to another. It's just something for you to be aware of.

Java Blend provides the Java ODL, Java OML, and Java OQL bindings. Persistence by reachability has been replaced by the explicit `Database` methods of `makePersistent` and `deletePersistentObject`. `DCollection` is supported, but not the other types of collection interfaces. The `Database`, `Transaction`, and `OQLQuery` classes are provided, but the methods they provide differ in small ways from those defined in ODMG 2.0. Where ODMG 2.0 defines how to execute dynamic OQL queries, Java Blend supports only the execution of static OQL queries. Finally, Java Blend supports both pessimistic concurrency control, which is specified in ODMG 2.0, and optimistic concurrency control, which is mentioned as a desirable extension for products.

It is possible that some of these differences were ironed out with the publication of ODMG 3.0 in late 1999. ODMG has also stated its intention to begin developing a certification suite for its Java binding. Looking a bit further into the future, there is another effort that you should be aware of. Sun Microsystems has created the Java Community

Company	Product
Ardent Software	O_2 System
Computer Associates	Jasmine
Object Design	ObjectStore, PSE for Java
Objectivity	Objectivity/DB
Objectmatter	BSF
POET	POET Object Server
Versant	Versant ODBMS

TABLE 10.2 *Companies and products that support ODMG 2.0.*

Process to help develop and revise Java technology specifications. JSR-000012, Java Data Objects Specification, is one of the specifications that are being developed under this process. This specification addresses the need to store Java objects in transactional data stores and to treat relational data as Java objects. ODMG has agreed to contribute the ODMG 3.0 specification to the group that is working on Java Data Objects.

10.6.4 Other Products That Support ODMG 2.0

Java Blend is not unique in its support of the Java Bindings of ODMG 2.0. Table 10.2 shows a list of products (possibly incomplete, though we have tried to be thorough) that support this specification as well.

10.7 Chapter Summary

We've seen how to create a mapping between persistence-capable classes and a database, starting with either of them and generating the other. Java Blend, as an implementation of the ODMG 2.0 specification, hides the underlying DBMS and provides persistence-capable classes that are very natural for a Java programmer to work with.

Although SQL operations are executed transparently by the Java Blend runtime environment, the query language that provides non-procedural access to persistent objects, OQL, is strongly based on SQL.

During our work with Java Blend 1.0, we encountered several limitations and a couple of outright bugs. This situation is fairly normal for a "version 1.0" product. It is our understanding that the new version of Java Blend on the way has addressed these problems, but we have not (yet) had an opportunity to evaluate that release.

WEB ENHANCED

Additional information on Java Blend can be found at *www.sun.com /software/JavaBlend.*

CHAPTER

11

GUI Java Application Builders

11.1 Introduction

In this chapter, we take a fairly cursory look at several GUI (graphical user interface) products meant for building Java applications. All of these products provide tools of various sorts for accessing data in SQL (and other) databases, but their support for some of the technologies we've discussed in this book—such as embedding SQL statements in Java code—ranges from nonexistent in some products to fairly impressive in others, at least for embedded SQL in Java. (The other aspects of SQLJ—invoking Java methods from SQL code and using Java classes in SQL databases—aren't meaningful to a GUI application builder; they are more relevant to a database management system.)

We show enough of each product to give you a feel for its use in database applications, but the truth is that we don't have the space or time to show you every aspect of the products—even the database-related aspects. Instead, we try to focus on those features that illustrate the products' relationship to the various technologies on which this book has focussed. But for those readers who haven't had an opportunity to use any of these products, we'd like to briefly describe what they do and how they're used. The rest of you can take a short break and rejoin us in a few minutes.

11.2 Why Use a GUI Application Builder for Java?

As a reader of this book, you are probably a user of Java, meaning that you probably write code in the Java programming language. Java has been said to be relatively easy to write, especially when compared with that other well-known object-oriented language, C++. However, like all programming languages, Java has tedious requirements as well as more elegant capabilities. Application building products, especially the "visual" ones, are extremely helpful to avoid the more tedious aspects of writing in Java. These tools typically involve capabilities that allow an application writer to visually construct a user interface to an application by "dragging and dropping" components onto a representation of a screen and often allow additional drag and drop operations to create skeleton code structures that can then be completed by adding Java statements that perform the application's required functions.

A number of these tools are on the market, and it wouldn't be possible for us to cover them all. Instead, we'll focus on three with which we have some experience and then briefly mention a few others.

All of the products use what the industry has called a "visual programming" paradigm: that is, the products give their users the ability to create an application, including a user interface, by dragging various components onto a form. Most of these components will be visible on the form when the application runs, but some of them represent entities that are somewhat abstract—like a transaction, database connection, or query—and that have no visible structure to display on a user interface. In general, the components provided by these products are found on one of (usually) several *palettes*, each containing one or more components. Typically, the product will include components that are used by the application to display text on the form (often called label boxes), components that allow user input text to the application (text boxes), components that simulate buttons on the form (check boxes, radio buttons, and command buttons), and so forth. As we discuss some of the products in this chapter, we'll show you the products' windows containing the palettes to give you a better picture of how this works.

Once you have positioned the components you need onto the user interface form, you begin to write code controlling the actions required to respond to user input and to manage application output to the user. In some cases, you're simply going to have to bite your lip and dig down into your code-writing skills; in others, you might be able to use the product's facilities to get at least a skeleton of the code written for you by the product itself—possibly using some sort of "wizard" built into the product.

Even more importantly, all of these products give you an interactive development environment (the acronym IDE is often used to describe them). The principal benefit of an IDE is that program compilations and debugging is done in the same environment used for developing the code, so you get quick, interactive feedback tied directly to the code you're building on any errors or other problems encountered. Since these products generate a lot of code on your behalf (for example, a text box that you position on a form with a simple drag-and-drop operation might require dozens of lines of Java code to actually create and set up), it's a lot less confusing if you don't have to debug the real code but only the code you wrote yourself. IDEs such as the ones in these products are fabulous timesavers because of this capability.

11.3 PowerJ, JDeveloper, and Visual J++

PowerJ, JDeveloper, and Visual J++ are, in many ways, quite different from one another. If you were to start each of these products on different computers, you might at first glance not recognize them as competitors with one another. Nonetheless, they are each intended to solve the same problem in approximately the same way—by building Java programs using a visual metaphor. The differences, however, are not just cosmetic; some of them are quite substantial. For example, Microsoft's Visual J++ is intended for use in building Java programs that run (primarily, if not exclusively) in the Windows environment, whereas Oracle's JDeveloper and Sybase's PowerJ produce code that is far less sensitive to the underlying operating system facilities.

11.3.1 PowerJ by Sybase

Sybase's PowerJ product does not (as of Version 2.5) support SQLJ Part 0 (embedded SQL statements in Java code, also known as SQL/OLB). That omission does not mean, of course, that you are prohibited from taking the Java code created by PowerJ, editing it to add embedded SQL statements as specified in the SQL/OLB standard, processing the resulting code with the SQLJ Part 0 Reference Implementation (or other preprocessor), recompiling the resulting Java code, and then using it. However, PowerJ isn't really set up for this process and we don't recommend using this approach—in fact, we have chosen not to demonstrate it, simply because it is so awkward. Instead, we show how you might choose to write JDBC code in your PowerJ applications.

On the other hand, you probably won't have much reason to fall back into JDBC directly when you're building applications with PowerJ. Most of the time, you will be able to use the data-oriented components provided with PowerJ to accomplish all the database operations you need. Although we're going to demonstrate how you could use JDBC, it's only fair to recognize that we didn't have to do so: The specific item we chose to add to our sample application in this section could have been added much more easily using PowerJ's built-in components! So, should you spend the time to read this section? We think so, because we demonstrate a capability that, while probably not required very often, may sometimes be essential to getting your job done.

Before we get into this capability, however, let's take a look at how PowerJ handles database operations in the absence of supporting your own SQL statements in its Java code. The distribution kit for PowerJ includes a number of sample applications, so we'll use one of them to illustrate this capability. We're using the sample application called "BoundControls." In Sybase terminology (and that of many other vendors, too), a *bound control* is a button or collection of buttons on a form that is "bound" to a specific database query and that executes that query—possibly in different ways—when the button (or one of the buttons) is pressed by the user. Figure 11.1 shows what the application looks like when it's being executed.

In this screen shot, the bar filled with various symbols, such as ◄ and ►|, is the actual bound control; this particular control is called a `dataNavigator`. Each button on that control has a specific meaning—for example, ► means "move to the next row of the result set returned by the query to which the control is bound."

Now, you may be very familiar with PowerJ; then again, you may not. So we'll take just a bit more time to explain how it is used. When

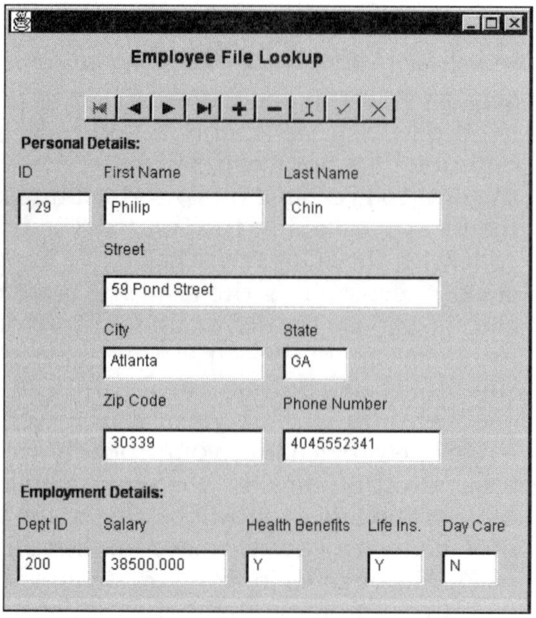

FIGURE 11.1 *Sybase PowerJ BoundControls sample application.*

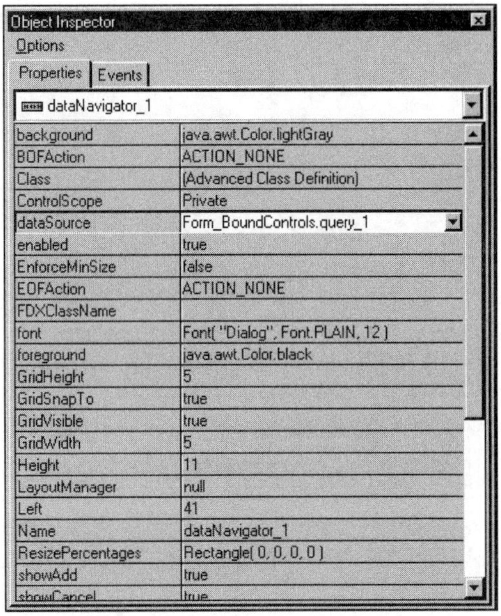

FIGURE 11.2 *Object inspector in Sybase PowerJ for* `dataNavigator_1`.

developing an application in PowerJ, like any other GUI application builder, you normally start off by building the visual representation (or "form") that you want to see when the application runs. Figure 11.1 shows what the application looks like after it's finished, but you should recognize that the form may have grid lines or other markings when you're working on the development screens, as you'll see in Figure 11.6. As you place each object (control, field, label, or whatever else) onto the form, you typically use the "object inspector" to set various characteristics of the object. Figure 11.2 shows the object inspector when we've selected the bound control we're discussing.

In this screen shot, the object we're inspecting is named `dataNavigator_1`; we have highlighted the object's `dataSource` attribute, showing that its value is `Form_BoundControls.query_1`. That is a critical piece of information because it informs the underlying Java class code (which we can't show, mostly because it's proprietary to Sybase) that the various buttons on this control operate on the result set created by that query. The query is another object that is placed on the form; it's visible in the design view of the form, but invisible when the application is running.

But let's look at what the object inspector shows about that query, `query_1`. Figure 11.3 shows this information. In this screen shot, we've

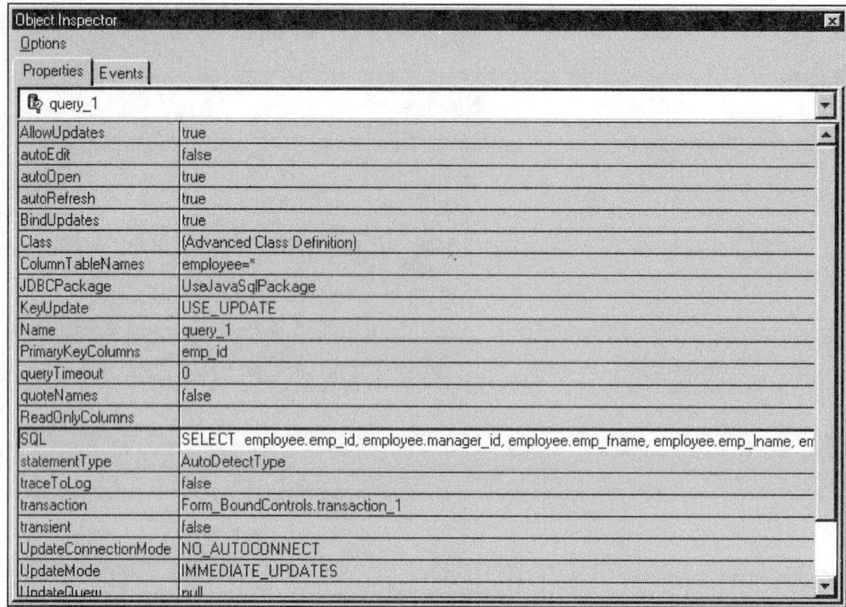

FIGURE 11.3 *Object inspector in Sybase PowerJ for `query_1`.*

selected the object property named `SQL`, which you can see apparently contains an SQL statement; the full text of that SQL statement is shown in Example 11.1.

EXAMPLE 11.1 SELECT STATEMENT USED IN `query_1`.

```
SELECT    employee.emp_id, employee.manager_id,
          employee.emp_fname, employee.emp_lname,
          employee.dept_id, employee.street, employee.city,
          employee.state, employee.zip_code, employee.phone,
          employee.status, employee.ss_number,
          employee.salary, employee.termination_date,
          employee.bene_health_ins, employee.bene_life_ins,
          employee.bene_day_care, employee.sex
FROM      DBA.employee employee
```

Not far beneath the selected property, you can see that there's a property named `transaction`, whose value is `Form_BoundControls.transaction_1`. As you may infer, that implies another (invisible at runtime) object to represent a database transaction. Figure 11.4 shows

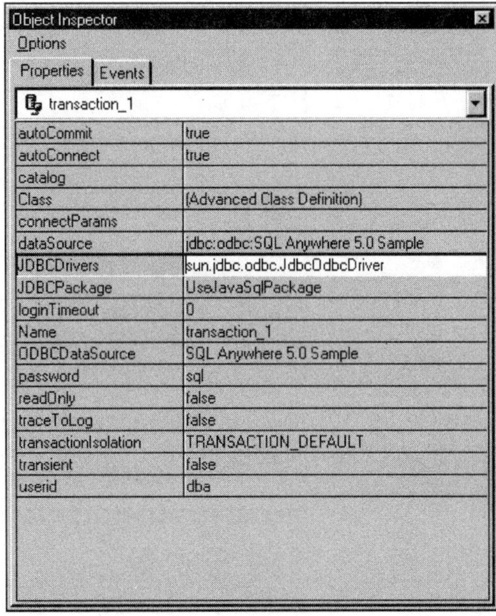

FIGURE 11.4 *Object inspector in Sybase PowerJ for* `transaction_1`.

the object inspector's view of `transaction_1`. Here, we've highlighted the `JDBCDrivers` property of the object, in part to show that this sample application uses a Type 1 JDBC driver (a JDBC-ODBC bridge) as we described in Chapter 4.

Of course, there's a way to associate each column returned by `query_1` with a text field—named `textf_fname` ("text field for first name")—on the form. You can see this in the screen shot shown in Figure 11.5. Note the highlighted attribute named `dataColumns`, indicating which column of the result set returned by the SQL statement is used to fill in the text field. Just below that attribute, you'll notice the `dataSource` attribute, tying this text field directly to `query_1`. (By the way, `textf_fname`—and each of the other text fields that display database data on this form—is also a bound control, just like the `dataNavigator` control.)

When the application generated by this example is run (as a Java applet), the generated code attaches to the database identified in the `dataSource` property of the `transaction_1` object, after which a new transaction is started. Next, the application executes the SQL statement specified in the `SQL` attribute of `query_1`. That statement causes a result set to be returned from the attached database to the application, and the application associates that result set with the

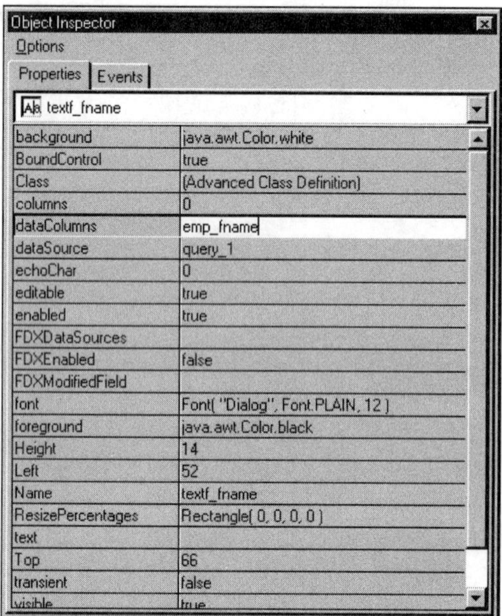

FIGURE 11.5 *Object inspector in Sybase PowerJ for* `text_fname`.

bound control `dataNavigator_1`, causing the columns of the first row of the result set to be associated with the various text fields (e.g., `textf_fname`) on the form and the values in the row displayed in their associated fields. Whenever the user clicks on one of the buttons in that bound control, the action associated with that button is performed. For example, when the user clicks on the ▶ button, the bound control causes the next row's column values to be associated with the appropriate text fields and displayed.

Now, there's not a lot of code generated by PowerJ that's associated with these controls. Instead, the code is mostly buried in the class definitions associated with Sybase's

```
powersoft.powerj.db.Transaction,
powersoft.powerj.db.Query,
```

and

```
powersoft.powerj.ui.DataNavigator
```

classes. That code, unfortunately, is not available for us to show you.

As we said above, PowerJ does not support embedded SQL in the generated Java code directly, but you can always manually extract the generated code and compile it yourself. That is not the easiest of things to do, but it's more reasonable to write code that uses JDBC to access the database—and that's what we'll demonstrate with PowerJ. (We note, however, that we are aware that Sybase plans to support embedded SQL in Java code in a future release of PowerJ, so—if you've chosen this tool for your shop—keep your eyes open for this enhancement.)

Because of the tight connection between PowerJ's `dataNavigator` control and the result set columns that it associates with fields on the form, it's a little awkward to consider some additional SQL operation that we might want to perform outside that context. (Remember: since we don't have the code associated with the `dataNavigator` class, we can't "get inside" it to enhance and recompile that code. Therefore, any embedded SQL we create has to be in either code we write as part of our application or, at a minimum, in code generated by PowerJ as part of the application.) Consequently, we've decided that we'll illustrate the process by adding a new field on the same form and populating it (when the applet starts) with the total number of rows satisfying the query. But we're not using the `query_1` object; instead, we're manually reproducing the query in the SQL statement that we need in our embedded SQL statement. Of course, our change would have been simpler if we had chosen to build a second query object returning a single column and row containing the row count of the first query and then had bound our new text field to the query. But that wouldn't be as illustrative, now would it?

In Figure 11.6, you can see the design view of our form after we've added a new label and a new text field in the top right corner of the form. That's where we'll be displaying the total number of employee rows in our result set. Figure 11.6 also shows the object inspector's view of the new text field. We've highlighted the `BoundControl` property to show that this object is not bound to any query (compare with Figure 11.5's view of the `textf_fname` object; while you're at it, observe that this not-a-`BoundControl` text field simply doesn't have properties named `dataColumns` or `dataSource`).

Figure 11.7 contains an image of PowerJ's main screen, including the palette from which we chose the new text field and label that we put onto the application's form. (If you have never worked with an IDE like PowerJ, you may wonder why the main screen is so "vertically challenged." The answer lies in the various other windows—such as the various form windows, property windows, and so forth—that PowerJ displays on which the developer does the work; the main screen is used primarily to initiate actions on other windows.)

Now that we've added the new field, with a corresponding label for the convenience of the user, to our sample application's form, it's time to modify the code. Example 11.2 shows the code that PowerJ shows to the application developer. This is *not,* by the way, the code that PowerJ generates for compilation by Java! Although you can see the generated

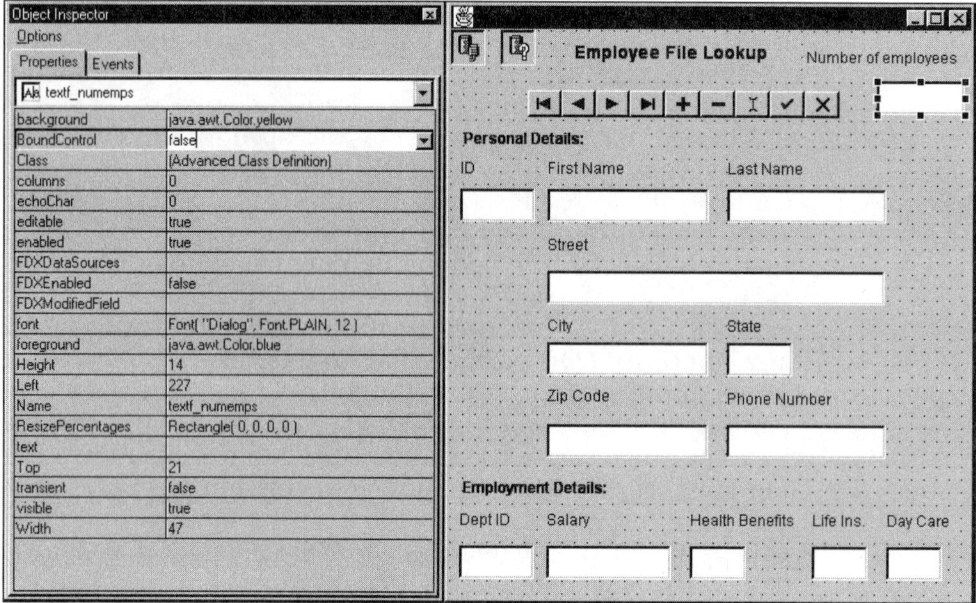

FIGURE 11.6 *Bound control and object inspector.*

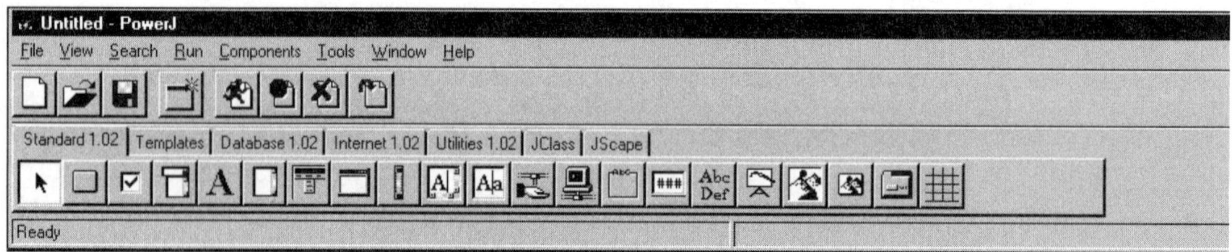

FIGURE 11.7 *PowerJ main screen.*

code, you normally won't want to attempt to modify it—doing so will take you outside of PowerJ's scope, and you're on your own after that.

We quickly observe that there is no obvious place to put any code that will be executed when the applet starts running, but you Java programmers will rapidly figure out that we can choose to add an event handler that runs at the time that our form is created (which, at least in PowerJ-generated code, occurs after the text field on the form is created). Let's take that approach—we'll add an appropriate event handler, and then we'll write some JDBC code to retrieve the information we want along with the code to display the retrieved value in that new text field.

EXAMPLE 11.2 POWERJ'S GENERATED CODE.

```
// custom imports for Form_BoundControls

// add your custom import statements here

class Form_BoundControls
        extends java.awt.Frame
        implements java.awt.event.WindowListener
{

    public Form_BoundControls()
    {
        super();
    }

    public void processEvent(java.awt.AWTEvent event)
    {
        defaultProcessEvent(event);
    }

    public java.awt.Container getContentPane()
    {
        return this;
    }

    public void unhandledEvent( String listenerName,
                                String methodName,
                                java.lang.Object event )
    {

    }

    public boolean Form_BoundControls_windowClosing
                  (java.awt.event.WindowEvent event)
    {
        setVisible( false );
        destroy();
        return false;
    }

    // add your data members here
}
```

We've chosen to add the new method just preceding the `unhandledEvent` method in the code we showed you just a couple of paragraphs above, although it really doesn't matter where it goes. Because we're using JDBC facilities, we'll have to add the `import` statement shown in Example 11.3 to the class definition for the form to make the JDBC classes available to us.

EXAMPLE 11.3 NECESSARY `import` JAVA STATEMENT.

```
import java.sql.*;
```

The new code we've inserted looks like that shown in Example 11.4.

EXAMPLE 11.4 INSERTED CODE.

```
public boolean Form_BoundControls_objectCreated
                (powersoft.powerj.event.EventData event)
    {

      // Declare a Connection variable, but don't initialize it

      Connection con = null;

      // Declare a String variable and initialize it to a specific
      //   JDBC URL value

      String url = "jdbc:odbc:SQL Anywhere 5.0 Sample";

      // Attempt to load and register a specific JDBC driver
      //   Failure throws ClassNotFoundException; just print a msg

      try {
         Class.forName("sun.jdbc.odbc.JdbcOdbcDriver");
      }
      catch (ClassNotFoundException cnf) {
         System.out.println (cnf.getMessage ());
         return false;
      }

      // Attempt to connect to the database at the URL
      //  Failure throws SQLException; just print a msg
```

```
try {
   con = DriverManager.getConnection
           (url, "dba", "sql");
}
catch (SQLException sqe) {
   String this_message = sqe.getMessage ();
   System.out.println (this_message);
   return false;
}

// Allocate a variable for our SQL statement

try {
   Statement stmt = con.createStatement();

// Create a String to contain the text of a SELECT statement

   String stmtsource =
          "select count(*) from dba.employee";

// Invoke the executeQuery method of the Statement object,
//    with the text of the SELECT statement to be executed

   ResultSet rs = stmt.executeQuery (stmtsource);

// Process the result set---remember, there's only 1 row

   while (rs.next()) {

      // Retrieve the count value in the result set's only
      // column, casting it to a String for display purposes
      String empcount = rs.getString(1);

      // Now, display the retrieved value
      textf_numemps.setText(empcount);
      }
}
catch (SQLException sqe) {
   System.out.println (sqe.getMessage ());
   return false;
}

return false;
}
```

Some of that code should look familiar—you've seen code very much like it in Chapter 4 when we discussed JDBC 1.0.

In Figure 11.8, you can see the application's display, with the new text field duly filled in by our new code.

And we have thus demonstrated how to use one of the Java/SQL technologies described in this book—JDBC—with a specific GUI Java application builder—Sybase's PowerJ.

Keeping in mind the fact that we could have used PowerJ's facilities directly to display the number of rows in the database, using a text box as a bound control associated with another query object, you've got to ask yourself how often you're likely to want to write JDBC code—or even SQL embedded in Java code—when using an IDE like this. We doubt that it's going to happen very often, but still believe that you should know how to do it for those rare situations when you need something that a provided component doesn't give you.

PowerJ provides a wide selection of components that can be used as bound controls, including components such as text fields, list boxes, and choice boxes (in fact, we often think of this kind of component as "data-aware," as opposed to "data-oriented" components like the data navigator component used in our sample application). We decided not to attempt to describe all of those components because there are so many and because the list wouldn't contain any surprises or obvious omissions. However, you'll probably be interested in knowing the major

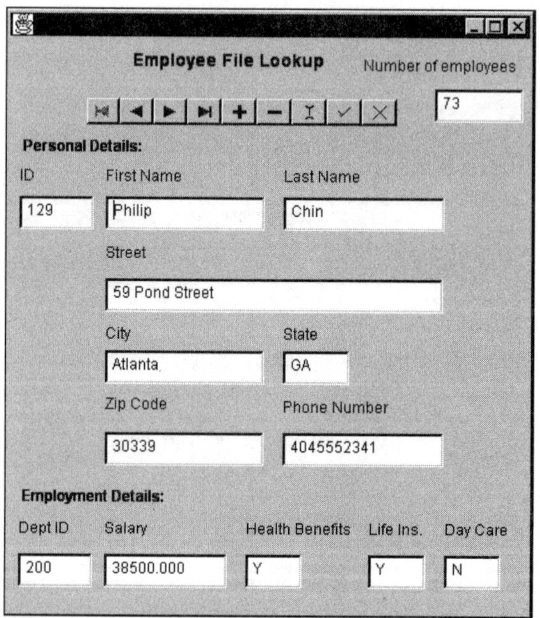

FIGURE 11.8 *Modified PowerJ application screen shot.*

Control name	Control purpose
Query	Submit SQL queries for execution and process any result sets
Transaction	Create a database connection and perform common tasks such as commits and rollbacks
Data navigator	Used to allow the user to navigate through the rows of a result set resulting from a query; also used to update, delete, or insert rows and to signal completion of a transaction

TABLE 11.1 *PowerJ data-oriented controls.*

components that PowerJ provides specifically for working with data. Table 11.1 contains that information.

As you'd expect, PowerJ provides a great many more object classes for use in applications that deal with databases, but those classes are used in conjunction with the components shown in Table 11.1. There are a surprisingly small number of data-oriented controls provided by PowerJ, but they are powerful enough (when combined with the related object classes) to build very sophisticated data management applications.

11.3.2 JDeveloper by Oracle

Oracle's JDeveloper product, unlike Sybase's PowerJ, *does* support embedding SQL statements in the Java code that you write as part of the applications developed in this IDE. Although the details of JDeveloper are quite different from those of PowerJ, the overall philosophy and goals are the same. For example, JDeveloper has a very different selection of components available on its palettes, the selection of palettes is quite dissimilar, and the sequence of operations that you use to create an application is unlike that of PowerJ. Nonetheless, the applications built by both PowerJ and JDeveloper use many common concepts, such as projects, frames, text controls, and so forth; in addition, both products produce Java applications, applets, servelets, and so forth, and do so while allowing you to debug in the context of the visual and source-language environment.

Instead of going through the same sequence of steps we showed you in our PowerJ discussion, we decided to avoid a lot of repetition and get more quickly to new information—JDeveloper's ability to let you use SQLJ Part 0 in the Java code you develop with this product.

In JDeveloper, as in PowerJ, you create a project (using, if you prefer, one of the wizards provided) and build your application's forms by placing components onto the skeleton structure and then writing code to provide the semantics you want those components to have. Also like PowerJ, JDeveloper provides a number of components that you can bind to your database—bound controls. Consequently, you probably won't often find the need to use JDBC or SQL/OLB in the applications you develop with JDeveloper, but the product gives you that flexibility if you need it. The JDBC support is equivalent to PowerJ's, and you can add JDBC code to your JDeveloper applications just as easily as to your PowerJ applications—in practically identical ways. In addition, if you'd prefer to avoid the tedium of JDBC coding, you can use the techniques we showed you in Chapter 5 and simply add those new statements to the Java code being constructed by JDeveloper. The most significant new requirement when doing this turns out to be the fact that you must save your source code with a different file name extension—it must be saved as `xxx.sqlj` instead of `xxx.java`!

Let's consider one of the sample applications that comes with JDeveloper. The application we're going to use here is one that Oracle provided specifically to illustrate the use of embedded SQL code in Java. It's called "Feedback" and provides a user interface that permits a person using a Web browser (one that supports Java, of course!) to submit feedback to the enterprise building Web pages for some purpose, such as an e-commerce application. The applet appears in Figure 11.9.

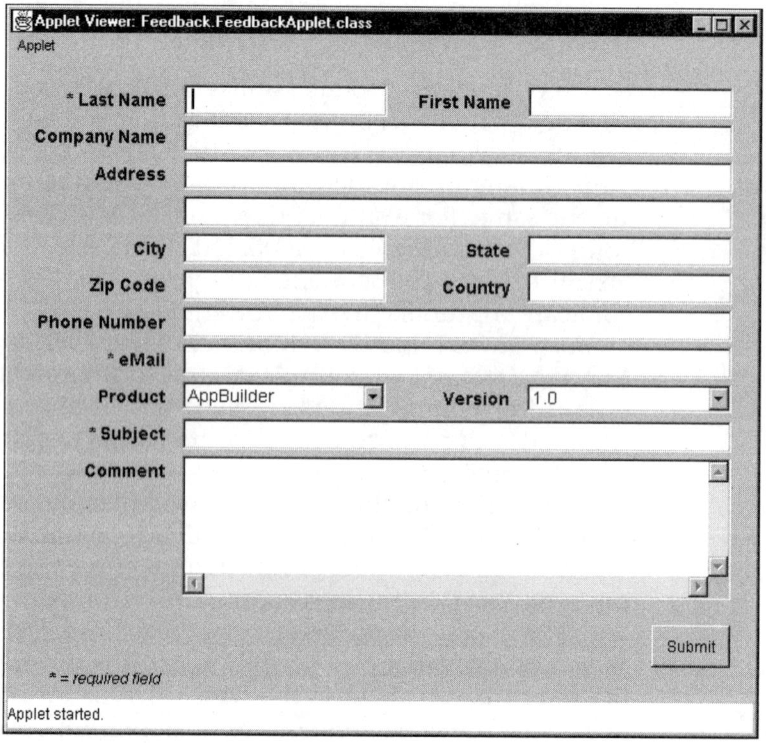

FIGURE 11.9 *JDeveloper sample applet appearance.*

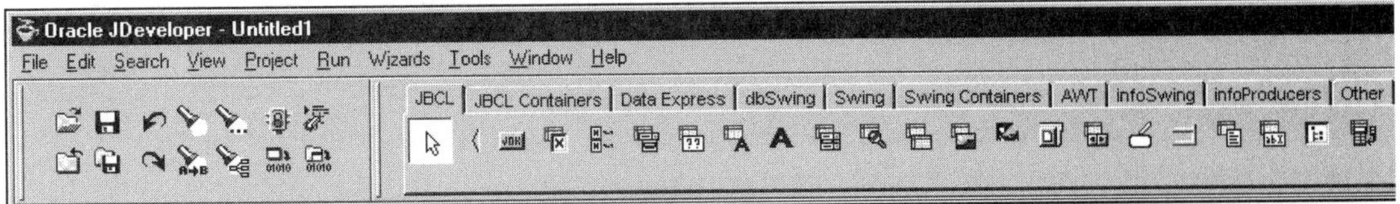

FIGURE 11.10 *JDeveloper main screen.*

Of course, since this is an *applet,* it would appear only in the context of a Web page being displayed by a Java-enabled browser (such as Netscape Navigator 4.0 or above or Internet Explorer 4.0 or above). As you can see, this form and its controls are rather like something that you could have built with PowerJ. Even so, we think you'd like to see what JDeveloper's main screen looks like, with its palettes displayed. Figure 11.10 shows that screen shot.

You will quickly notice that JDeveloper has more palettes than PowerJ and that the palettes have completely different names (which doesn't necessarily mean that one product is better than the other, only that they are different).

We could, of course, show you other screen shots to illustrate similarities (such as the existence of an object inspector) and differences (such as the way class hierarchies are displayed) between the products, but that's rather unimportant to the issue at hand. Instead, let's take a look at some of the code that JDeveloper provided for this applet.

Now, the code to implement this applet is rather lengthy, and we don't think it's all that interesting for the purposes of this discussion, so we've simply abstracted the portion of the code that's relevant, as shown in Example 11.5.

The interesting piece of that code is in **boldface** so you won't miss it. It's an ordinary SQL INSERT statement written using the SQLJ Part 0 convention (`#sql {...}`). Now, *this* is the sort of thing that's awkward to do with bound controls (which, after all, are really designed for data retrieval and display, not updating).

Once you have designed your application (or applet) and have written all of its code—including any embedded SQL code, such as that shown above—it's time to build and test. In JDeveloper, when you build a project, and that project contains files whose file names have the extension `sqlj`, JDeveloper simply invokes the SQLJ translator first to translate those files into pure Java code (with, naturally, the same file name and an extension of `java`). The Java files thus generated are then automatically translated into Java byte code by the built-in Java compiler to generate the appropriate class files. *Et voilà*—your Java code with embedded SQL statements has become ordinary Java classes in byte code, ready to be interpreted by your favorite Java Virtual Machine.

EXAMPLE 11.5 APPLET CODE.

```
void btnSubmit_actionPerformed(ActionEvent e) {
    lblErrorInfo.setText("");
    if (validateForm())  {
       String lastName = getText(txtLastName);
       /* several irrelevant lines deleted */
       String commentAbstract =
          getText(txtCommentAbstract);
       try {
          #sql {INSERT into feedback
                  (id, lastname, firstname, phone,
                   email, company, addressone, addresstwo,
                   city, state, zipcode, country, product,
                   version, commenttype, status,
                   commenttext, commentdate,
                   commentabstract)
                  VALUES (feedback_seq.nextval, :lastName,
                          :firstName, :phone, :eMail,
                          :company, :addressOne,
                          :addressTwo, :city, :state,
                          :zipCode, :country, :product,
                          :version, :commentType, :status,
                          :commentText,
                          TO_DATE(:entryDate,
                                  'mon dd hh24:mi:ss YYYY',
                                  'NLS_DATE_LANGUAGE =
                                  American'),
                          :commentAbstract) };
       /* several irrelevant lines deleted */
       }
       catch (SQLException ex) {
       /* several irrelevant lines deleted */
       }
    }
  }
}
```

Of course, you won't be surprised to learn that JDeveloper allows you to set a number of options dealing with just how the embedded SQL translation is performed (for example, whether the SQL code is to be checked against some database schema for table and column validity) and how the Java compilation itself is done. Figure 11.11 shows the dialog box used for this purpose. You should particularly note the tab

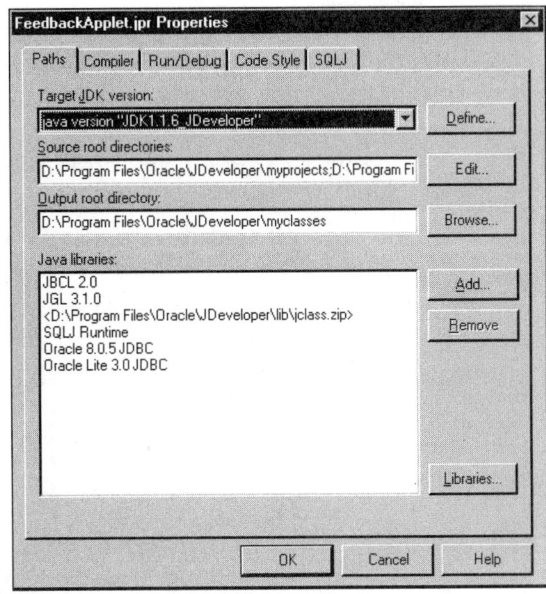

FIGURE 11.11 *JDeveloper project properties.*

(not selected in this screen shot) labeled "SQLJ" and the fact that one of the Java libraries listed for inclusion in the compilation is named "SQLJ Runtime"; both of these relate to the embedded SQL statement in our code abstract above.

It gets better: When you're ready to debug your application, JDeveloper doesn't bother to show you the generated Java code that resulted from preprocessing the `.sqlj` files. Instead, you debug by using the `.sqlj` files themselves! For example, you can set breakpoints on a source line containing embedded SQL code, such as our `#sql {SELECT...}` statement above. When you run the program, the debugger will stop at that breakpoint like any other, and the statement will be highlighted in the debug window of JDeveloper. You're debugging directly in the SQLJ source code, not in the generated Java source code.

JDeveloper offers you quite a choice of components that can be used as bound controls. Of course, this includes components such as text fields, list boxes, choice boxes, and so forth. We aren't listing all of those components, both because the selection is large and because it contains no surprises (not even surprising omissions). But we think (as we did in the PowerJ discussion) that you might be interested to know at least some of the controls specifically designed for working with data. Table 11.2 presents these data-oriented controls. Naturally, there are many more object classes that you would use in manipulating data

Control name	Control purpose
Navigator control	Navigates to selected row of data, which is then displayed by data-aware components such as text fields
Database	Encapsulates a database connection through JDBC to a database server; also provides lightweight transaction support
Table data set	Creates a storage data set from a source other than an SQL database (for example, a text file)
Query data set	Contains the data returned by execution of a query
Query resolver	Manages changes made to a data set and governs whether and how those changes are applied to the data source
Parameter row	Provides additional abstraction of returned data set values for use in queries
Data set view	Presents an additional view of data returned in a storage data set (for example, to permit multiple ways of ordering the data)
Session info	Contains all information related to a database connection; acts as a parent to row set info controls
Row set info	Defines master-detail relationships between rows of data; describes the table rows that the application will access

TABLE 11.2 *JDeveloper data-oriented controls.*

in applications you might build in JDeveloper, but these are the major components available on this product's palettes that you will use when designing those applications.

One more thing: if you are familiar with similar development tools, then you are probably used to having "wizards" to assist you with certain tasks. Unfortunately JDeveloper does not appear to provide any wizards that will generate embedded SQL statements in the Java code you're building—you're on your own for that.

11.3.3 Visual J++ by Microsoft

The third product that we've actually had a chance to use is Microsoft's Visual J++. As you are undoubtedly aware, there has been some controversy over Microsoft's relationship to Java. Microsoft naturally has aligned its Java strategy with its Windows strategy, and it has been said that code produced by Microsoft's Java products runs better on Windows than on other operating systems. We don't intend to get into that debate—not in this book, certainly! But we have noted that many of the object classes provided in the Visual J++ implementation are oriented toward Windows support (for example, the Windows Foundation Classes, or WFC, are given more prominence in the documentation than the Java Swing classes, which we were unable to locate at all). Also, we note that Visual J++'s data-oriented classes tend to encourage the use of OLE DB and ActiveX Data Objects (ADO), which is probably to be expected—after all, the other products are certainly more closely oriented to their vendors' other technologies than to competing vendors' products!

Since we've already shown you one sample application in some detail (the employee lookup application in our PowerJ discussion), including modifying it to use JDBC in addition to the data-aware and data-oriented components, and we've shown how embedded SQL can be added to Java code in another example (the feedback applet in the JDeveloper discussion), we won't go into as much detail in this section discussing Visual J++. After all, Visual J++ does not support the SQL/OLB facility to embed SQL statements in your Java code—unlike PowerJ, Visual J++ is unlikely to ever include this capability—and Visual J++ does support JDBC just as well as the other products. Therefore, it would be difficult to demonstrate anything especially new that is directly related to the subject of this book. (We could, if we chose, demonstrate plenty of Microsoft-specific features, but there are better resources for you to use to learn that material.)

Instead, we jump straight to the identification of those data-related components available on Visual J++'s palettes. Table 11.3 contains this information.

There are several other data-oriented components that we do not show in Table 11.3 because they are so specialized for Microsoft Windows environments. These components include a largish set of components designed for use strictly with ADO, some directed as Microsoft's Index Server, some used with Microsoft Message Queue products, and so

Control name	Control purpose
Data navigator	Allows the user to change the current record in a record set managed by an ADO
Data source	Provides data to another component; combines the capabilities of an ADO connection, an ADO command, and an ADO record set
Data binder	Creates and manages the bindings between the fields in a record set and the bindable properties of other WFC components; participates in causing updates to data to be reflected in the data source
Record set	Controls the flow of data from a data source, through a data binder, to the application and back
Record set navigation bar	Provides a set of buttons that the user can manipulate to move through the rows of a record set and to update those rows, if desired

TABLE 11.3 *Visual J++ data-oriented controls.*

forth. If you are concerned strictly with Windows applications, then Visual J++'s support for these other Microsoft technologies will be interesting to you, and you can learn more about them from the product documentation.

Like the other products, Visual J++ provides many object classes for you to use when building data-oriented applications, but you use those classes in conjunction with the components in Table 11.3 and the other data-aware components we haven't included.

11.4 Other Products

Among the other products in this genre that you might encounter are Borland's JBuilder, IBM's Visual Age for Java, Symantec's Visual Café, and Tek-Tools Kawa. Although we have no real experience with any of these products directly, we have managed to do enough research to give you some minimal information about their relationship to this book's subject matter.

First, we know that Oracle's JDeveloper is directly derived from Borland's JBuilder. In fact, Borland licensed the product to Oracle, who made fairly minor changes (largely to identify it as an Oracle product) and then added a number of additional object classes to support a number of additional visual components, mostly related to data management. We believe that most of what we said about JDeveloper—except anything specifically dealing with the new classes that Oracle provided—is appropriate for JBuilder, although we have not actually used Borland's product. Just to be clear: JBuilder does not include any explicit support for SQLJ Part 0 (SQL/OLB) capabilities.

We have had brief exposure to IBM's Visual Age for Java, but unfortunately have not had the opportunity to use the product. It appears to be (as we'd expect) closely related to IBM's other Visual Age suite of products, which may be an advantage if you have experience with those products. However, our initial impression is that IBM has put a lot of effort into making Visual Age for Java a powerful and versatile tool for building portable Java applications. Without experience of our own to report—or even reliable information from others who have used the product—we can only say that it seems like a tool worth investigating.

Symantec's Visual Café is a very popular product, judging from the number of places we see it advertised and the number of reviews that it has gotten. Its reviews have mostly been very positive, but we have neither used it ourselves nor heard firsthand reports from experienced Java programmers who have used it. This product comes in several configurations, including a packaging intended for "enterprise application development" and one intended for personal use. We suspect that the personal use package has been more widely sold, as our experience suggests that corporate developers seem to use PowerJ, JDeveloper, Visual J++, and JBuilder more often.

In addition, we have had no exposure at all to Tek-Tools Kawa, but have recently seen positive reviews of the product in several trade journals. Without either direct or indirect experience, however, it is impossible for us to evaluate its capabilities or popularity.

We've also heard about—but have had no experience at all with—some "pure Java" tools that you might wish to investigate if you're pursuing application development using integrated development environments. These include the following:

- JDesignerPro, a product made by BulletProof Corporation, which contains some database support, some of it in the form of an "SQL wizard" and some in the form of JDBC facilities.
- NetBeans Developer, by NetBeans, Inc., which appears to support the creation of Enterprise Java Beans from database tables, although we have no details on the product features that you'd use to accomplish this.
- Java Workshop, published by Sun Microsystems themselves, but it is unclear to us whether any database-specific support (beyond JDBC access, that is) is provided.

All of these products provide an interactive development environment capability and run on Windows NT, UNIX, and other platforms.

11.5 Chapter Summary

In this chapter, we've given you an overview of several products that are used to develop Java applications in an interactive development environment. We concentrated on the relationship between these products and the facilities they provide for accessing databases, particularly SQL databases. We illustrated how you might use these products along with the skills you're developing (from reading this book, of course!) in using JDBC and SQL/OLB, as well as summarizing the data-related components they provide for performing database operations without explicit coding on your part.

CHAPTER

12

Future Developments and Standards Processing

12.1 Introduction

We've covered a lot of ground in this book so far. We've introduced the subject of using Java and SQL together, we've provided summaries of each language (principally for the benefit of readers who are familiar with one but not the other), we've examined the three parts of SQLJ—and the corresponding standards—in detail, we've given you a fairly close look at SQL:1999's user-defined types and its underlying object model, and we've talked about Java Blend, Sun's approach to putting a Java-flavored topping on SQL databases.

But, considering the technologies involved—Java itself, the Internet and World Wide Web—the situation as we've shown it is unlikely to remain static. In fact, we are confident that new developments will arise between the time we finish writing this book and the time that you are reading it. We're all living life in "Web time" and things change ever more rapidly. Because of that, we believe that we owe it to you to dust off the old crystal ball and give you our thoughts on where the technology is headed, both in the short term (a year or so from publication) and the longer term (up to five years).

Obviously (to us, probably more so to you), we can't see into the future with any real clarity. What we say in this chapter is based on our experience in this fast-moving industry and on talks we've had with some of the "movers and shakers" who are making it all happen. Naturally, we have a higher degree of confidence in our short-term observations than in the longer-term ones, if only because the development efforts related to the shorter time frame are already under way, whereas those required for the more distant future are probably not even fully thought out yet.

In spite of all the risk and uncertainty, we're willing to go out on the proverbial limb to try to give you a peek at the future. You are naturally free to influence that future yourself, which we encourage you to do—by purchasing products that best meet your needs and even by participating in the development of the technologies that will emerge over the next few years (we certainly plan to be a part of it).

Additionally, it is in this chapter that we summarize the de jure standards processing of Java, JDBC, and the various aspects of SQLJ technology. You probably won't be surprised to learn that these specifications are traveling several different paths toward their destinies. We'll try to make it as clear as possible what has already happened and what we expect to happen in this area.

12.2 Starting the New Millennium

The group of people who started getting together back in early 1997 to develop a specification for embedding SQL statements in Java programs continues to meet about once a month, in addition to exchanging ideas and proposals through frequent email. Although (as we told you earlier in this book) this group of experts, who call themselves "the SQLJ group," have never formally constituted themselves into a consortium—mostly because of the legal, financial, and administrative overhead involved—they have the support of the companies for whom they work. Because of this support, along with the fact that they are quite productive and contribute something rather important to the industry, we believe that they will continue to work on the issues of using SQL and Java together for some time to come.

In fact, as this chapter is being written, the group is putting together a new Web site (*www.sqlj.org*) and getting even more organized about the documents—including both the proposals and the specifications—they produce. Furthermore, the membership of the group remains pretty constant, although we note that new participants occasionally show up and become active.

In the short term—that is, roughly during the remainder of 2000, the SQLJ group will be completing the publication of the second part of the two-part SQLJ standard. "Completing" is likely to involve little more than the following:

- Careful review of the features in the specifications for completeness and possible errors.

- Editorial cleanup, mostly to ensure clarity and lack of ambiguity.
- Technical alignment with what most vendors have committed to implement.

We don't believe that major new technical features are likely to be added to any of the SQLJ specifications in the next year or two.

Later in this chapter, we'll talk about the standardization process itself. For the purposes of the present discussion, it's sufficient to say that the SQLJ group intends to be foremost in driving the standardization of the specifications it develops. Since the bulk of the worldwide expertise in these technologies is made up of people in the group, that seems like a reasonable thing to do. Of course, that doesn't imply that nobody else will be participating—far from it! But we would be quite surprised if major developments in this area happened over the next year or two without significant participation from the SQLJ membership.

By the way, if you or your organization has an active interest in participating in the ongoing evolution of these specifications and standards, you can find contact information at the group's Web site that will allow you to make an informed decision about joining the group and attending its meetings.

Another shorter-term task involves enhancements to SQLJ Part 0 (SQL embedded in Java). Part of this job—alignment of the new ANSI X3.135.10-1998, known as SQL/OLB (or Object Language Bindings) with SQL:1999—is already under way. You'll see more about this in Section 12.4, but it's worth mentioning here that the international community has begun to consider adopting SQL/OLB as a new part of the ISO SQL standard, with the provision that it be oriented toward SQL:1999 instead of SQL-92.

The ANSI standard for SQL/OLB that was approved late in 1998 was oriented toward SQL-92 for a very pragmatic reason: Everybody involved wanted to ensure that the standard would be widely implemented and used without having to wait for vendors to complete implementation of a new version of the SQL standard. In fact, OLB-98, as we sometimes call it, depends only on the most widely implemented features of SQL-92, those specified in the Entry SQL level of that standard and those features beyond Entry SQL that are commonly implemented by at least several SQL vendors.

However, the ISO group responsible for the international standard for SQL made the decision not to merely rubber stamp the ANSI OLB-98 standard, but to progress a significant revision that supports—and takes advantage of—some new technical features in SQL:1999. Obviously, the SQL vendors will not implement SQL:1999 immediately. In fact, the Core SQL conformance criteria are significant enough that most vendors are not expected to conform until late 2000 or early 2001. Only then will it become clear what SQL:1999 features are also going to be widely implemented (and widely required by application developers).

Instead of waiting for SQL:1999 to be widely implemented, the SQLJ group hopes to rapidly revise OLB-98 to align with the newly published revision of the JDBC API specification, JDBC 2.0, and just those SQL:1999 features that are required for the JDBC 2.0 alignment. This work should be complete by mid-2000, and we believe it's possible that an ISO publication of SQL/OLB aligned with JDBC 2.0 could be published as an international standard in late 2000.

Many participants in standardization activities (including SQL and SQLJ standardization) have noted that, without any testing and branding facilities, it's difficult for a customer—or, indeed, a vendor—to know whether a product *really* conforms to a standard or not. The SQLJ group started work in 1999 to identify a mechanism by which a test suite can be developed (almost certainly seeded by tests contributed from SQLJ participants) and a testing agency identified. Whether such a testing agency must, or will, be a body that is independent from the SQLJ participants, or whether it might be the SQLJ group itself, is a question that as of yet has not been completed. Nonetheless, we are confident that some form of testing capability—even if it means self-certification—will emerge.

12.3 The More Distant Future

As the timeline lengthens toward the year 2010, our vision (naturally) gets somewhat dimmer. That limitation doesn't change our belief that the SQLJ group will continue to develop specifications, but it does make it more difficult to predict even approximately what the results will be. However, one task is clearly going to occupy a significant fraction of the SQLJ group's time: complete alignment of all of the SQLJ specifications with SQL:1999.

At the end of the preceding section, we told you that SQLJ Part 0, standardized as SQL/OLB, should be republished as part 10 of the ISO SQL standard in 2000, enhanced to align with the recent revision to the JDBC specification. In the longer term, we expect SQL/OLB to be revised and extended to be aligned with quite a bit more of SQL:1999, including (but not limited to) all of the Core SQL conformance criteria.

From Chapters 3 and 7, you will be aware that SQL:1999 adds support for object orientation to the SQL standard's capabilities. Some of the work involved in evolving SQL/OLB will be related to SQL:1999's object capabilities, but not a lot of it. However, alignment of the two parts of the new SQLJ standard, NCITS 331, will be more significantly affected by those capabilities.

We expect the SQLJ group to spend significant amounts of time discussing and building additional language features that align better with SQL:1999. This includes both parts of the SQLJ standard (Part 1, *SQL Routines Using the Java™ Programming Language,* and Part 2, *SQL Types Using the Java™ Programming Language*). The first version of those two parts were (unlike the SQL/OLB specification) not limited to strictly SQL-92 alignment; for example, NCITS 331.2 (that is, part 2) includes syntax explicitly designed to align with SQL:1999's user-defined type facilities. However, much more can be done to make it easier for application writers to seamlessly move between the two ways—SQL structured types and Java classes—of dealing with specialized types for applications.

We have also begun to see signs that Sun Microsystems may finally be ready to submit its dynamic Java interface specification, JDBC, to a more public forum (such as the Java Community Process being set up for maintenance of the Java specifications) for maintenance, enhancement, and standardization. The SQLJ group is certainly a strong candidate for taking over this specification, should Sun decide to take this step. We don't believe that the SQLJ group, should it be selected by Sun as the appropriate vehicle for JDBC maintenance, would make dramatic changes to the specification. Still, issues have arisen every now and then to which a solution would be enhancements to JDBC, so it's possible that new versions of that interface may in the future be published as a de jure standard after development by the SQLJ group. Whether this formal standardization will be undertaken through ANSI, ISO, or both is, of course, far from clear at this time.

One thing is, however, quite clear: The individuals and companies involved in progressing de facto and de jure standards involving the use of SQL and Java together are all committed to the principle of application portability, including the Java notion of "write once, run anywhere." Perhaps this goal will not always be achieved completely, but we're confident that the specifications will come quite close even if they don't get all the way there.

12.4 Standards Processing of Java, JDBC, and SQLJ Technologies

The technology we've discussed in this book—including JDBC and SQLJ, and other issues associated with Java, especially in conjunction with SQL—is proving to be extraordinarily important to a very wide variety of commercial interests. As you are no doubt vividly aware, organizations all over the world have begun using these technologies to implement Web applications, including e-commerce and all the other "e-words," in addition to other more pedestrian applications.

Nothing gives a CIO or IT manager heartburn more quickly than a rumor that the supplier of a critical technology is going bankrupt, being acquired by a competitor, or refocusing on some different strategy. Nobody likes being abandoned, but it's especially painful when your business is at stake! You've probably experienced the fear and loathing of cancelled products, projects that are never completed, and even infrastructure technology that has fallen by the wayside. And, of course, you've faced situations where manufacturers and software publishers have changed their standards and formats without asking how *you* will be affected (many of us recall—not very fondly—the change from Microsoft's Word 95 storage format to its Word 97 format).

Well, to use a cliché, change happens. Nothing you or we can do will ever stop the forces of change or insulate you from its effects—including having your critical technologies become orphaned or radically altered by their creators. But there is hope!

When a technology has become a standard, whether it is merely a de facto standard or a full-fledged de jure standard, it becomes a little more dependable and stable. It's somewhat less subject to the whims of a single owner, and more vendors are willing to undertake the sometimes substantial risks of using the technology in their products. Obviously, standards come and go, and not every standard is worth the paper it takes to print it. Some very carefully and publicly developed standards, such as the Ada programming language, haven't proved durable in actual use. If you developed a strategic dependency on such standards, you weren't saved by the mere fact that they were not privately owned. Similarly, some very private specifications, like Visual Basic, have been around—although significantly enhanced—for years and show no signs of vanishing. Nonetheless, we believe that when all else is equal, it's an advantage when technologies you care about most are standards that can be widely implemented by many suppliers.

Java

When Sun Microsystems released the specifications for its Java programming language, (most of) the programming world was thrilled: Here, at last, was a language that promised to be very widely implemented, safe and secure even in network environments, truly object oriented, and *universally portable* (whatever that means). The parade was rained on in very short order, though, when other vendors started changing, enhancing, and otherwise "messing with" the specifications. Microsoft, for one, released extensions to Java in support of its Windows environment, resulting in lawsuits, industry confusion, and general unpleasantness. Many feared that Java would never deliver on its promise, in part because it was far from clear how the language would evolve—would it be forever controlled by its single-corporation owner, or would the larger community have a meaningful say in its destiny?

In response to those concerns, Sun applied to ISO (the International Organization for Standardization) in 1997 for the right to submit its specifications to be balloted as international standards. After a somewhat fierce debate, both within the United States and internationally, Sun was given the status of "PAS submitter" (a PAS is a publicly available specification). With this status, Sun was then able to submit its Java specifications to ISO for a single ballot, called a fast-track ballot. If the result of that ballot, voted on by all national bodies that are members of Joint Technical Committee 1 of ISO and IEC (International Electrotechnical Commission), were to have been successful, then the Java specification would have immediately become an international standard. However, Sun decided not to submit Java for this fast-track ballot. Instead, Sun negotiated with ECMA (formerly the European Computer Manufacturer's Association) to submit Java to its TC41 for standards processing. Once (if?) that happens, then ECMA may be able to submit its Java standard to ISO for fast-track processing. Time will tell . . .

That last paragraph undoubtedly raised a few questions in your minds, such as "What are all these committees?" and "Exactly what steps are involved?"—so we've prepared the diagram in Figure 12.1 to illustrate the structure of the relevant parts of ISO and the flowchart in Figure 12.2 to show you the steps that Java is expected to follow to formal standardization.

In Figure 12.1, it's apparent that Joint Technical Committee 1 answers to two "masters." Although IEC is a *joint* parent of JTC 1, in practice it is usually ISO whose administration governs JTC 1's operations. JTC 1 has a number of subcommittees, currently about 20, with responsibilities ranging from developing a glossary of terms used in information technology through formats used to record data on hard drives to networking, programming languages, and database access. Many subcommittees further partition their work among various working groups. SC 32, Data Management and Interchange, contains five working groups (WG 3 is responsible for the SQL standard) and two rapporteur groups (which are less formal than WGs and are groups of experts that are supposed to reach *rapport* on some technical subject).

If and when Sun submits Java to ECMA for processing, and when (and if) ECMA submits Java to ISO for formal standards processing, the ISO fast-track ballot will be initiated and handled by JTC 1, not (as some might expect) by JTC 1/SC 22, Programming Languages. It was once widely anticipated that the standard that would result from a successful ballot would be assigned to JTC 1/SC 22 for maintenance—in fact, SC 22 has created a new Java-oriented WG in anticipation of that possibility. However, that no longer seems likely; instead, Java will probably continue to be developed by Sun using its Java Community Process.

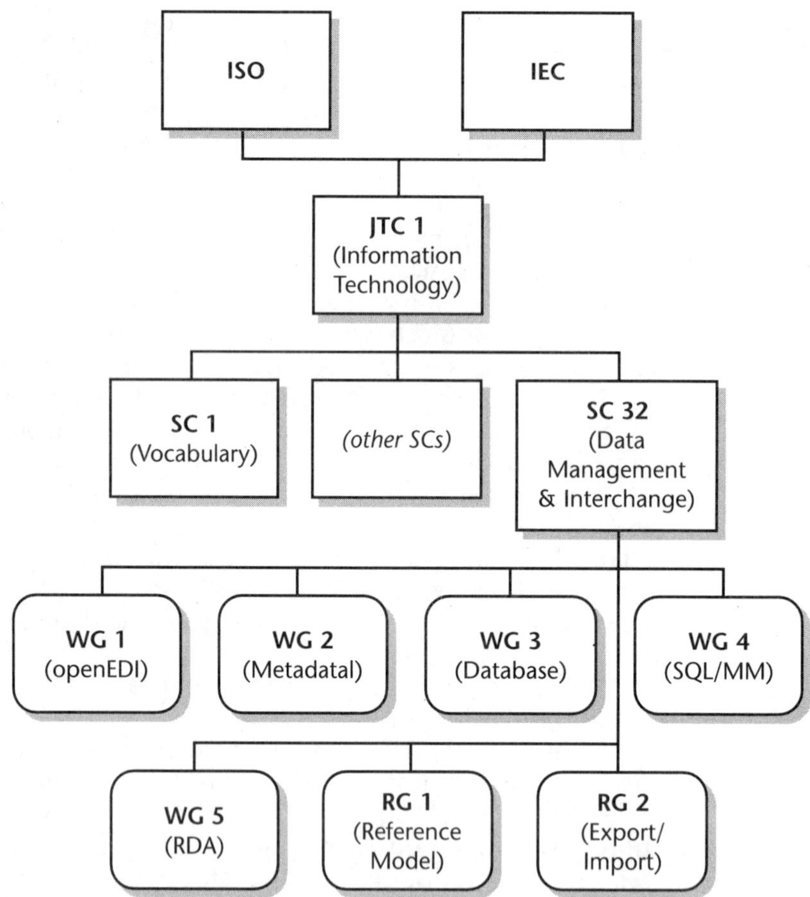

FIGURE 12.1 *Structure of ISO.*

Figure 12.2 outlines the major steps that Java will follow after Sun submits it for standardization. We're inclined to believe that the ballot will be successful, possibly with minor editing. However, it's possible that major problems will be identified during the ballot; if that happens, then Sun—as the submitter of the PAS—can choose whether to withdraw its submission (possibly reworking it privately and resubmitting it later) or release it to JTC 1 for "normal processing." We cannot imagine that Sun would choose the latter alternative; something as valuable as the right to develop the Java specification will certainly be kept by Sun.

JDBC

And that idea brings up the question of JDBC standardization! JDBC, as you know from reading earlier chapters in this book, is the de facto

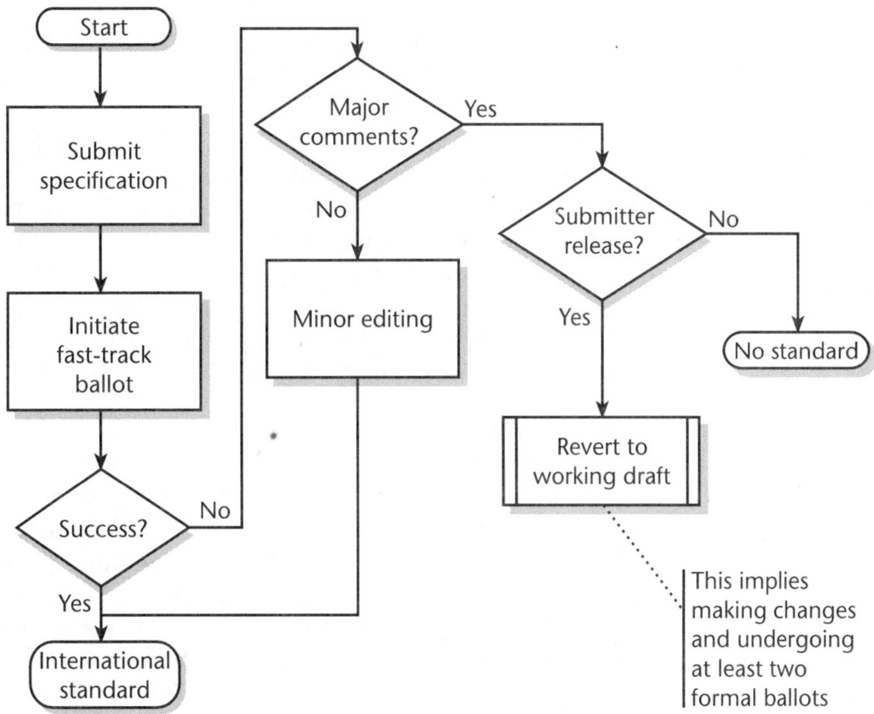

FIGURE 12.2 *Java standardization steps.*

standard for accessing relational database systems from Java programs. A very reasonable question to ask is: Will Sun ever seek de jure standardization for JDBC?

Although we won't say "never," we do know that Sun has been asked this question a number of times and its answer has always been "Not yet." We are uncertain whether that means that Sun will be willing to submit JDBC to some formal standards body once it has reached a certain development milestone, or if it merely wishes to wait until it sees how the Java specification's submission works out before releasing yet another document into the jaws of the standards community.

As we said in Section 12.3, we've recently heard Sun employees suggest that they may be willing to consider turning maintenance and enhancement of JDBC over to some industry group, such as SQLJ. Doing so would at least provide the status of a more public forum, removing some concerns related to proprietary standards. Whether Sun would also permit SQLJ, or whatever other group is selected, to submit JDBC for de jure standardization is another question, but we're inclined to believe that it would be allowed under the right circumstances.

SQLJ

You've read several times in this book that the three specifications being developed by the SQLJ group are being progressed as formal standards. However, they are not all done using the same mechanisms. The reason for using multiple approaches is a little obscure, but we can characterize it as an issue of timing and resource availability.

SQLJ Part 0, as you know by now, specifies ways in which you can write binary-portable applications in Java with embedded SQL statements—applications that will work on any SQL database system that provides the SQLJ Part 0 components. We've already said that SQLJ Part 0 has been published in the United States as part 10 of the SQL standard (ANSI X3.135.10-1998) and that it has also been submitted to ISO for balloting.

Figure 12.3 illustrates the steps that were taken to turn SQLJ Part 0 into part 10 of the ANSI SQL standard, and Figure 12.4 shows the steps that are required in the ISO process to accomplish the same goal.

What's not apparent from Figure 12.3 and Figure 12.4 is the fact that the ANSI process tends to slow down toward the end because the public review (or reviews) aren't held until after all development has occurred. By contrast, the ISO process permits document changes to be made as a result of all CD (committee draft) and FCD (final committee draft) ballots, but does not permit changes to the very last ballot (FDIS—final draft international standard). This fact makes it a bit cumbersome to progress an ANSI and an ISO standard simultaneously, especially when coupled with the fact that ANSI technical committees frequently meet six times per year, whereas ISO WGs rarely meet more than two or three times a year.

As mentioned earlier in this chapter, SQLJ Part 0 has already been published as a de jure standard in the United States but is still wending its way through the ISO process. In fact, by the time you read these words, it's possible that the ISO document will be well on its way toward publication, after having been aligned with the JDBC 2.0 specifications.

That leaves us with SQLJ Parts 1 and 2 to cover. Because of several factors (expertise residing primarily in the SQLJ group, the ANSI Technical Committee H2, Database, being fully occupied with completing SQL:1999, and so forth), the SQLJ group requested that NCITS permit it to submit these two specifications for a fast-track ballot to become an American national standard. NCITS granted that permission, and you can follow the process that each part has to take in Figure 12.5.

In Figure 12.5, you'll see a box that contains the phrase "BSR number"; that's a number assigned by the NCITS Board of Standards Review that, assuming the document is eventually approved as an American national standard, becomes the number of the standard itself. In the

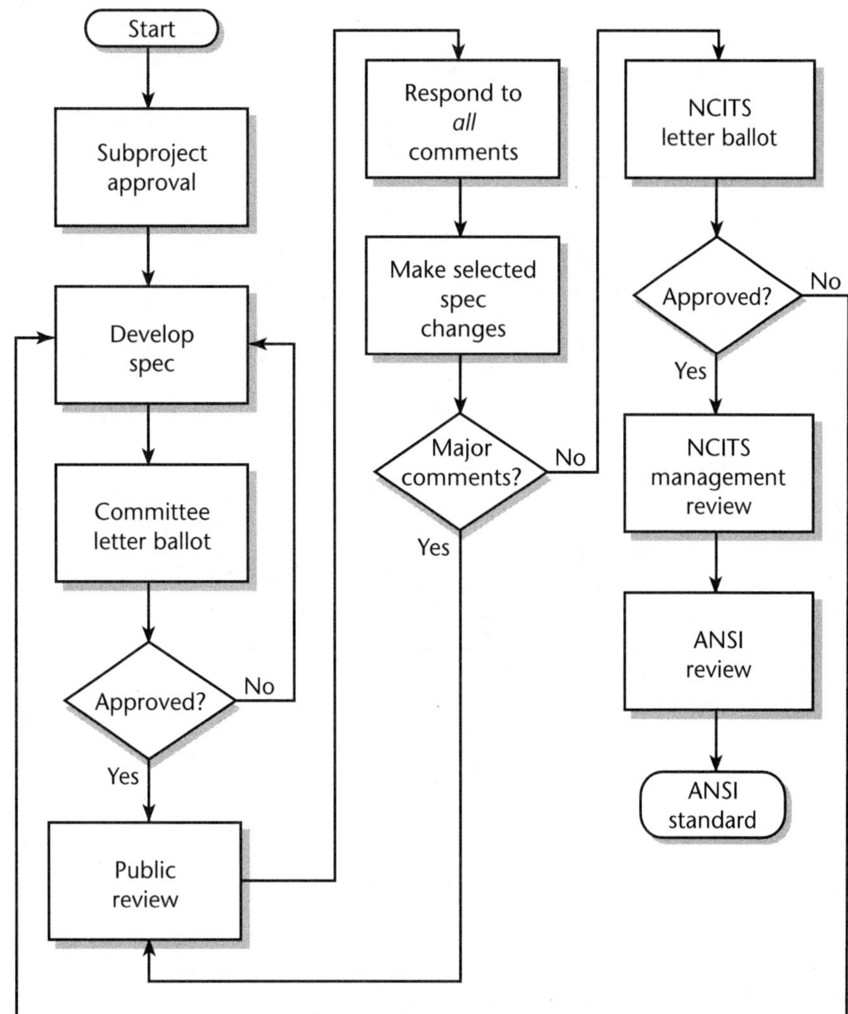

FIGURE 12.3 *ANSI progression using normal processing.*

case of SQLJ Parts 1 and 2, the BSR number assigned is NCITS 311, so part 1 is officially ANSI NCITS 331.1-1999. Part 2, when published, will be ANSI NCITS 331.2-*yyyy* (where *yyyy* is the year of publication).

SQLJ Part 2 had not been submitted for fast-track processing at the time we completed writing this book but is expected to be submitted some time early in 2000 and may already have become a standard by the time you're reading this book.

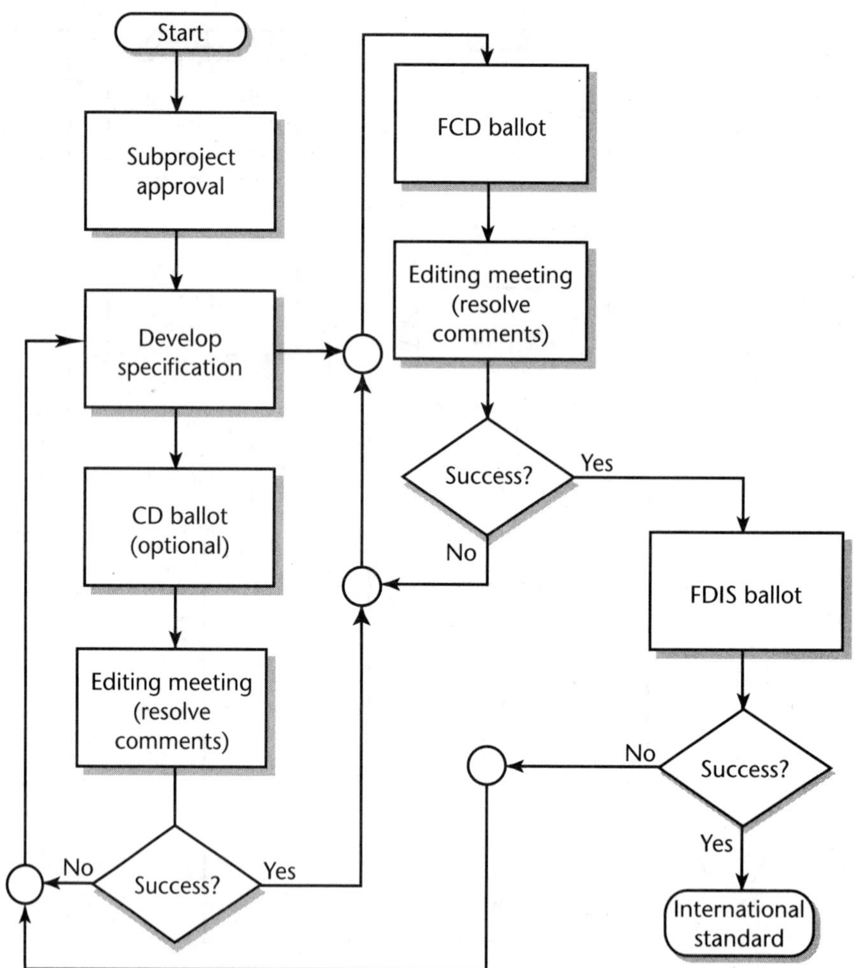

FIGURE 12.4 *ISO progression using normal processing.*

The obvious next question is "Will ANSI NCITS 331 ever become an ISO standard?" and, frankly, we don't know the answer to that one. There is certainly interest in the international standards community to adopt that technology. One possibility is for ANSI to submit both parts of ANSI NCITS 331 for an ISO fast-track, analogous to the path that Java is taking (ANSI, like any other National Body, is an approved submitter of documents for fast-track processing). Another possibility is for some ISO group—probably JTC 1/SC 32—to independently progress a new standard identical to, or very closely related to, the ANSI standard; this option has the disadvantage of requiring a new project ballot to be

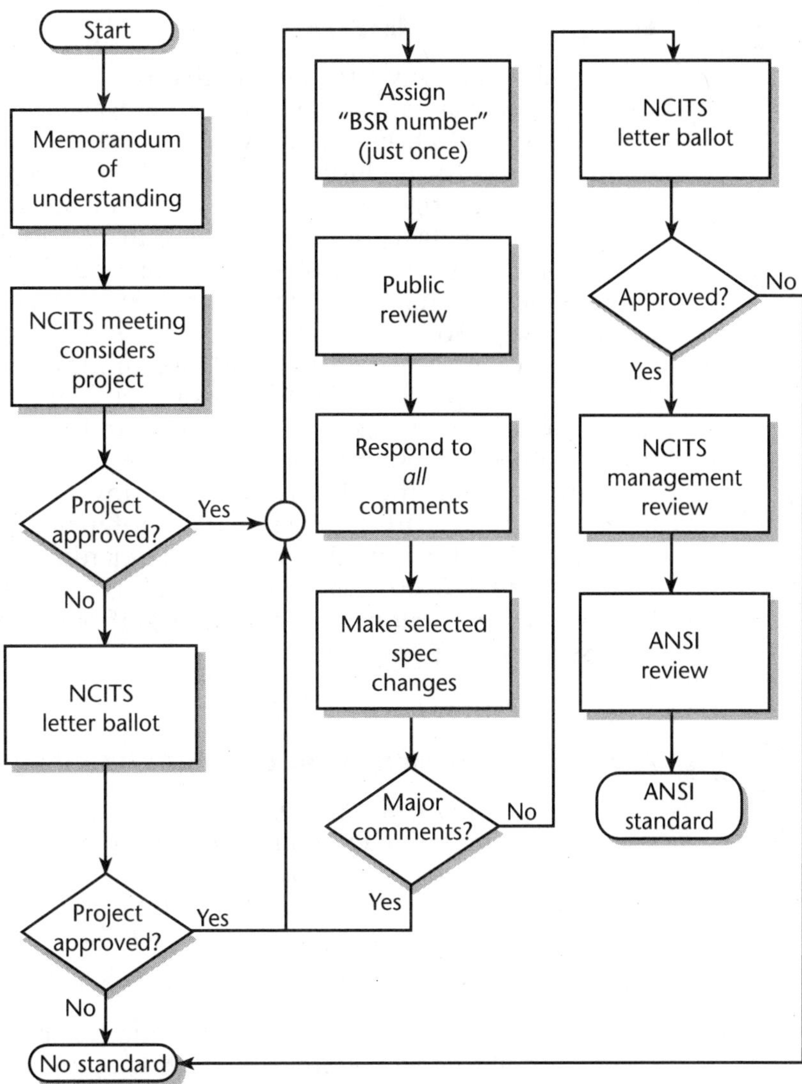

FIGURE 12.5 *NCITS fast-track processing.*

conducted at the JTC 1 level. Still another possibility that we've heard discussed is creation of yet two more parts to the SQL standard and adoption of the SQLJ documents for those two new parts of SQL. It's far from clear which of these would be the most appropriate, but we suspect that there *will* be ISO standards corresponding to the two SQLJ parts that ended up as ANSI NCITS 331.

12.5 Less Formal Standardization

We certainly do not want to imply that the only standards—much less the only *good* standards—are those promulgated through some de jure standards organization such as ANSI or ISO. Far from it! In fact, many useful standards—including many standards that really matter the most—have never gone through de jure standardization; instead, they have become de facto standards, sometimes through the efforts of a less formal group (such as the SQLJ group or X/Open—now The Open Group) and sometimes through the actions of a single company, such as Sun or Microsoft.

Sun's decision to give the broader community the ability to influence the development of Java and its various components through the Java Community Process (JCP) is proving to be an extremely effective way to gather the resources necessary to create a real, meaningful standard and to avoid the pitfalls of attempting to do so within a single organization. We think it's especially noteworthy that Java Blend's object/relational mappings are being standardized through the JCP (a group called JSR-000012 Java Data Objects is responsible for this work). We endorse these efforts but still find significant value in more formal processes where appropriate.

12.6 Acceptance, Implementation, and Wide Use

We're certainly not the first to observe that today's world economy seems to ensure rapid acceptance of almost everything claiming to be Web-oriented. Stock offerings of companies founded to do business on, or with, or associated with the World Wide Web virtually explode as investors clamor to acquire new issues. New products designed to exploit the Web, or to make it easier for enterprises to do so, are guaranteed to attract interest.

One of the primary factors in Java's rapid rise is its focus on Web-oriented applications. Certainly, the ability to use Java and SQL together will only amplify that success, if only because e-commerce demands the ability to make information resident in databases available to Web applications and customers. Consequently, the pace of developments in technologies such as JDBC and SQLJ continues to be astonishing. We find it difficult to be sure we're always up to date, even though we're active participants!

Although Java was first designed (in 1991, under the name "Oak") as part of a Sun Microsystems research project related to development of software for consumer electronics such as home appliances (stoves, refrigerators) and entertainment systems (televisions, stereos), it didn't start receiving wide attention until late 1994 and early 1995, when Sun introduced the HotJava Web browser. HotJava supplied the first vehicle for downloading and executing platform-independent applications, called *applets,* from the Web. The rest is history-in-the-making. Thus, in a very few years, Java went from virtually unknown in the computer industry to one of the more important programming languages in our toolboxes today.

Similarly, JDBC was designed—very quickly—in early 1996. Without a Java-oriented interface to SQL database systems, Java applications would have to depend on existing non–object-oriented, less secure interfaces such as ODBC (Open Database Connectivity). However, the advantages of JDBC's inherent Java nature brought it instantly into the consciousnesses of Java programmers. In only a couple of years, JDBC became *the* accepted interface for accessing databases from Java code.

Less than a year after JDBC was published, a group of experts from several relational database companies came together in an effort to define a specification permitting the writing of embedded SQL statements in Java programs. This effort resulted in the specification now called SQLJ Part 0 (and SQL/OLB). This group, which you now know as the SQLJ group, concurrently wrote the two additional specifications known as SQLJ Part 1 and Part 2. One company whose experts participated in SQLJ from the beginning (Oracle Corporation) developed a "reference implementation" of SQLJ Part 0 and has put it into the public domain. Several other companies use that reference implementation as the foundation for their products that support SQL embedded in Java. We've included that reference implementation on the CD-ROM that came with this book.

It's difficult to estimate the rate at which the SQLJ and related technologies will be embraced by the vendor community—in part because that depends on estimating a more elusive variable: how rapidly the applications development community will demand their implementation. Still, even though the technology is relatively young, we know that several SQL vendors (for example, Oracle, Sybase, and IBM) are very committed to implementing and delivering some or all of the technologies we've described in this book before the end of the millennium. Some application developers will enthusiastically begin using those new product versions right away, but we suspect that the usual technology adoption curve will apply—there will be early adopters, but the large bulk of customers will wait a year or two to be sure that the products aren't dead ends.

We believe that there are at least two additional factors—besides the rapidity of vendor implementation—that will have a large influence on customer demand. The first is training. Until there are training courses in place to teach users how to apply the technology and how to build functional systems using them, adoption will necessarily be slow. In addition, significant toolsets are not yet available that application developers can use to build systems using the SQLJ technologies—even though the development tools do support JDBC already. It seems likely that the IDE (interactive development environment) tool builders will start to support the various SQLJ technologies fairly soon, after which users will get more exposure to them and will begin to at least experiment with their use.

In short, the progression of technology in this area is nothing short of staggering, and it shows no signs of letting up. Companies on both sides of the marketplace—vendors and implementors, as well as buyers and developers—are rapidly adopting Java, and Java and SQL together, as important components of their business strategies. JDBC continues to enjoy vigorous development and wide popularity, while the SQLJ-based technologies are attracting new implementations constantly and are being used in a great many corporations building Web-based application systems.

However, we do see signs of at least one factor that may temporarily slow down some of the absorption rates. Many organizations spent large fractions of their resources—financial and human—on resolving issues related to the Y2K problem. Happily, Java and SQL do not make that problem worse; in fact, the SQL standard has never supported datetime datatypes without four-digit year support—meaning, we suppose, that there is a Y10K problem, which bothers us only a little. Java's support of datetime is also not a contributor to the Y2K issue, although its support of dates (in class `java.util.Date`) centers its dates on 1900 instead of year 0, making all dates earlier than 1900 appear as negative values. Whether this diversion of attention will have as significant an effect on the growth of Java as it is predicted to have on some other aspects of the computer industry remains to be seen, but we're sure that any such impact will be short-lived.

12.7 Chapter Summary

In this rather short chapter, we've discussed the current and near-term activities of the SQLJ group, who we believe will continue to develop most (but probably not all) of the specifications related to using SQL and Java together. We've even pointed you to the Web site that the group has developed to help manage and promote the results of its work.

We've also outlined some of the major activities that we think may come along in the next few years related to this technology. But we must emphasize one fact: Things change very quickly in this business, and Java-related technologies change at least as fast as any other. Although we're moderately confident about the activities that we've suggested will take place over the next five years or so, we want to stress that it's possible—even probable—that things will go further and faster than we imagine today. But we don't think this technology is likely to be derailed and simply fail, certainly not in the next half-decade.

In the longer term—five to ten years—it's much more difficult to predict. Ten years ago, virtually nobody expected the Internet to become as important to worldwide business as it is today, and Java wasn't even a glimmer in your eye yet. We won't be surprised if 2005 brings changes just as dramatic, but we will be surprised if Java and SQL (and, for that matter, COBOL!) are no longer important to corporations large and small.

Finally, we gave a reasonably complete picture of how this technology relates to various standards activities in different forums.

12.8 A Final Word

We've been asked a number of times our opinion about the ultimate value of using Java and SQL together, particularly using Java data in SQL tables. In the words of one colleague,

> *Just as a random futures comment of my own, I've been telling people that when we get SQLJ Part 2 accepted, we will have met the marketplace need/definition of "object relational." The ability to use an object either inside or outside the DBMS and have it be the same object, with no impedance mismatch, will be (to coin a phrase) "way cool." I can't help but wonder whether or not [Jim and Andrew] agree.*

We do agree—the power that application developers will gain from being able to seamlessly exchange data between all components of their application systems will prove to be among the best aspects of Java. This certainly does not mean that there is no place in modern information systems for SQL/PSM (or one of the proprietary analogs) or for SQL:1999's structured types. But it does give Java users an incredibly powerful tool!

APPENDIX

A

Relevant Standards Bodies

A.1 Introduction

If you would like to acquire a copy of the ANSI SQL/OLB-98 standard, you can do so only through the American National Standards Institute, whose contact information is included in this appendix. The same is true of the standard for SQLJ Part 1 and the anticipated SQLJ Part 2 standard, as well as for all parts of the SQL standard. Of course, as these standards move through the ISO process and become international standards, you can acquire copies of them from your National Body.

In this appendix, we provide the names, addresses, telephone numbers, and (where available) fax numbers, email addresses, and even URLs of the Web pages for the national standards bodies for several countries. If we have omitted your country, we apologize; however, it is not feasible to list every country, so we've focussed on those countries that we believe are most likely to have interested readers.

Some countries have adopted the ISO standard and put their own standard number on it. However, this practice is not widespread and often lags publication of the ISO standard by as much as two or three years, so we haven't attempted to provide that data here.

The information we present here was current at the time of publication but is—as is so much technical information today—always subject to change.

A.2 Contacting ISO

You can contact ISO at this address:

- **International Organization for Standardization (ISO)**
  1, rue de Varembé
  Case postale 56
  CH-1211 Genève 20
  Switzerland
  Telephone: +41.22.749.0111
  Telefax: +41.22.733.3430
  Email: central@iso.ch
  WWW: *www.iso.ch*

A.3 Selected National Standards Bodies

- **Australia**
  Standards Australia (SAA)
  P.O. Box 1055
  Strathfield — N.S.W. 2135
  Telephone: +61.2.9746.4700
  Fax: +61.2.9746.8450
  Email: intsect@saa.sa.telememo.au
  WWW: *www.standards.com.au*
- **Canada**
  Standards Council of Canada (SCC)
  45 O'Connor Street, Suite 1200
  Ottawa, Ontario K1P 6N7
  Telephone: +1.613.238.3222
  Fax: +1.613.995.4564
  Email: info@scc.ca
  WWW: *www.scc.ca*
- **People's Republic of China**
  China State Bureau of Technical Supervision (CSBTS)
  P.O. Box 8010
  Beijing 100088
  Telephone: +86.10.6.203.2424
  Fax: +86.10.6.203.1010

- **Denmark**
  Dansk Standard
  Kollegievej 6
  DK-2920 Charlottenlund
  Telephone: +45.39.96.61.01
  Fax: +45.39.96.61.02
  Email: dansk.standard@ds.dk
  WWW: *www.ds.dk*
- **France**
  Association Française de Normalisation (AFNOR)
  Tour Europe
  F-92049 Paris La Défense Cedex
  Telephone: +33.1.42.91.55.55
  Fax: +33.1.42.91.56.56
  WWW: *www.afnor.fr*
- **Germany**
  Deutsches Institut für Normung (DIN)
  Burggrafenstrasse 6
  D-10772 Berlin
  Telephone: +49.30.26.01-0
  Fax: +49.30.2601.1231
  Email: postmaster@din.de
  WWW: *www.din.de*
- **Hungary**
  Magyar Szabványügyi Testület (MSZT)
  Üllöi út 25
  Pf. 24.
  H-1450 Budapest 9
  Telephone: +36.1.218.3011
  Fax: +36.1.218.5125
  Email: sze1545@helka.iif.hu
- **India**
  Bureau of Indian Standards (BIS)
  Manak Bhavan
  9 Bahadur Shah Zafar Marg
  New Delhi 110002
  Telephone: +91.11.323.7991
  Fax: +91.11.323.4062
  Email: bisind@del2.vsnl.net.in

- **Ireland**
  National Standards Authority of Ireland (NSAI)
  Glasnevin
  Dublin-9
  Telephone: +353.1.807.3800
  Fax: +353.1.807.3838
  Email: nsai@nsai.ie
  WWW: *www.nsai.ie*
- **Israel**
  Standards Institution of Israel (SII)
  42 Chaim Levanon Street
  Tel Aviv 69977
  Telephone: +972.3.646.5154
  Fax: +972.3.641.9683
  Email: standard@netvision.net.il
- **Italy**
  Ente Nazionale Italiano di Unificaziono (UNI)
  Via Battistotti Sassi 11/b
  I-20133 Milano
  Telephone: +39.2.70.02.41
  Fax: +39.2.70.10.61.06
  Email: webmaster@uni.unicei.it
  WWW: *www.unicei.it*
- **Japan**
  Japanese Industrial Standards Committee (JISC)
  c/o Standards Department
  Ministry of International Trade and Industry
  1-3-1, Kasumigaseki, Chiyoda-ku
  Tokyo 100
  Telephone: +81.3.3501.2096
  Fax: +81.3.3580.8637
  WWW: *www.hike.te.chiba-u.ac.jp/ikeda/JIS*
- **Republic of Korea**
  Korean National Institute of Technology and Quality (KNITQ)
  1599 Kwanyang-dong
  Dongan-ku, Anyang-city
  Kyonggi-do 430-060
  Telephone: +82.3.4384.1861
  Fax: +82.3.4384.6077

- **The Netherlands**
  Nederlands Normalisatie-instituut (NNI)
  Kalfjeslaan 2
  P.O. Box 5059
  NL-2600 GB Delft
  Telephone: +31.15.2.69.0390
  Fax: +31.15.2.69.0190
  WWW: *www.nni.nl*
- **Norway**
  Norges Standardiseringsforbund (NSF)
  Drammensveien 145 A
  Postboks 353 Skoyen
  N-0212 Oslo
  Telephone: +47.22.04.92.00
  Fax: +47.22.04.92.11
  Email: firmapost@nsf.telemax.no
  WWW: *www.standard.no*
- **Russian Federation**
  Committee of the Russian Federation for Standardization, Metrology and Certification (GOST R)
  Leninsky Prospekt 9
  Moskva 117049
  Telephone: +7.095.236.4044
  Fax: +7.095.237.6032
  Email: gosstandart@sovcust.sprint.com
- **Spain**
  Asociación Española de Normalización y Certificación (AENOR)
  Génova, 6
  E-28004 Madrid
  Telephone: +34.1.432.6000
  Fax: +34.1.310.4976
  WWW: *www.aenor.es*
- **Sweden**
  SIS—Standardiseringkommissionen i Sverige (SIS)
  Box 6455
  S-113 82 Stockholm
  Telephone: +46.8.610.3000
  Fax: +46.8.30.7757
  Email: info@sis.se
  WWW: *www.sis.se*

- **Switzerland**
  Swiss Association for Standardization (SNV)
  Mühlebachstrasse 54
  CH-8008 Zurich
  Telephone: +41.1.254.5454
  Fax: +41.1.254.5474
  Email: post@snv.snv.inet.ch
- **United Kingdom**
  British Standards Institute (BSI)
  389 Chiswick High Road
  GB-London W4 4AL
  Telephone: +44.181.996.9000
  Fax: +44.181.996.7400
  Email: info@bsi.org.uk
  WWW: *www.bsi.org.uk*
- **United States of America**
  American National Standards Institute (ANSI)
  11 West 42nd Street, 13th Floor
  New York, NY 10036
  Telephone: +1.212.642.4900
  Fax: +1.212.398.0023
  Email: info@ansi.org
  WWW: *www.ansi.org*

A.4 Purchasing Standards Electronically

When SQL:1999 finished its progression through the ISO and ANSI procedures, its five parts were annointed as international standards and endorsed as USA standards. Unlike all previous SQL standards, though, the parts of SQL:1999 are *not* available on paper from ISO or ANSI.

Instead, they are available only in electronic form, as PDF (Adobe Acrobat Portable Document Format) files. You can purchase them from the following two Web stores:

- American National Standards Institute (ANSI)
  webstore.ansi.org
- National Committee for Information Technology Standards (NCITS)
  www.cssinfo.com/ncitsgate.html

Both Web sites sell the parts of the ISO/IEC 9075:1999 for U.S. $20/part.

Additional Web sites in other countries may offer similar purchase capabilities, but we are not aware of any at the present time.

APPENDIX B

Database Schema Used in Our Example

B.1 Introduction

This appendix contains the database schema that we have used throughout the book. We have included sample data for each of the tables, but in most cases the sizes of the tables precluded our including them in their entirety. This schema and all of the data that we have used can be found on the CD-ROM included with this book.

B.2 The movies Table

```
CREATE TABLE movies (
   title              CHARACTER VARYING (100),
   director           CHARACTER VARYING (50),
   year_introduced    CHARACTER (4),
   runs               INTEGER,

   CONSTRAINT runs_range
      CHECK (runs BETWEEN 0 AND 480),

   CONSTRAINT movies_pk
      PRIMARY KEY (title)
   );
```

title	director	year_introduced	runs
A Fish Called Wanda	Charles Chrichton	1988	108
A Passage to India	David Lean	1984	163
A Room with a View	James Ivory	1986	117
Aanslag, De	Fons Rademakers	1986	144
Affliction	Paul Schrader	1997	113
Amadeus	Milos Forman	1984	158
An Officer and a Gentleman	Taylor Hackford	1982	122
Antonia	Marleen Garris	1995	102
Arthur	Steve Gordon	1981	117
As Good As It Gets	James L. Brooks	1997	138
.	.	.	.
.	.	.	.
.	.	.	.

B.3 The awards Table

```
CREATE TABLE awards (
    award           CHARACTER VARYING (20),
    person          CHARACTER VARYING (60),
    title           CHARACTER VARYING (100) REFERENCES movies,
    award_year      CHARACTER (4)
    );
```

award	person	title	award_year
Supporting Actor	Kevin Kline	A Fish Called Wanda	1988
Supporting Actress	Peggy Ashcroft	A Passage to India	1984
Writer	Ruth Prawer Jhabvala	A Room with a View	1986
Foreign Language	(null)	Aanslag, De	1986
Supporting Actor	James Coburn	Affliction	1998
Picture	(null)	Amadeus	1984
Director	Milos Forman	Amadeus	1984
Actor	F. Murray Abraham	Amadeus	1984
Writer	Peter Shaffer	Amadeus	1984
Supporting Actor	Louis Gossett Jr.	An Officer and a Gentleman	1982
Foreign Language	(null)	Antonia	1995
Supporting Actor	John Gielgud	Arthur	1981
Actor	Jack Nicholson	As Good As It Gets	1997
Actress	Helen Hunt	As Good As It Gets	1997
.	.	.	.
.	.	.	.
.	.	.	.

B.4 The votes Table

```
CREATE TABLE votes (
   title          CHARACTER VARYING (100) REFERENCES movies,
   voter          CHARACTER VARYING (10),
   vote           INTEGER
   );
```

title	voter	vote
A Fish Called Wanda	Andrew	7
A Fish Called Wanda	Jim	8
A Passage to India	Andrew	9
A Passage to India	Jim	8
A Room with a View	Andrew	6
A Room with a View	Jim	4
Affliction	Andrew	5
Amadeus	Andrew	10
Amadeus	Jim	7
An Officer and a Gentleman	Andrew	6
An Officer and a Gentleman	Jim	8
Arthur	Andrew	5
Arthur	Jim	5
.	.	.
.	.	.
.	.	.

B.5 The movies_in_stock Table

```
CREATE TABLE movies_in_stock (
   title             CHARACTER VARYING (100) REFERENCES movies,
   quantity          INTEGER,
   sale_price        DECIMAL(4,2),
   YearToDateSales   DECIMAL(6,2),

   CONSTRAINT stock_pk
      PRIMARY KEY (title)
   );
```

title	quantity	sale_price	YearToDateSales
Blazing Stewardesses	131	21.95	8942.85
Deep Impact	21	24.95	1247.50
Independence Day (ID4)	12	19.95	1995.00
Lost in Space	34	4.95	103.95
Mars Attacks!	17	17.95	2566.85
Plan 9 from Outer Space	9	10.00	680.00
Terminator 2: Judgment Day	42	12.95	3082.10
The Terminator	28	17.95	1310.35

B.6 The movie_stars Table

```
CREATE TABLE movie_stars (
   title             CHARACTER VARYING (100),
   star_first_name   CHARACTER VARYING (25),
   star_last_name    CHARACTER VARYING (25),

   CONSTRAINT movie_stars_pk
      PRIMARY KEY (title, star_first_name, star_last_name),

   CONSTAINT movie_star_movies_fk
      FOREIGN KEY (title)
         REFERENCES movies
   );
```

title	star_first_name	star_last_name
Conan the Barbarian	Arnold	Schwartzenegger
Conan the Destroyer	Arnold	Schwartzenegger
Deep Impact	Elijah	Wood
Deep Impact	Morgan	Freeman
Deep Impact	Robert	Duvall
Deep Impact	Téa	Leoni
Deep Impact	Vanessa	Redgrave
Eraser	Arnold	Schwartzenegger
Independence Day (ID4)	Bill	Pullman
Independence Day (ID4)	Jeff	Goldblum
Independence Day (ID4)	Judd	Hirsch
Independence Day (ID4)	Will	Smith
.	.	.
.	.	.
.	.	.

Movie and Vote Classes

C.1 Introduction

This appendix contains the `Movie`, `Vote`, and `VoteOutOfRange` classes that were developed piecemeal in Chapter 6 and Chapter 8. The comments that introduce the variables and methods may seem verbose. They are structured comments used by the `javadoc` tool to generate HTML documentation for these classes.

C.2 The `Movie` Class

```
package Cinema;

import java.util.*;
import java.io.*;
import java.sql.*;

/**
 * This class represents a movie object. It allows votes to
 * be registered, which are used in the ordering of movies
 * to one another.
 *
 * @author   Andrew Eisenberg
 * @version  1.0
 * @since    JDK 1.1.6
 */
```

```
public class Movie implements java.io.Serializable {

   public String                      title;
   public int                         length;
   public String                      description;

   private Hashtable                  votes = new Hashtable ();


   /**
    * Constructor for a Movie
    *
    * @param  title          The title of the movie.
    * @param  length         The length of the movie in minutes.
    * @param  description    A brief description of the movie.
    */

   public Movie (String title, int length, String description) {
      this.title = title;
      this.length = length;
      this.description = description;
   }

   /**
    * Clear the votes that have been cast for a movie.
    *
    */

   public void clearVotes() {
      votes.clear();
   }

   /**
    * Clear the votes that have been cast for a movie.
    *
    * @return    The average of the votes received, 0 if no votes
    *            have been received.
    */

   public int clearVotes2() {
      int r;
```

```
      r = this.tallyVote();
      this.clearVotes();

      return r;
   }

   /**
    * Register a vote for a movie.
    * A voter may vote more than once, but only the most recent
    * vote counts.
    *
    * @param   whoVotes    The name of the voter.
    * @param   vote        The vote itself.
    */

   public void addVote (String whoVotes, Vote vote) {
      votes.put (whoVotes, vote);
   }

   /**
    * Tally the votes that have been received.
    *
    * @return   The average of the votes received, 0 if no votes
    *           have been received.
    */

   public int tallyVote () {
      Enumeration values;
      Vote                currentVote;
      int                 valuesTotal = 0;
      int                 valuesCount = 0;

      if (votes.size () == 0)
         return 0;

      values = votes.elements ();

      try {
         while (true) {
            currentVote = (Vote) values.nextElement ();
            valuesTotal += currentVote.getValue ();
            valuesCount++;
         }
      }
```

```
      catch (NoSuchElementException e) {
         return (int) (valuesTotal / valuesCount) ;
      }
   }

   /**
    * Produce a string representation of this Movie.
    *
    * @return   The string representation.
    */

   public String toString () {
      return "\"" + title + "\""
             + ((length == 0) ? "" : (", " + length + " minutes"));
   }

   /**
    * Compare two movies based on their respective tallies.
    *
    * @return    <code>-1</code> for less than,
    *            <code>0</code> for equal to, and
    *            <code>+1</code> for greater than.
    *
    */

   public int compareTo (Movie comparand) {
      int tally1 = this.tallyVote ();
      int tally2 = comparand.tallyVote ();

      if (tally1 < tally2)
         return -1;
      else if (tally1 > tally2)
         return 1;
      else if (this.votes.size () < comparand.votes.size ())
         return -1;
      else if (this.votes.size () > comparand.votes.size ())
         return 1;
      else return 0;
   }
```

```
/**
 * Produce a string of stars, reflecting a 1-10 rating.
 *
 * @param    rating     The rating for a film.
 * @return   A string, with between 1 and 10 stars.
 *
 */

public static String stars2 (int rating) {
   String result = "";

   while (rating-- > 0) {
      result += "*";
   }

   return result;
}

/**
 * Produce a string of stars, reflecting a 1-10 rating.
 *
 * @param    rating     The rating for a film.
 * @return   A string, with between 1 and 10 stars.
 *           A null rating will return an empty string
 *
 */

public static String stars2 (Integer rating) {
   String result = "";
   int r;

   if (rating != null) {
      r = rating.intValue();
      while (r-- > 0) {
         result += "*";
      }
   }

   return result;
}
```

```
/**
 * Produce a string of stars, reflecting a 1-10 rating.
 *
 * @param    rating     The rating for a film.
 * @param    result     The 0th element of this array will
 *                      contain the string of stars
 *
 */

public static void toStarsProc2 (int rating, String[] result) {
   String s = "";

   while (rating-- > 0) {
      s += "*";
   }

   result[0] = s;
}

/**
 * Produce a string of stars, reflecting a 1-10 rating.
 *
 * @param    io         The 0th element of this array should
 *                      contain a 1-10 rating. Upon
 *                      completion, the 0th element will
 *                      contain the string of stars.
 *
 */

public static void toStarsProc2 (String[] io)
   throws NumberFormatException {

   String s = "";
   int rating = Integer.parseInt(io[0]);

   while (rating-- > 0) {
      s += "*";
   }

   io[0] = s;
}
```

```
   /**
    * Produce a string of stars, reflecting a 1-10 rating.
    *
    * @param    rating     The rating for a film.
    * @return   A string, with between 1 and 10 stars.
    *
    */

   public static String starsWithException (int rating)
      throws SQLException {

      if (rating < 0 || rating > 10) {
         throw new SQLException ("Invalid rating value", "38111");
      }

      String result = "";

      while (rating-- > 0) {
         result += "*";
      }

      return result;
   }

}
```

C.3 The Vote Class

```
package Cinema;

import java.util.*;

/**
 * This class represents a vote from 1 to 10, where 10 is best and
 * 1 is worst.
 *
 * @author   Andrew Eisenberg
 * @version  1.0
 * @since    JDK 1.1.6
 *
 */
```

```
public class Vote {

   int                        value;
   public final static int    minVote = 1;
   public final static int    maxVote = 10;


   /**
    * Constructor for a Vote.
    *
    * @param       voteValue        Value of the Vote.
    * @exception   VoteOutOfRange   Vote outside of the range
    *                               of 1 to 10.
    */

   public Vote (int voteValue) throws VoteOutOfRange {
      if (voteValue < minVote || voteValue > maxVote)
         throw new VoteOutOfRange ();
      value = voteValue;
   }

   /**
    * Gets the value of a Vote.
    *
    * @return   Value of the Vote.
    */

   public int getValue () {
      return value;
   }
}
```

C.4 The `VoteOutOfRange` Exception Class

```
package Cinema;

public class VoteOutOfRange extends Exception {
}
```

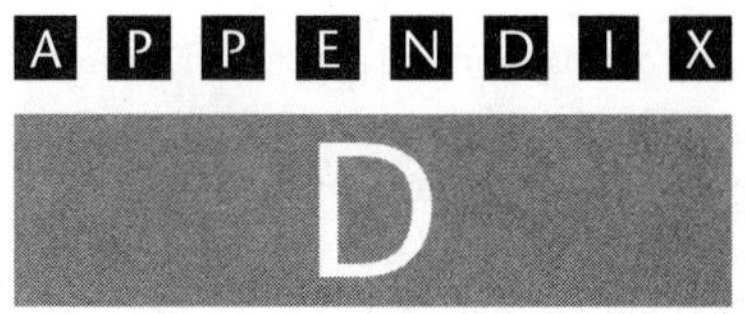

SQL/PSM Syntax

D.1 Introduction

This appendix contains the syntax used to create procedures and functions in SQL. The syntax in this appendix is taken from SQL:1999. It is not the complete syntax for these features—we have rearranged it a bit to make it more readable, and we have pruned it to remove extraneous features and options.

D.2 SQL PSM Syntax

```
<schema procedure> ::=
     CREATE PROCEDURE <schema qualified routine name>
       <SQL parameter declaration list>
       [ <routine characteristic>... ]
       <routine body>

<schema function> ::=
     CREATE FUNCTION <schema qualified routine name>
       <SQL parameter declaration list>
       <returns clause>
       [ <routine characteristic>... ]
       <routine body>
```

```
<SQL parameter declaration list> ::=
     <left paren>
       [ <SQL parameter declaration>
         [ { <comma> <SQL parameter declaration> }... ] ]
     <right paren>

<SQL parameter declaration> ::=
       [ <parameter mode> ] [ <SQL parameter name> ]
       <parameter type>

<parameter mode> ::=
       IN
     | OUT
     | INOUT

<parameter type> ::=
     <data type> [ <locator indication> ]

<locator indication> ::=
     AS LOCATOR

<returns clause> ::= RETURNS <returns data type>

<returns data type> ::= <data type> [ <locator indication> ]

<routine characteristic> ::=
       <language clause>
     | SPECIFIC <specific name>
     | <deterministic characteristic>
     | <SQL-data access indication>
     | <null-call clause>
     | <dynamic result sets characteristic>

<language clause> ::=
     LANGUAGE <language name>

<language name> ::=
     ADA | C | COBOL | FORTRAN | MUMPS | PASCAL | PLI | SQL

<parameter style clause> ::=
     PARAMETER STYLE { SQL | GENERAL }

<deterministic characteristic> ::=
       DETERMINISTIC
     | NOT DETERMINISTIC
```

```
<SQL-data access indication> ::=
       NO SQL
     | CONTAINS SQL
     | READS SQL DATA
     | MODIFIES SQL DATA

<null-call clause> ::=
       RETURNS NULL ON NULL INPUT
     | CALLED ON NULL INPUT

<dynamic result sets characteristic> ::=
     DYNAMIC RESULT SETS <unsigned integer>

<routine body> ::=
       <SQL routine body>
     | <external body reference>

<SQL routine body> ::= <SQL procedure statement>

<external body reference> ::=
     EXTERNAL [ NAME <external routine name> ]
     [ <parameter style clause> ]
```

APPENDIX

E

SQLJ Part 0 Syntax

E.1 Introduction

This appendix contains the syntax defined in SQLJ Part 0 (also known as SQL/OLB). Some of the nonterminals refer to elements defined in either Java or SQL.

E.2 Names and Identifiers

```
<modifiers> ::=                   !! Java class modifier keywords
                                  !! (e.g., static, public, private,
                                  !! protected, etc.)

<java class name> ::=             !! Java class name


<java id> ::=                     !! Java variable name

<java datatype> ::=               !! Java datatype


<java primitive datatype> ::=     !! one of the following Java types:
                                  !! boolean, byte, short, int, long,
                                  !! float, or double.
```

```
<java constant expression> ::= !! legal Java constant expression

<java literal> ::=             !! Java literal
```

E.3 <host expression list>

```
<host expression list> ::=
     <host expression> [ { <comma> <host expression> }... ]

<host expression> ::=
     <colon> [ <parameter mode> ] <expression>

<expression> ::=
       <simple variable>
     | <left paren> <complex expression> <right paren>

<simple variable> ::=          !! Java SimpleName
                               !! (as specified by JAVA
                               !! in section 19.5)

<complex expression> ::=
       <Rval expression>
     | <Lval expression>

<Rval expression> ::=          !! Java AssignmentExpression
                               !! (as specified by JAVA
                               !! in section 19.12)

<Lval expression> ::=          !! Java LeftHandSide
                               !! (as specified by JAVA
                               !! in section 19.12)

<Rval expression value> ::=    !! Property of <Rval expression>

<Lval expression value> ::=    !! Property of <Lval expression>

<Lval expression location> ::= !! Property of <Lval expression>
```

E.4 <parameter mode>

```
<parameter mode> ::=
       IN
       OUT
       INOUT
```

E.5 <with clause>

```
<with clause> ::= with <left paren> <with list> <right paren>

<with list> ::= <with element> [ { <comma> <with element> }... ]

<with element> ::= <with keyword> <equals operator> <with value>

<with keyword> ::=
       <predefined with keyword>
     | <user defined with keyword>
```

E.6 <implements clause>

```
<implements clause> ::= implements [ <interface list> ]

<interface list> ::=
     <interface element> [ { <comma> <interface element> }... ]

<interface element> ::=
       <predefined interface class>
     | <user defined interface class>

<user defined interface class> ::= !! any user-specified
                                   !! interface class

<predefined interface class> ::= sqlj.runtime.ForUpdate

<predefined with keyword> ::=
       sensitivity
     | holdability
     | returnability
     | updateColumns

<user defined with keyword> ::= <java id>

<with value> ::= <java constant expression>

<with type> ::= <java datatype>
```

E.7 <SQLJ clause>

```
<SQLJ clause> ::= #sql <SQLJ specific clause> <semicolon>

<SQLJ specific clause> ::=
        <connection declaration clause>
      | <iterator declaration clause>
      | <executable clause>
```

E.8 <connection declaration clause>

```
<connection declaration clause> ::=
     [ <modifiers> ] context <java class name>
     [ <implements clause> ] [ <with clause> ]
```

E.9 <iterator declaration clause>

```
<iterator declaration clause> ::=
     [ <modifiers> ] iterator <java class name>
     [ <implements clause> ] [ <with clause> ]
     <left paren> <iterator spec declaration> <right paren>

<iterator spec declaration> ::=
        <positioned iterator>
      | <named iterator>
```

E.10 <positioned iterator>

```
<positioned iterator> ::= <java type list>

<java type list> ::=
     <java datatype> [ { <comma> <java datatype> }... ]
```

E.11 <named iterator>

```
<named iterator> ::= <java pair list>

<java pair list> ::=
     <java pair> [ { <comma> <java pair> }... ]

<java pair> ::=
     <java datatype> <java id>
```

E.12 <executable clause>

```
<executable clause> ::=
     [ <context clause> ] <executable spec clause>

<executable spec clause> ::=
       <statement clause>
     | <assignment clause>
```

E.13 <context clause>

```
<context clause> ::=
     <left bracket> <context spec clause> <right bracket>

<context spec clause> ::=
       <connection context>
     | <execution context>
     | <connection context> <comma> <execution context>
```

E.14 <statement clause>

```
<statement clause> ::=
     <left brace> <statement spec clause> <right brace>

<statement spec clause> ::=
       <sql clause>
     | <positioned sql clause>
     | <select into clause>
     | <fetch clause>
     | <commit clause>
     | <rollback clause>
     | <set transaction clause>
     | <procedure clause>
     | <set statement clause>
```

E.15 <sql clause>

```
<sql clause> ::=                 !! SQL statement as defined
                                 !! in SQL-92
```

E.16 <positioned sql clause>

```
<positioned sql clause> ::=
    <update sql statement> WHERE CURRENT OF <iterator host expression>

<iterator host expression> ::= <host expression>

<update sql statement> ::=      !! SQL UPDATE or DELETE statement,
                                !! without WHERE clause
```

E.17 <select into clause>

```
<select into clause> ::=
     SELECT <select list>
       <into clause>
       <table expression>

<select list> ::=               !! As defined by SQL-92

<table expression> ::=          !! As defined by SQL-92

<into clause> ::= INTO <host expression list>
```

E.18 <fetch clause>

```
<fetch clause> ::=
     FETCH <iterator host expression> <into clause>

<iterator host expression> ::= <host expression>

<into clause> ::= INTO <host expression list>
```

E.19 <set statement clause>

```
<set statement clause> ::=
     SET <target host expression> <equals operator> <value expression>

<value expression> ::=          !! As defined by SQL/PSM-96

<target host expression> ::= <host expression>
```

E.20 <commit clause>

```
<commit clause> ::= COMMIT [ WORK ]
```

E.21 <rollback clause>

```
<rollback clause> ::= ROLLBACK [ WORK ]
```

E.22 <set transaction clause>

```
<set transaction clause> ::=
     SET TRANSACTION <transaction mode> [ <comma> <transaction mode> ]

<transaction mode> ::=
       <access mode>
     | <isolation level>

<access mode> ::=
       READ ONLY
     | READ WRITE

<isolation level> ::=
     ISOLATION LEVEL <isolation>

<isolation> ::=
       READ COMMITTED
     | READ UNCOMMITTED
     | REPEATABLE READ
     | SERIALIZABLE
```

E.23 <procedure clause>

```
<procedure clause> ::=
     CALL <sql procedure name> <left paren>
       [ <value expression> [ { <comma> <value expression> }... ] ]
     <right paren>

<sql procedure name> ::=
     [ [ <identifier1> <period> ] <identifier2> <period> ] <identifier3>
```

E.24 <assignment clause>

```
<assignment clause> ::=
     <Lval expression> <equals operator>
         <left brace> <assignment spec clause> <right brace>

<assignment spec clause> ::=
       <query clause>
     | <function clause>
     | <iterator conversion clause>
```

E.25 <query clause>

```
<query clause> ::=             !! SQL query statement
                               !! as defined by SQL-92
```

E.26 <function clause>

```
<function clause> ::=
     VALUES <left paren>
         <sql function name> <left paren>
             [ <value expression list> ] <right paren>
         <right paren>

<value expression list> ::=
       <value expression>
     | <value expression list> <comma> <value expression>

<sql function name> ::=
     [ [ <identifier1> <period> ] <identifier2> <period> ] <identifier3>

<value expression> ::=         !! as defined by SQL-92
```

E.27 <iterator conversion clause>

```
<iterator conversion clause> ::=
     CAST <result set expression>

<result set expression> ::=
     <host expression>
```

E.28 SQL blocks

```
<SQL block clause> ::=
     BEGIN
       { <statement spec clause> }...
     END
```

APPENDIX

F

SQLJ Part 1 Syntax

F.1 Introduction

This appendix contains the syntax defined in SQLJ Part 1. Some of the nonterminals refer to elements defined in either Java or SQL.

F.2 Names and Identifiers

```
<sql_identifier> ::=            !! SQL identifier

<java_identifier> ::=           !! Java identifier

<sql_datatype> ::=              !! SQL data type

<jar_name> ::=
     [ [ <catalog_id> . ] <schema_id> . ] <jar_id>

<catalog_id> ::= <sql_identifier>

<schema_id> ::= <sql_identifier>

<jar_id> ::= <sql_identifier>
```

F.3 SQL-Java Paths

```
<sql_java_path> ::= [ <path_element>... ]

<path_element> ::= ( <referenced_class>, <resolution_jar> )

<referenced_class> ::=
       [ <packages> . ] *
     | [ <packages> . ] <class_name>

<packages> ::= <package_name> [ . <package_name> ]...

<package_name> ::= <java_identifier>

<class_name> ::= <java_identifier>

<resolution_jar> ::= <jar_name>
```

F.4 SQLJ Procedures

```
sqlj.install_jar (url IN VARCHAR(*), jar IN VARCHAR(*),
                  deploy IN INTEGER)

sqlj.replace_jar (url IN VARCHAR(*), jar IN VARCHAR(*))

sqlj.remove_jar (jar IN VARCHAR(*), undeploy IN INTEGER)

sqlj.alter_java_path (jar varchar(*), path varchar(*))
```

F.5 DDL Statements

F.5.1 CREATE PROCEDURE/FUNCTION Statement

```
<create_procedure_statement> ::=
     CREATE PROCEDURE <sql_procedure_name> ( [ <sql_parameters> ] )
     <sql_properties>
     [ DETERMINISTIC | NOT DETERMINISTIC ]
     <external_java_reference>

<create_function_statement> ::=
     CREATE FUNCTION <sql_function_name>
        ( [ <sql_parameters> ] ) RETURNS <sql_datatype>
```

```
     <sql_properties>
     [ DETERMINISTIC | NOT DETERMINISTIC ]
     [ RETURNS NULL ON NULL INPUT | CALLED ON NULL INPUT ]
     <external_java_reference>

<sql_procedure_name> ::=
     [ [ <identifier1> . ] <identifier2> . ] <identifier3>

<sql_function_name> ::=
     [ [ <identifier1> . ] <identifier2> . ] <identifier3>

<identifier1> ::= <sql_identifier>

<identifier2> ::= <sql_identifier>

<identifier3> ::= <sql_identifier>

<sql_parameters> ::= <sql_parameter> [ { , <sql_parameter> }... ]

<sql_parameter> ::=
     [ <parameter_mode> ] [ <sql_identifier> ] <sql_datatype>

<parameter_mode> ::= IN | OUT | INOUT

<sql_properties> ::=
     [ <data_access_indication> ] [ DYNAMIC RESULT SETS <integer> ]

<data_access_indication> ::=
       NO SQL
     | CONTAINS SQL
     | READS SQL DATA
     | MODIFIES SQL DATA

<external_java_reference> ::=
     EXTERNAL NAME '<method_name> [ <java_method_signature> ]'
     LANGUAGE JAVA
     PARAMETER STYLE JAVA

<method_name> ::= <jar_name> : <java_method_name>

<java_method_name> ::= <java_class_name>.<method_identifier>

<java_class_name> ::= [ <packages>. ] <class_identifier>
```

```
<packages> ::= <package_identifier> [ .<package_identifier>... ]

<package_identifier> ::= <java_identifier>

<class_identifier> ::= <java_identifier>

<method_identifier> ::= <java_identifier>

<java_method_signature> ::=
     ( [ <java_parameters>  ] ) returns <java_datatype>

<java_parameters> ::= <java_datatype> [ { , <java_datatype> } ]
```

F.5.2 DROP PROCEDURE/FUNCTION Statement

```
<drop_routine_statement> ::=
     DROP [ PROCEDURE | FUNCTION ] sql_routine_name
     [ ( <sql_datatype> [ { , <sql_datatype> }... ] ) ]
     RESTRICT
```

F.5.3 GRANT Statement

```
<grant_statement> ::=
     GRANT USAGE ON JAR <jar_name> TO <grantee> [ {, <grantee> }... ]

<grantee> ::= <sql_identifier>
```

F.5.4 REVOKE Statement

```
<revoke_statement> ::=
     REVOKE USAGE ON JAR <jar_name> FROM <grantee> RESTRICT

<grantee> ::= <sql_identifier>
```

F.6 Deployment Descriptor Files

```
<descriptor_file> ::=
     SQLActions [ ] =
     { [ " <action_group> " [ , " <action_group> " ] ] }

<action_group> ::= <install_actions> | <remove_actions>

<install_actions> ::=
     BEGIN INSTALL [ <command> ; ]... END INSTALL

<remove_actions> ::=
     BEGIN REMOVE [ <command> ; ]... END REMOVE

<command> ::= <sql_statement> | <implementor_block>

<implementor_block> ::=
     BEGIN <implementor_name> sql_token... END <implementor_name>

<implementor_name> ::= <sql_identifier>
```

APPENDIX G

SQL UDT Syntax

G.1 Introduction

This appendix contains the syntax used to create user-defined types in SQL. The syntax in this appendix is taken from SQL:1999. It is not the complete syntax for these features—we have rearranged it a bit to make it more readable, and we have pruned it to remove extraneous features and options.

G.2 SQL User-Defined Type Syntax

```
<user-defined type definition> ::=
     CREATE TYPE <user-defined type body>

<user-defined type body> ::=
     <user-defined type name>
     [ <subtype clause> ]
     [ AS <representation> ]
     [ <instantiable clause> ]
     <finality>
     [ <reference type specification> ]
     [ <cast option> ]
     [ <method specification list> ]
```

```
<subtype clause> ::=
     UNDER <supertype name>

<supertype name> ::=
     <user-defined type>

<representation> ::=
       <predefined type>
     | <member list>

<member list> ::=
     <left paren> <member> [ { <comma> <member> }... ] <right paren>

<member> ::=
       <attribute definition>

<instantiable clause> ::=
       INSTANTIABLE
     | NOT INSTANTIABLE

<finality> ::=
       FINAL
     | NOT FINAL

<reference type specification> ::=
       <user-defined representation>
     | <derived representation>
     | <system-generated representation>

<user-defined representation> ::=
    REF USING <predefined type> [ <ref cast option> ]

<derived representation> ::= REF FROM <list of attributes>

<system-generated representation> ::= REF IS SYSTEM GENERATED

<ref cast option> ::=
     [ <cast to ref> ]
     [ <cast to type> ]

<cast to ref> ::=
     CAST <left paren> SOURCE AS REF <right paren>
       WITH <cast to ref identifier>
```

```
<cast to ref identifier> ::= <identifier>

<cast to type> ::=
     CAST <left paren> REF AS SOURCE <right paren>
       WITH <cast to type identifier>

<cast to type identifier> ::= <identifier>

<list of attributes> ::=
     <left paren> <attribute name>
        [ { <comma> <attribute name> }...]
     <right paren>

<cast option> ::=
     [ <cast to distinct> ]
     [ <cast to source> ]

<cast to distinct> ::=
     CAST <left paren> SOURCE AS DISTINCT <right paren>
     WITH <cast to distinct identifier>

<cast to distinct identifier> ::= <identifier>

<cast to source> ::=
     CAST <left paren> DISTINCT AS SOURCE <right paren>
     WITH <cast to source identifier>

<cast to source identifier> ::= <identifier>

<method specification list> ::=
     <method specification> [ { <comma> <method specification> }... ]


<method specification> ::=
       <original method specification>
     | <overriding method specification>

<original method specification> ::=
     <partial method specification>
     [ SELF AS RESULT ]
     [ SELF AS LOCATOR ]
     [ <method characteristics> ]
```

```
<overriding method specification> ::=
     OVERRIDING <partial method specification>

<partial method specification> ::=
     [ INSTANCE | STATIC ] METHOD <method name>
         <SQL parameter declaration list>
       <returns clause>
       [ SPECIFIC <specific name> ]

<method characteristics> ::=
     <method characteristic>...

<method characteristic> ::=
       <language clause>
     | <parameter style clause>
     | <deterministic characteristic>
     | <SQL-data access indication>
     | <null-call clause>
     | <transform group specification>

<attribute definition> ::=
     <attribute name>
     <data type>
     [ <reference scope check> ]
     [ <attribute default> ]
     [ <collate clause> ]

<attribute default> ::=
     <default clause>
```

SQLJ Part 2 Syntax

H.1 Introduction

This appendix contains the syntax defined in SQLJ Part 2. Some of the nonterminals refer to elements defined in Java, SQL, or SQLJ Part 1.

H.2 Names and Identifiers

```
<sql_identifier> ::=            !! SQL identifier

<java_identifier> ::=           !! Java identifier

<sql_datatype_name> ::=
     [ [ <identifier1> . ] <identifier2> . ] <identifier3>

<identifier1> ::=               !! Defined in SQLJ Part 1

<identifier2> ::=               !! Defined in SQLJ Part 1

<identifier3> ::=               !! Defined in SQLJ Part 1

<sql_attribute_name> ::=        !! Defined in SQL:1999

<sql_datatype> ::=              !! Defined in SQL:1999

<sql_method_name> ::=           !! Defined in SQL:1999
```

H.3 DDL Statements

H.3.1 CREATE TYPE Statement

```
<create_type_statement> ::=
     CREATE TYPE <sql_datatype_name>
     [ UNDER <sql_datatype_name> ]
     EXTERNAL NAME '<class_name>' LANGUAGE JAVA
     ( [ <members> ] )

<members> ::= <member> [ { , <member> }... ]

<member> ::= <attribute_spec> | <method_spec>

<attribute_spec> ::=
     <sql_attribute_name> <sql_datatype>
     EXTERNAL NAME '<java_field_name>'

<method_spec> ::=
     <function_method_spec> | <static_field_method_spec>

<function_method_spec> ::=
     [ STATIC ] METHOD <sql_method_name> <sql_function_signature>
     <sql_properties>
     [ DETERMINISTIC | NOT DETERMINISTIC ]
     [ RETURN NULL ON NULL INPUT | CALL ON NULL INPUT ]
     EXTERNAL NAME '<java_method_name> [ <java_method_signature> ]'

<static_field_method_spec> ::=
     STATIC METHOD <sql_method_name> ( ) RETURNS <sql_datatype>
     EXTERNAL VARIABLE NAME '<java_field_name>'

<sql_function_signature> ::=
     ( [ <sql_parameters> ] ) RETURNS <sql_datatype> [ SELF AS RESULT ]

<sql_parameters> ::=            !! Defined in SQLJ Part 1

<sql_properties> ::=            !! Defined in SQLJ Part 1

<class_name> ::= <jar_id> : <java_class_name>

<java_class_name> ::= [ <packages> . ] <class_identifier>
```

```
<jar_id> ::= <sql_identifier>

<packages> ::=
     <package_identifier> [ {. <package_identifier> }... ]

<package_identifier> ::= <java_identifier>

<class_identifier> ::= <java_identifier>

<java_field_name> ::= <java_identifier>

<java_method_name> ::= <java_identifier>

<java_method_signature> ::=    !! Defined in SQLJ Part 1
```

H.3.2 CREATE ORDERING Statement

```
<create_ordering_statement> ::=
     CREATE ORDERING FOR <sql_datatype_name> <ordering_form>

<ordering_form> ::=
       EQUALS ONLY BY <ordering_category>
     | ORDER FULL BY <ordering_category>

<ordering_category> ::=
       MAP WITH <ordering_routine>
     | RELATIVE WITH <ordering_routine>
     | RELATIVE WITH COMPARABLE INTERFACE
     | STATE

<ordering_routine> ::=
       FUNCTION <sql_function_name>
     | METHOD <sql_method_name>

<sql_function_name> ::=
     [ [ <identifier1> . ] <identifier2> . ] <identifier3>
```

H.3.3 DROP TYPE Statement

```
<drop_datatype_statement> ::=
     DROP TYPE <sql_datatype_name> RESTRICT
```

H.4 SQLJ Member References

```
<member_reference> ::=
       <instance_expression> . <member_name>
     | <sql_datatype_name> :: <sql_method_name>

<instance_expression> ::=
       <sql_expression>
     | <member_reference>

<sql_expression> ::=            !! SQL:1999 expression

<member_name> ::= <sql_attribute_name> | <sql_method_name>

<column_reference> ::=
     [ [ [ <catalog_name> . ] <schema_name> . ] <table_name> . ]
     <column_name>
```

H.5 SQLJ Method Call

```
<method_call> ::=
       <member_reference> ( [ <parameters> ] )
     | NEW <sql_datatype_name> ( [ <parameters> ] )

<parameters> ::= <parameter> [ { , <parameter> }... ]

<parameter> ::= <sql_expression>
```

H.6 Deployment Descriptor Files

```
Name: file_name
SQLJDeploymentDescriptor: TRUE


<descriptor_file> ::=
     SQLActions [ ] =
     { [ " <action_group> " [ , " <action_group> " ] ] }

<action_group> ::= <install_actions> | <remove_actions>

<install_actions> ::=
     BEGIN INSTALL [ { <command> ; }... ] END INSTALL
```

```
<remove_actions> ::=
     BEGIN REMOVE [ { <command> ; }... ] END REMOVE

<command> ::= <sql_statement> | <implementor_block>

<sql_statement> ::=            !! SQL statement

<implementor_block> ::=
     BEGIN <implementor_name> <sql_token> ... END <implementor_name>

<implementor_name> ::= <sql_identifier>

<sql_token> ::=                !! SQL token
```

The `PlayingCard` Classes

I.1 Introduction

This appendix contains several classes that were developed piecemeal in Chapter 2. These classes are `PlayingCard`, `PlayingCardAceLow`, `PlayingCardEnum`, and `Deck`. The comments that introduce the variables and methods may seem verbose. They are structured comments used by the `javadoc` tool to generate HTML documentation for these classes.

I.2 The `PlayingCard` Class

```
import java.io.*;
import java.util.*;


/**
 * This class represents a playing card.
 *
 * @author   Andrew Eisenberg
 * @version  1.0
 * @since    JDK 1.1.6
 *
 */
```

```
public class PlayingCard  implements Serializable {

   /**
    * The suit of Hearts
    *
    */

   final public static int HEART    =  0;

   /**
    * The suit of Diamonds
    *
    */

   final public static int DIAMOND  =  1;

   /**
    * The suit of Spades
    *
    */

   final public static int SPADE    =  2;

   /**
    * The suit of Clubs
    *
    */

   final public static int CLUB     =  3;

   /**
    * An indication that no suit is applicable to this card.
    *
    */

   final public static int NOSUIT   =  4;
   final static int MAXSUIT  =  4;
```

```
/**
 * The rank of Two
 *
 */

final public static int TWO      =  0;

// The ranks of THREE, FOUR, FIVE, SIX, SEVEN, EIGHT,
// NINE, TEN, JACK, QUEEN, and KING would go here.

/**
 * The rank of Ace
 *
 */

final public static int ACE      = 12;

/**
 * The rank of Joker
 *
 */

final public static int JOKER    = 13;

final static int MAXRANK  = 13;

/**
 * The number of cards in a full deck.
 *
 */

final public static int DECKSIZE = 54;

final static String[] suitNames = { "Hearts",
                                    "Diamonds",
                                    "Spades",
                                    "Clubs",
                                    ""
                                  };
```

```
final static String[] rankNames = { "Two",
                                    "Three",
                                    "Four",
                                    "Five",
                                    "Six",
                                    "Seven",
                                    "Eight",
                                    "Nine",
                                    "Ten",
                                    "Jack",
                                    "Queen",
                                    "King",
                                    "Ace",
                                    "Joker"
                                  };

/**
 * A complete deck of 54 cards.
 *
 */

static public PlayingCard[] CARDS = null;

/**
 * The rank of the playing card.
 *
 * @serial
 */

private int rank;

/**
 * The suit of the playing card.
 *
 * @serial
 */

private int suit;

/**
 * Constructor for a PlayingCard.
 *
 * @param       rank        The rank of the playing card.
 * @param       suit        The suit of the playing card.
 */
```

```
public PlayingCard (int rank, int suit) {

   this.suit = suit;
   this.rank = rank;
}

/**
 * Constructor for a PlayingCard.
 *
 * @param       rank         The rank of the playing card.
 */

public PlayingCard (int rank) {
   this.rank = rank;
   this.suit = NOSUIT;
}

/**
 * Get the rank of the playing card.
 *
 * @return   The rank of the card.
 */

public int getRank () {
   return rank;
}

/**
 * Get the suit of the playing card.
 *
 * @return   The suit of the card.
 */

public int getSuit () {
   return suit;
}

/**
 * Get the suit number and name of the playing card.
 *
 * @param suitOut        Array in which to return the suit.
 * @param suitNameOut    Array in which to return the suit name.
 */
```

```
public void getSuitAndName (int[] suitOut,
                            String[] suitNameOut)
{
   suitOut[0] = suit;
   suitNameOut[0] = suitNames[suit];
   return;
}

/**
 * Determine whether the suit of the playing card is black.
 *
 * @return   True if the card is black.
 */

public boolean black () {
   return black (suit);
}

/**
 * Determine whether the suit of the playing card is red.
 *
 * @return   True if the card is red.
 */

public boolean red () {
   return red (suit);
}

/**
 * Determine whether the playing card is equal to another
 * playing card. Equals considers both rank and suit in
 * this determination.
 *
 * @param    comparand     The card to test against.
 * @return   True if this card is equal to the comparand card.
 */

public boolean equals (PlayingCard comparand) {
   return (this.suit == comparand.suit &&
           this.rank comparand.rank);
}
```

```
/**
 * Determine whether the playing card is equal to another
 * playing card that has the rank and suit provided.
 * Equals considers both rank and suit in this
 * determination.
 *
 * @param    rank     The rank of the card to test against.
 * @param    suit     The suit of the card to test against.
 * @return   True if this card is equal to a card with the
 * rank and suit provided.
 */

public boolean equals (int rank, int suit) {
   return (this.rank == rank && this.suit == suit);
}

/**
 * Determine whether this PlayingCard is greater
 * than the comparand PlayingCard. Aces are considered high.
 *
 * @param    comparand     The card to test against.
 * @return   True if this card is geater the comparand card.
 */

public boolean greaterThan (PlayingCard comparand) {
   return (this.rank > comparand.rank);
}

/**
 * Determine whether this PlayingCard ties the comparand
 * PlayingCard. Only rank is considered in this comparison.
 *
 * @param    comparand     The card to test against.
 * @return   True if this card ties the comparand card.
 */

public boolean ties (PlayingCard comparand) {
   return (this.rank == comparand.rank);
}
```

```
/**
 * Format a playing card.
 *
 * @return   A String representation of this playing card.
 */

public String toString() {
   String result = "";

   try {
      result += rankNames[rank];
      if (suit != NOSUIT) {
         result += " of " + suitNames[suit];
      }
   }
   catch (Exception e) {
   }

   return result;
}

/**
 * Determine whether a suit of cards is black.
 *
 * @param    suit      A suit of cards;
 *                     HEART, CLUB, SPADE, or DIAMOND.
 * @return   True if the suit of cards is black.
 */

public static boolean black (int suit) {
   return (suit == SPADE || suit == CLUB);
}

/**
 * Determine whether a suit of cards is red.
 *
 * @param    suit      A suit of cards;
 *                     HEART, CLUB, SPADE, or DIAMOND.
 * @return   True if the suit of cards is red.
 */

public static boolean red (int suit) {
   return (suit == HEART || suit == DIAMOND);
}
```

```
/**
 * Determine whether a combination of rank and suit are valid.
 *
 * @param    rank      A rank of cards; TWO, THREE, ..., JOKER.
 * @param    suit      A suit of cards;
 *                     HEART, CLUB, SPADE, or DIAMOND.
 * @return   True if the combination of rank and suit is valid.
 */

public static boolean valid (int rank, int suit) {
   if (rank < 0 || rank > MAXRANK || suit < 0 ||
        suit > MAXSUIT)
   {
      return false;
   }
   else if (rank == JOKER && suit != NOSUIT) {
      return false;
   }
   else if (rank != JOKER && suit == NOSUIT) {
      return false;
   }
   else return true;
}

/**
 * Provides an enumeration for a complete deck of playing cards.
 *
 * @return   An Enumeration for a deck of playing cards.
 */

public static Enumeration deck () {
   return new PlayingCardEnum();
}

static {
   CARDS = new PlayingCard[DECKSIZE];

   int i = 0;
   for (int r = 0; r <= MAXRANK; r++) {
      for (int s = 0; s <= MAXSUIT; s++) {
         if (r != JOKER && s != NOSUIT) {
            CARDS[i++] = new PlayingCard (r, s);
         }
      }
   }
```

```
      CARDS[i++] = new PlayingCard (JOKER, NOSUIT);
      CARDS[i++] = new PlayingCard (JOKER, NOSUIT);

   }

}
```

I.3 The PlayingCardAceLow Class

```
public class PlayingCardAceLow extends PlayingCard {

   /**
    * Constructor for a PlayingCardAceLow.
    *
    * @param      rank        The rank of the playing card.
    * @param      suit        The suit of the playing card.
    */

   public PlayingCardAceLow (int rank, int suit) {
      super (rank, suit);
   }

   /**
    * Determine whether this PlayingCardAceLow is greater
    * than another PlayingCard. Aces are considered low.
    *
    * @return   Whether this card is geater than another card.
    */

   public boolean greaterThan (PlayingCard comparand) {
      if (this.getRank() == ACE) {
         return false;
      }
      else if (comparand.getRank() == ACE) {
         return true;
      }
      else return super.greaterThan(comparand);
   }


}
```

I.4 The PlayingCardGui Class

```
public class PlayingCardGUI extends PlayingCard {

   /**
    * A URL to a Gif file that can be used as the image for
    * the back of a playing card.
    *
    * @serial
    */

   public java.net.URL backgroundGIF = null;

   /**
    * Constructor for a PlayingCardGUI.
    *
    * @param       rank         The rank of the playing card.
    * @param       suit         The suit of the playing card.
    * @param       url          The URL of a GIF file for the
    *                           back of the playing card.
    */

   public PlayingCardGUI (int rank, int suit, String url) {
      super (rank, suit);
      try {
         backgroundGIF = new java.net.URL(url);
      }
      catch (java.net.MalformedURLException mue) {
      }
   }

}
```

I.5 The PlayingCardEnum Class

```
import java.util.*;

/**
 * This class represents an enumeration of a deck of playing cards.
 *
 * @author   Andrew Eisenberg
 * @version  1.0
 * @since    JDK 1.1.6
 *
 */

public class PlayingCardEnum implements Enumeration {
   private int currentCard = 0;

   /**
    * Constructor a PlayingCardEnum that represents a deck
    * of cards.
    */

   public PlayingCardEnum () {
   }

   /**
    * Determine whether there are any more cards left.
    *
    * @return   True if there are more cards.
    */

   public boolean hasMoreElements () {
      return (currentCard < PlayingCard.DECKSIZE);
   }

   /**
    * Get the next playing card.
    *
    * @return Object   The next playing card.
    */
```

```
   public Object nextElement () throws NoSuchElementException {
      if (currentCard == PlayingCard.DECKSIZE) {
         throw new NoSuchElementException();
      }

      return PlayingCard.CARDS[currentCard++];
   }

}
```

I.6 The Deck Class

```
import java.util.*;
import java.lang.Math;

/**
 * This class represents a PlayingCard Exception
 *
 * @author   Andrew Eisenberg
 * @version  1.0
 * @since    JDK 1.1.6
 *
 */

class DeckInUse extends Exception {
}

class DeckIsFull extends Exception {
}

/**
 * This class represents a deck of playing cards.
 *
 * @author   Andrew Eisenberg
 * @version  1.0
 * @since    JDK 1.1.6
 *
 */
```

```
public class Deck {

   private PlayingCard[] deckOfCards =
   new PlayingCard[PlayingCard.DECKSIZE];
   private int cardsLeft;
   private int cardsRemoved;
   private Random rnd = new Random();

   /**
    * Constructor for a deck of playing cards.
    *
    * @param       e         An Enumeration of playing cards from
    *                        which the deck will be built.
    */

   public Deck (Enumeration e) {
      int i = 0;

      while (e.hasMoreElements()) {
         deckOfCards[i++] = (PlayingCard) (e.nextElement());
      }
      cardsLeft = PlayingCard.DECKSIZE;
      cardsRemoved = 0;
   }

   /**
    * Constructor for an empty deck of playing cards.
    *
    */

   public Deck () {
      cardsLeft = 0;
      cardsRemoved = PlayingCard.DECKSIZE;
   }

   /**
    * Shuffle the deck of cards.
    *
    */

   public void shuffle () {
      cardsLeft = PlayingCard.DECKSIZE - cardsRemoved;

   }
```

```
/**
 * Specifies whether any cards are left in the deck.
 *
 * @return   Whether any cards are left in the deck.
 */

public boolean moreCards () {

   return cardsLeft != 0;
}

/**
 * Deal a card from the deck.
 *
 * @return   The top card from the deck.
 */

public PlayingCard dealCard () {
   PlayingCard chosenCard = null;

   if (cardsLeft == 0) {
      return null;
   }

   int chosenCardPosition = Math.abs(rnd.nextInt())%cardsLeft;
   chosenCard = deckOfCards[chosenCardPosition];
   deckOfCards[chosenCardPosition] = deckOfCards[--cardsLeft];
   deckOfCards[cardsLeft] = chosenCard;

   return chosenCard;
}

/**
 * Add a playing card to the deck. The card will not
 * be seen until the deck is shuffled.
 *
 * @param     newCard   PlayingCard to add.
 * @exception DeckIsFull   The deck of cards is already at its
 * maximum size.
 */
```

```
    public void addCard (PlayingCard newCard) throws DeckIsFull {

       if (cardsRemoved == 0) {
          throw new DeckIsFull();
       }
       deckOfCards[PlayingCard.DECKSIZE - (cardsRemoved--)] =
                   newCard;
    }

    /**
     * Remove a playing card from the deck. The removed card will
     * not return after the deck is shuffled.
     *
     * @exception DeckInUse   A card cannot be removed while cards
     * have been dealt from the deck.
     */

    public void removeCard (int rank) throws DeckInUse {
       int i = 0;
       PlayingCard chosenCard = null;

       if (cardsLeft != PlayingCard.DECKSIZE - cardsRemoved) {
          throw new DeckInUse();
       }

       while (i < PlayingCard.DECKSIZE - cardsRemoved) {
          if (deckOfCards[i].getRank() == rank) {
             chosenCard = deckOfCards[i];
             deckOfCards[i]
                = deckOfCards[PlayingCard.DECKSIZE - ++cardsRemoved];
             deckOfCards[PlayingCard.DECKSIZE - cardsRemoved] =
                                                  chosenCard;
          }
          else {
                i++;
                }
       }

       cardsLeft = PlayingCard.DECKSIZE - cardsRemoved;
    }
}
```

INDEX

D

E

N

Q

R

U

V

W

ABOUT THE AUTHORS

Jim Melton is editor of ISO/IEC 9075 and representative for database standards at Oracle Corporation. Previously he was senior architect and representative for database standards at Sybase Inc., and prior to that he held the position of consulting engineer at Digital Equipment Corporation, where he was a relational database system implementor, corporate database architect, and database standards representative. He has been in the computer industry since 1969 and in the database industry since 1976. From 1986 to the present he has been the database representative for his company to ANSI X3H2, and for the United States to ISO/IEC JTC1/SC32/WG3. He is the liaison between database committees and international committees; and editor of SQL-92, SQL/CLI-95, SQL/PSM-96, and SQL:1999, and emerging next-generation SQL standards (all parts). He is the author of *Understanding SQL's Stored Procedures: A Complete Guide to SQL/PSM,* co-author of *Understanding the New SQL: A Complete Guide,* a former columnist for *Database Programming & Design* magazine, a frequent speaker at industry events, and the author of many peer-reviewed articles.

Andrew Eisenberg is currently manager of standards and consortia at Progress Software Corp. Prior to this he held the positions of senior architect at Sybase, consulting engineer in the Database Systems Group at Digital Equipment Corp., and development manager at Computer Corp. of America (CCA). He represents Progress Software Corp. on the NCITS H2 Database Committee, the World Wide Web Consortium (W3C) XML Query Work Group, and the Transaction Processing Performance Council (TPC). He has represented his previous employers on the Object Management Group (OMG) and the SQLJ informal group of companies. He has been a member of the H2 Database Committee since 1985 and was an active participant in the development of SQL-92, SQL/PSM, and SQL:1999.

LICENSE AGREEMENT
For Oracle JDeveloper Suite 2.0

NOTICE TO USER: BY INSTALLING OR USING THIS SOFTWARE YOU ACCEPT ALL THE TERMS AND CONDITIONS OF THIS AGREEMENT. PLEASE READ IT CAREFULLY.
THE FOLLOWING TERMS AND CONDITIONS ("AGREEMENT") SHALL GOVERN YOUR INSTALLATION AND USE OF THE ACCOMPANYING SOFTWARE PROGRAMS AND RELATED EXPLANATORY MATERIALS (THE "PROGRAM") UNLESS THIS SOFTWARE IS SUBJECT TO A SIGNED TRIAL LICENSE AGREEMENT WITH ORACLE INC. IF YOU DO NOT ACCEPT OR AGREE WITH THESE TERMS, YOU MANY NOT INSTALL OR USE THE PROGRAM AND YOU SHOULD PROMPTLY RETURN THIS PACKAGE (INCLUDING ALL SOFTWARE AND DOCUMENTATION HEREIN) TO ORACLE OR THE PARTY THAT PROVIDED YOU WITH THIS PROGRAM.

UPON YOUR ACCEPTANCE OF THIS AGREEMENT, ORACLE GRANTS YOU A LIMITED, NON-EXCLUSIVE LICENSE TO USE THE PROGRAM AS FOLLOWS:

1. **USE OF PROGRAM.** You may install and use the Program (and accompanying documentation) internally in your organization solely for evaluation purposes on a single computer system for personal development purposes only. You may not use the Program for any development, commercial or production purpose, and you may not use the Program for processing data of your own or any other third party. The Program may not be transferred, sold, assigned, rented, timeshared, sublicensed or otherwise conveyed (whether by operation of law or otherwise) to another party without Oracle's prior written consent. If the Oracle Program licensed hereunder is a suite of several component software products, use of all components of such Program is limited to the same computer system and the components of this Program may not be unbundled and used on different or additional computers. THIS PRODUCT MAY CONTAIN A TIME CLOCK CAUSING IT TO CEASE TO OPERATE AT THE END OF THE EVALUATION PERIOD.

If you desire to use the Program for production purposes you will need to contact Oracle and acquire a license for such a Program.

2. **COPY RESTRICTIONS AND OTHER RESTRICTIONS.** You may not copy the Program except that you may either install the Program on your hard disk or make one copy for inactive back-up and archival purposes for your own use. Except as expressly permitted in the Documentation, you may not modify or adapt the Program in whole or in part (including but not limited to translating or creating derivative works) or reverse engineer, decompile or disassemble the Program (except to the extent applicable laws specifically prohibit such restriction). You may not use the Program for timesharing, rental or service bureau purposes. You shall not remove any copyright notices or other proprietary notices from the Program or Documentation and you must reproduce such notices on all copies or extracts of the Program and Documentation. You may not run any benchmark tests with the programs.

3. **COPYRIGHT AND OWNERSHIP.** The Program is owned by Oracle, its subsidiaries, or their suppliers, and is protected by copyright laws and international treaty provisions. You acquire only the non-exclusive right to use the Program as permitted herein and do not acquire any rights of ownership in the Program or any other implied rights or licenses under any intellectual property rights of Oracle.

4. **SUPPORT.** The Program is provided to you free of charge on an "AS IS" basis and is unsupported. This Agreement does not entitle you to any maintenance or other services or any updates, bug fixes, maintenance releases or new versions of the Program.

5. **U.S. GOVERNMENT RESTRICTED RIGHTS.** The Program is Commercial Computer Software. Use, duplication and disclosure of the Program and Documentation by the U.S. Government is subject to restrictions set forth in this license or in a written agreement specifying the Government's right to use the Program. Oracle reserves all unpublished rights under U.S. copyright laws.

6. **TERMINATION.** Your license to use the Program will automatically terminate as of the date 90 (ninety) days after your receipt of the Program. YOU ACKNOWLEDGE AND UNDERSTAND THAT THE PROGRAM MAY CONTAIN A DEVICE WHICH SHALL CAUSE IT NOT TO OPERATE AFTER SUCH PERIOD. In addition, Oracle may immediately terminate this Agreement on notice to you. Upon termination, you shall cease using the Program and shall destroy all copies of the Program (and associated Documentation) in any form. All disclaimers of warranties and limitations of liability shall survive any termination of this Agreement.

7. **WARRANTY DISCLAIMER.** The Program is provided AS IS, without any warranty whatsoever. **ORACLE DISCLAIMS ALL WARRANTIES AND CONDITIONS, EXPRESS OR IMPLIED, INCLUDING WITHOUT LIMITATION THE IMPLIED WARRANTIES OR CONDITIONS OF MERCHANTABLE QUALITY, NONINFRINGEMENT, AND FITNESS FOR A PARTICULAR PURPOSE. NO WARRANTY IS MADE REGARDING THE RESULTS OF ANY PROGRAM OR THAT THE PROGRAM'S FUNCTIONALITY WILL MEET YOUR REQUIREMENTS.**

8. **LIMITATION ON LIABILITY. NEITHER ORACLE, ITS SUBSIDARIES NOR ANY OF ITS LICENSORS SHALL BE LIABLE FOR ANY LOSS OR DAMAGE HEREUNDER, INCLUDING, WITHOUT LIMITATION, ANY INNACURACY OF DATA, LOSS OF PROFITS, OR DIRECT, INDIRECT, SPECIAL, INCIDENTAL OR CONSEQUENTIAL DAMAGES, EVEN IF SUCH PARTY HAS BEEN ADVISED OF THE POSSIBILITY OF SUCH DAMAGES.**

9. **EXPORT.** You agree to fully comply with all laws and regulations of the United States and other countries ("Export Laws") to assure that neither the Program, related technical information or any direct products thereof are (1) exported, directly or indirectly, in violation of Export Laws, or (2) are used for any purpose prohibited by Export Laws, including, without limitation, nuclear, chemical or biological weapons production.

10. **GOVERNING LAW; COMPLETE AGREEMENT.** THIS AGREEMENT CONSTITUTES THE COMPLETE AGREEMENT BETWEEN THE PARTIES WITH RESPECT TO THE PROGRAM AND IS GOVERNED BY THE LAWS OF THE STATE OF CALIFORNIA, U.S.A (EXCEPT FOR CONFLICT OF LAW PROVISIONS). The United Nations Convention on the International Sale of Goods is expressly excluded. If any provision of this Agreement is held to be unenforceable, such provision shall be limited, modified or severed as necessary to eliminate its unenforceability, and all other provisions shall remain unaffected.

SYBASE, INC. EVALUATION LICENSE AGREEMENT

(THIS IS A LICENSE AND NOT A SALE)

NOTICE TO USER: BY INSTALLING OR USING THIS SOFTWARE YOU ACCEPT ALL THE TERMS AND CONDITIONS OF THIS AGREEMENT. PLEASE READ IT CAREFULLY.

THE FOLLOWING TERMS AND CONDITIONS ("AGREEMENT") SHALL GOVERN YOUR INSTALLATION AND USE OF THE ACCOMPANYING SOFTWARE PROGRAMS AND RELATED EXPLANATORY MATERIALS (THE "PROGRAM") UNLESS THIS SOFTWARE IS SUBJECT TO A SIGNED TRIAL LICENSE AGREEMENT WITH SYBASE, INC. IF YOU DO NOT ACCEPT OR AGREE WITH THESE TERMS, YOU MANY NOT INSTALL OR USE THE PROGRAM AND YOU SHOULD PROMPTLY RETURN THIS PACKAGE (INCLUDING ALL SOFTWARE AND DOCUMENTATION HEREIN) TO SYBASE OR THE PARTY THAT PROVIDED YOU WITH THIS PROGRAM.

UPON YOUR ACCEPTANCE OF THIS AGREEMENT, SYBASE GRANTS YOU A LIMITED, NON-EXCLUSIVE LICENSE TO USE THE PROGRAM AS FOLLOWS:

1. **USE OF PROGRAM.** You may install and use the Program (and accompanying documentation) internally in your organization solely for evaluation purposes on a single computer system for an evaluation period of sixty (60) days. You may not use the Program for any development, commercial or production purpose. The Program may not be transferred, sold, assigned, sublicensed or otherwise conveyed (whether by operation of law or otherwise) to another party without Sybase's prior written consent. If the Sybase Program licensed hereunder is a suite of several component software products, use of all components of such Program is limited to the same computer system and the components of this Program may not be unbundled and used on different or additional computers. THIS PRODUCT MAY CONTAIN A TIME CLOCK CAUSING IT TO CEASE TO OPERATE AT THE END OF THE EVALUATION PERIOD.

If you desire to use the Program for production purposes you will need to contact Sybase and acquire a license for such a Program.

2. **COPY RESTRICTIONS AND OTHER RESTRICTIONS.** You may not copy the Program except that you may either install the Program on your hard disk or make one copy for inactive back-up and archival purposes for your own use. Except as expressly permitted in the Documentation, you may not modify or adapt the Program in whole or in part (including but not limited to translating or creating derivative works) or reverse engineer, decompile or disassemble the Program (except to the extent applicable laws specifically prohibit such restriction). You may not use the Program for timesharing, rental or service bureau purposes. You shall not remove any copyright notices or other proprietary notices from the Program or Documentation and you must reproduce such notices on all copies or extracts of the Program and Documentation. Results of benchmark or other performance tests run on the Program may not be disclosed to any third party without Sybase's prior written consent.

3. **COPYRIGHT AND OWNERSHIP.** The Program is owned by Sybase, its subsidiaries or their suppliers and is protected by copyright laws and international treaty provisions. You acquire only the non-exclusive right to use the Program as permitted herein and do not acquire any rights of ownership in the Program or any other implied rights or licenses under any intellectual property rights of Sybase.

4. **SUPPORT.** The Program is provided to you free of charge on an "AS IS" basis and is unsupported. This Agreement does not entitle you to any maintenance or other services or any updates, bug fixed, maintenance releases or new versions of the Program.

5. **U.S. GOVERNMENT RESTRICTED RIGHTS.** The Program is Commercial Computer Software. Use, duplication and disclosure of the Program and Documentation by the U.S. Government is subject to restrictions set forth in this license or in a written agreement specifying the Government's right to use the Program. Sybase reserves all unpublished rights under U.S. copyright laws.

6. **TERMINATION.** Your license to use the Program will automatically terminate as of the date ____ (_0) days after your receipt of the Program. YOU ACKNOWLEDGE AND UNDERSTAND THAT THE PROGRAM MAY CONTAIN A DEVICE WHICH SHALL CAUSE IT NOT TO OPERATE AFTER SUCH PERIOD. In addition, Sybase may immediately terminate this Agreement on notice to you. Upon termination, you shall cease using the Program and shall destroy all copies of the Program (and associated Documentation) in any form. All disclaimers of warranties and limitations of liability shall survive any termination of this Agreement.

7. **WARRANTY DISCLAIMER.** The Program is provided AS IS, without any warranty whatsoever. **SYBASE DISCLAIMS ALL WARRANTIES AND CONDITIONS, EXPRESS OR IMPLIED, INCLUDING WITHOUT LIMITATION THE IMPLIED WARRANTIES OR CONDITIONS OF MERCHANTABLE QUALITY, NONINFRINGEMENT, AND FITNESS FOR A PARTICULAR PURPOSE. NO WARRANTY IS MADE REGARDING THE RESULTS OF ANY PROGRAM OR THAT THE PROGRAM'S FUNCTIONALITY WILL MEET YOUR REQUIREMENTS.**

8. **LIMITATION ON LIABILITY. NEITHER SYBASE, ITS SUBSIDARIES NOR ANY OF ITS LICENSORS SHALL BE LIABLE FOR ANY LOSS OR DAMAGE HEREUNDER, INCLUDING, WITHOUT LIMITATION, ANY INNACURACY OF DATA, LOSS OF PROFITS OR INDIRECT, SPECIAL, INCIDENTAL OR CONSEQUENTIAL DAMAGES, EVEN IF SUCH PARTY HAS BEEN ADVISED OF THE POSSIBILITY OF SUCH DAMAGES.**

9. **EXPORT.** You agree to fully comply with all laws and regulations of the United States and other countries ("Export Laws") to assure that neither the Program, related technical information or any direct products thereof are (1) exported, directly or indirectly, in violation of Export Laws, or (2) are used for any purpose prohibited by Export Laws, including, without limitation, nuclear, chemical or biological weapons production.

10. **GOVERNING LAW; COMPLETE AGREEMENT.** THIS AGREEMENT CONSTITUTES THE COMPLETE AGREEMENT BETWEEN THE PARTIES WITH RESPECT TO THE PROGRAM AND IS GOVERNED BY THE LAWS OF THE STATE OF CALIFORNIA, U.S.A (EXCEPT FOR CONFLICT OF LAW PROVISIONS). The United Nations Convention on the International Sale of Goods is expressly excluded. If any provision of this Agreement is held to be unenforceable, such provision shall be limited, modified or severed as necessary to eliminate its unenforceability, and all other provisions shall remain unaffected.

ABOUT THE CD-ROM

System Requirements

This CD-ROM was created in ISO 9960 format with Joliet extensions and is intended for use on IBM-compatible PCs running Windows 95 and later or Windows NT 4.0 and later. Long file names (up to 64 characters in length) are used on this CD-ROM.

Getting Started

Open Welcome.html in the top-level directory with your web browser. You can use any reasonably current browser for this purpose (such as Netscape Navigator or Microsoft Internet Explorer). This file describes the contents of the CD-ROM in detail, suggesting different ways in which these contents may be used, and provides references to pages on the World Wide Web that you may find useful.

Description of the CD-ROM Materials

This CD-ROM contains a varity of materials that we hope will allow you to more fully explore some of the topics that we have presented in our book.

We include Windows versions of Sybase's SQL Anywhere Studio 6.0.3 (evaluation copy), Oracle's SQLJ Reference Implementation Translator v1.0.1.1, Informix's Cloudscape v2.0.3 (evaluation copy), and Oracle's JDeveloper 3.0 (evaluation copy) on this CD-ROM. Versions of these programs for platforms other than Windows can be found at

> *www.sybase.com/products/anywhere/*,
>
> *www.sqlj.org/implement/oracle/index.html*,
>
> *www.cloudscape.com/*, and
>
> *www.oracle.com/tools/jdeveloper*,

respectively. Additionally, the example files contained on the CD-ROM can be downloaded from Morgan Kaufmann's Web site at *www.mkp.com/books_catalog/catalog.asp?ISBN=1-55860-562-2*.

CD-ROM Directory Structure

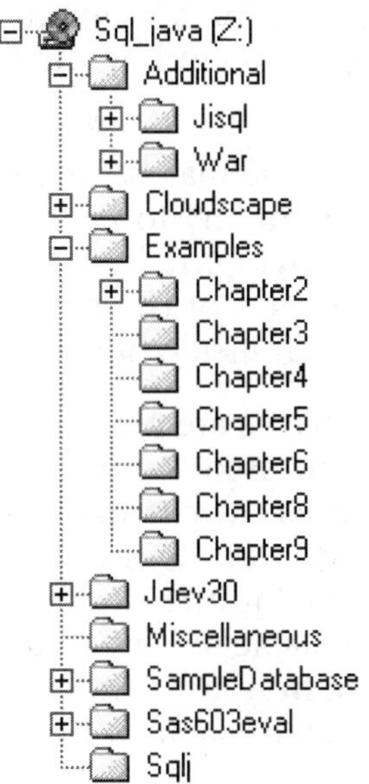

Directory	Description
`drive:\Examples`	Most of the examples used in the book. Includes `.bat` files to compile and run them.
`drive:\SampleDatabase`	The sample database used throughout the book (an ASA 6.0 database), as well as the files and scripts necessary to build the database from scratch.
`drive:\Additional\War`	The children's card game of War, which uses the `PlayingCard` class (and several related classes) developed in Chapter 2.
`drive:\Additional\Jisql`	A "JDBC Interactive SQL" tool, written in Java and using JDBC. This utility was used to build the sample database and run some of our examples.
`drive:\Sas603eval`	Sybase's SQL Anywhere Studio 6.0.3 (evaluation copy) with a 60-day license. Included in this product is Adaptive Server Anywhere 6.0.3.
`drive:\Sqlj`	Oracle's SQLJ Reference Implementation Translator v1.0.1.1.
`drive:\Cloudscape`	Informix's Cloudscape v2.0.3 (evaluation copy) with a 30-day license.
`drive:\Jdev30`	Oracle's JDeveloper 3.0 (evaluation copy).

CD-ROM Directory Description

Copyright Note

The software and data are provided on the accompanying CD-ROM. By opening the package you agree to be bound by the following agreement: